will altern....... ....
Mr. Roche's views are personal,
rather than partisan; their roots are
in intellect, rather than in ideology.
Each discussion of an issue, no
matter how controversial, reveals the
author's thorough understanding of
and earnest respect for the views of
those who disagree with him. An
historian, not a prophet, writes here,
and his essays eschew pat answers in
a way that will intrigue the thinking
reader of whatever political
persuasion.

Students, legal scholars, historians,
educators, political scientists, and the
ordinary reader who is curious about
the important issues of our times will
find this volume a valuable one.

JOHN P. ROCHE, a self-styled
"unfashionable professor" in an era
of intellectual fads, is currently
Henry Luce Professor of
Civilization and Foreign Affairs at
the Fletcher School of Law and
Diplomacy, Tufts University.

Also by John P. Roche

Shadow and Substance
The Quest for the Dream
The Dynamics of Democratic Government
  (in collaboration with Murray S. Stedman, Jr.)
Courts and Rights
The American Image: The Political Process
  (in collaboration with Leonard W. Levy)

SENTENCED TO LIFE

SENTENCED TO LIFE

John P. Roche

MACMILLAN PUBLISHING CO., INC.

NEW YORK

COLLIER MACMILLAN PUBLISHERS

LONDON

Library of Congress Cataloging in Publication Data

Roche, John Pearson, 1923–
    Sentenced to life.

    CONTENTS: Kennedy and the politics of modernity.—
The uses of American power.—Gideon of the right. [etc.]
    1. United States—Politics and government—1945—
Addresses, essays, lectures. 2. United States—Constitutional
law—Addresses, essays, lectures.
I. Title.
E839.5.R57   320.9′73′092   73–13361
ISBN 0–02–604350–5

*Macmillan Publishing Co., Inc.
866 Third Avenue, New York, N.Y. 10022
Collier-Macmillan Canada Ltd.*

First Printing 1974

Printed in the United States of America

Acknowledgments

Grateful acknowledgment is made to the following companies and publications for permission to reprint some of the essays in this volume: "Kennedy, Johnson and the Intellectuals" © 1964 by The New York Times Company (originally entitled "How the President Can Use the Intellectuals") is reprinted by permission. "John Marshall: Major Opinions and Other Writings" is from *John Marshall: Major Opinions and Other Writings*, edited by John P. Roche, copyright © 1967, by the Bobbs-Merrill Company, Inc., and is reprinted by permission of the publisher. "Constitutional Law: Distribution of Powers" is reprinted, with permission, from *The International Encyclopedia of the Social Sciences*, © 1968 by Macmillan Publishing Co., Inc.

To the Memory of Two Friends:

LYNDON JOHNSON

HAROLD WEISBERG

each of whom, in his distinctive fashion,
taught me—in the words of the Preacher—
that "in much wisdom is much grief: and he
that increaseth knowledge increaseth sorrow."

SENTENCED TO LIFE

Preface

ABOUT TEN YEARS ago I sat down to write the preface to my last collection of essays, *Shadow and Substance*, which Macmillan published in 1964. At the time, John F. Kennedy was in the White House, Nikita Khrushchev was bounding around, Vietnam was a tiny cloud on the horizon—most of the emphasis was on Laos—and David Halberstam in Saigon was calling for the overthrow of President Ngo Dinh Diem so that the full forces of effective anti-Communism could be unleashed against Hanoi. Ironically, in my capacity as National Chairman of Americans for Democratic Action, I was suggesting in season and out that the Kennedy Administration, far from being the "best and the brightest," could not get Congress to pass the Ten Commandments, to say nothing of civil rights legislation.

The intervening decade seems to have lasted a century. I confess that I have found little reason to alter my fundamental beliefs, although I have learned the hard way that it is not enough to have the courage of your convictions. You must also have the courage of their consequences. To be specific, when someone today proposes that we support the overthrow of the white racist regime in South Africa, my initial reaction is "Fine, but how much are you prepared to pay to do it?" This is sometimes denounced as "conservatism," or worse, but I prefer to consider it Augustinian liberalism, based on my pessimistic conviction that the fire-eaters will precipitously vanish when the guns start firing.

So here I am at fifty, somewhat battered by my years at point on Vietnam, but still an unashamed antitotalitarian liberal, one who does not believe that wolves have vanished from the world. I freely concede that in part this volume is a brief for the defense, but it is not an *apologia*. The texts (which have been edited only to catch typographical errors in the originals and to eliminate self-plagiarism in those few instances where I used the same formulation in essays addressed to different audiences) speak for themselves. At points they disclose what I now consider errors of judgment. I am, for example, convinced that I grossly misconstrued Chinese Communist intentions in the early 1960s. Also, I had a Korean complex about domestic reaction to the war in Vietnam, anticipating an assault from the Right, not the Left. But enough flagellation; the reader can swing his own whip.

The essays fall naturally under three headings. Those on politics and education are in simple chronological order, while the legal studies have been grouped by subject matter. I am grateful to the Macmillan Company for this opportunity to gather them under one roof. And finally I want to express my love and sympathy to Connie and Joanna, who have made a life sentence tolerable—indeed, often joyous.

JOHN P. ROCHE
June, 1973   *Weston, Massachusetts*

Contents

●

Law

POLITICS

Kennedy and
the Politics
of Modernity

To THE AMERICAN HISTORIAN of the future, who can rely only on the cold record, the accomplishments of the Kennedy Administration may appear quite insubstantial. The Ph.D. candidate in 1980 will probably begin his dissertation by remarking that President John F. Kennedy had less than three years in which to make his mark and one can never know what triumphs might have stamped his remaining five years in office. This lightning rod up, he will then turn to the legislative record as well as to the administration's accomplishments in foreign affairs and, I suspect, indicate at some length that Kennedy was not a "great President," that his domestic policy was strangled in Congress, and that his foreign policy had two major successes—Cuba in 1962 and the Test-Ban Treaty—to balance the failure of the "Grand Design" for the Atlantic Community, the Alliance for Progress, the Bay of Pigs and the withering away of NATO and SEATO.

In objective historical terms, such an account will be essen-

Reprinted, with permission, from *The New Leader*, August 17, 1964.

tially correct. It is going to be as difficult to substantiate the proposition that John Kennedy was a magnificently talented politician twenty years from now as it would be to demonstrate that a pitcher who spent the years 1961–63 warming up in the bullpen had the greatest curve of our time. The only meaningful statistic in politics or baseball is the ratio of games won to games lost, and by this standard Kennedy hardly ranks among our effective Presidents.

Yet at the basic level of American political reality, the young historian of the future will be wrong, profoundly wrong. His legislative statistics and sour observations on the Grand Design will be unimpeachable, but what he will probably overlook is Kennedy's impact on American opinion, on our self-image—in a phrase, Kennedy's subtle introduction of *the politics of modernity.* We are not here talking about superficial mannerisms, but about a fundamental approach to the nature of politics—or even a redefinition of the political.

It is my contention that the Thousand Days marked a sharp transition in American attitudes. A whole series of issues were muted and a new set emerged to replace them. The forties and fifties were characterized by a universe of political discourse which had its roots in World War II and the postwar collapse of the "Grand Alliance"; between 1961 and 1964, the whole international system founded on bipolarity began to crumble. And it was Kennedy's genius that he realized the extent to which our foreign policy was dying from hardening of the categories and set out to lead the American people to a new framework of analysis.

Liberals have been accused of holding a naive faith in the progressivism of the American people. Historically there may have been some merit to this charge, but it appears to me that some of our recent problems have arisen from the converse, from an overaddiction to a secularized version of the doctrine of Original Sin. The fifties, and particularly the presidential election of 1952, tended to generate a profound liberal pessimism which rested at base upon an unarticulated distrust of public opinion.

The fifties were indeed a hard decade for liberalism. I suspect that many liberals have not yet recovered from the deadening impact of the 1952 election. For twenty years the liberal movement had enjoyed that wonderful feeling of exhilaration that accompanies victory; Truman's 1948 triumph, in particular, seemed to indicate that there was a cosmic endorsement for the objectives of liberal Democrats. Then came Korea, McCarthyism and November 1952. Stevenson's defeat was especially devastating because for the first time we had a presidential candidate who *really* talked our language. Never in this century has a nominee for President campaigned as *seriously*—in our sense of the word—as did Stevenson in 1952. (Kennedy was deadly serious in 1960, but his style was entirely different: Stevenson was a serious Greek, Kennedy a serious Roman. Intellectuals have always preferred Greeks to Romans.)

We all died a little on that somber November night as we learned that the Age of Banality had begun. And I suspect that we all began, at various levels of consciousness, to question the viability of the democratic process. The fearful beatings we took in the early fifties tended to encourage a siege mentality. We had been brutally whipsawed: Can one ever forget being simultaneously denounced as pro-Communist for "losing China" and as a "war party" for intervening in Korea?

The 1952 election results appeared to indicate that we had lost what we had blissfully assumed was a permanent majority among the American people for the forces of Enlightenment. In retrospect it seems clear to me that the remarkable aspect of the 1952 election was that Stevenson did as well as he did: While the American people were clearly counting on Eisenhower to get them out of the front lines and back to normalcy, when one analyzed figures one could learn that the election was anything but a repudiation of liberalism. (Even among Irish Catholics, who were allegedly raving with the McCarthyite virus, 55 percent of the votes were cast for Stevenson.) While Eisenhower carried 297 congressional districts, the Republican candidates for the House were victorious in only 221. And Stevenson, running against a picture on the American wall—the Liberator of Europe —still amassed more votes than any previous *winning* candidate for President.

Liberal pessimism was, of course, reinforced by the terrible drubbing Stevenson took in 1956, though even a biased view of the '56 campaign must take into account that it was a shambles.

The one echo of the intellectual vitality of the '52 campaign—Stevenson's call for a ban on nuclear tests—was so hedged about with qualifications and defensive rhetoric that it did actually sound like a political maneuver.

In short, we liberals went "underground." We continued to express ourselves and to advance vigorously unorthodox positions on such issues as the recognition of Red China, anti-Communist legislation or nuclear testing, but the old punch was gone. We spent an unduly large proportion of our time talking to each other—and the rest in the psychologically satisfying but essentially negative task of excoriating the Eisenhower Administration. We did not undertake the task of public education or stimulate a climate of opinion in which vital questions (such as the absurdity of the Dulles doctrine of "massive retaliation") could be canvassed. We issued press releases from our bunkers, but did not emerge to take the offensive.

In other words, we took the '52 and '56 election results as evidence that we had lost contact with the American people, and this conviction undermined our *élan,* our will to fight and above all to provide the advance guard for new political ideas and formulations. And this happened concurrently with our exodus not only from the seats of power (unfortunately we have never had the power attributed to us by either the messianic Left or the *National Review*) but also from the political communications network. Our friends were out of office in the national administration: we no longer had the privilege of going to the White House or the Department of State to complain. We felt lonesome and alienated—a fact which, I suspect, contributed to the fantastic increase in assaults by liberal intellectuals on the horrors of "mass culture."

This is a severe and perhaps overstated indictment, but it limns what I take to be the essentials of the liberal malaise. The consequences of this defeat syndrome were many and varied, but the key one for our purposes here was that in its reaction to the alleged reactionary rigidification of American opinion the liberal community tended to become hermetic and to a considerable degree nonpolitical—a large segment took refuge in cultural elitism and abandoned the masses to their materialistic revels. Yet, on close analysis, was American public opinion (that amorphous statistical entity) anything near as rigid or as reactionary as the pessimists seemed to believe? Perhaps the notion of an inherently McCarthyite public was just as absurd as the earlier concept of the innately liberal public?

We must not forget the role trust plays in the political process. Being issue-oriented, liberals sometimes delude themselves into believing that politics is—or should be—an intellectual enterprise. This leads to the view that nobody should ever take a position on anything until he has studied the facts for himself and reached an independent judgment. I would be the last person to depreciate the role of intelligence in the political process, but I would strongly argue that an intelligent approach to political decisions can quite reasonably involve the application of the division of labor. The notion of 190 million Americans engaged in technical research on the problems of a test-ban treaty is in fact rather terrifying, for it would indicate an absence of that trust in leadership which is the necessary foundation for any stable society.

Take the Kennedy-Nixon debates as a case in point. Does anyone seriously think that the watchers were scoring the results with a copy of *Time's* current events test? They were scoring it, but in an entirely different fashion; they were certainly not under the illusion that excellence as a Quiz Kid was a qualification for the presidency. Intellectual evaluation was, of course, part of the total, but essentially the watchers were attempting to determine—on the basis of a whole range of considerations both conscious and unconscious—which of these men could be trusted with the destiny of the Republic. And before the angry reader accuses me of anti-intellectualism, he should meditate on the ironic fact that if *only* college graduates had the franchise, Richard M. Nixon would be President of the United States.

My feeling, therefore, is that those who decided to vote for John Kennedy after watching him on the Great Debate were not registering their support for the specific propositions he advanced, which were not much out of the ordinary, but were naming him their opinion-executor. Effectively they were saying that Kennedy (or Nixon) was the man to whom they delegated their decision-making in national affairs or international affairs—just as, at a different level, congressmen also exercise delegated trust. A failure to understand this key proposition led to much pessimism about the possibilities of American ratification of the test-ban treaty.

So-called "manipulation" of public opinion is not the issue. What is involved is *trust,* and an inability to appreciate this concept and its vital consequences has crippled the peace movement. When a "peace candidate" rode forth in the fall of 1962, he did so with the commendable mission of informing the public on the crucial issue of war and peace. The difficulty was that to the average voter—who strongly believes in peace—the essence of a "peace candidate's" message seemed to be: "The President and the Congress are eager to see us all blown up." He attempted to cut the bond of trust between the population and its political leaders, and failed completely. The public trusted John Kennedy in the Cuban confrontation—and in the test-ban negotiations; after all, he was elected to handle precisely such questions.

This detour leads us back to the problem in the early fifties. Then precisely the opposite development occurred: The "public" (again a statistical fiction) *lost* faith in its political leaders, and transferred its trust to Dwight D. Eisenhower. It would be nice to blame this transfer on History or some other transcendent factor, but I regret to say that—while I think the decision of the electorate was wrong—there was a real foundation for public concern and dismay. From 1950 on, the Truman Administration was a wreck, and liberal forces in the political sector were in fearful disarray. True, the Republicans were playing dirty, but the Marquis of Queensbury has never been a mentor for American politics—does anyone recall the "missile gap"? And to a liberal who is also a historian, the hard fact emerges that the *political* counter-offensive to McCarthyism was a dismal flop. When Truman vetoed the McCarran Internal Security Act of 1950, for example, only ten Senators supported him; and the grotesque Internal Security Act of 1954 passed 79–0.

The lesson should be clear by now: the overarching importance of liberal leadership in the political sector, and the secondary character of cultural or purely issue-oriented emphases. Contrast, for instance, the tremendous battle the liberals fought against McCarthyism in the society at large with the collapse of anti-McCarthyism in the political arena. This curious situation encouraged the pessimism of European observers who, assuming that Washington, D.C., was the United States, announced that McCarthyism was carrying everything in its path and the nation was on the abyss of fascism. In fact, McCarthyism was not an organized political movement with deep roots in the country, but a psychosis that thrived on the disorganization and timidity of its opponents, and on the opportunism of the so-called "conservatives," Democratic and Republican, who were glad to employ any stick to beat the liberal dog.

The enormous support that developed for the nuclear test-ban, as well as the growing weight of public endorsement for a strong civil rights bill in 1963–64, should suggest that the ice pack of internal insecurity and "hard-nosed" anti-Communism of ten years ago has broken up. Essentially, I believe, the Thousand Days of John F. Kennedy marked a transition point in American politics: It undermined the power of Yahoo Republicanism and of Southern racism, though in the name of efficiency and modernity rather than for liberal ideological reasons. But however motivated, the New Frontiersmen brought a whole new operational framework to national and international politics, and opened up American politics in a fashion reminiscent of the early years of the New Deal.

Examples of what I have called the Kennedy Breakthrough can be drawn from a number of areas of domestic and foreign policy, but I shall confine myself to two instances drawn from each area. In foreign relations Kennedy inherited the Manichean universe of John Foster Dulles and Dean Acheson. Dulles' foreign policy was in fact a logical extension of Acheson's: "Liberation" was always implicit in "containment," though Truman and Acheson had the prudential sense not to convert operational logic into a *reductio ad absurdum*. In essence, Dulles was a caricature of Acheson. More important, the policy which Acheson and Kennan devised in 1947 was designed to cope with immediate Soviet expansionism, to mobilize American opinion to a "hard line" which was absolutely necessary in the context of the times. Ironically, just as Stalin died, Dulles became President of the United States for Foreign Affairs and set to work to "correct" the policies of the five previous years. With a fixated legalism, Dulles seemed to think that he could at the appellate level reverse the decisions made at the trial; for six years he rebriefed the past and in his dream-world took Stalin to the "brink."

But Stalin was dead and Dulles' exercises in brinksmanship were fantasies, founded—as Hans Morgenthau noted at the time—on the archaic premise of nuclear monopoly. One may suspect that Khrushchev only learned that he had been humbled at the brink from subsequent Dulles memoirs in the *Saturday Evening Post*. Indeed, Dulles' *de facto* foreign policy probably encouraged the flexible Soviet leader, who must have decided early in his career that Dulles confused rhetoric with action. During the Hungarian Revolution, for example, the Soviets were obviously in a quandary (they were afraid—and understandably so—of an American response to military intervention in Budapest) until Dulles thoughtfully took them off the hook by assuring Khrushchev that the United States would not intervene in the internal affairs of the Soviet bloc. From this point on Khrushchev had Dulles tagged as a moral isolationist—a spiritual America Firster—who would never risk Chicago to save Budapest. Only in this fashion can we explain the expansion of Khrushchev's political vocabulary from that time on to include, almost as a standard incantation, the threat of a "hail of rockets" to those nations who persisted in anti-Soviet coalitions.

To put it bluntly, American foreign policy as it emerged from the fifties was an eerie compound of high-flown anti-Communist morality and operational cowardice. The American people had been (willingly) lulled to sleep by assurances that the forces of Satan were cowering before the Sword of the Righteous. Indeed, I cannot find *one* instance in the eight years of the Eisenhower Administration when the people were told by their leaders that real risks were present, that the road was perilous. The threat of Communist expansion had allegedly been exorcised. But Khrushchev, who had survived the *Yezhovshchina* and knew a risky road when he saw one, was not fooled: On a perfectly solid empirical basis, he calculated that in any confrontation the United States would take all steps short of action that would risk a thermonuclear exchange. As he told Robert Frost and several other visiting Americans, "the United States is too liberal to fight." Since it was in his power to define the "risk" of thermonuclear war, he was able to shape American foreign policy.

Thus Kennedy inherited a policy that consisted of ferocious abstract attacks on the wickedness of Communism and tactical paralysis. From the short-range viewpoint of the American "man in the street," this was ideal: He could rejoice in the ferocious rhetoric and relax. It made the neo-isolationists happy because it warmed their hearts to hear an American Secretary of State "tell off the Reds"—and yet justified budget cutting. It even warmed the hearts of the group I once called the "Eisenhower Marxists," whose dialectical sense led them to support the President as a "peace candidate," i.e., a loser in the cold war. Behind the psychological Maginot Line of "massive retaliation" all was calm and peaceful—while in the outside world American policy was dying the Chinese death of a thousand cuts.

The essence of any sane American policy in 1961 was an absolute reversal of priorities: a diminution of chiliastic rhetoric and calls to immediate "total victory," and a stepping-up of concrete, tactical responses to the endless Communist probes. Above all, Kennedy had to change the universe of discourse by convincing the Soviets that nuclear war must be abandoned as an instrument of policy because it was a real possibility. And he had to bring home to the American people the fact that Communism could not be exterminated, if we so willed, unless we were ready to go down in a common grave; that massive resurrection would be, for most of us, the precondition to massive retaliation.

In sum, Kennedy had to obtain freedom of maneuver by escaping from the trap of Soviet nuclear initiatives—the "hail of rockets"—and from the ideological bonds created by rigid, hard-line, millennial anti-Communism. He had to discredit both ends of the "better Red/dead than dead/Red" syllogism. Specifically, he had to ask the American people to trust him with their destinies in a war of maneuver—not Armageddon—where it might be necessary to stop short of "total victory"; where it might be imperative to negotiate with the "enemy," even to do business with the "enemy"; where tactical demands might require retreat in the interest of long-run objectives.

Kennedy achieved these objectives in two superbly organized campaigns: the first against the Soviet Union in October 1962, and the second against the frozen American Right in the struggle for the Test-Ban Treaty. The Cuban confrontation is surely the most remarkable application of political physics the world has ever seen: The Soviet miscalculation was met with precisely determined optimum-force responses; there was no chauvinism, no howling for total victory, no effort to mislead the American people about the gravity of the crisis. Initially, imitating Soviet tactics in East Germany, we simply tore up the roads to Cuba and prepared for gradual intensification of the pressure; from the outset Khrushchev was provided with room for retreat. The Soviets were clearly terrified; they were used to Dulles—who would have left the missiles in Cuba, organized a Caribbean security treaty, and denounced the evils of Communism before the American Legion.

This halfway house between defeat (which would have left the missiles in Cuba or brought a nuclear holocaust) and total victory (which would have seen the elimination of the Castro regime) brought the Chinese out screaming: the Chinese Right in the United States and the Chinese Left in the Soviet bloc. But the American people, who had knowingly put their lives in the balance for almost a week, were prepared to accept the President's prudential guidance, i.e., they abandoned the Goldwater Standard of anti-Communism.

This became clear during the prolonged battle for Senate approval of the Test-Ban Treaty. The Right brought out all the old drums and beat them frantically for six months. The President and his advisors in Congress and the administration mounted a coldly rational campaign: The treaty was not presented as a miraculous cure for cold war tensions but as a beginning, a first step; the Soviets were not billed as reformed sinners, but as partners in a quest for mutual interest—survival; there was no apocalypticism—only a sober appeal for common sense.

Against the opposition of great congressional barons, public opinion gradually mobilized behind the President. The Gallup Poll, for example, indicated a fantastic growth in favorable opinion between July and September 1963—a surge of pressure so great that it led to a vote of 81–19. The conclusion was obvious: The American President was dealing with the Enemy and the American people were willing to trust him with the unfortunate, undesirable, but necessary task. The Right had called the spirits from the vasty deep, had invoked all the magic in the arsenal of the fifties, but the spirits from the vasty deep had not responded: The ship of state had finally broken out of the ice pack of McCarthyism.

It is important to note that Kennedy's policies here, as elsewhere, were not "liberal" in the usual ideological sense of that word. One could even argue that his notions of how foreign policy should be conducted were, if anything, in the classic tradition of statecraft as represented in our time by, say, George Kennan and Sir Harold Nicolson. The significant thing is thus not the content of his policy, but the fact that he won public acceptance for a diplomatic posture that has traditionally been associated with aristocratic regimes and unrepresentative elites. It was Kennedy's accomplishment that the American public showed itself willing to send him out to handle the incredibly delicate task of maintaining freedom *and* peace in a contingent universe.

A final contrast, perhaps, will underscore this accomplishment: When in 1958 President Eisenhower announced over television that we might have to consider the possibility of undertaking certain conceivable warlike actions in the Formosa Straits, the public response was quantitatively and vigorously negative—before the State Department suppressed statistics, communications were allegedly running on the order of 500–1 *against*. The reaction to Kennedy's statement on the Cuban blockade was, on the other hand, overwhelmingly favorable. Eisenhower had painted himself into a strategic corner by his constant refusal to challenge the American people, particularly by his suggestion in the 1952 campaign that the Korean War was a Democratic blunder. Again at the time of Hungary and Suez he prescribed tranquilizers. His role was to exorcize the turbulent past. Without for a moment suggesting that he was right in calling for a policy of (ambiguous) vigor in the Formosa Strait, I would suggest that *any* concretely vigorous foreign policy he might have suggested would have received the same negative response. He was in the position of a man who has become a prisoner of his own press releases. Kennedy sensitized American opinion to the perils of the nuclear age and carried his constituents with him—nervously but with commitment—to the abyss in the most awesome display of democratic solidarity since the Battle of Britain.

On the domestic scene, much the same process occurred,

though less dramatically. The conduct of foreign relations was ideally suited to Kennedy's approach. Traditionally the President has far greater scope for initiative in the international sector than at home, and far less attrition from Congress. I suspect that, despite his years in the House and Senate, Kennedy was really quite bored by Congress: He was never a good listener unless he could set up the conversational options, and his congressional career must therefore have contained a good deal of cruel and unusual punishment. And in the handling of domestic policy, the President must to a considerable degree throw himself on the mercy of the national legislature; he has a good deal less "power" in this context than is ordinarily realized.

It must be conceded that Kennedy never really developed an effective relationship with Congress. For one thing, he suffered from what Kierkegaard somewhere called the "paralysis of knowledge"—he knew too much about the congressional capacity for sabotage to commit himself to a militant challenge to legislative power. Yet at the same time it was perfectly clear that he considered Congress an appalling barrier to the creation of an efficient, modern government. Unlike Harry Truman or Lyndon Johnson, he had never been an "insider," a member of the club—secretly he may have felt that such membership was equivalent to high status in the Society for the Preservation of the Whooping Crane. He had no patience with ancient rubes in their anecdotage and, no matter how many times he paid tribute to their "statesmanship" at press conferences, the old magnates knew an enemy when they saw one and had their revenge.

Thus his legislative program was quietly strangled in the House Rules Committee or in the anterooms of the Senate, and the bills that emerged were often far removed in substance from those that he proposed—one may, for instance, surmise that the tax bill, minus tax reforms, that the House passed (and which later became law) would have been denounced by liberals as "class legislation" had Eisenhower been President.

Despite the pathetic legislative record of the Thousand Days, however, there is another aspect of Kennedy's domestic program which must be taken into consideration—his impact on American public opinion. Alas, we can never know whether this impact would have been reflected in Congress, say, in 1965–66, but

Kennedy's groundwork might very well have brought delayed but substantial rewards in two areas in particular: fiscal policy and civil rights. Let me again stress that, while Kennedy's efforts contributed to a "liberal" climate of opinion, he was not in my opinion proceeding according to any ideological system. He simply wanted to eliminate from American politics and administration a collection of inefficient, unfunctional superstitions.

The first to be brought under public scrutiny was belief in the moral wickedness of deficit spending and the whole notion of the inherent godliness of the balanced budget. Here the President, with the aid of a series of charts, attempted to bring Keynes to the consciousness of the American public via a TV lecture. It was (as he later commented wryly to me) a "C minus performance." Still, for the first time a President of the United States impeached the validity of the most deeply rooted economic myth in our collective consciousness.

It seems difficult to believe, but until 1962—despite all the empirical data that has been accumulating for the last quarter-century—the balanced budget had maintained its sacramental standing in American politics. Of course, if the average citizen adopted the principle of the balanced budget, the economy would probably collapse: He is in hock for his house, his car, his refrigerator, his boat, his kitchen stove—all purchased today on the premise of future affluence. And the investment policies of business are predicated on similar optimism and willingness to take a risk. But somehow the realities of economic life have never been permitted to intrude into the inviolate atmosphere of economic myth.

Kennedy, with his customary intellectual ruthlessness, seized the nettle, proposing major tax reductions with the concomitant of an unbalanced budget as a technique for stimulating long-range economic growth. The clamor was fantastic: The banshees wailed in the hills, solemn legislators predicted that the creditors would evict us from the country. Henry Hazlitt and Raymond Moley held a death-watch for American capitalism in the pages of *Newsweek*. But eventually (after the President's assassination) the principle was enacted into public policy. True, President Johnson did rush to the rescue of classical mythology by demanding "economy" in government, thus eliminating the most effective form of economic stimulation—direct government expenditure—in favor of the indirect techniques of leaving expansion in corporate and private hands (where the savings factor can act as a massive restraint). Yet the deed was done, the precedent established. Kennedy made it clear that in his opinion the emperor had no clothes, and it is doubtful whether all the incantations that classical economic fakirs intone can ever restore the myth to its pristine position.

Kennedy's part in the civil rights area was far more passive. While it was always clear where his sympathies in this matter lay, he seemed for too long a time to cherish the unrealistic hope that a reconciliation was possible between the Southern white politicians and the Northern liberals which could prevent a public confrontation. Tensions within the national Democratic coalition, which led to some Southern defections in 1960, could be increased to the point where the antique alliance would fall apart—and with it, perhaps, his majority in 1964. Moreover, Kennedy had, in my judgment, one great blind spot: He was simply incapable of understanding extremism. The day he was shot, he had spent an hour in the plane pressing two Texas representatives on the Birchers and the radical Right—and persistently he returned to the same question: "What do they *really* want?" Similarly, he seems to have assumed at the outset that the Southern Democrats were merely putting up a militant racist front in order to establish a hard bargaining position, that they did not *really* believe the anachronisms they promulgated.

The outcome of this presidential restraint was a tremendous effort on the administrative level to work out the civil rights issue below the threshold of political visibility, an effort which culminated with the dispatch of the Attorney General to Birmingham, literally to "fix the ticket," i.e., get the reasonable brokers together in a room and hammer out a face-saving compromise. The Attorney General apparently got an education in Alabama: He was alleged to have said on his return that it was like "going to another country." John Kennedy and his brother here confronted the thing which above all others makes a modern, urbane utilitarian nervous: raw ideology unmitigated by any rationality or willingness to compromise.

The President had no temperamental fondness for moral civil

wars, but whatever his reservations the fact remains that once the genie was out of the bottle, he shifted his whole approach and threw his influence behind a strong civil rights bill. In addition, he announced flatly (with none of Eisenhower's reservations) that there were no two ways of looking at the civil rights matter: The white supremacists were simply wrong. Although it is difficult for one who was urging the President in season and out to raise the battle flag and exercise moral leadership to admit it, there were undoubtedly great benefits that accrued from Kennedy's low-key handling of the civil rights issue. Most important perhaps was the impact of his flat, factual, unadorned, unemotional statements on public opinion. He made the whole quest for equality sound so *sensible,* so commonsensical, while racists appeared worse than immoral—they were stupid Neanderthalers trying to hold back the tide of modernity.

We liberals, who have been fighting for civil rights over the years, have every reason to be proud of our accomplishments—I for one refuse to flagellate before the image of St. James Baldwin for the alleged sins of "white liberals"—and it is clear to me that our travail was necessary before the American people would treat racial equality as a meaningful component of national idealism. But if what we accomplished was necessary, it was not sufficient. When the history books are written, it will, I suspect be seen that the final civil rights breakthrough occurred under the (curiously reluctant) auspices of President John Kennedy. For it is now, in 1964, patent that the institutional back of white supremacy has been broken, and that the racists themselves are conducting a sullen, bitter retreat into historical oblivion. It may be a generation before we have genuine equality at the social and economic levels, but the political and legal fortress of American apartheid has been fatally undermined.

If I am correct in my reading of the state of mind of contemporary public opinion, the time has come for a basic reassessment of the liberal posture. It seems apparent to me that John Kennedy's Thousand Days closed the books—in a psychological sense—on much of the recent political past: closing in the process many of our accounts, as well as those of our opponents. He brought us into the modern world, and in a symbolic way the reaction to his murder indicated a new mood of public maturity. To the great dismay of European ideologues—to whom, ironically, the excesses of the McCarthy era were proof of American puerility—we did not launch a great hysterical witch hunt for "conspiracy," but rejected social paranoia for the commonsense assumption that the deed was done by an isolated psychotic. Those of the far Right and the millennial Left who have patiently cultivated the seeds of a conspiracy theory have been left arguing with each other on whether Kennedy was killed by the Communists for double-crossing his master Khrushchev, or by the CIA for signing the Test-Ban Treaty. The cracked drums are beating in a void.

As a committed liberal activist, I regret that I can supply no institutional prescriptions, no certain chart of where liberals should go from here. In short, I can issue negative injunctions with some confidence—I know what we *should not* do. And, as a political scientist and historian (there is no such thing as "Liberal History") I am afraid that we are in for perilous times, that we run the risk of becoming ideological dinosaurs unless we respond to the challenge of the open future.

I must therefore end on an abstract note—with apologies, since my views may be a bit embarrassing to my utilitarian friends who get nervous when anyone talks about morality. But either we are moralists or we are nothing, and the nub of our dilemma is that the times imperatively require a rebirth of liberal morality, or of liberal political theory, to use a less loaded term. Over the past half-century we have exhausted our stock of ideas, those we inherited from Victorian liberalism and Victorian socialism, and unless we are prepared to spend our time as social and political plumbers, playing with the pipes and unclogging drains, we must turn to the task of reformulating our premises. This is not a call to "repudiate" anything—we need theory, not polemic—for the historical fact is that with the weapons we held we took the United States away from the Yahoos and created the foundations of a decent society.

From this perspective the Goldwater nomination is a desperate, flailing assault by the Yahoos aimed at the politics of modernity. I am convinced that Goldwater can be beaten and beaten badly, but I am equally aware of the fact that history is unilinear, that progress is not automatic. Our first priority is thus a total commitment to the kind of effective political action which alone can guarantee the results on November 3—which can make the Goldwater crusade the political equivalent of the Pawnee Ghost Dance.

Unless I am drastically wrong in my reading of the fundamental mood of the American people, we stand at the threshold of a new era—an era in which the categories "liberal" and "conservative" as we know them may have as much meaning as Whig and Tory. It is our obligation to take the grand principles of our tradition, the great ideal of a self-governing community living in justice and freedom, and apply them radically and without trepidation to novel circumstances. Put another way, we must reassert our offensive political function, climb out of our defensive redoubts, and justify our noble claim as prophets of democratic morality.

The Uses of
American Power

No PROBLEM is more perplexing to liberals than the appropriate utilization of international power. For as long as I can remember, we have been arguing about the proper content of a "liberal" foreign policy or, to put it another way, to what extent American power should be employed in world politics to advance "good" objectives and frustrate "bad" ones. It is this issue which underlies liberal criticism of the foreign aid program, though unfortunately perfectly legitimate and cogent critics often find themselves carrying spears in Otto Passman's version of *Götterdammerung*.

In concrete terms, should we consciously use pressure, at whatever level may be necessary, to encourage and maintain democratic regimes and to undermine the authority of the undemocratic? In extreme situations, should we be prepared to use military means to aid democratic governments threatened from without (e.g., Israel, India) or from within (e.g., the Dominican Republic, Honduras, Venezuela)? Should we have lowered the

Reprinted, with permission, from *The New Leader*, March 2, 1964.

boom on the Diem Administration? Should we support the hard British position against Indonesia's Sukarno? What should we plan to do in British Guiana when the British liquidate, as they certainly will within the year?

Year in and year out we have faced these issues on an *ad hoc* basis, but we have never seized the nettle. While we believe that the power of the state should be employed to achieve racial justice, economic abundance, adequate education and decent facilities for the sick and aged, in the United States we somehow wince at the thought of utilizing the same state to improve the international environment. We have in us a deep streak of moral isolationism: American power in the world arena is unclean and, worse, must be unclean. And we labor under a burden of guilts: Because Theodore Roosevelt stole Panama from Colombia, we are supposed to stand by abashedly while a tinhorn military gangster butchers our comrades in Honduras.

In effect, we thus endorse the proposition that the Hondu-ranians would prefer a dictatorship to a free government backed by the United States. Our "nonintervention" in the Dominican Republic reflected the same absurd premise; we "nonintervened" in favor of a wretched junta and against a democratic gov-ernment.

Liberals are no more sinful in this rudderless drifting than other Americans, but I submit that we have a special obligation to coherent intellectual leadership which precludes our endorse-ment of that "pragmatism" which is simply an excuse for not having a policy. No red-blooded American can object to playing by ear, but perhaps one may timidly ask *what* is being played.

The liberal's problem is in part historical. We are simultane-ously the heirs of nineteenth-century liberalism *and* of the demo-cratic internationalism of social democracy. These two value systems were at one time compatible. When in April 1917, for example, the American Socialist party at its St. Louis convention condemned the entrance of the United States into World War I, it was asserting both the liberal imperative of national integrity and socialist internationalism. But between the end of the First World War and the outbreak of the Second, the two traditions parted, leaving ideological schizophrenia in their wake: The British Labour party in the late thirties found itself simultaneously endorsing collective security against Hitler (in the liberal tradition) and opposing rearmament (in the name of proletarian internationalism). American liberals and socialists went through similar, and even more complex, convolutions trying to figure out how to help the Spanish Republic without providing "objective support" to militarism. Out of kindness to a great many people (myself included), I shall omit examples.

The essence of the liberal tradition in this context was stated (on its death-bed) by Woodrow Wilson in his principle of national self-determination. Liberalism, in short, emphasized the integrity of the national unit and the maintenance of international order on a pluralistic basis. The internal structure of a nation was irrelevant to its status in the international forum; the only standards of behavior were formalized at the international level as nonaggression and nonintervention in the internal affairs of other states. Liberalism thus anathematized all crusades; like the rain, the approval of liberals fell equally on the just and the unjust, provided they left their neighbors alone. Similarly, enormous sanctity was accorded to treaties and other rituals of international "order": A nation which violated a treaty was far more despicable than one which murdered half its population. (Happily, certain primitive nations were restrained by treaty from murdering the Christian part of their populations; thus certain great powers had the right to intervene in Turkey to protect Christian minorities.) "International law" was elaborated as the moral etiquette of international relations.

The other side of this coin was, of course, colonialism and imperialism, which were justified by distinguished liberals (and by Karl Marx, for his own reasons) because they brought "enlightenment" to the benighted, non-Western pagans. In the same fashion that Jefferson in the Declaration of Independence could affirm the equality of all men with the unarticulated corollary that Negro slaves were not "men," John Stuart Mill could proclaim the virtues of "liberty" and exclude from its coverage "barbarians" or races in their "nonage" (e.g., the Indians). But once a nation was admitted to the liberal club, the fiction of equality took over. It was just damned hard to get admitted; essentially, as Mill also noted, the proof of one's readiness for nationhood was the capacity to throw out the occupying power! Q.E.D.

Socialist internationalism operated from radically different premises. At base it countered a nation-to-nation with a people-to-people model which completely denied the presuppositions of liberalism—except as a phenomenon in the sociology of knowledge, i.e., as a necessary stage of historical development. (This latter aspect of Marx's historicism often led to curious alignments; just as Marx praised the *objective* role of British imperialism in India, some socialists supported imperialism as the impregnation of "feudal" or "primitive" societies with the fetus of capitalism, which would in turn give birth to socialism.) It would, however, be a mistake to overemphasize the Marxist-historicist component in socialist internationalism, particularly in its Anglo-Saxon version. My own reading, at least, suggests that in Britain and the United States socialist internationalism was far more a secularization of Christian ideals of brotherhood than an exercise in dialectics.

Marxist and non-Marxist internationalists were in substantial agreement that the nineteenth-century nation-state was a reactionary enterprise which stood in the way of genuine internationalism. Some felt, with Eduard Bernstein and the British Fabians, that the immediate need was to achieve a socialist state; others seem to have assumed that the abolition of the state per se would lead to some millennium. But whatever their vision of the future, they converged in a revolutionary tactic of "intervention." Freedom and justice were the goals, socialism the vehicle, and they were prepared to undermine and overthrow any regime which denied its population the right to choose its own course, i.e., any regime which suppressed freedom of choice. The leaders of the Second International were first of all democrats; it never entered their minds to impose socialism. They simply took for granted the proposition that socialism would triumph in any democratic society, and the establishment and maintenance of democratic rights would thus lead automatically to a popular mandate for socialism. Indeed, Bernstein argued that the only source of violence in the transformation of a capitalist society to socialism would be found in the efforts of a moribund ruling class to eliminate the democratic institutions which were bringing its downfall.

This is wandering a bit far afield, but it is vital to an understanding of our contemporary dilemmas to appreciate the sources of our ambivalence. Alas, one more variable has to be thrown into the equation: the character of "state" action. The liberals treated states as atoms motivated by self-interest in an international system where "order" was the prime virtue; a "good" state was one that played the game according to the rules and the liberal ban would fall equally on a democratic state attempting to subvert its totalitarian neighbors and a totalitarian state engaged in similar activity. The socialists thought of themselves as representatives of a class with no fatherland. Until World War I and the formation of the Soviet Union, they had no favorite states. Some were greater evils, some lesser, but they were all capitalist. World War I destroyed the dream of internationalism and left fearful guilts—both contributed to the status of the USSR: One could expiate his guilt for chauvinism (or if he was not guilty, his often greater shame because the masses had deserted him) by adopting the USSR as a step-fatherland.

Thus there entered into the lexicon of the Left a new concept, that of the "good state." Here was a concept which, needless to say, was utterly absurd from the liberal viewpoint, and was a logical monstrosity from the vantage point of socialist internationalism. The organization of the Comintern formalized the structure and symbolized the new theory: The working class now had a general headquarters, the "world revolution" a homeland. The fascist states imitated this model in their own fashions.

The Spanish Civil War supplied a laboratory for the case analysis of these three models of international relations. Classical liberalism provided a policy of "nonintervention" in which decent people and totalitarians agreed under the aegis of the League of Nations not to intervene in the "internal affairs" of a sovereign state. The Fascists and the Communists intervened (paying no attention to the nonintervention agreement) to support their own agents. And the pathetic remnant of socialist internationalism denounced all the states involved and called on the working class everywhere to save the Spanish Republic in some unspecified fashion. (I recall advocating a general strike, though the logic of this position escapes me; it was probably the impact of Rosa Luxemburg on a fifteen-year-old.)

World War II indicated to me that the liberal model and the ideal of proletarian internationalism were equally antiquated, that they were theoretical siamese twins of nineteenth century origin. It was clear in cold retrospect that from 1935 on, nothing short of anti-Nazi *state* action could have deterred German aggression, that the classical liberal "boys will be boys" approach to the barbarities of Nazism *and* the socialist internationalist view that state action, i.e., war, would be as immoral and self-defeating as nazism itself, were both in practical terms absurd. Similarly, the appalling butchery of Soviet Communism and the expansionist drives of Stalinism would never be inhibited by "spontaneous" working-class action. In the postwar period, those anti-Stalinists who opposed state action were merely indulging in the luxury of signing their own death warrants—if they were unfortunate enough to be outside the reach of Western power. Ironically, the Nazis and the Stalinists in the 1930s, and those like Churchill who demanded a commitment of national power against the totalitarians, were right in their assessment of the situation; the liberals, clinging to their nineteenth-century state system, and the socialist internationalists, with their dreams of spontaneous popular resistance, were wrong.

Thus, whether we like it or not, the fact is that since 1947 the cause of freedom has rested on American power, on "good" state power. And we of the American liberal-Left, with our differing backgrounds, have never been willing to face up to this fact and to its consequences. Our sense of reality has been strong enough to lead us to support such openly military proposals as NATO, but only with uneasy consciences and a hope that we could quickly get back to issues less close to the bone, e.g., technical assistance, the Marshall Plan, support for the UN, etc. However much we may trust the state in domestic affairs—and our program is built on that proposition—we somehow feel that American power in the international arena is corrupt, a manifestation of "imperialism" or "colonialism." When we hear the clarion call of the "young radicals," denouncing the U.S. and the USSR in equally strident terms for the menace of nuclear annihilation, we may suffer from acute guilt feelings and (fogetting our own experience) glorify the zeal of the young. The wonderful thing about childhood is that one can outgrow it, but all of us have regrets—at various levels of consciousness—that we have left that marvelous Manichean universe where black is black, white is white, and grey is outlawed. (Every so often even I, hardened bureaucrat and Establishment man that I am advertised to be, long to proclaim the General Strike.)

In this connection I might note that my wife and I both learned to sing "We Will Overcome" in 1939 (along with Jim Farmer, Bayard Rustin and a number of others), but we were clobbered in our struggle for equal rights. The reason was simple: We did not have state power on our side. Without in any way depreciating the dedication of contemporary civil rights militants, I would suggest that having the national government in the struggle does provide some big battalions for the forces of righteousness. One can even become a civil rights martyr today, though the first time Bayard Rustin got sent down to the chain gang he vanished without a trace and we could hardly get a newspaper to handle the story. (As Orwell noted, if one wants to be a martyr, he has to choose his enemies pretty carefully.)

In domestic affairs, then, liberals want to see the national government exercise its power to expand freedom, nourish equality, eliminate unemployment and succor the sick and aged. Is there any logical reason why we should not utilize the same approach in the international arena? Why should we not urge that American power be employed to protect and strengthen democratic regimes and harass and undermine the undemocratic? If one believes that freedom, justice, equality, are not subordinate to national boundaries, it seems to me to follow that we should consciously shape our policy in terms of revolutionary, democratic internationalism.

The immediate objection to this view is to label it American chauvinism or liberal "imperialism." (Given the obsolescence of this criticism, I am surprised that no one has trotted out the antique epithet "social patriot"!) In point of fact, what this viewpoint involves is a set of evaluative principles which are applied across the board—to the United States (where we have been battling for justice, equality and decency to the best of our ability) as much as to any other society. What we deny is the existence of a double moral standard: Some years ago when I was lecturing in France, for example, I had the American authorities in acute distress because of my strictures on the subject of racial discrimination, and the French in an uproar because of my observations on torture in Algiers. In the liberal view, nothing is more absurd than the assumption that a dotted line on a map muffles moral principles.

To the charge of moral authoritarianism from the ethical relativists, little reply need be made. A number of us put in three or more years of our lives fighting against this inane solipsism in its concrete form: that killing Jews and other deviants was an "old German custom" which "they think is right." We are not absolutists in the metaphysical sense, but we believe that one has to make an absolute, total commitment on behalf of the truth but dimly seen. In particular, we must assert man's supremacy over his instruments, i.e., his right to retain the power of choice. Thus, when we oppose the suppression of opposition in any society it is not in the name of the "American Way of Life" or even of *jus naturale,* but rather because such action forecloses the very possibilities of further decisions—except by violence. (And it might be added that we have opposed precisely such tendencies *in* the United States, e.g., the Smith Act, the McCarran Act, etc.)

Acceptance of this position does not involve a commitment to constant "liberation" in *practical* terms. We live in a world which is beyond control in any simple sense, and we have to recognize not only that there may be no solutions to many problems (only outcomes), and that our capacity for action must be limited by recognition of risks. In other words, one can oppose the "liberation" of Eastern Europe, or Cuba, on prudential grounds (as I do), but retain the policy as the long-range objective with whatever tactics may be appropriate. If we accept this view, we would not simply relax in the luxury of a 1964 détente with Khrushchev (one obviously founded, on his part, on Soviet self-interest) but would take advantage of Soviet difficulties to mount a campaign of "competitive peaceful coexistence" throughout the world. (This need not be advertised in *Amerika* or shouted from the house-tops in Washington; it could conceivably even take the form of expressions of sympathy to the Chinese Communists that they are having such troubles with their imperialist neighbor, the USSR.

After all, if they had listened to us, they would have appreciated the exploitative, colonialist character of the Soviet regime.) In short, there has to be a pragmatic flexibility but one founded on a coherent policy of democratic internationalism. And this is totally different from John Foster Dulles' Byzantine combination of appeals for "liberation" and, when the Hungarians rose in defiance, assurances to Khrushchev that the United States would, of course, not intervene in the internal affairs of the Soviet bloc.

As I observed at the outset, liberal difficulties in these matters have arisen from the fact that we wander back and forth, as issues arise, between two antithetical polar positions. Because we are instinctively antipower while intellectually quite sophisticated, we usually emerge with a position that is sound, though for the wrong reasons. We are always looking for good, nineteenth-century liberal "cover," which in our time means the involvement of some international organization.

When Truman intervened in Korea, for example, we were rescued from our reflexes by the fiction of UN forces: We are wholly committed to the UN. Today in Latin America we piously support OAS or "multilateral" action, though we are all aware that the OAS is merely a morgue where policies are stacked until they can be given quiet burial—i.e., an institutionalized channel for inaction. (Similarly, if the Korean invasion occurred today I am certain there would be no UN support for resisting aggression; two years ago the Indians, who had recognized Peking and even agreed on *Panch Shila,* the five principles of coexistence, found the UN otherwise occupied when the Chinese came over the border.)

I am convinced, therefore, that we are in for a long period of marginal turbulence in international relations. We are going to be confronted by a series of Vietnams, Panamas, Malaysia-Indonesias, Congos, Cypruses and the like. And whether liberals like the prospect or not, American power is going to be involved directly or indirectly at every point. The nineteenth-century alternatives of intervention versus non-intervention are dead: To refuse to intervene is itself a form of intervention. (In September 1939 when Eamon de Valera announced Eire's neutrality to the parliament, an opposition member arose and inquired who the Irish were neutral *against!*)

We cannot escape from a confrontation with reality by a fetishistic deference to the UN or the OAS—both of which could be useful forums for mediation, but they are not independent power centers. Moreover, I am not sure that we want them to become independent power centers; leaving the UN out of the discussion, it is quite conceivable to me that the United States might be censured by a solid majority of the OAS on a secret ballot because it has an inherently unstable democratic government! This, however, is a topic for another article; the problem here comes down to a ruthlessly simple question: Should American power be employed in behalf of democratic ideals? While reserving the right to argue tactics on the prudential level, it seems to me that we must wholeheartedly endorse a strategy of democratic intervention and cast off once and for all the ideological encrustations of nineteenth-century liberalism *and* nineteenth-century socialism.

Gideon
of the Right

I WAS ENDOWED with what one of my friends once called a "secret police memory." This faculty creates problems on occasion (I am always suspicious when I come up with some seemingly original notion and go carefully through the literature to make sure I have not unobtrusively borrowed a remembered formulation from an unremembered source!), but it also has its virtues. As I was watching Barry Goldwater at the Cow Palace and listening to various interviews conducted by "enemy" newsmen, I had an almost overpowering sense of *déjà vu*. I had been here before; at some time in the past I had witnessed this same sort of pageant featuring this same sort of man.

This obsession ruined my sleep for two nights and then the answer came to me in a literal moment of truth and, at four in the morning, I grabbed two books from the shelf and began to read. Here are some of the passages, slightly changed for reasons that will appear shortly, that had lived on in the human equivalent of the computer data-bank:

Reprinted, with permission, from *The New Leader*, August 3, 1964.

"I'm no expert on the John Birch Society. But the Birchers I've met have been very good Americans." "I am not following their [the Birch Society's] line. If they want to follow my line I say God bless 'em. I admire their utter devotion to a cause they think is just."

Obviously this is not Barry Goldwater—if it were, this article would be pointless. It is *Henry A. Wallace* in 1947 discussing the role of the Communists in his movement—and I have simply substituted the Birch Society where Wallace mentioned the Communists.

Goldwater is the Henry Wallace of the American radical Right with a striking collection of Wallace's characteristics. Indeed, to use that jaded term, Goldwater has Wallace's "style" down cold. He is no more of a "fascist" than Wallace was a "communist." Like Wallace he is rigid, he has no feel for political nuances, for relaxed polemic; he would prefer to be left alone with his hobbies. He, too, excoriates the present in the name of an allegedly betrayed heritage and appeals to what Reinhold Niebuhr, in *The New Leader,* has called "the politics of nostalgia." In short, he has that same combination of abstract chiliasm tempered by acute boredom with "practical politics." And again like the Gideon of 1948, he is a reluctant leader who was dragged into the fray by his supporters and, I suspect, in private moments keeps asking himself, "What the hell am I doing *here?*"

This characterological similarity works itself out in other ways. Goldwater appears to have Wallace's rhetorical liability: His formal speeches are wooden and sententious and his informal ones direct and indiscreet. Indeed, Goldwater's acceptance speech—which might have been subtitled "My Life and Its Meaning"—ranks favorably with the following abstract ruminations delivered by Wallace on December 16, 1947, when he announced his mission:

"We have assembled a Gideon's army—small in number, powerful in conviction, ready in action. We have said with Gideon, 'Let those who are fearful and trembling depart.' For every fearful one who leaves there will be a thousand to take his place. A just cause is worth a hundred armies. We face the future unfettered by any principle but the general welfare. We owe no allegiance to any group which does not serve that welfare. By

God's grace, the People's Peace will usher in the Century of the Common Man."

It is predictable that Goldwater's praetorian guard will exercise the same vigilance to protect him from off-the-cuff interviews that the Communists and their allies employed to prevent their candidate from letting down his hair. I recall Jimmie Wechsler noting at one point in the '48 campaign that it was easier to interview the Pope than Henry Wallace.

There is no point to overworking the analogy, but I think it has real institutional significance. The Goldwater candidacy will have exactly the same divisive impact on the Republican party that Wallace's crusade had on the liberal movement. For it is simply not true to say, speaking technically, that Goldwater has captured the Republican party. He has captured the nomination, and some local parties in the states, but you can't capture (except in symbolic terms) something that does not exist. The Republican National Committee may have become the Dean Burch Society—but national committees are virtually powerless entities.

The only national institution of any consequence that a party has is its nominating convention every four years. Goldwater's nomination is a ticket good for this ride alone; his victory did not give him jurisdiction over, say, the Massachusetts Republican party. (On the contrary, the leaders of that party in Massachusetts are engaged in a war to the knife with Goldwater's local pirates who want to seize the organization—in one sense, the local GOP regulars have a stake in Goldwater's defeat!)

Just as there was no liberal organization—no structured monolith—for Wallace and his supporters to capture, there is no Republican party, but rather fifty-one Republican parties (fifty states and the District of Columbia), each with its own personnel, who are not responsible except in liturgical terms to the presidential nominee. Moreover, the first obligation of these local and state political organizations is to survive (at worst) and win office (at best) at the local and state levels. What goes on at the top of the ticket is important to them mainly insofar as it contributes to their parochial success or failure.

This is as true of the Democrats as of the Republicans. When in 1956 most Southern Democratic leaders abandoned Stevenson for Eisenhower, they did so in terms of an explicit bargain: They gave the GOP the top of the ticket and the Republicans in turn left them alone at the bottom.

From now until election day, state and local Republican organizations are going to be engaged in the process of assessing the implications of Goldwaterism. And if the prodigious energy of his rightwing enthusiasts has brought him initial victory, this same zeal will generate countless problems in the months to come. Admittedly, in many sections of the country Goldwaterism reflects the genuine conviction of local Republicans. Ironically, this is true in areas of Democratic preponderance (California, Texas, Arizona) rather than in states where the GOP holds power (New York, Pennsylvania, Michigan, Oregon). This conforms with a standard political maxim that ideological militance is a direct coefficient of practical impotence.

Thus the full impact of Republican internecine conflict will be felt in areas of greatest GOP power, states where the Goldwaterites will be more concerned with destroying "traitors" and seizing the party machinery than with beating the Democrats. The situation in Massachusetts provides a classic example.

Thomas Waring, a long-time loser within the state Republican party and a militant "conservative" (he once managed Robert Welch's primary campaign for Lieutenant Governor), returned from San Francisco brimming with fervor. His man had won and he immediately appointed himself the Grand Inquisitor of New England Republicanism, which was patently deficient in Grace. On arriving at Logan Airport in Boston, he delivered himself a string of excommunications worthy of a Reformation Pope. He cast out of the True Church just about every significant Republican politician in New England, including the Governors of Maine and Rhode Island and the senior Senator from Massachusetts.

Now this is good clean fun, but it is not the way to win elections. In fact, just as the savage Communist attack on liberal institutions in 1947–48 generated a counter-offensive, Waring's assault is uniting his opponents as they have not been united previously. (The Maine GOP, for example, has already turned down a bid for power by Goldwater's local missionaries.) And this will create baleful problems for the Goldwater campaign staff. When they deal with the Republicans in New York, Pennsylvania or Massachusetts, will they do business with the regulars, or with the Goldwater rebels? Either way they are whipsawed: If they work through the regular organization, the nominee will be accused of betraying his saints for cheap vote-getting objectives; if they work through the saints, the regular organization will abandon ship.

Goldwaterism has, in other words, injected into American national politics an ideological virus that has not been seen on a large scale since 1948. A disciplined minority pulled off a masterful coup at the Cow Palace; now the essentially nonideological majority of the Republican coalition must pay for its incompetence, for the amateur hour that Rockefeller, Romney & Company sponsored at the convention.

Goldwater can win: I once held four natural kings in a poker game and was beaten by four natural aces. But the odds are that just as the Communists ended up with a paper organization in the Progressive party, while the liberal movement reconstituted itself more powerfully without them, the Birchers will find on November 4 that they have captured themselves. And far from vanishing with its nominee, the Republican coalition will reconstitute itself and be back at the post, perhaps with increased vigor, for the election of 1968.

Kennedy, Johnson and
the Intellectuals

I T WAS DIFFICULT, if not impossible, in the first months after Dallas to attain any real perspective on the accomplishments and stature of John Fitzgerald Kennedy. Sober judgment was swept aside by *The Times* by grief for a man who was a symbol of our nationhood. There was, in addition, the starkness of Greek tragedy about the whole incredible affair: the master rationalist—urbane, sardonic, committed to purposeful restraint—struck down by a nihilist.

The shock waves from the assassination hit the intellectual community hard, both here and abroad. For reasons worth exploring, John Kennedy, who was highly suspect in 1959 and 1960, had succeeded in three years in attaining a standing among intellectuals unmatched by any previous President. I found some reactions to the President's death a bit embarrassing. When a group of America's most distinguished—even dedicated—non-political figures poured out their grief in *The New York Review of Books,* I could almost visualize John Kennedy's sardonic grimace. He despised mawkish sentimentality.

"The worst insult to a dead man's memory," runs an old Irish proverb, "is to lie about him." In that spirit, let me make clear my view that while John Kennedy was a superbly talented human being—ranking with Theodore Roosevelt and Woodrow Wilson in terms of sheer intellectual capacity—he was not, on the record, a "great President." (What another five years in office might have demonstrated is, alas, a matter of opinion—not political science.)

Kennedy's triumphs were in the sector of politics where administration is decisive. Never had the top levels of the federal bureaucracy been so effectively managed and coordinated; the creation of a meaningful defense department ranks as a spectacular achievement. Foreign relations were handled with a perceptiveness and unified command that dazzled many observers; the Cuban confrontation of October 1962 was a model of effective democratic statecraft.

But these are areas in which the President has enormous authority, where his writ—if not unchallenged—runs without direct congressional checks. In domestic affairs, however, where "politics" in its broad sense dominates the field, Kennedy often seemed baffled and overwhelmed. It is clear that even as a member first of the House and then of the Senate he had little affection or respect for Congress as an institution. This is understandable in a political scientist—I share this attitude myself—but it is hardly part of the prescription for a chief executive, particularly when he is incapable of dissembling his jaundiced views. True, Kennedy always treated Congress with elaborate solicitude, but it was that of a kindergarten teacher who suspects that one of the children has secreted a hand grenade on the premises.

It seemed to me that in his relations with Congress, Kennedy was temperamentally incapable of leading lost causes, or causes which seemed lost in a rational appraisal of the odds. Thus in May 1963, when an Americans for Democratic Action group implored him to exercise strong leadership in civil rights, "to nail the battle flag to the mast," he responded with great sympathy and then gave us first a masterfully concise twenty-minute lecture on the problems of federalism, and then an equally cogent twenty-minute exposition of presidential difficulties with Congress.

He mentioned that a Southern representative for whom he had a high regard had just called him to say that he would have to vote "wrong" in the Rules Committee on an impending measure. "What can I say to him?" the President asked. "He has to protect himself in Alabama." (Carl Elliott might as well have voted his convictions—for he was defeated in the Alabama primary this June.)

What I am suggesting—and I made this same critique during the President's tenure—is that Kennedy's great asset as an administrator—his uncanny capacity to analyze a problem and to appreciate its various dimensions—was a liability in congressional relations.

Congress is a curious body with a built-in resistance to presidential authority. A chief executive who tries to play by congressional rules, to "go along," inevitably discovers that he is handling loaded dice. It was Kennedy's misfortune that, knowing the dice were loaded, he still played with them because he could think of no alternative. He flooded the Hill with splendid messages and proposals and then watched with angry resignation as they went down before the inexorable butchery of Congress or were put to death in the Rules Committee's silent gas chamber. (Most of his major proposals were never voted down by the Rules Committee; they were simply ignored.)

To put it another way, Kennedy was a dogged, even heroic, rationalist. This gave him enormous strength in certain situations, but it also made him insensitive to ideologies and political extremism. As I noted years ago, he was intellectually liberal but temperamentally conservative; he could never get steamed up over abstractions, and he tended to consider ideology as a cover for pragmatic, negotiable interests. Most of the time it probably is, but one must be able to recognize the exceptions.

Over civil rights, for example, I think that both the President and the Attorney General initially considered Southern extremism as nothing more than a hard bargaining position. Indeed, the Attorney General went to Birmingham in 1963 with a mission analogous to that of a mediator in a labor dispute—get the boys together and split the difference. He returned a sadder but wiser man, appalled by his first immersion in the acid of pure ideology. "It was like being in a different country," he allegedly reported— something that any Freedom Rider could have told him. But he had to learn for himself. Up to that point, Freedom Riders as well as white supremacists were all "extremists," muddying the waters of rational political bargaining.

Rationalism was the essence of Kennedy's "style"—and clearly the basis for his enormous popularity among intellectuals. Kennedy was our first "modern" President, the first to emerge from the political vortex of urban America, the first to represent the urbane sophistication of the Northeast. That he was of Irish ancestry and a Catholic was incidental; what was significant was that he read *The New Yorker*.

Intellectuals are urban creatures and they reacted enthusiastically to Kennedy's rhetoric, his sharp wit, his self-ridicule, his refusal to be "corny"—with all the rural associations that word evokes.

Kennedy's inability to cope with Congress confirmed, if anything, his reputation among intellectuals. From long experience I have become convinced that most intellectuals are secret Platonists who feel that somehow the messy, human aspects of life and politics should be brought under the control of enlightened men. In their view, politics should be a "science" and the politician a "political scientist." The image that emerged from Kennedy's encounters with Congress was thus one that appealed to Platonic sensibilities: the young, modern President with his Harvard-trained view of the national interest perpetually set upon by rustics, overwhelmed by parochialism. Those of us who argued that his leadership of Congress left much to be desired were chastized for not realizing that congressional strength was unbeatable, that no one at the White House could cope with the "legislative system."

It is not my purpose here to defend Congress. As Don K. Price noted long ago, it is a "collective noun," an anarchic body which desperately needs overall leadership from the very President it is determined to humble. The nub of Kennedy's problem, I am convinced, was not that he did not accept Congress on its own terms (no man can do that and claim his salary as President), but that he considered it an anachronism, a living fossil cluttering up the landscape of efficient politics.

As Lyndon Johnson's stunning performance indicates, however, senators and representatives will accept some pretty rough handling from a President who takes their function (if not their performance) seriously. Like other men, they too want to be loved—but love was not in the Kennedy political lexicon. It is almost incomprehensible, for example, to an apostle of his brand of modern politics that a long-time senatorial opponent of closure could promise his *friend* the President a vote for closure if it were needed.

"The voice was the voice of Humphrey," as one liberal senator said later, "but the hands were the hands of Johnson." Senator Richard Russell made much the same point, commenting wryly that youngsters like Mike Mansfield and Hubert Humphrey hadn't brought him down. There was another force in the background. Indeed, the hand of Johnson has been much in evidence these last six months: Congress has been acting like a legislature rather than a legislative Death Row.

Yet, despite his accomplishments, President Johnson has achieved little standing among intellectuals. Given the urban orientation referred to earlier, they have tended to see in him a reincarnation of William Jennings Bryan, the rural cornhusker. The contrast with President Kennedy is, of course, striking—for lack of a stronger word. Some years ago I escorted Kennedy to a Brandeis University function where he was to give a speech. While we were waiting for the program to begin, he took out a yellow pad, asked me what the celebration was about, wrote two pages of notes and then delivered a fine thirty-minute speech complete with an exact, fairly long quotation from Justice Louis Brandeis. He had a fantastic memory and a gift for the *mot juste* and the well-turned ironic phrase.

In contrast, President Johnson recently delivered the commencement address at Swarthmore College, and although it read well, the appalling news came from a Pennsylvania friend that the President has used a TelePrompTer! This bulletin left me unmoved—Johnson's speech at the signing of the Civil Rights Act was a superb statement of moral leadership. It would not have mattered if he had read it from a notebook, the back of an envelope or a blackboard.

A comparison of President Kennedy's news conferences, where suddenly that wit would flash like a dagger, with Johnson's, characterized by his circumspect geniality, makes the same point. Johnson seems to come from a different universe; his rhetoric is extravagant, his hats are wide—everything about him seems to symbolize a reversion to the political style of yesteryear.

Similarly, Johnson's very success in managing the creaky congressional machinery has generated suspicion. It seems unfair to sensitive critics that the same legislators who cut down John Kennedy and ignored his excellent messages should respond to wheeling and dealing, to "vulgar Machiavellianism." Moreover, Johnson—like FDR, whom many intellectuals also distrusted—is patently no Platonist. He is the kind of man who might well do something in order to win votes—thus indicating, in the best Platonic sense, an imperfection of soul.

Of course, President Kennedy may on occasion have shaped his policies to the end of winning votes, but Johnson is not being compared with Kennedy the politician, whose shenanigans in the 1952 senatorial election in Massachusetts, when he refused to acknowledge that Adlai Stevenson was also on the ticket, would arouse professional envy even on the Texas hustings. Rather, he is compared with the thoughtful Kennedy, the introspective patron of culture, the omnivorous reader (of books!). Intellectuals liked him and were prepared to forgive him much because he liked them.

Lyndon Johnson, on the other hand, seems to fall into the category of anti-intellectual politicians—or, at least, he has given little indication that he feels that intellectuals have a meaningful, creative role in American society. John Kennedy did not appreciate criticism—who does?—but he obviously recognized that criticism was a natural function of the intellectual and that it had both public and private utility. In contrast, I do not know anyone who questions President Johnson's intelligence, but give and take between the White House and the nation's intellectuals has virtually ceased.

Now I am not suggesting that the Republic will collapse if the President does not get to know the editors of *Partisan Review*.

Nor am I arguing that Lyndon Johnson should attempt to follow the Kennedy pattern—he must be himself. But I am concerned about the integration of intellectuals into the political life of American society.

Despite the Marxist claim that alienation from the central values of American life is a sign of mental health, it seems to me that we have seen the emergence of an intellectual community in the United States over the past thirty years which is committed to the attainment of democratic ideals. This sense of commitment burgeoned during the Thousand Days of John Kennedy but now seems to be in decline. Part of the responsibility for this decline rests, as I have suggested, upon the intellectuals themselves, who have forgotten too quickly the lesson once learned from Harry Truman: that the presidency has a remarkable impact upon allegedly provincial politicians.

The nub of this problem is a conflict of parochialisms, and intellectuals have their own brands of snobbery. Yet in all fairness I think a heavy burden of responsibility for this deterioration of relations lies on the White House. It would be ironic if, in this year of fence-mending, no efforts were made to re-establish the critical dialogue that existed between John Kennedy and the intellectuals. And it would be tragic if the Johnson Administration did not understand why these efforts are worthwhile. After all, the vision of "The Great Society" can hardly be fleshed out without the often irritating but essential participation of visionaries and critics.

The Liberals
and Vietnam

$\mathbf{E}$VER SINCE THE PACE of the hostilities in Vietnam accelerated, and particularly since the administration's decision to bomb North Vietnam, there has been a certain element of hysteria in liberal circles. About once every three days, for example, some multipurpose, ad hoc committee of protest invites me to join in the liturgical ceremony of signing an ad in the New York *Times*.

Now I do not "approve" of war or violence, but I also disapprove of treating complex policy issues by revival meeting techniques. I confess that I was born without an apocalyptic chromosome, yet I still insist that liberal intellectuals should not behave like a secular branch of the Holy Rollers. What particularly disturbs me is the growth of part-time pacifism, or liberal isolationism. Fine liberals, who would storm Congress to aid a beleaguered Israel, suddenly shift gears when Asia is involved and start talking about "the inevitability of Chinese domination" and the "immorality" of bombing North Vietnam. Let me make it

Reprinted, with permission, from *The New Leader*, April 26, 1965.

perfectly clear that a pacifist can on principle argue that the use of force in international affairs is immoral. Though I do not hold this position, I recognize its principled foundation. But a pacifist is thus forbidden by his moral imperatives from having any favorite wars.

Leaving aside pacifism, on what grounds can one argue that our Vietnamese policy is *immoral?* (Not mistaken, but immoral.) There is only one other foundation for such a position, namely, that North Vietnam is a historically progressive regime confronted by a reactionary, imperialist creation in South Vietnam. One who holds this view can quite legitimately condemn our actions as an immoral effort to block the course of history. If we are not pacifists, nor spiritual supporters of Hanoi, we find ourselves in a different universe, one dominated by standards of wisdom and prudence, not by the moral trumpets of the apocalypse. We find ourselves arguing about: How should force be employed? Under what circumstances? To what ends? With what intensity?

This is not a universe of denunciation, but of calculation and serious evaluation of options. Above all, we must—to the extent that it is possible—work out a strategy for Asia which is more than a series of ad hoc responses to crises. My thoughts are directed to that end, and when I am done it will be noted that I have not proposed a "solution in Asia." This is not because I am hedging my bets; it is simply because I do not accept the Platonic notion that somewhere in the *geist,* awaiting our use, there is a "solution." I am prepared to settle for a favorable outcome.

Any intelligent examination of the role of the United States in Asia must begin with a realistic appraisal of the opposition, and a realistic appraisal cannot be based on wishful thinking. Too often, because we are opposed to war, we liberals start with the conclusion that war is unthinkable, convert it into a premise, and then—in order to reassure ourselves—convert our opponents into genial pragmatists like ourselves. I recall distinguished liberal and socialist leaders informing us that Hitler was just a rational spokesman for German national interest, an understandable consequence of the "evils of Versailles." Beginning with the unarticulated premise that war was the ultimate evil, many fine liberals convinced themselves—and many of us—that Nazism was largely a creation of British propaganda, that if Germany were granted her "legitimate aspirations," the Nazi threat would subside into harmless *gemutlichkeit.*

It is perfectly legitimate to argue, as many pacifists do, that war *is* the ultimate evil. But the logical conclusion of this view is the advocacy of submission rather than a fanciful re-evaluation of the character of the enemy. One argues that however wicked the Nazis, or Communists, may be, submission is better than war. One does not argue that the Nazis, or the Communists, are really a bunch of decent chaps who have been misunderstood; or worse, that the statement that Nazis, or Communists, are devoted enemies of freedom and justice is propaganda for war spread by evil warmongers. A true pacifist, in short, does not decapitate the messenger who brings bad tidings.

I regret that I may be a messenger of bad tidings, but I am convinced that the absence of liberal realism in the analysis of international relations has a dangerous effect on national opinion. And on international stability: Have we ever been closer to Armageddon than in October 1962, when Khrushchev thought the Americans were "too liberal to fight?"

This examination of United States options in Asia will begin with an analysis of the character of the main enemy—Red China. Whether we like the idea or not, the Red Chinese have been at war with us since 1950. The war burned hot in Korea for three years, and it has been lukewarm ever since. But it is war—the highest Chinese authorities have said so and we have no reason to question their sincerity.

The Chinese are authentic Leninists, which means that in the post-1923 context they are ideologically Trotskyites. Of course, organizationally they are Stalinists—Trotsky in power would have been a Stalinist *vis-à-vis* opposition groups who pretended to speak for the proletariat. Trosky's complaint was not against monolithicism *per se,* but against monolithicism in the hands of his enemies. The ritual curses which the Chinese Communists have poured upon the memory of Trotsky must thus be disregarded—they have roughly the same historical standing as Henry VIII's denunciation of Martin Luther, which won the king the papal accolade of "Defender of the Faith."

What has impelled the Sino-Soviet schism is not a rarified

question of ideology, but a concrete question of Chinese national interest. The Soviets, good Stalinists, even under the regime of Stalin's vilifiers, have imposed "socialism in one country" upon the Chinese. To put it another way, the Chinese as advocates of "combined development," i.e. "permanent revolution," have expected the Russians to provide the technological bases for Chinese primitive capital accumulation, to make it possible for an agrarian society to build capitalism with socialist institutions, to telescope the whole capitalist epoch by creating capitalism without capitalists. The Chinese, good Trotskyites *malgré eux*, therefore demanded from the Russians enormous capital-creating capital in order to bridge the abyss between agrarian serfdom and socialism, and the Soviets, good Stalinists even as they denounced the "cult of personality," refused to take up their fantastic burden. The Chinese were, in effect, told to earn their own way; indeed, East Germany has received more economic assistance from the USSR than Red China.

Leaving aside the intriguing question of whether Trotsky in power in the USSR, or Lenin had he survived, would not have adopted "socialism in one country" as a national imperative in the Twenties and Thirties, we can, I submit, evaluate Maoist doctrine as pure Leninism of, say, 1919. The basic assumption is that socialism is at war with capitalism on every front and that "negotiation" or "peace" are merely tactical expedients employed by the socialist society in its confrontation with temporarily, or locally, more powerful enemies. The only *real* solution to a struggle between socialism and capitalism can be the eventual total defeat of the latter.

If this hypothesis is correct, it is unnecessary to worry about any great Chinese concern with "saving face." This is a bourgeois luxury. Lenin once observed that a good Bolshevik would if necessary "crawl on his belly" in the interest of the Party, and Trotsky noted that "revenge is not a political sentiment." Decisions are made in terms of the balance of forces, not as an outgrowth of a feudal sense of honor or some equally antiquated and unproletarian rationale.

In 1931 Trotsky (writing with regard to the possibility of a Nazi takeover in Germany) advised that the USSR should attack immediately. "In the face of a mortal enemy, when the logic of the situation points to inevitable war, it would be irresponsible and unpardonable to give that enemy time to establish himself, to consolidate his positions . . . and to work out the plan of attack." (Germany was then disarmed in accordance with the Versailles Treaty and the USSR had probably the largest army in the world.) Stalin refused to follow this authentic Leninist counsel, but it is clear to me that the Chinese Communists operate on precisely this premise. As *Red Flag* put it on March 4, 1963 ("More on the Differences Between Comrade Togliatti and Us"), "the axiom that 'war is the continuation of politics by other means,' which was affirmed and stressed by Lenin, remains valid today." The Chinese assault on India in 1962 was patently designed, in this spirit, to destroy the illusion that India was a first-rank Asian power; it was a cold-blooded, calculated thrust out of Clausewitz by Lenin.

Given this set of assumptions, it seems apparent that the reason the Chinese have dubbed the U.S. a "paper tiger" is that from their perspective we have refused to use our power in Asia in conformity to their canons. In other words, had the situations been reversed, they would have attacked us long ago, particularly since the Soviet Union made it clear by 1960 that it would not extend deterrent coverage to China: that a strategic air attack on Red China (whether nuclear or conventional) would not automatically bring the USSR into the war. The Chinese, in short, trapped in a frozen ideology, cannot believe that the U.S.—despite its enormous advantage in strategic power—is restrained by "moral" considerations from undertaking a pre-emptive strike. The logical alternative for them is to assume that we have lost the capacity to kill, that we are degenerate and ambivalent—a society on the edge of dissolution, a fourth-century Rome.

Yet the Chinese, unlike the Nazis, are totally lacking in a *"Götterdammerung* Complex." Admitting in Mao's phrase that "power comes from the barrel of a gun," they are prepared to back away from bigger guns. Compromise and negotiation are instruments in policy making, but—like Brest-Litovsk—tactics merely. As *Red Flag* put it (January 1, 1963): "It is precisely in accordance with Lenin's teachings that we Chinese Communists distinguish between different kinds of compromise, favoring compromises which are in the interests of the people's cause and of world peace, and opposing compromises that are in the nature of treachery." To paraphrase Lenin's *Leftwing Communism,* the Chinese support negotiations and compromise the way a rope supports a hanged man.

The Chinese have a very clear strategic design for Asia: They look upon themselves as the double heirs of Chinese nationalism and proletarian internationalism. There is no need to tarry here with the question of what form the thrust of Chinese power would take if it were unchecked, whether it would create Stalinist-style puppet states in neighboring countries or settle for substantive domination over client regimes maintaining the semblances of sovereignty.

What is significant is that by a series of historical accidents the United States finds itself containing Red China, but (in contrast to the Chinese) while we have enormous power, we have no strategy. Nothing could bring this out more starkly than the fact that the map shows two main lines of great power confrontation in Asia: India-China and Indonesia-Malaysia (Britain), and our power is being dissipated in a Balkan war. Our Vietnamese enterprise is thus an expedition to Salonika; we are in the right war, but the wrong place. The future of Asia cannot be determined in Indochina; indeed, once we recognize where the real axes of conflict are it is obvious that our commitment to the Asian Balkans is strategically counter-productive. If a full war broke out, Vietnam would not be merely irrelevant, it would be a net liability: a force like the Salonika Expedition of World War I which could not go forward, and equally—in political terms—could not be liquidated.

Let us examine the course of American commitment in Asia. As a consequence of the war with Japan and its aftermath, the United States for the first time became really involved in Asia. Despite much 20/20 hindsight it seems apparent that no one in 1945 from President Roosevelt and General MacArthur down had any premonition of future problems. China was still Nationalist, Mao was under Stalin's curse as a probable loser (Stalin probably assumed that the United States would never permit its client Chiang Kai-shek to be defeated by the Reds: thus the Soviets stripped Manchuria before they departed), Japan was disarmed and, by MacArthur's constitution, permanently disclaimed military power.

Indeed, MacArthur's demilitarization of Japan in itself indicated the absence of any Machiavellian plots in American "ruling circles." Had Americans anticipated any long-range threat in Asia, they would surely not have removed the Japanese piece from the strategic chessboard. MacArthur, with characteristic disingenuousness, later implied that the Japanese peace pledge was the work of sinister subversives, but contemporary accounts indicate that he on several occasions took personal credit for this act of statesmanship.

The collapse of Nationalist China, the Korean War, the rise of Indonesia, the Indochinese conflict, suddenly gave Asia an entirely different appearance. American power in Asia was at its nadir in 1950 and all over the map strange and ominous events were occurring. Our response was, and has been ever since, one hastily improvised reaction after another. What strategic principle could, for example, justify abandoning the French in Indochina in 1954—and then becoming deeply involved there ourselves a decade later? The difference is that in 1954 we were primarily concerned about the character of our "colonialist" ally; today we are focusing on the character of the enemy. (I am not arguing that we should have rushed to aid the French, but that our decisions have been made on an ad hoc basis.)

If this assumption is sound, the Johnson Administration is logically correct in hurting North Vietnam. Hanoi, according to this scenario, would ask Peking for massive aid and the latter would refuse more than token assistance on the ground that if it should intervene in force, American airpower would devastate China's industrial sector virtually unchallenged by the obsolete air force in Red hands—and the USSR would confine itself to ritual complaints and minor aid while putting a basketball team in space. Hanoi, deserted and vulnerable to air strikes, would therefore choose to close down its support for the Vietcong and negotiate some time-gaining settlement such as neutralization of the whole area under great power guarantees.

The Johnson Administration's tactic (and I use that word deliberately) has been ferociously attacked as immoral, vicious and provocative at innumerable political prayer meetings in recent weeks. However, if one is neither a pacifist nor a spiritual supporter of Hanoi and Peking (nor an isolationist, who thinks American involvement in the outside world is somehow unethical), it is hard to take such a frenetic line. There is nothing more immoral about bombing staging areas in North Vietnam than there is in North Vietnamese support for Vietcong terrorists in the South (who have murdered from 20,000 to 30,000 village officials in the past six years).

"The use of force is moral when I approve of it" is a rationale with a certain existential charm, but it can hardly provide guidance for liberals who are concerned with fundamental sources of principled action. We should know by now that we cannot select our favorite wars and refuse to support any political regime which has a lower liberal quotient than the late Spanish Republic in an hour of crisis. There is no principled basis for part-time pacifism. Thus I submit that the defense of the autonomy of South Vietnam is a legitimate cause, that we are under no more obligation to recognize the 17th parallel as a limit to our actions than has Hanoi, that unless the USSR gives deterrent coverage to China we need not expect a "general war" in Southeast Asia, that, in sum, there is tactically considerable merit to the administration's measured escalation.

Yet I am opposed to it. For even if (as I expect would be the case) no general war occurred as a consequence of continuous pounding of North Vietnam, Hanoi could drag us from a marginal intervention (30,000 troops) into a full-scale Balkan War *without* overt Chinese assistance. At a certain point, Hanoi could well decide that North Vietnam has nothing further to gain by holding back its army (300,000) and go in (without China) on the ground, not merely into South Vietnam but also into Laos. Such a decision could be made in desperate hopes of forcing the hands of Peking and Moscow. We should not become so obsessed with avoiding Munich that we forget the lesson of Sarajevo.

Whatever response Hanoi received from China or the USSR (and were we to assault the industrial cities of North Vietnam, there would be incalculable tensions and pressures in the Communist worlds and possibilities of irrational reactions), we would find ourselves in a major enterprise. If it were to be fought effectively, we should have to make a substantial ground commitment—perhaps, as Hanson Baldwin says, a million men—and to what end? Simply to hold on to a Balkan enclave where no crucial decisions about Asia are at issue.

The real problem with Balkan Wars is that they cannot be won *in* the Balkans. In many ways the Vietnamese War resembles the Greek Civil War of 1945–50. If one goes back and reads the journals of opinion of that era, he learns that the guerrillas were seemingly triumphant, that the Greek government was corrupt and incapable of mobilizing the resources of the people, that the "masses" only wanted to be left alone. One important difference should be noted: unlike South Vietnam, Greece had a discrete national tradition.

Like Vietnam, however, Greece demonstrated the futility of the concept of "civil war." In areas of great power commitment there are no more "civil wars" in the old sense of private internecine fights. Spain in the thirties rather than the United States of 1861–65 provides the model, with the great powers providing client elites with overt or covert support. The Greek Communists failed in their assault, but hardly because of Greek considerations. They failed because the Yugoslavs, at a crucial moment, defected from the Soviet camp and, apparently, because Stalin distrusted Markos. The Bulgars and Albanians (who were isolated) could not provide the logistical support for the Communist guerrillas; the back of the rebellion was broken and Stalin— who *may* earlier have been following Yugoslav initiatives against his better judgment—liquidated his losses.

No one can expect history to repeat itself in mechanical terms, but it does make sense to suggest that the key relationship in Indochina is that between Hanoi and Peking. (The Soviet Union despite its latest rhetorical flourishes, has—I suspect—effectively departed from Southeast Asia.)

The "domino theory" has been used to justify a major effort in Indochina, but I fail to see the logic of the argument. We can keep the South Vietnam "domino" standing indefinitely if we make the necessary commitments. If we cannot win any prize in the Balkans, neither can we be defeated there. But the other dominos can fall even if South Vietnam remains upright. If Hanoi launched a ground offensive, Laos, Cambodia, even Thailand, would be vulnerable and—given our full concentration in Saigon—all the dominos between the Kra Isthmus and the Indian frontier could topple. (If, indeed, they are *now* standing. There is, for example, some reason to believe that Burma is a geographical fiction.)

To return to the main theme, we have a tactic in Indochina but no strategy in Asia. We can hold the solitary domino in South Vietnam, but the other dominos could go over anytime Hanoi (not necessarily Peking) intervenes in force on the ground.

Do we really want to up the ante in Indochina? Bombing the North is a way of saying to Hanoi that we find its intervention in the South intolerable. In strategic terms, Communist intervention is nasty and uncooperative; it is hardly intolerable. The British recently sent 50,000 troops to defend Malaysia, and we are distressed about a commitment of 30,000 in South Vietnam. What has really aggravated us, I suspect, is not the behavior of Hanoi so much as the perpetual circus in Saigon, the apparent inability of the South Vietnamese elite to create a viable government. (There is an interesting analogy between our problems in Saigon and the difficulties the Allies had with the White Russians in 1918–20—see Winston S. Churchill's *The World Crisis*, vol. vi, *The Aftermath*.)

The enormous frustrations of American policy makers confronted by Saigon's incapacity to govern, to create a state (without which an effective army cannot exist), and by the equal unwillingness of the South Vietnamese to permit the Americans to operate a protectorate, have led to demands for "action" against somebody. In the words of Edmund Burke, criticizing British policy toward America, the government was seized by "a general notion that some act of power was become necessary." We could hardly bomb Saigon, so the planes went north. There were other options which did not risk international complications: As S.L.A. Marshall pointed out (*New Leader*, March 15, 1965), we could have moved to establish ground security by increasing our troop commitment moderately.

Hanoi, in my judgment, has from the outset exercised strategic direction over the Vietcong (which is not to say that Hanoi has had operational control over guerrilla units on a day to day basis). But I rather suspect that by this time the Vietcong has become a semiautonomous operation, which may even be prepared to blackmail Hanoi on occasion. Thus the notion that Ho can blow a whistle and call off the Vietcong—which underpins our attacks on the North—may be questionable. Indeed, Vietcong terrorism against Americans could be designed to keep Hanoi on the hook, though this seems unduly clever and clever explanations of political behavior are rarely correct. The less said about the American *White Paper* the better: The Vietcong has its ideological inspiration in the North, but its weaponry has come largely from South Vietnam's army, indirectly from the U.S.

To put the pieces together in a coherent fashion, let me set out in analytical fashion the main points of the argument:

1) We are caught in a minor Balkan War involving potentially enormous commitments in a sector of Asia where no crucial determinations can be made.

2) Our escalation of the war against Hanoi is a logical step only if we are prepared to fight a major Balkan War on the ground—not necessarily involving overt Chinese intervention. (Great power action in the Balkans usually sees one engaged with the other side's second or third team.)

3) Such a major Balkan War in Asia, as envisaged by Hanson Baldwin, would be essentially defensive: to hold one domino. We would certainly never *march* north.

4) In the absence of a viable South Vietnamese state, the U.S. would have to run this war from start to finish. It would soon be known as the "American War" in Vietnam—and as "Johnson's War" in Republican circles in the United States.

5) Thus it is in American national interest to have a minimal involvement in Indochina and, one could argue, in the Chinese Communist interest for us to get enmeshed in the jungles with their second and third teams. Consequently, we should not raise the ante with Hanoi, but should intensify our commitment in the South to the level where only conventional techniques (not guerrilla tactics) could seriously hurt us; we should establish ground security and plan to hold on indefinitely. And we could put far more effort than we have done so far into developing a viable state in South Vietnam—a political and economic, as well as military commitment. Moreover, we should undertake political initiative (such as President Johnson's implied offers of economic

assistance to a nonaggressive North Vietnam) which could encourage argument between Hanoi and Peking, and nourish Ho's
anti-Chinese tendencies.

6) This un-American policy of giving the enemy a chance to
make a few mistakes, of giving Hanoi and Peking some opportunity to argue, of letting the Sino-Soviet schism fester, of waiting
out the consequences of the death of the old guard in Hanoi and
Peking, has a great positive advantage as well. It gives us a
chance to think through an Asian strategy.

Our strategic priority in Asia can only be the buttressing of
Indian strength to the point where India becomes a first-class
Asian power capable of providing a counterpoise to China. This
is far more than a military problem. In fact, the first step should
be an enormous program of economic aid for India. The Indian
elite, too many of whom have the reflexes of leftwing British
intellectuals, can be counted on to make the going sticky. But—
as distinct from Saigon—at least there is an Indian elite with a
sense of national consciousness and, since the Chinese attack, a
realization that moral aphorisms in international affairs are, regrettably, no substitute for national power. In essence we must
make it possible for the Indians to have guns and butter: We
must see to it that the increase in Indian defense expenditures
does not decrease the already marginal living standards of the
population, but that the latter simultaneously increase.

Paradoxically, we should do for India what the Soviet Union
has refused to do for China: institute a democratic version of the
policy of "combined development." All the other dominos on the
mainland of South Asia are minute by comparison with India. If
all of them fall and India holds, there is still a future for democracy in Asia. If India falls, or disintegrates, under internal and
external stresses, the show is over and our operations in South
Vietnam will resemble Gallipoli rather than Salonika. We may
have the power to blow up Asia, but we will have no alternative
to destruction. We will not have an Asian policy but a no-Asia
policy.

A Professor Votes <u>for</u> Mr. Johnson

"The British people must face the unpleasant fact that they are no longer in a position to insist on their ideas of justice and democracy in Europe or the Far East. . . ."—The *New Statesman and Nation*, October 15, 1938 (with reference to Nazi Germany and Japan, the then "natural" powers in Europe and Asia).

NEVER in American history has an administration taken such a series of giant steps toward the attainment of liberal objectives as we have seen under the presidency of Lyndon B. Johnson. In this session Congress acted like a legislature; major pieces of social policy (some, like Medicare, after almost a generation in limbo) escaped from the gas chamber which the "conservative coalition" formerly sponsored on Capitol Hill. Indeed, liberals may now have to convene an emergency session to formulate new policy objectives. And the civil rights movement is likely to be foreclosed by a new organization: the National Association for the Advancement of Everyone, Lyndon B. Johnson, president and executive director.

Yet this stunning performance has received virtually no notice, let alone applause, from liberal intellectuals. They are off in full pursuit of the President for his "provocative" foreign policy. Indeed, never in my memory has the intellectual community been so bitterly antiadministration.

Since it has become a sign of sophistication today to make contemptuous remarks about "cold warriors" and to smirk knowingly at the Neanderthal notion that Communism had to be contained, I should like to make it perfectly clear that I am an unabashed, veteran cold warrior. Moreover, I submit that our success in containing Communism has made all the smirking possible. With logical contortions worthy of the late Senator McCarthy, our opponents have tried to link us ideologically with the John Birch Society—though the epithet "McCarthyite" is reserved by them for those (like Dean Rusk) who suggest that psychologists, biochemists and baby doctors who sign petitions on Vietnam in *The Times* may have no expert qualifications. (A while ago, a representative of the multipurpose *ad hoc* committee of protest which operates out of Cambridge asked me to sign a *Times* petition denouncing Dean Rusk for attempting to terrorize the academic community and suppress academic freedom. The notion of "Ruskism" replacing "McCarthyism" as a specter haunting the groves of academe broke me up for two days, but my solemn caller was not amused and lectured me on my blindness to the harbingers of "fascism.")

The main focus of the cold war has shifted from Europe (where containment worked) to Asia (where we have been appallingly backward in establishing *any* overall policy), but to me the fundamental principles are as valid today as they were twenty years ago. The essential proposition has always been that time is on our side; that if we can hold the line against Communist aggression, transformations will in time occur in Communist systems that will undermine their expansionist drives. If we can, in short, contain Communist imperialism in the *Jihad* phase, we can anticipate détente and, as the ideological fire burns down, hope for internal liberation and entente.

Already we have seen the demolition of Communism as a world system. In 1948, the Yugoslavs set up the first heretical caliphate and the Chinese have for the past five years been constructing another. A number of commentators on Asia are Waiting for Tito—in fact, we are faced now with a Tito (in organizational terms) when we confront Communist China. There is no logical reason why the polycenters of world Communism should be nonexpansionist, but many seem to have made the assumption that since Yugoslavia turned inward any subsequent polycenters will also abandon aggression.

However, although Hanoi is obviously detached from direct control by Peking, it is quite capable of undertaking aggressive drives of its own, particularly when these happen to coincide with the interests of Peking. Recall that Titoism flared up in Yugoslavia because of a direct conflict between the national interests of the two regimes: the Soviets wanted Yugoslavia to develop what amounted to a colonial economy, while Tito rejected the "international division of labor" that would have hindered Yugoslav modernization. In contrast, there is no necessary conflict between Chinese and North Vietnamese objectives or interests. There could be in ten years, or twenty, but we cannot put the Vietnamese crisis on ice and wait. (I think that stalling is precisely the tactic we have tried to employ—but Hanoi has been unwilling to cooperate). Waiting for Tito is thus a wishful excuse for inertia: We already have one Tito in Peking and two-thirds of one (at least) in Hanoi, but it is quite possible to have a Tito without Titoism, i.e., without a "national Communism" which eschews expansion and turns inward.

If Waiting for Tito is illusory, what then are we to do in Asia? The optimal policy is one best described (may my ancestors forgive me!) as building an "Ulster" in the South, establishing ground security and holding onto the main population centers for an indefinite period. The minute one says this, he is attacked for proposing a "military" solution. Everywhere one turns these days, he hears liberals advocating a "political" solution, usually coupled with a demand that we replace soldiers with agronomists and support a program of economic development "which alone can win the allegiance of the peasantry." When one begins to examine these slogans carefully, however, he finds little substance.

What does it mean to ask for a political solution? *Negotiations.* With whom? *Hanoi, Peking, the Vietcong.* But they refused to negotiate. *That is because we have been bombing.* But they refused to negotiate before we started bombing. *Our preconditions were unacceptable, we wouldn't talk to the Vietcong.* The President has made it clear that this is no real obstacle. And Hanoi and Peking have established their precondition: unconditional surrender. *But President de Gaulle, and Pope Paul, and U Thant, and Harold Wilson, and . . . all favor negotiations. We must find a political solution. . . .*

The fact is, I have yet to meet anybody who does not favor negotiations—except the Asian Communists who, understandably, saw no reason why they should not play out what seemed until recently to be a winning hand. As Hanoi informed a representative of Ghana who recently dropped in to urge negotiations, "The fighting in Vietnam must end with a Communist victory." The President could, I suppose, negotiate with the Pope, U Thant and General de Gaulle just to keep in practice, but until Hanoi realizes it is not fighting the French and alters its preconditions there is no real business to be done in Vietnam. We can hardly accept surrender as a precondition for discussing the status of South Vietnam.

So, with complete endorsement of the principle that we should seek a political solution (if anyone can devise one acceptable to both sides), let us turn to the other half of the proposition: that we should develop nonmilitary alternatives to win the allegiance of the countryside.

Again, there is no dissent in the American government from this reasonable objective. The difficulty is that *until* internal stability is attained in South Vietnam, it is literally impossible to implement economic and social programs. Great efforts have been made to train teachers and village officials—who go bravely off into the bush and are murdered by the Vietcong. Some 30,000 such cadres have been killed in the past five years in one of the most savagely mounted campaigns of élite demolition ever seen. The Vietcong has turned terror into a science and has in the process bled white the infrastructure of the South Vietnamese state.

It might be added that in 1945–46 the Vietminh handled

potential opponents in the North with a prophylactic expertise which made the East European Communists look like blundering humanitarians: an estimated 10,000 "unreliables," i.e., independent radicals, hemi-demi-semi-Trotskyites and eccentric Marxists, were summarily executed by General Giap's police—Giap then doubled in brass as Minister of the Interior. This helps to account for "Uncle Ho's" high standing in the hearts of his people, that consensus which some observers have found so moving.

No one in his right mind, even among us cold warriors, has ever believed that military power alone could solve the crises engendered by Communist expansion. What we have argued is that military power is a necessary prerequisite for economic and social development. We have to be able to protect agronomists, doctors, teachers, community workers from the calculated campaign of terror.

There is nothing new and startling about this relationship between military and nonmilitary responses to Communist imperialism: it is precisely the pattern followed in Western Europe where the United States held the marches while providing enormous economic assistance to the war-stricken nations behind the shield. The main difference is that, except for Greece, we had no major insurgency problems in Europe. And it is curious to note that in the period of 1946–49 our intervention in the Greek "civil war" was denounced in liberal circles in the United States because it substituted military for economic and social measures. Then, as now, military measures "solve" nothing, but they can make other kinds of solutions possible.

What, then, can one say about our involvement in South Vietnam? In any rational sense, can it be condemned as "provocative"? Has our conduct of the war been "irresponsible"? Is there any justice in the accusation that Johnson has adopted Goldwater's policy? Above all, what is the source of the ferocious animosity toward Johnson among liberal intellectuals?

Let us begin with the last question. It is important to sort out the categories of criticism that have been developing even though at times they merge into one seething maelstrom. It is clearly unfair, for example, to dump into the same categorical pigeonhole I. F. Stone, Staughton Lynd, Hans J. Morgenthau, Senator Wayne Morse and Walter Lippmann.

I. F. Stone has been busy grinding his "progressive" axe for over thirty years and once wrote a case study in existential documentation to "prove" that the United States launched the Korean War; only Khrushchev could convince him that the Moscow trials had been a travesty of justice. Staughton Lynd, who recently at an anti-Vietnam teach-in at Harvard called for the organization of an "isolationist" party in the United States, is a "New Left" type of the purest apocalyptic strain—he is still trying to figure out why there was no pogrom of American radicals after the murder of John Kennedy, and I suspect he never will get that one unwound.

Hans J. Morgenthau, by contrast, is a scholarly, urbane European intellectual: his major premise is that Americans cannot be trusted with power, and since Johnson (like Kennedy, who got the same treatment) is an American, there is little more to say. Wayne Morse is in the great tradition of populist eccentrics; it is hard to know at the moment whether he is mad because we are in Vietnam, or because we are there without a formal declaration of war by Congress. Finally, Walter Lippmann is off in his sphere-of-influence corner arguing that we have no business monkeying around in China's "natural" zone of power. He is quite consistent: he opposed frustrating Japan's ambitions in China on the same ground in the 1930s, when the Japanese seemingly had a cosmic *imprimatur*.

To label this congeries "isolationist," or even "neo-isolationist," is patently unfair. (And I have omitted all reference to bona-fide pacifists, such as the leaders of the Society of Friends and the American Friends Service Committee, who have the broadest international concerns but reject violence.) All that they have in common is a momentary coincidence of views, views that happen to bring a startling response from the intellectual sector, particularly from young intellectuals (like myself in 1940) who have no interest in being shot at in the jungles of Asia. Ideals have a remarkable way of serving self-interest and it is quite understandable that college students (who have been virtually untouched by the draft for a decade) should take a dim view of increased military commitments in Asia and look around for some High Theory to maintain their civilian status.

This reluctance is understandable (and should not be confused with cowardice), but what is less understandable is the failure of their intellectual elders to provide any rational leadership. And this in turn, I am convinced, arises not from reasoned convictions about the futility of war in Vietnam but from a simple, irrational distrust of Lyndon B. Johnson.

Thus, as I remarked at the outset, Johnson's fantastic success with his domestic program has, if anything, been greeted among liberal intellectuals with a sort of grudging malice: "Wheeling and dealing" has triumphed where the urbane talents of John Kennedy failed; "politics" has overshadowed intellect. In the view of the intellectuals, Lyndon Johnson is (as the British would say) "unclubbable." Moreover, they sense in the President a distrust of intellectuals and feel unloved, and (speaking as a former dean of faculty) I can testify that a bunch of unloved intellectuals can create more problems than a visitation of the plague.

Paradoxically, in the light of their professed standards, intellectuals have an unbelievable propensity for converting political relationships into love affairs. In this fashion, perhaps, they can transmute the dross of politics—full of messy, unpredictable variables—into the gold of power, vicariously exercised. To be loved by the powerful (or to think that one is loved) thus brings fulfillment and exorcises alienation. To be rebuffed by the powerful arouses a bitterness and cynicism that is immune to redemption by works: If Johnson achieved world disarmament tomorrow, proclaiming that swords should be beaten into plowshares, someone would surely say he did it on behalf of the Texas plowshare manufacturers.

Now when I look for love, I don't go into politics after it. Political allegiance often has a foundation in friendship, but the cement of politics is trust—and one can trust people he dislikes intensely (and, conversely, distrust individuals of whom he is personally very fond). The key question, in my opinion, is not, "Do I love Lyndon Johnson?" (whom I have seriously talked to once and who doubtless does not know me from Adam), but, "Do I trust Lyndon Johnson?" The first question is existential and irrelevant; the second is essential, political and significant. And the answer to this second question can only be formulated on the basis of performance, not on divination of motives or other inner considerations.

When, for example, Johnson moved forcefully to the leadership in the struggle for equality, and made it clear by his subsequent actions that he plans to maintain this leadership, I did not attempt to plumb his motives. I happen to think that he genuinely believed what he said, but what if his motives were mixed? Ideally, I would like to associate only with those who are right for the right reasons, but next in order of preference are those who are right for the wrong reasons.

What about Johnson's conduct of American foreign policy? Does it merit the trust it has received from the overwhelming mass of the American people? Or are the liberal intellectual critics (a category that includes self-styled "radicals" whose "radicalism" consists of rhetorical extravagance) right in believing that "Johnson can't be trusted" with our destiny?

On the basis of his performance to date, I believe that President Johnson deserves our trust. It is hard to establish standards of bookkeeping for matters of this sort, but in my view he has taken a very soundly pessimistic view toward the multilateral nuclear force, mishandled the Dominican situation and acted with careful restraint in Vietnam. And the Dominican crisis was clearly of a different magnitude from the MLF or Vietnam.

What appalled me about the administration's handling of the Santo Domingo situation were the defects it revealed in the decision-making process in Washington. As Senator Fulbright recently pointed out in a trenchant analysis, the President was mouse-trapped by bad intelligence. Wessin y Wessin seemingly sold the same dubious list of Communist infiltrators and plot scenario to the Embassy, the MAAG and the CIA in Santo Domingo, each reported it to Washington, and when the President called for top-level advice the outcome was merely proof of the formula that $(3 \times 0)^n = 0$. Once it became clear that the imbroglio in Santo Domingo was far more complex than an attempted Castro *putsch,* the engine was thrown into neutral and we refused to restore Wessin and Imbert to power.

The administration's quiet disposal of the multilateral nuclear force proposal seems to me far more significant than is generally appreciated. From the Soviet viewpoint, MLF appeared as a technique for bootlegging nuclear arms into Germany. (The Russians, having suffered a net population decrease of roughly 40 million as a consequence of World War II, are understandably less pro-German than some of the rest of us.) Johnson's strongly worded statements against nuclear proliferation, buttressed by the silent demise of MLF, are concrete evidence to the Soviets that the United States wants to encourage détente, that our limited war in Vietnam is not aimed at them, that—in short—we are not cranking up the machine for a general confrontation.

MLF had a Rube Goldberg quality about it from the moment it emerged as an initiative designed to head off an independent French deterrent. Once the French had ignored it and plunged ahead, MLF existed only as a grotesque caricature of that concept of Atlantic community so cherished by John Kennedy, as a possible goad to German military ambition and as a senseless provocation to the Soviet Union. I hope it will shortly be interred with appropriate formal rites.

Finally, has the President's conduct of the war in Vietnam been "reckless," "immoral" or contrary to the national interest? I do not think so.

What has to be realized is that the Communist party of Vietnam, the Lao Dong, its state in the North, and its proto-state in the South, are at war with us. We have made it clear that we have no territorial designs on North Vietnam—there is no fustian talk of "liberation"—but they demand the unification of North and South under Communist auspices. Even our bombing pattern in the North has followed a careful etiquette of "controlled response": we have observed what Herman Kahn would call the "city threshold" and only went after a few of the SAM missile launchers when they began to broaden their protective mission beyond Hanoi-Haiphong. We are, in short, fighting a carefully limited war in the effort to attain a perfectly reasonable objective: not the destruction of the Hanoi regime, but the maintenance of the integrity of the Saigon Government from Communist aggression masked as "civil war."

At this point, one can engage in an interminable discussion of the vices of the South Vietnamese government, but such excursions are largely irrelevant. No strategist in his senses would have argued that after refusing to confront Hitler in the Rhineland, in Austria and in Czechoslovakia, the ideal spot was Poland. Yet Poland was the symbolic break in the policy of appeasement, the place where the line was drawn. Although a number of us denounced the war and inquired bitterly why we should fight for a crew of Polish fascists, the character of the Polish government was in fact beside the point.

South Vietnam, which is certainly not a fascist state, has today the same sort of symbolic significance. We can pull out, but if we do, Laos and Cambodia will fall like ripe plums when the Lao Dong shakes the tree. Then comes Thailand, for which a Communist proto-regime—a "liberation front"—has already been organized in the Pathet Lao-dominated area of Laos. Malaysia will then be in a vise between Indonesia and a Communist-dominated Indochina—and Communist insurgents will resume the labor which the British and Malayans suppressed at such great cost in the fifties.

I do not believe that this gloomy prognosis is overdrawn; looking at a map of Southeast Asia is itself a depressing experience. Our decision on what to do in Vietnam is therefore inevitably a decision about our policy in the whole region; while in theory we could shift our defense emphasis to Thailand, in psychological terms this would be disastrous now that the gauntlet has been thrown down in Vietnam: The Thais would have no confidence in our sticking power. I think, in sum, that we have no option but to sweat it out in Saigon, build up American forces and create an impregnable Asian Ulster.

This might take a troop commitment of 200,000–250,000 men—a thought that seems to appall many critics. On the other hand, the United States is reputed to be a great power and for a great power this is a trivial frontier force (the British, with roughly a quarter of our population, have over 50,000 troops in Malaysia alone). The remarkable thing to an observer with any historical perspective is not that we now have to commit troops to the Asian marches, but that we have had over a period of twenty years of confrontation with Communism *only one* major frontier war: Korea.

The real problem is, of course, American public opinion. The Communists have for fifty years treated frontier wars as empirical exercises, as a perfectly valid technique of exercising power in favorable circumstances. In the late thirties, for example, the Soviets and the Japanese—without anybody ever bothering to declare war—were fighting major pitched battles along the Manchurian frontiers. The Soviet invasion of Finland in 1940 was based on a strategic need to provide defense in depth for Leningrad—a sound Bolshevik rationale in the mind of Trotsky as well as of Stalin. The Greek uprising, the Chinese invasion of Tibet and later of India, the Korean War, Malayan and Philippine insurgency were all Communist frontier probes at one force level or another.

I have omitted Castro's rising in Cuba because I am certain, on Theodore Draper's evidence, that Fidel was a surprise convert to Marxist-Leninism *after* the success of his revolution. Similarly, I suspect Castro's subversion department was startled by the revolt in Santo Domingo last spring. My hunch is that Castro's infiltration squads are concentrating on big objectives such as Venezuela, Colombia and Peru rather than trying to become the trustees in bankruptcy of the Dominican Republic. Even Communist subversion has a sense of realistic priorities: A Bolivian ex-Communist once told me that in the early fifties he had reported to a Soviet official in La Paz that the country was ripe for a Communist coup and the latter (who had been drinking) stared at him and replied, "Only dedicated enemies of the Soviet Union would try to saddle us with Bolivia."

The Communists take border wars for granted, though the rules have changed somewhat since the Cuban confrontation of 1962, with the Soviet Union becoming far more careful about peripheral probes. We in the United States, however, consider such undertakings as un-American and public opinion is likely to polarize on a "get out" or "go up" basis (with the same people, notably Republican Midwestern congressmen, veering unnervingly from one extreme to the other).

The Republicans would like nothing better than once again to set up the Korean whipsaw, denouncing the Democrats as the "war party" on Mondays, Wednesdays and Fridays, and as the "party of appeasement" on Tuesdays, Thursdays and Saturdays. The stage was set for this by General Eisenhower at the GOP convention last year when, with his characteristic clarity, he told the assembled delegates that it was surely no accident that—however justified the decisions might have been—all recent wars started under Democratic Presidents.

The task of the President in this era of twilight wars which must remain limited is to reject both the "get out" and "go up" extremes and to convince the American people that "total victory" and "unconditional surrender" are slogans from the lexicon of the prenuclear epoch. While Lyndon Johnson's "style" may be disconcerting to an Ivy League constituency, it is crystal clear from his speeches and comments that he has undertaken this fearful political burden. There is no constitutional requirement that liberal intellectuals must love the President, but on his record to date in both foreign and domestic policy I submit that he deserves their trust.

Can a Free Society
Fight a Limited War?

IN THE SPRING of 1966, the President asked me to go to Vietnam to get the "feel" of the place and some sense of the possibilities for the development of representative institutions. Since that time (despite rumors in the New York *Times* that I was playing therapist to disaffected intellectuals), I have lived day in, day out, week in, week out, with the problems of Vietnam. And I have watched, impotent and heartsick, while the War has eroded the position of the Johnson Administration.

As an old fashioned liberal cold warrior, I have seen and still see nothing immoral about fighting to contain aggressive totalitarianism. Suppressing my human fears, I was prepared to go to the brink with John Kennedy over Berlin and Cuba, and last year I was equally prepared to support the Israelis to the hilt had the Soviets intervened to rescue their incompetent Arab clients. In sum, just to get the record clear at the outset, I take for granted the vital role that the United States must play in helping to achieve a stable world, and I believe that South and Southeast

Reprinted, with permission, from *The New Leader*, October 21, 1968.

Asia present a major challenge to stability in our generation. I may be wrong—I have never been able to attain the witless certainty of the True Believer, and have lost a lot of sleep as a result. But right or wrong, this is what I believe. The unfortunate thing about this world is that one always has to make a 100 percent action commitment on the basis of inadequate evidence. If you wait for all the precincts to report, you do not make history—you write it.

On occasion, I have reacted bitterly to criticism and have been particularly hard on the communications media. But bitterness destroys the analytical capacity—and the hard fact in my judgment is that (whatever the distortions of the media and the critics may have been) Vietnam has poisoned our political atmosphere for a far more fundamental reason than a failure of communication between the Johnson Administration and the people.

The basic issue in Vietnam is this: Can a free society fight a limited war? That is, a strategic war, a war without hate, a war without massive popular involvement. To put it differently, the war in Vietnam is being fought for an abstraction: American national interest in a nontotalitarian Asian future. And it is being fought by a new set of rules, rules which began to emerge during the Korean War but were forgotten in the subsequent years. It is very difficult to tell a young soldier, "Go out there and fight, perhaps die, for a good bargaining position." It is almost impossible to explain to Congressmen that Vietnam is a crucial testing ground—on one side for a brilliantly mounted "war of liberation"; on the other, for our capability to cope with (and in the future deter) such liberators. What sense, moreover, can the average American make of our offer of future economic assistance to a nonaggressive Hanoi? What, in short, has happened to the concept of "the enemy"?

As one of the early advocates of flexible response and limited war, I have watched the defection of the liberal intellectuals with somber anguish. The record is perfectly clear: Limited war was conceived of *by liberals* as *the liberal* alternative to massive retaliation and/or isolationism. It was the liberal answer to John Foster Dulles that was to find classic formulation in the speeches of President John F. Kennedy and in Robert McNamara's spectacular reorganization of the Department of Defense. At root, the theory asserted that instead of relying on apocalyptic nuclear power to deter aggression, the United States would be capable of a flexible, measured response to the forces deployed on the other side of the hill—enough force and no more than was necessary to frustrate aggression. Kennedy and McNamara realized that the very character of nuclear war made any other response an all or nothing proposition; one either pushed the button or capitulated.

John Foster Dulles managed to combine verbal brinkmanship with *de facto* isolationism (the siamese twins of Republican defense policy to this day), but to many of us liberals it seemed that American power under Eisenhower and Dulles was undergoing the death of a thousand cuts. So we assailed Dulles, called for an active foreign policy and beat the drums for flexible response: the defense posture that did not leave the United States with the two crisis options of nuclear weapons or appeasement. Indeed, in November 1962, the *New Republic* editorially took an unblinking view of the possibilities of a land war in Asia—and chose it as preferable to another nuclear confrontation on the Cuban model.

We assumed, naively as it turned out, that the knowledge that the U.S. could transport 100,000 men 12,000 miles in forty-seven hours and thirty-two minutes (or some such logistical triumph) would itself act as a deterrent. Discussions of military strategy began to sound more and more like seminars in game theory. There was a kind of antiseptic quality permeating the atmosphere; one often had the feeling he was attending a chess match.

This, in part, was the source of many later problems. An expert chess player can at a certain point confidently tell his opponent "mate in twelve moves." Normally the opponent, if he is worth playing with, concedes and starts a new game. The atmosphere made those of us who come from the harsh training of poker decidedly uneasy. We knew that nobody has ever folded a full house because he suspected another player of holding four of a kind. Education in these matters always costs money. In international relations it costs more than money—human lives are involved.

Vietnam has provided an agonizing education on the limitations of our theory of limited war. The worst of it is that what I believe to be the real "lessons of Vietnam" have been largely ignored on the political circuit this fall. The hustings are full of politicians solemnly intoning "No More Vietnams." But try to find out what this means. The late Senator Robert Kennedy was relatively clear. In his lexicon it merely meant "Don't support losers." (If one changed a few words in Kennedy's major address on the subject and travelled back thirty years in time, his speech becomes a devastating case against anti-Franco intervention in the Spanish Civil War. Franco did, after all, become the very model of a polycentric fascist, a nationalist "Tito" in Hitler's New Order.) Assuming the winner is identifiable from the outset, this advice can be helpful.

But what is one to make of Senator Eugene McCarthy's gloss on "No More Vietnams"? It was a bit murky, but the gist of his admonition seemed to be that we should only help *good* nations. Even weak ones, for he specifically mentioned India.

Now ever since I took seriously President Kennedy's statement that we are "the watchmen on the walls of world freedom"—only to learn later from reading Arthur Schlesinger's *Bitter Heritage* that Kennedy did not really mean it—I have been reading the small print rather carefully. So when I came upon McCarthy's nomination of India as a possible substitute for Vietnam, I was, to say the least, startled. The small country of South Vietnam has swallowed up half a million American troops. Can one conceive the magnitude of the troop commitment that would be necessary to bolster India's feeble defenses? Or of the bill for the military hardware that would come due if the Indian army were to be equipped properly?

Since I take McCarthy's intelligence for granted, his statement could only make sense if 1) he had an ironclad promise from Peking that India will not again be invaded; or, 2) he was silently and surreptitiously returning to the Dulles strategy of nuclear containment. If the latter is the case, McCarthy's "No More Vietnams" formula involves the abandonment of limited war and a rejuvenation of the nuclear strike. Thus militant "liberals" are in the odd position of embracing the H-bomb as the key instrument of American policy.

The Republican position is quite simple. Richard Nixon will, of course, submit that the Democrats get the country into wars they cannot *end*—citing Korea. This is shorthand for the proposition that the Republicans know how to deal with Communists, that President Eisenhower ended the Korean War by threatening to use nuclear weapons on the sanctuary, that limited war is a "no win" policy and a gross misuse of our incredible national power.

I believe today—as I believed in 1956—that this nuclear strategy would in the long run be disastrous for the United States. But it has the enormous political advantage of being abstract. In October 1962, we lived through the most perilous week in the history of mankind, but there was no blood on the TV screens. The "dirty little war" in Vietnam, on the other hand, is infinitely and, with TV, intimately bloody. While one can argue that fewer Americans have died there in the last six years than die annually in the United States from drunken driving, that one MIRV would destroy more people than have been killed in all of Vietnam in twenty years, he can expect no sympathetic response. Vietnam is *war*—nuclear holocaust is a remote fantasy.

Paradoxically, the marginal character of the war in Vietnam has contributed to its political liabilities. It is not a big war; it is not, comparatively speaking, costing much—3–4 percent of the Gross National Product compared with roughly 11 percent for Korea—but it has no built-in support in the electorate. The President could have drummed up support by hitting the traditional chord of messianic anti-Communism, by engaging in old-style McCarthyism. There were some in Washington, in fact, who advised him three years ago that he could not fight an invisible war, that unless he provided the American people with a vivid "enemy," he would face massive defections.

But Lyndon Johnson flatly refused to whoop up Yahoo chauvinism. At least half a dozen times, I have heard him say that he remembered the anti-German hysteria of World War I and the consequences of Joe McCarthy in the fifties; that he was not going to be the President "who got Americans hating." The historical irony of this is that by prohibiting a return to the old reactionary McCarthyism, he generated the new liberal McCarthyism, which has loosed more hate in the United States than "old Joe" could ever have dreamed of.

The rhetoric of limited war is in itself a major problem.

Johnson was carved up by his critics for telling the troops at Camranh Bay to "bring home that coonskin." Perhaps the figure of speech could have been improved upon, but what American commander-in-chief could address his troops in the field and urge them to die, if necessary, for a stalemate? The British in the nineteenth century could play strategic chess with their regulars and mercenaries—invading such unlikely places as Tibet, Ethiopia, Zululand and Afghanistan—with no repercussions at home unless (as in the First Afghan War) they lost. Once they achieved their usually limited objectives, a treaty was forthcoming and the troops pulled out. Individual families would mourn a sergeant killed in the Sixth River War, or a sepoy butchered at Kabul, but except for disasters these wars were fought outside the forum of British public opinion.

If Ho Chi Minh had permitted the war in Vietnam to remain invisible—with only professional soldiers involved—the pattern of the nineteenth century might have been retained. But Ho Chi Minh has always been a problem. While we may be fighting a limited war against him, he has declared total war against us— and he has played his hand brilliantly. His central goal (learned from his experience with the French and from the lessons of Algeria) was to escalate the war in Vietnam to the point where it became *politically* unjustifiable in the United States. Put differently, he would not permit Johnson to fight an invisible war and—knowing the major tenets of the doctrine of limited war— he proceeded in 1965–68 to utilize his assets to the maximum. To be specific, the United States had foresworn any direct attacks upon the legitimacy of the Hanoi government, had barred the use of nuclear weapons, had—in short—recognized Ho's *political* sanctuary.

True, we denied him military sanctuary by bombing the North, but he obviously wrote off bombing as a painful harassment and countered at our weakest point: ground control in the South. Over the DMZ, and in from Laos and Cambodia, came the regulars of the North Vietnamese Army to buttress the guerrillas already on the ground. The infiltration began well before the decision to bomb the North and—with a great deal of coming and going across unmarked frontiers—has probably exposed over 500,000 North Vietnamese troops to combat in the South.

This commitment of PAVN (Hanoi's regulars) was a death blow to the concept of the invisible war. Airpower enthusiasts to the contrary, there is only one way to fight infantry—with other infantry. Airpower provides mobile artillery, but nobody ever pacified a province with an F-4. In 1965 and 1966—for reasons we will explore subsequently—there was suddenly an acute shortage of riflemen in the Republic of Vietnam.

So far, we have been cutting across time and history with a certain amount of recklessness in the interest of exploring the various consequences of our commitment to limited war in Indochina. Let us now proceed in a more orderly historical fashion. What we tend to forget is that in the years of the Kennedy Administration, Vietnam was not center-stage—the real crises were in Berlin, Cuba and, of all places, Laos. The Soviet willingness to make a Laotian deal, which appeared to be completely ignored by Hanoi, suggested that perhaps the big powers could bilaterally close down Indochina as a source of instability by simply getting the children out of the game.

The difficulty was that the Soviets either could not, or did not choose to, go through with their end of the bargain. (In my judgment, their efforts were simply spiked by Hanoi's intransigence; Khrushchev overestimated his influence on the Viet Minh hardliners and was probably later incensed by their effrontery in disregarding the Geneva Agreement of 1962.) Thus, instead of Laos returning to its status as a kingdom with a thousand years on LSD, the Pathet Lao guerrillas, aided as in South Vietnam by PAVN regulars, took over the task of protecting the Zone of Communication: the Ho Chi Minh trail.

The significance of this double-cross cannot be underestimated. What the Laos agreement of 1962 represented was a willingness by the United States and the Soviets to respect a genuine neutralization of that country, to achieve a "political solution." This had been a liberal demand in the United States for years. I, for example, had supported it vigorously at various conventions of Americans for Democratic Action, and liberal spokesmen had been unsparing in their attacks on Kennedy, and Eisenhower before him, for supporting a rightwing military junta in Laos. Now the authentic, 24-karat "neutralist" Souvanna Phouma was brought back to Vientiane and given our blessing to opt his nation out of the Asian cold war. Had he been successful, we hoped to follow the same pattern in all Indochina.

The Laotian agreement was a horse dead at the post, however; a complete nonstarter. And all the evidence that I have seen indicates that President Kennedy, who had a cold eye, realized this—and realized that Laos was, with the possible exception of Bhutan, the worst place in the world to try to match Communist military pressure. So, writing Laos off as tactically hopeless, Kennedy turned his attention to Vietnam where the situation was very different, particularly in terms of accessibility. His reply to Hanoi's repudiation of the Laotian settlement was to reinforce the defenses of the Republic of Vietnam.

There have been a number of accounts by associates of the late President Kennedy to the effect that he wanted out of Vietnam too. Regrettably, these lack empirical foundation—and quoting the dead is an ancient form of historical fraud, immune to either proof or disproof. The fundamental evidence—notably his support of Secretary of State Dean Rusk and McNamara—suggests that he was unhappy about the situation in Vietnam (as who with any knowledge of the place was not?), but felt the line had to be drawn and enforced in that nation. On this basis Kennedy made the quantum jump: Disregarding the Geneva Accord of 1954 (which we had unofficially respected but never signed), he increased the number of American "advisors" from roughly 750 (as authorized at Geneva) to over 16,000. In addition, "Green Berets" were bootlegged into Vietnam under covert auspices.

This is no place to investigate the internal affairs of the Saigon government. Suffice it to say that the Diem regime, after a seemingly amazing start in the 1950s, was in deep trouble in 1962–63. Objectively viewed, Diem was in an impossible enfilade: The Americans would not let him run an efficient dictatorship (like the one in Hanoi), and he was incapable of building effective representative-government. Confronted by the chaos in Saigon, which became much worse after the fall of the Diem government in November 1963, the Americans gradually made—without really recognizing its import—a critical decision: to fight the war independently.

The basic premise, which I do not believe I have ever seen clearly articulated, was that the United States, with its massive technological assets, would directly force the Hanoi leaders to pull back their troops. We would, in other words, "punish" the Democratic Republic of Vietnam (DRV). Once Ho and his chief strategist, General Giap, knew what they were up against, they would agree "mate in twelve moves" and give up the game. This shortcut had two admirable arguments in its favor: First, we could effectively ignore the condition of the Saigon government; second, we could employ our airpower assets with a relatively slight loss of American lives. The unfortunate consequence was that the South Vietnamese Armed Forces (ARVN) were treated as orphans and given essentially a spectator role in the U.S.–Hanoi competition.

Unfortunately, too, Ho and Giap were never programmed by the Pentagon's game-theorists. They were determined to prevent the United States from fighting a cut-rate war. Down the Ho Chi Minh trail came the trained regiments of the PAVN with the mission, not of defeating the United States on the ground, but of forcing the Americans to fight a ground war in full, costly visibility. To a considerable extent these soldiers were on a suicide mission, but when one appreciates that their goals were *political* rather than military the "kill-ratio" loses much of its impact. North Vietnamese Premier Pham Van Dong had announced the scenario as far back as 1962 when he told the late Bernard Fall: "Americans do not like long inconclusive wars—and this is going to be a long inconclusive war."

President Kennedy presided over the transformation of American strategic theory from massive retaliation to flexible response, but at the time of his murder (less than a month after Diem fell) the United States had only put this doctrine into action in the Cuban missile crisis. Lyndon Johnson, then, inherited from Kennedy a strategy, a Cabinet and a seemingly trivial conflict in Vietnam. As he went on to election in his own right in 1964, Vietnam was still on the back pages—but there was great stirring in Hanoi and PAVN engineers and support troops were busy building base camps in the Central Highlands of South Vietnam. Indeed, communications with the Vietcong were being developed to the point where, in the remarkably short period of six months, the guerrillas were rearmed with the 7.62 weapons family, most notably the AK-47 automatic rifle. (Not only was the AK-47 incomparably superior to the Garands and M-1s of ARVN, but no American rifle before the M-16 could match it. In fact, I have seen Marines up in I Corps who carry the AK-47 in preference to the M-16.)

There is no need to recapitulate in detail the events of the next few years. President Johnson, who was only alerted to the full gravity of the Vietnamese crisis in the fall and winter of 1964–65, has been savagely assaulted for deserting the Kennedy doctrine for a "military solution." Nothing could be further from the truth: Johnson committed American air power and then, in the summer of 1965, ground forces to frustrate a "military solution," a Hanoi victory. (Lincoln did not want a "military solution" to the Secession Crisis of 1861, but despite his wishes half a million Americans died. Like Ho and Giap, Jefferson Davis and Robert E. Lee were most uncooperative.)

In 1964–65, the Americans began looking for trained Vietnamese soldiers to meet Ho Chi Minh's challenge on the ground in the South; they found a poorly trained, miserably equipped, dispirited ARVN. Despite our experience in Korea, where in 1950–51 American divisions had scouts out on their flanks to make sure the ROKS were still there—although five years later South Korea had probably the finest army in Asia—ARVN had remained a stepchild. So American soldiers and Marines, instead of providing a steel frame for the training of ARVN, had to take the field themselves. There simply was no time for the necessary training (the lead time in Korea had been a good year and a half). The "Americanization" of the ground war was thus a consequence of military necessity.

Yet military necessity, while an explanation for what has occurred over the past three years, is not an excuse. Why did Presidents Kennedy and Johnson and Secretary McNamara consistently neglect ARVN? One can suggest a number of partial answers: The American officers in the field obviously felt that nothing short of a drastic purge of the officer corps would do any good—and such a purge was politically impossible in Saigon; the Pentagon's budget experts, faced with the need to cut, would patently give higher priority to the needs of an American service than to ARVN; and Congress *in 1962–63*—the key years—would clearly have taken a dim view of a massive and expensive rearmament and training program. Vietnam was a kind of low-level infection which they hoped would go away. (And had the President endorsed such a program, the organized liberal community in the United States—with me in the forefront in my capacity as National Chairman of Americans for Democratic Action—would have denounced him to the rafters for supporting the "reactionary, unrepresentative Diem clique.")

But these are partial answers. I think the real key to ARVN's neglect was the Pentagon game-theorists' belief in their own press releases; they believed that pressure on Hanoi, "turning the screw," would lead Ho to make the logical calculation that he had more to lose than gain by continuing the conflict. Unfortunately, this was based on a complete misreading of the mind and character of a dedicated and ruthless Leninist—one who, in Koestler's phrase, is prepared to sacrifice one generation in the interest of its successor.

What Ho Chi Minh has done, to return to the main theme, is to hit the doctrine of limited war at its weakest point: domestic opinion. The Johnson Administration, hit by ground war on a scale never anticipated and by the accompanying casualty lists, tried to maintain the ground-rules of limited war. What this often amounted to was simply "hunkering up like a mule in a hailstorm" as the apocalyptics of the left- and rightwing spokesmen for national frustration raged throughout the land. The crux of the matter is that while any two-bit demagogue can make the eagle scream in a nice, neat "us or them" confrontation, explaining the rationale of limited war is incredibly difficult.

Adding to the burden was the disaffection of the young, notably the college elite who compensated for their deferment—with the noxious psychic compound of safety and guilt it provided—by a torrent of abuse of the President and the administration worthy of a sixteenth-century lunatic sectarian. Though this in aggregate probably influenced relatively few young people—who are as leery of religious extremism as the rest of us—the cold fact is that American youth has a genuine grievance. Never in our history has a war been fought with so little involvement by the society as a whole. Which is another way of saying that Vietnam really has been an adult's war and a young man's fight.

Who has been hurt? The economy roars along, the Dow-Jones creeps up, unemployment is down, incomes are at a record high, corporate profits are pushing the roof. The answer is that nobody except the young men directly at war—and indirectly their families—has been hurt. In existential terms, the young have been left alone with the war. When I was in Danang last year, a Marine major put it to me. "Oddly enough in the light of all the agitation," he said, "I have never seen Marines with such good *political morale*. Not even in World War II, and certainly not in Korea. Can't the administration get the people to take this war seriously? Couldn't Johnson at least ration tires so they would know there is a war on?"

These are the things we never thought of when, with all the zeal of innocence, we liberals advanced our doctrine of limited war. Now in 1968 those who have stayed the course, who have had the courage of their consequences, stand appalled by the revival of isolationism—and its identical twin, nuclear deterrence. They stand appalled, too, by the fact that a great President, Lyndon Johnson, has gone into political limbo because of his indomitable commitment to a sound but unpopular policy, flexible response and limited war.

Johnson can look with confidence to the judgment of future historians, but the immediate problem remains. If the "lesson of Vietnam" is that a free, democratic society cannot fight a limited war, what strategic options are still open? Must we revert to the balance of terror? Or, as some notable liberals today seem to think, can we build affluence in one country and somehow escape the broils of the outside world?

I confess that, battered as I am, I still believe that flexible response is not only a sound but a *liberal* alternative to the only other strategies I see on the horizon. And I would suggest that those who are busy leaping up and down about Vietnam take a brief pause in their exercise to inform us precisely *how* they plan to employ American power in the interest of international stability and world order.

Except for the pacifists (and those who are pro-Hanoi), I have yet to find a critic who—when pushed back on his premises—did not end up embracing some variety of isolationism. There is nothing wicked or un-American about being an isolationist, but it is a doctrine that American liberals outgrew a quarter of a century ago. It would be tragic if a united front of Nixonites and followers of Eugene McCarthy, playing up to the understandable frustrations of the American people, undermined our commitment to limited war and returned us to the Age of Dulles. Perhaps we should recall that while limited war is nasty, for most of us resurrection would be a precondition for appreciating the strategic virtue of nuclear retaliation.

Moralism and Foreign Policy

THE OUTSTANDING CHARACTERISTIC of American foreign policy today is the retreat from what might be called "moralism." In the hands of a cool President and a positively remote Secretary of State, the United States is abandoning its moralistic thrust of the last thirty years for the solid ground of "vital national interests." No longer are we to be "the watchmen on the walls of world freedom," as John F. Kennedy viewed our role, or the advocates of a universal "Great Society," which Lyndon B. Johnson saw as a legitimate American aspiration.

In practical terms this amounts to abandoning our concern with the behavior of other nations unless their actions pose something called a "direct threat" to our interests. Like the rain, which falls equally on the just and the unjust, American policy in the Middle East will be "evenhanded"; in Africa it will buttress the "territorial integrity" of existing states, in Latin America it will welcome dictatorships and democracies with equal warmth, in

Reprinted, with permission, from *The New Leader,* February 16, 1970.

Asia it will (as an antiwar military officer put it to me in Saigon) "let the gooks fight it out."

This policy of disengagement can, of course, be wrapped in high rhetoric. President Nixon, for example, did a masterful job of justifying to Congress the demolition of the Alliance for Progress, explaining that only innate modesty has led us to halt our attempts to shape the Latin American future. While the conservatives, who have for years opposed pouring resources into "rat-holes," winked at each other knowingly, Senator Frank Church (D.-Id.) rushed to give a liberal *imprimatur* to this strategy of national selfishness. Church does not want to give funds to undemocratic regimes, the conservatives do not want to give money to anybody, but pragmatically there is full agreement: no money.

Similarly, when Senator Mike Mansfield (D.-Mont.) argues for a cutback in American commitments, he and his Senate Foreign Relations Committee colleagues claim to be doing penance for our "arrogance." A certain amount of humility is no doubt healthy, but the argument supports the conservative position best formulated as "Who needs them?"

On that level of analysis the conservatives are, of course, right. We don't need "them"—the Thais, the Vietnamese, the Germans, the Indians, the Israelis. The only power in the world that can directly threaten the United States is the USSR, so why should we become exercised over who controls Saigon, Bengal, Djakarta, Ouagadougou or Jerusalem? Joseph Kraft put this sentiment in its classic form in his May 29, 1967, syndicated column when he pointed out that in Vietnam and the Middle East no "American vital interests are at stake. On the contrary, this country will also get along nicely no matter what happens in the Middle East or Southeast Asia."

The conservatives are further correct in their assessment that advances in military technology have made isolationism (or disengagement, for those who choke on a word) functional for the United States. Once upon a time, we needed bases to contain Communist power; our military effectiveness depended on airfields in Britain, Western Europe, Libya, etc. This gave us, in the hardnosed view, a vital interest in the security of those states.

Now a news item about the closing of Bada Beir, the communications base in Pakistan, describes the situation tersely: "Technological progress in electronic surveillance made the base in Pakistan no longer necessary. . . . Today 'spy-in-the-sky' satellites orbit over Soviet central Asia and Communist China." The ICBM and Polaris submarine have rendered the rest of the world militarily expendable. This is obviously a powerful argument, but are its premises valid?

The conservative case for an essentially isolationist foreign policy rests on the proposition that remarkably few things could happen in this world which would vitally affect our national interests. Therefore we should disengage behind, in Walter Lippmann's phrase, "blue water." A few solid commitments would remain: the Monroe Doctrine, and our alliances with insular powers such as Japan, Britain and Australia. Events in the developing world outside of Latin America we would view with friendly disinterest. What concern of ours is it whether black or white prevails in Rhodesia? Whether Communists or non-Communists in Vietnam? Arabs or Jews in Israel?

If one extracts moralism as a basic component of foreign policy, the conservative position is impregnable. Our continental fortress is only vulnerable to the Soviet Union, but for twenty-five years the USSR has been hoping the U.S. would agree to a spheres-of-influence division of the world. If we settled for the Western Hemisphere, Britain and Western Europe, Japan and Australia, and abandoned moralism (that is, the Cold War), the sources of conflict with Russia would presumably vanish: The two superpowers would go about their business in their own bailiwicks. (If the New Left historians are correct in asserting that the cold war arose from American provocations, this division should bring détente in short order; here, as elsewhere, the New Left provides conservative advance men.)

The high priest of this view of national interest is the distinguished historian and diplomat George F. Kennan. Back in 1951, he presented the essence of his position in a small tour de force, *American Diplomacy*. With a surgeon's scalpel, he opened up American twentieth-century diplomacy and found it to be suffering from a pervasive malignancy: moralism—or, in his precise formulation, "the legalistic-moralistic approach to international problems."

With regard to Japan, for example, Kennan's tightly argued thesis was that an intelligent approach to our relations with the Orient might have avoided Pearl Harbor. But failing to appreciate the forces that drove the Japanese to expand, and carried away by sentimental attachment for China, we "hacked away, year after year, decade after decade" at the Japanese encroachment on the Asian mainland.

"Had we been over a long period of time more circumspect in our attitudes toward the Japanese, more considerate of the requirements of their position," Kennan wrote, "there was a possibility that the course of events might have been altered." When we disregarded "power realities in the Orient," we bought unnecessary trouble.

Kennan's central argument is profoundly pessimistic. Most of our interventions, he suggested, have created problems greater than those they were designed to meet—an inevitable result, perhaps, since they were founded on crusading fervor rather than rational calculation of real interests. In reality, he observed, we cannot shape the world to our ideals, we cannot alter history; thus, he went on, "the great misfortune of the West, I suspect, was not Hitler but the weakness of German society which made possible his triumph."

This world view necessitates a spectator role—except where vital interests are at stake, say, in Latin America. It is an argument with great intrinsic appeal to the American people—who, after all, did not go to war with Nazi Germany until Adolf Hitler declared war on the U.S. Yet it seems important to note that for the last twenty-five years the moralists have made the foreign policy decisions, and only with Vietnam and the ensuing desertion of liberal intellectuals did this begin to change.

The conservative justification for isolationism—that the United States can manage very nicely no matter what happens at most places in the world—is coldly realistic. The liberal rationale, while it results in roughly the same policy, is quite different, resting on a curious amalgam of pacifism, anti-imperialism and anticapitalism.

Here is a seminal statement of the central theme: "The destiny of Europe and Asia has not been committed, under God, to the keeping of the United States; and only conceit, dreams of grandeur, vain imaginings, lust of power or a desire to escape from our domestic perils and obligations could possibly make us suppose that Providence has appointed us his chosen people for the pacification of the earth."

It has a familiar ring, and could be Senator Eugene McCarthy or Professor Henry Steele Commager discussing Vietnam at a hearing of the Senate Foreign Relations Committee. It could be a resolution by Americans for Democratic Action or an editorial in the *Christian Century*. It is, in fact, an excerpt from Charles A. Beard's *Giddy Minds and Foreign Quarrels* (1939).

The liberal argument further suggests that our arrogance will destroy our democratic values: "If we go in, decency, tolerance, kindliness, truth, democracy and freedom will be the first victims," wrote Norman Thomas and Bertram D. Wolfe in *Keep America Out of War* (1939). In other words, our primary mission is to bring the democratic ideal to fruition in the United States. How can we spend money to defend Southeast Asia when there is still poverty and discrimination at home?

The appalling reality of modern totalitarianism muffled this liberal isolationist theme in the decade following World War II. The moralists took command of containing Communist power, much to Kennan's dismay. As the chief theoretician of containment, he believed that dealing with the Soviets was a task for foreign service officers and other gentlemen, not for impassioned crusaders. What emerged from the practice of containment was an alliance between those who thought that checking Communist power was a vital American interest (conservatives), and others who believed that the United States was morally obligated to oppose totalitarianism (liberals).

This inherently schizophrenic coalition limped along through the fifties, but disintegrated under the impact of Vietnam. The young generation, never having seen at first hand the enormities of totalitarianism, simply defected. Ironically, they unwittingly returned to the positions that those of us who opposed World War II had abandoned in December 1941!

There is nothing wicked about this rejection of moralism ("the tired clichés of the cold war," etc.); however, it puts the conservative isolationist position beyond reproach. What, for instance, can a rational analyst of national interest make of a

President who would say: "What do you do when little Israel calls on you for assistance and help? I'll tell you what you do. You do what is right. . . . You stand up for freedom, whatever the price." Or of a President who announces that we are the "watchmen on the walls of world freedom"? The only possible conclusion is that these men—Lyndon B. Johnson and John F. Kennedy—were intoxicated by power.

I would be the last person to deny that moralism can get us into trouble, or—on the other hand—to defend indiscriminate and nonprudential efforts to liberate the world. But I am convinced that a United States dedicated to isolation and national affluence, while most of the world degenerated into squalor and totalitarianism, would be a moral monstrosity.

The Jigsaw Puzzle
of History

SOME YEARS AGO, in reviewing Arthur Schlesinger's *A Thousand Days* for *Harper's* Magazine, I suggested that there was some resemblance between the volumes then flowing from Schlesinger, Sorensen, Salinger and other lesser luminaries at Camelot, and the medieval monastic chronicle. If anything, events since that time have reinforced this prejudice.

To be specific, I doubt that any historically valid treatment of the Kennedy-Johnson era can emerge for at least another decade, if then. I confess that when I emerged from the White House I signed up to do an "insider volume," but sober, professional second thoughts have led me to put that project on ice until at least 1980.

The problem is that I simultaneously know too much, and not enough. I know what I thought was happening, what others on the staff thought was happening, what the press thought was happening. But I cannot fully document what happened. And I have seen enough highly classified documents to know that what most of the observers thought was happening was at best half-right, at worst dead wrong. (We will explore a few cases of this sort later.) This has steered me in a different direction as far as writing is concerned: I am now preparing what is frankly and unashamedly an *ex parte* memoir, *From Camelot to the Alamo*. It is based on what I believed was true, on the picture as I conceptualized it, of the Kennedy-Johnson era. As I pointed out so long ago with respect to Schlesinger's fine book, it will not be a *history* but should be helpful to those who try objectively to put the pieces together.

This is not the place to explore in detail the various "inside" stories that have emerged from the Kennedy-Johnson era, except to note that too frequently they are disguised autobiography and/or therapy. I have nothing against autobiography, but I get a bit tired of grievances posing as high theory. For example, several chroniclers emphasize President Johnson's "isolation" and the extent to which his "courtiers" protected him from reality. Translated, this means "Why didn't Lyndon talk to me?" Similarly, we are told that no one dared to challenge the President on his Vietnam policies, that he went up in smoke if anyone suggested a bombing halt. Translated, this means "I didn't dare argue because he might have fired me."

Now it so happens that I opposed the bombing *strategy* against North Vietnam from the day it was inaugurated, wrote an article condemning it which appeared in the spring of 1965 in the Washington *Post* and elsewhere, and never changed my views. Note my formulation: I supported the defense of South Vietnam but opposed the whole notion of a cut-rate, airpower war. (I did not see it as a moral issue: sending bombs by air mail is no less moral than employing parcel post, as the North Vietnamese did.) President Johnson was fully aware of my position, which I called to his attention about once a month in various contexts. Indeed, on several occasions he asked me to send copies of my memorandums to Secretary of State Dean Rusk and Secretary of Defense Robert S. McNamara. As a courtesy I always sent copies to Walt Rostow, but since I neglected to send any to the New York *Times* (I was not working for them), it was officially True that nobody in the administration ever questioned the President's policies.

This is not to assume a heroic pose—several of my friends in the White House (who did not have university tenure) lost their voices arguing with the President on issues ranging across the board from foreign policy to crime bills to increasing taxes. But— and this is the crux of the matter for the historian—not only was there verbal argument, respectful but nonetheless sharp, but there were pieces of paper: "Secret—Eyes Only" memos to the President from his staff. There were full transcriptions of various crucial meetings. Each of us has a set of our memos, but only the presidential archives in Austin contain the whole range. Including most significantly what the President said to Dean Rusk or Robert McNamara after he had read whatever stuff we sent him.

The net result is that most White House "revelations" would be thrown out of a court of law in about thirty seconds; they simply lack any probative substance. I know what the President said to me over the unmonitored direct line, and Harry McPherson and Joe Califano know what I told them the President told me. Then one of Califano's assistants might pass on to a speechwriter with an ego deficiency what he had heard (via Califano) that the President told me. The speechwriter, who was tucked away somewhere in the Executive Office Building preparing "Rose Garden prose," i.e., talks to visiting Elks, might decide to build up his credit as an insider by calling a newspaper correspondent: "You know, I was with Johnson when he was talking to Roche this morning about the problem of jets for Peru and the old man was really climbing the wall."

Next day, Page One: "Informed White House sources indicate that the President referred obscenely to de Gaulle in connection with a rumored French agreement to sell supersonic jets to Peru." To the end of time, who will believe that the original discussion related to the British sale of Hawker Hunters to, say, Pakistan? This is hypothetical, but just so—and only to protect the guilty.

A classic example of this sort of embellishment can be found in Eric F. Goldman's *Tragedy of Lyndon Johnson*. Professor Gold-man, accustomed to the genial environment of Princeton, got himself involved with the West Side Jacobins in connection with a White House Arts Festival, and several of them decided to convert the affair into an anti-Vietnam happening. There was, as you may recall, a bit of a stir and, indeed, it is difficult not to feel considerable sympathy for Professor Goldman. At the same time, the President—for equally good reasons—was not amused and, apparently, simply froze Goldman out of any White House functions. But Goldman relates that he took his troubles to an old friend of the President, who called presidential appointments secretary Marvin Watson, to get a reading. The old presidential friend talked to Watson and then told Goldman that Watson suggested, in vivid obscene language, that the professor take a jump in the river.

Several aspects of this should be noted. First, Goldman does not say that Watson used the obscenity; he says X quoted Watson to that effect. Second, Goldman was clearly not the President's favorite at the time, so the story has some deductive persuasiveness. But the hooker is that Watson is a devout churchman who simply never uses that kind of language—to those of us who know Watson (and he is a close personal friend of mine) Goldman's anecdote has the same persuasiveness as a story headlined "Pope Paul Busted on Pot Charge." But how can one prove a negative? Particularly when it is confronted on the second bounce.

Admittedly, this is a trivial instance, but it highlights a whole genre, one almost would say a business: namely, the surfacing of presidential quotes, and of attributions to other high officials, which are impossible to validate or to refute. I recall vividly a phone conversation with President John Kennedy in late September or early October 1962, in which he scorched me for at least fifteen minutes. I had written an article suggesting less profile and more courage on a number of pressing issues, notably civil rights, and he caught me at 7:30 A.M. as I was drinking my first cup of coffee. For me it was a Bay of Pigs: I didn't get a word in edgewise and he was running about 400 a minute.

When he hung up, I went back to my breakfast and figured that this was the penalty one paid for being national chairman of Americans for Democratic Action—a job which required one to try to keep a liberal President in fighting trim. I didn't know that I had been blasted by a future martyr—Jack Kennedy had been sore at me off and on since I went to work for him in 1957. The consequence was, of course, that I did not rush to my commonplace book and record Kennedy's sentiments—I just figured that the next time he needed ADA support, he would be in a friendlier mood. (As, in fact, he was.)

A couple of months later I ran into Larry O'Brien, who filled me in on some details. He had gone to see the President in his bedroom and Kennedy had thrown the magazine at him—the one with my offensive article—and said, "What the hell is Arthur [Schlesinger] getting paid for? He is supposed to keep these bastards on a leash." I thought this was pretty funny and remembered it, but I wonder if O'Brien has the slightest recollection. There is no particular reason why he should—what was for me a startling experience was probably for him a commonplace event. But in legal terms, there is no way of proving a thing—I could have dreamed it all up.

While I can honestly say that I have never knowingly invented a quote for presidential attribution, I must in all candor concede that on occasion things got a bit complicated. For example, President Johnson would in succession call Califano, Christian, McPherson and me to get our reading on some problem. Usually his calls were slightly therapeutic; i.e., he would be madder than hell about some column and would explore the author's credentials and ancestry in some detail. We would immediately caucus and try to work out a sensible, common position, and in the course of our meditations each would repeat the pithier components of the President's analysis. By the time we got finished, it was often hard to recall which things he had said to whom and within a week, I suspect, each of us fed the whole works into his personal memory bank. The smart thing to do would have been to have our secretaries monitor and transcribe the conversations, but this was absolutely forbidden (except, I believe, to Walt Rostow— who had to have his instructions on crucial matters of foreign policy down in black and white). Lyndon Johnson wanted privacy with his staff, even at the expense of historical exactitude.

Another of Goldman's difficulties which might be mentioned at this point is that he believed what he read in the papers. In his book—of which very little is actually firsthand recollection—he lavishes praise on Hubert Humphrey for his spontaneity and wit in the 1964 campaign (which was, in fact, a fearful drag). To exemplify his point he takes a speech Humphrey delivered in Toledo, Ohio, on October 6, 1964, and suggests that it was

Hubert at his best. Improvised wit, searching commentary—these were the essentials of the vice presidential candidate's vivid presentation.

The only problem is that this speech was neither spontaneous nor delivered! It was written by me—and with all due immodesty I can state it was a good speech—and under the arrangement we had with the Senator, unless he vetoed it, the Democratic National Committee sent out a press release based on our (the Washington staff's) draft. This was done for morning release on the seventh of October, and—since it was a slow day elsewhere and the speech had some zip—it hit the headlines in three leading papers.

Meanwhile, out in Toledo, Humphrey—instead of giving my twenty-minute speech—talked for an hour and forty minutes. He gave one-third of each of five bad speeches. Why? Because someone on the plane into Toledo had persuaded him that my speech would lose Ohio, and seven volunteer speechwriters (every man seems to consider himself a speechwriter—in fact, speechwriting is a real art) had put together a monstrosity (which I later heard on tape). The correspondents on the plane heard the first ten minutes and retired to the nearest bar, so the only coverage the event received was 1) in the Toledo papers which were accurate; and 2) in the *Times*, Baltimore *Sun* and Washington *Post*, whose stories were based on the DNC press release and totally inaccurate. As I recall, this was the speech in which Humphrey actually told the assembled Democrats that Jack Kennedy was watching from heaven to see how they voted! It was not one of his better days.

Let us turn to another area of instant history which is going to be a source of major problems to the historian of the future: the conflict in authorities on the same event. On September 2, 1963, President Kennedy gave Walter Cronkite of CBS an exclusive interview, most of it centering on the status of the Diem regime in Vietnam. Roger Hilsman, then Assistant Secretary of State, Far East, noted in his book that television forced a decision. "The subject of Vietnam and the Buddhist crisis," wrote Hilsman, "was an inevitable question. . . . The White House staff [composed] a proposed response that was an innocuous as possible [but] the

President tossed it aside and bit the bullet. 'I don't think,' the President said, 'that unless a greater effort is made to win popular support that the war can be won out there . . .'"

Hilsman goes on to state that the "meaning of [a] reference to the need for 'changes in policy and personnel' was that the President had decided that the tension between the United States and the Diem regime would continue until the policy of repression against the Buddhists and the students had been abandoned . . ."

Of the same situation, Schlesinger wrote that President Kennedy "tossed aside a moderate statement his staff had prepared" and went on to sock Diem with a hardline position. In short both Hilsman and Schlesinger indicate that Kennedy, in his Cronkite interview, deliberately rejected a moderate view and substituted what was, in effect, an ultimatum to Diem to shape up or ship out. Sorensen makes no substantive comment.

However, another precinct—one far closer to the actual TV interview than either Hilsman or Schlesinger—has also reported (and with an entirely different reading of the course of events). Pierre Salinger, press secretary, who handled the logistics of the Cronkite interview, later wrote that this TV special "had an unfortunate aftermath. CBS shot half an hour of questions and answers, mostly on Vietnam, but cut the footage to twelve minutes for actual broadcast. The result was a partial distortion of JFK's opinion of President Diem. In the actual interview, which was filmed, President Kennedy spoke of his respect and sympathy for Diem. When the film was shown to the public, only the unfavorable presidential remarks remained."

I later asked Pierre Salinger how this could have happened: it is inconceivable that a network would edit an interview with the President without going over the cuts with the White House. He said it was one of those things that fell through the slats when the President was out of town—like the famous "Do not abort" cable sent to the embassy in Saigon (encouraging an anti-Diem coup) when the President was at Hyannis in late August 1963. These things happen in every administration, providing fodder for later paranoids: Why was the warning to General Short at Pearl Harbor on December 6, 1941 sent by Western Union?

From my knowledge of the government, I am absolutely ready to believe that the answer was incompetence. But what know they of incompetence who only footnotes know?

Let us examine the focus of another, more recent conflict of sources: the famous "Battle of Johnson's Speech." In March 1969, a year after the Johnson speech which cut back the air war on North Vietnam and announced his retirement from the presidential competition, the New York *Times* ran two articles on the reasons for this shift and the bureaucratic infighting that accompanied it. Subsequently, the man who claimed to be the *deus ex machina* of the whole shift in Vietnam policy, Townsend Hoopes, published a book, *The Limits of Intervention*, which attempted to bolster this claim.

Frankly, this put me in a difficult position. It was folly to allow Hoopes to pre-empt the historical stage (since, in fact, he was poorly informed), but any serious reply had to be based on highly classified materials (which Hoopes didn't even know existed). The fact is that when Lyndon Johnson asked people to keep their mouths shut, they did—or were put on ice in one of the many comfortable welfare programs that exist in the government. I spent, at the President's request, a good part of six months trying to figure out what went wrong in Vietnam, and I had access to all relevant documents going back to 1963–64. But, to repeat, I reported to him, not to the New York *Times*. Moreover, there was a certain moral question involved in anticipating the President's memoirs—as well as the nice legal question of declassifying "Top Secret, Sensitive, Eyes Only" memorandums.

So I called the former President and suggested he break loose enough material to demolish Hoopes, but he felt that he would have an opportunity to deal personally with the question in a forthcoming series of TV interviews with the ubiquitous Walter Cronkite. On February 6, 1970, he went into the whole affair on TV, reading from some of the memos, only to be greeted by hoots of derision from Hoopes (who accused him of "standing history on its head") and others. Hoopes accused Johnson of lying when the latter said he had instructed Rusk and Clifford by memo on February 28, 1968, to undertake a searching reappraisal of all aspects of our Vietnam policy. Hoopes said flatly that "the Pentagon officials concerned are quite clear that they never received such a document." Hoopes cited a host of hearsay witnesses, and made the flat statement: "Clifford is certain that his instructions from the President were entirely oral, and rather narrow in scope . . ."

This time I challenged Hoopes in print, pointing out that there was a memo of February 28, 1968; it went to the principal officials (including McNamara, who was retiring on the twenty-ninth; it called for a total, across-the-board evaluation of our options in Vietnam; and that Clark Clifford had signed a receipt for his copy and referred to its headings in a reply written March 4. I still did not feel it proper to distribute copies, but the odds seemed pretty good that if Hoopes, Clifford or any of the others involved called me a liar, some documentation might surface from Austin. I guess those involved thought so, too—there was not one effort to refute my contentions.

Finally, in this context, take the role of Dean Rusk, who was, in March 1968, the principal supporter of an unconditional, partial (above the 20th parallel) bombing halt. Schlesinger once referred to Rusk, whom I gather he did not like, as a "Buddha" who never contributed to policy discussions. Rusk's reply was that when Schlesinger was in the room he kept his mouth shut, since otherwise his words would be all over Georgetown in half an hour. My view is that Rusk overdid the secrecy bit—I think sometimes he kept secrets from himself just to stay in trim—but in direct private consultations with the President, McNamara, Clifford and perhaps two or three others he was a sharp, discerning participant.

By the fall of 1967, although he was pessimistic about any positive result (with justification, as events have demonstrated), Rusk had decided that a cutback in the bombing of North Vietnam might lead to negotiations. (The idea of cutting back to the 20th, by the way, had been around for some time: McNamara and Assistant Secretary of State William Bundy had staffed it out in the spring of 1967.) This came out in a reply Rusk drafted in November 1967, to a memo (anonymous, but actually written by McNamara) which the President circulated to a dozen trusted advisers recommending a total bombing halt, a troop ceiling for

Vietnam, and in general de-escalation and what is now known as "Vietnamization." Of those canvassed, only Rusk and Under Secretary of State Nicholas Katzenbach reacted sympathetically, though they argued for a partial rather than a total bombing halt to protect our troops in I Corps from invasion through the DMZ. Clifford, by the way, was hard as nails. On March 4, 1968, Clifford was still a hard hawk, but Rusk reintroduced the proposal for a bombing cutback, argued for it with the President, and found a receptive ear.

No disrespect is intended to Clark Clifford, who in my judgment did in the Department of Defense what should have been done two years earlier—that is, he began the Vietnamization of the war. My only point is that Rusk's proposal did not come out of the blue; he had made it six months earlier. But Hoopes simply was unaware that the November-December discussions had ever taken place.

Well, so much for "The Battle of Johnson's Speech," except to note that this was not really a historical argument at all. It was theological. As of 1970, liberal Democrats decided that the war in Vietnam must somehow be expunged from the party's record. The ideal way to accomplish this Orwellian objective was to show that a few sinister hawks foisted our Southeast Asian policy on an unwilling but helpless mass of liberal doves.

Hoopes and his associates were thus busy concocting a virtuous past; history has become an instrument of retrospective salvation. Indeed, as I look around today, I get the distinct impression that the only supporters of the Vietnam war in the top echelons of the Johnson Administration were the President, Dean Rusk, Walt Rostow and myself. The White House staff, the bureaucracy, Congress and even some high military positions were seemingly populated by secret doves. Washington, in short, was full of men wrestling with their consciences, and—as the paucity of resignations indicated—winning.

Indeed, it will be interesting to watch the historian of the future wrestling with the problem of defining a "dove." Professor Hans J. Morgenthau, for example, has been thought of as a leading dove, but the reader of his views on Southeast Asia finds himself a bit unnerved. True, Morgenthau opposed "peripheral containment" of Asian Communism (i.e., the war in Vietnam), but suggested in its place a straight Dulles strategy—nuclear bombs!

Or, take the confusing role of General James M. Gavin, who in 1966 became famous for his alleged opposition to bombing North Vietnam and his alleged advocacy of "enclaves." I say "alleged" because in testimony before the Senate Foreign Relations Committee in February 1966, General Gavin flatly denied that he wanted to stop bombing North Vietnam, denied that he wanted "a halt in the escalation" and denied that he recommended "withdrawal of American troops to defend a limited number of enclaves." Indeed, he urged that "the utility value [of Haiphong] should just be done away with since it is a major port of entry for military supplies"!

Perhaps some of the confusion arose because a year later, in testifying before the same committee, General Gavin announced that "I opposed the bombing of North Vietnam at the last hearings, and I still oppose the bombing of North Vietnam, and I think the bombing should be stopped." Since the politicians were already beginning to cover their tracks on bombing, one suspects they decided to let the General join the caper.

Politicians and generals can, perhaps, be forgiven for trying to cover their tracks, but the situation of a scholar is somewhat different. The personal theme of Hilsman's book, *To Move a Nation*, was that he resigned from the Johnson Administration because he saw it deviating from the flexible, political strategy toward Vietnam implemented by President Kennedy. The Johnson Administration, Hilsman wrote, "was obviously going to take the military path." In the course of writing his volume, Hilsman declassified a large number of his own Secret and Top-Secret memorandums; I am taking the liberty now of declassifying one that he somehow overlooked.

Dated August 30, 1963, it is a six-page Top-Secret memorandum to the Secretary of State from the Assistant Secretary, Far East (i.e., Hilsman). Subject: "Possible Diem-Nhu Moves and U.S. Responses." The background might be briefly noted. President Ngo Dinh Diem and his brother, Ngo Dinh Nhu, suspecting that the United States was plotting a coup in Saigon, began in the summer of 1963 to threaten the Americans with what we now call "Vietnamization." Among the sinister gambits allegedly considered were 1) a deal with Hanoi, 2) telling the Americans to go home and 3) calling for great-power neutralization of the whole of Indochina (patterned on the Laos model of 1962).

Hilsman projected eleven possible Diem-Nhu moves and suggested what contingency plans should be evolved to deal with each. Our concern here is with four of those moves:

"Diem-Nhu Move: *Severance of all aid ties with the U.S., ouster of all U.S. personnel (except for a limited diplomatic staff), and demand for the removal of all U.S.-controlled military equipment in Vietnam.*

"U.S. Response: *a) We should stall in removing U.S. personnel and equipment from Vietnam. This move by [Saigon] would again, however, underscore the necessity for speed in our counteraction. b) If Diem-Nhu move to seize U.S.-controlled equipment, we should resist by all necessary force.*

"Diem-Nhu Move: *Political move toward [Hanoi] (such as opening of neutralization negotiations), or rumors and indirect threats of such a move.*

"U.S. Response: *a) Ambassador Lodge should give Diem a firm warning of the dangers of such a course, and point out its continued pursuit will lead to cessation of U.S. aid. b) Encourage the generals to move promptly with a coup. c) We should publicize to the world . . . any threats or move by Diem or Nhu toward [Hanoi] in order to show the two-edged game they are playing and help justify publicly our counteractions. d) If [Hanoi] threatens to respond to an anti-Diem coup by sending troops openly to South Vietnam, we should let it [Hanoi] know unequivocally that we shall hit [Hanoi] with all that is necessary to force it to desist. e) We should be prepared to take such military action.*

"Diem-Nhu Move: *Appeal to de Gaulle for political support for neutralization of Vietnam.*

"U.S. Response: *a) We should point out publicly that Vietnam cannot be effectively neutralized unless the Communists are removed from control of North Vietnam. If a coalition between Diem and the Communists is suggested, we should reply that this would be the avenue to a Communist takeover in view of the relative strength of the two principals in the coalition. Once an anti-Diem coup is started in South Vietnam, we can point to the obvious refusal of South Vietnam to accept a Diem-Communist coalition.*

Diem-Nhu Move: *Continuation of hostilities in Saigon as long as possible in the hope that the U.S. may weaken because of the bloodbath which may involve U.S. personnel.*

U.S. Response: *a) We should maintain our* sangfroid *and encourage the coup forces to continue the fight to the extent necessary. b) We should seek to bring officers loyal to Diem over to our side. . . . We should encourage the coup group [to cut off Diem's supplies]. d) We should make full use of any U.S. equipment available in Vietnam to assist the coup group. e) If necessary, we should bring in U.S. combat forces to assist the coup group to achieve victory."*

Without laboring the obvious, Hilsman's definition of a "political solution" seems to have altered rather radically between August 1963, when he composed this bellicose memo, and February 1964, when he sensed a "military solution" in the offing and resigned. I might add that the key to any "political solution" in Indochina back in 1962–65 was "neutralization," along the lines of the Geneva Agreement on Laos. Thus Hilsman's view of neutralization, as expressed in the foregoing, is particularly pertinent. By 1963 standards, Hilsman made Dean Rusk sound like a pacifist.

There is one final problem of instant history that deserves brief analysis. That is the fact that at different periods in time people are asking different questions. The dispute over the Tonkin Gulf Resolution is a classic example of this kind of shift. In 1964, when the President asked Congress for a functional declaration of war (which is what the resolution was), the senators who held hearings asked Secretary McNamara *what* Hanoi's torpedo boats were trying to do to us. The hearings were heavily censored, but if one meshes them with those held by the Senate Foreign Relations Committee in 1968, the story becomes crystal clear: The American destroyers knew the North Vietnamese torpedo boats were out to get them because Hanoi's orders to its task force had been intercepted.

The reason for the excessive censorship escapes me—anyone with a fifth-grade education (here or in Hanoi) could figure out the main lines of the argument from the allusions in the uncensored portion of the report on the hearings. (Besides which I was told by a high Vietnamese official that the orders were transmitted *in clear,* i.e., they were not coded.) At any rate, in 1964 the Congress asked "What were they doing to us?" and the administration, with documents, indicated they planned to sink us. Congressmen and senators generally take a dim view of foreign warships trying to sink our destroyers; the President wanted to lay it on the line to Hanoi for deterrent purposes; the result: the Tonkin Gulf Resolution.

Unfortunately nobody cheers when deterrence works, but when it fails the trouble begins. And as the American people became increasingly infuriated with the war, their elected representatives began searching for protective cover. The simplest form of cover is the ancient slogan, "We were tricked!"—and out it came. One of the problems of being President is that you have no place to hide, no excuse when things get tough. As Kennedy said after the Bay of Pigs, "Success has a thousand fathers, but failure is an orphan."

Since President Johnson pulled a copy of the Tonkin Gulf Resolution out of his pocket every time a congressman or senator complained about the war—I suspect he kept one in his pajama pockets—the senators set out to undermine its validity. Now, instead of asking *what* the North Vietnamese PT-boats were trying to do, they asked a different and nastier question: *How successful* were they? In other words, the intention of the boats was at issue in 1964, their effectiveness in 1968. Manifestly they were unsuccessful—that had been apparent back in 1964—but now their lack of success became proof that the whole affair had been blown up out of all reasonable proportion simply to trick Congress.

Now this gets the analyst into a complex problem. Clearly the President, recalling Harry Truman's congressional difficulties over Korea, wanted to mass the Congress, and the nation. If the Tonkin Gulf Resolution had worked (as the Formosa Strait one did), we would have a different world about us. But it didn't, and the hard fact is we all (with a handful of exceptions) tricked ourselves.

So, farewell to instant history and God help the poor souls who try to put the jigsaw puzzle together when all the precincts have reported. As for me, I'm going to write it as I saw and believed it—but with a candid admission that any resemblance to events as they in fact occurred may be coincidental.

The Pentagon Papers

ROUGHLY TWENTY YEARS AGO, a law journal sent me a two-volume work in American constitutional history for review in 2,000 words. The study was bizarre, to say the least, and after inch-by-inch annotation, I was confronted with an impossible mission. I wrote the editors and told them that I would submit either a one-sentence review ("This is a fantasy: American constitutional history through the looking glass") or a 25,000-word analytical essay, taking the study apart section by section. I received no reply.

The *Pentagon Papers* falls into precisely the same category. An adequate one-sentence review would state: "While occasionally interesting and enlightening, the *Pentagon Papers* is fundamentally a historical junkpile which provides neither proof nor disproof for any hypotheses about the origins and character of the war in Vietnam." This proposition is one that I can document in 25,000 words, and fully intend to do so on another occasion. For

Reprinted, with permission, from the *Political Science Quarterly*, 87 (June 1972), 184–191.

our purposes, however, I shall take a different tack which will hopefully both confine me to the requested 2,000 words and prove useful to the profession. Instead of arguing the merits of the *Pentagon Papers*, I will raise certain questions for the benefit of those masochists who are prepared actually to read the mass of material. The intrepid few who last the course can respond to these questions in terms of their own application of the laws of evidence.

Certain issues of a marginal character can be eliminated, by *obiter dictum*, at the outset; they have only served to muddy the historical waters. There is, for example, no logical connection between the substantive merits of the *Pentagon Papers* and the question of censorship or the character of Dr. Daniel Ellsberg. In my judgment, the Attorney General was unwise to move against the New York Times: Inevitably, in the courtroom the parade of horribles began and before long the logical escalator put one in the position of either denying or affirming the right of the government to impose *any* sort of official secrecy. "Hard cases," as Justice Holmes put it, "make bad law"—a generalization which was validated by the murky holdings in the New York *Times* case.

Indeed, a cynic might suggest that most of the public interest in the *Pentagon Papers*, as well as the response of many reviewers, was based on the proposition that unless the documents were really vital, the United States would never have gone to such lengths to suppress them. As usual, cynics overestimate the rationality of the decision-making process.

Let us now turn to the questions that the hardy reader should keep in mind as he plows his way into the thicket. First, how authoritative are the *Pentagon Papers?* To put it another way, how accurate a reflection do they present of the decision-making process within the government of the United States? Presumably a well trained undergraduate, who had survived a course in American government and perhaps one on the presidency, should be equipped to answer this. Leaving aside the material in the papers pertaining to the period before 1961 (which is fundamentally of antiquarian interest only), what questions would our paradigmatic undergraduate ask himself?

"Where is the President?" is the obvious answer—and beyond

that, "Where is the Secretary of State?" We all know that the United States either enjoys or suffers under "presidential government" (the verb usage depending on one's attitude toward the incumbent president). Do the papers reflect this?

Not only are the President and the Secretary of State ghostly figures, but the papers rarely include even their written contributions to statecraft. What we find are drafts prepared by assistant secretaries for submission to secretaries for eventual consideration by the National Security Council and the President. Secretary of Defense Robert S. McNamara is represented in person from time to time, particularly in 1966–67, but his memos to the President do not include presidential replies nor the critiques of others, such as Secretary Rusk, Clark Clifford or Abe Fortas, to whom the President may have sent them for comment.

To take a case in point, the *Times* commentator indicates that the papers show there was a "consensus" to bomb North Vietnam within the administration before the 1964 presidential election.[1] But what do the papers document? Agreed, there were bombing scenarios on various drawing boards (indeed, the possibility of bombing the North had been raised in the 1961 Taylor-Rostow Report to President Kennedy), but what proof is there of a "consensus"? unless one believes there can be a policy consensus in the executive branch without the agreement of the President, he is confronted with an analytical *cul-de-sac*.

In this same context, the *Times* commentator notes earlier that in May 1964, Johnson was presented with a scenario that included bombing. The documentation is a draft prepared by Assistant Secretary of State for the Far East William P. Bundy and Assistant Secretary of Defense for International Security Affairs John McNaughton for *submission* to the Executive Committee of the National Security Council. The commentator implies that the President received this recommendation but "delayed another nine months the scenario's denouement in an air war."[2]

This clearly suggests a conscious decision—in context, a deceptive act. But what evidence is there that this recommendation

[1] *The Pentagon Papers: The Secret History of the Vietnam War as published by the New York Times* (New York, 1971), p. 318.

[2] *Ibid.*, p. 255.

was actually put before the President for decision one way or the other? None. In fact, as I know from my research on the presidential papers, it was deleted at the EXCOM level. But my personal knowledge is irrelevant to the point, namely, the evidential merit of the papers. All we know on this point from the documentation is that Bundy, McNaughton, et al. in May 1964 submitted to their principals a scenario that included bombing the North. (Parenthetically it might be noted that the President did not monitor the brisk chit-chat among assistant secretaries. Lyndon Johnson saw most of these documents for the first time when they appeared in the press.)

Space limitations require that we move to the next question that our well trained undergraduate will hopefully formulate: "What new information emerges from the papers?" What do they tell us about American policy in Vietnam that was not in substance already in the public domain? Obviously they provide cables, memos and other bureaucratic mementos that have never been revealed, but what do we learn that was not *contemporaneously* available in books, newspapers, columns to anyone who wanted to utilize it?

In other words, were key decisions hidden? Or did contemporary commentators simply not focus on the things we are concerned about today? Recall that in January 1966, the chairman of the Senate Foreign Relations Committee, Senator J. W. Fulbright, said to Secretary Dean Rusk: "I confess I was scarcely conscious about problems of any significance [in Vietnam] until the last few years because our attention was directed largely in Europe."[3] What was true of Fulbright was, *a fortiori*, even more true for the rest of us.

Let us take two examples from the papers. First, there was great dismay expressed last year when it "came to light" that the United States had instigated the coup that overthrew Ngo Dinh Diem on November 1, 1963. It is conceivable that most Americans believed that Tolkien's "hobbits" had done the job, but anyone who read the *New Yorker* in 1964 or *The Lost Revolution* in 1965

---

[3] U.S. Senate, Committee on Foreign Relations, *Hearings* on S. 2793, 89th Cong., 2nd Sess., 1956, p. 7.

knew from Robert Shaplen's account precisely what occurred in Saigon in the fall of 1963.[4] (Conceded: Shaplen did not name Colonel Lucien Conein as the Central Intelligence Agency's key man.) Indeed, if one read Morris West's jejeune novel *The Ambassador,* he came out with a pretty clear idea of the anti-Diem operation.[5]

Because of the Washington habit of "brackgrounding" columnists and top newsmen, I submit that very little occurred inside the bureaucracy that was not reflected in the press, usually quite accurately. (An important exception involved President Johnson's frank discussions with a tight circle of personal advisers.) Ironically, one of the conspiracies unearthed by the compilers of the papers probably reflects a failure in backgrounding, namely the allegation that National Security Action Memorandum No. 328 (April 6, 1965) included an authorization to change the mission of the Marine battalions at Danang from "defense" to "offense."[6]

Those unfamiliar with military usage may find a shift from a static to an active defensive posture a "change in mission," but what concerns us here is the alleged secrecy of the whole affair. The papers imply that the State Department only confirmed on June 8 that the Marines had allegedy changed their mission, and that this was done in such a way as to camouflage a quantum jump in strategy. Against this background, let me put two queries to the serious student: 1) when in fact did the Marines inaugurate active patrols? and 2) when was the fact that the Marines had inaugurated active patrolling announced at a Military Assistance Command, Vietnam (MACV) briefing in Saigon? A third question for those who do the necessary research: Why do you suppose the Saigon press corps did not feature this "change in mission"? Perhaps because the experienced war correspondents in Saigon did not recognize it as a "change in mission"? Could they have been correct?

Richard Harwood of the Washington *Post* has written in this connection:

[4] Robert Shaplen, "Letter from Saigon," *New Yorker,* XXXIX (Dec. 14, 1963), 201 ff.; XL (July 11, 1964), 37 ff.; XL (Sept. 19, 1964), 179 ff. Robert Shaplen, *Lost Revolution* (New York, 1965).

[5] Morris West, *The Ambassador* (New York, 1965).

[6] *Pentagon Papers,* p. 410.

[T]he *Post* and the *Times* and other large news organizations published thousands of stories, editorials and essays in 1964 describing the deteriorating military situation in Vietnam—just as it was described in the official memoranda and cables in the Pentagon papers. The various options and contingency plans being put before the President at that time were reported repeatedly and accurately—as they are now reported in the official papers . . . the public was simply not interested. Nor were most members of Congress.[7]

But again my role here is to ask questions, not to answer them. Let me conclude this section by challenging readers of the papers to uncover one significant policy issue that was not contemporaneously debated and explored in the media. They may find it useful to begin with the writings of I. F. Stone: Whatever one may think of his political views, he knew how to read.

Having looked into, first, the question of how authoritative are the papers as a source and, second, how much new information about policy issues does the volume provide, the reader might finally ask "What significant questions of policy do the papers ignore?" To put it another way, he should ask: "How coherent a history of our involvement emerges from the papers?" Drawing a figure of speech from Sherlock Holmes, let us search for some dogs that did not bark.

Beginning, as before, with 1961, a serious analyst of American policy toward Southeast Asia is immediately confronted with a serious gap in the narrative as found in the papers: There is no examination of the "neutralization" option, which flourished in the aftermath of the 1962 Geneva Agreement on Laos. In retrospect, the notion of the neutralization of all Indochina under great power auspices was doubtless a fantasy—Hanoi simply would not cooperate. But at the time a number of serious men, both inside and outside the government, took the possibility seriously.

Nor do we find any discussion of the decision inside the Kennedy administration that President Ngo Dinh Diem (and his brother Ngo Dinh Nhu) must not be permitted to make a private

---

[7] Richard Harwood, "Few 'Revelations' for Those Who Had Been Listening," Washington *Post*, June 24, 1971.

deal with Ho Chi Minh. Mieczyslaw Maneli, the Polish chairman of the International Control Commission in 1963–64, has recently presented serious evidence[8] that Diem and Ho were discussing a "political solution" (Maneli was the intermediary) which would, in essence, have led to South Vietnamese neutrality in the cold war—and an American departure from the premises. Washington, as some memos by Roger Hilsman, then Assistant Secretary of State for the Far East document,[9] found the prospect unthinkable: South Vietnam could not be permitted to desert the "Free World." Why did the compilers of the papers ignore this whole sequence? (They had the Hilsman memorandums at their disposal.)[10]

As it stands, the only significant mention of neutralization in the papers is in a cable from President Johnson in March 1964 to Ambassador Henry Cabot Lodge stating that he was intent on "knocking down the idea of neutralization wherever it rears its ugly head. . . ."[11] Without indulging in historical paranoia, one may legitimately inquire why the compilers dumped this body on Johnson's doorstep.

This sort of inquiry can be continued almost indefinitely, but without further help from me—at least on this occasion. What the conscientious analyst must do is to go through existing commentaries on our Vietnam policy, particularly Lyndon B. Johnson's *The Vantage Point* with its careful documentation of what occurred in the President's inner circle, and to compare the results with the narrative found in the papers.[12]

[8] Mieczyslaw Maneli, *The War of the Vanquished* (New York, 1971).

[9] See John P. Roche, "The Jigsaw Puzzle of History," *New York Times Magazine*, Jan. 24, 1971, and my exchange with Hilsman in the letters sections of subsequent issues.

[10] In December 1967, I provided Dr. Leslie Gelb, coordinator of "The McNamara History" (as it was then called), with my full dossier on the Diem coup, including the Hilsman memorandums cited above. None of this material appeared in the *Pentagon Papers*.

[11] *Pentagon Papers*, p. 252.

[12] Lyndon Johnson, *The Vantage Point* (New York, 1971). The Johnson memoirs indicate, for example, that the President began "rethinking" our strategic options long before Tet. To my personal knowledge, he was secretly dismayed with the military's "More of the Same" policy as early as May 1967. Before Christmas 1967, he had resolved not to give MACV any more

Let me confess, in conclusion, that I have done just this. In fact, I have gone through the full version of the papers—a cruel and unusual punishment if ever one existed. It would be both improper and impossible for me to render my verdict on our policy at this time. Improper because the precise point of this essay is that scholars must reach their own judgments on the evidence; impossible because I have been unable to conclude on the basis of all the evidence at my disposal whether certain critical decisions could have been averted given the political environment of the times—for example, would the American people, politicians and press have permitted the President to liquidate our commitment in 1963, 1964 or 1965?

Finally, one ultimate caveat: Anyone who wants to attempt the job can try to mold a conspiracy theory from these materials, but I hereby issue a formal warning. Go to it! But I will be waiting at the pass—with footnotes. To say that I am not prepared to offer a synoptic interpretation of our policy is not to imply that I am unprepared or unwilling to demolish alternative interpretations based on bad logic, bad evidence or both.

---

troops and was awaiting the installation of Clark Clifford as Secretary of Defense to initiate a total review of our options. Tet intervened and forced the pace.

The Vietnam Negotiations:
A Case Study
in Communist
Political Warfare

AS ONE who has followed the negotiations sequence in Vietnam with microscopic interest, first within the government and then outside, I must begin by congratulating the Hanoi politburo on one of the most spectacularly conducted exercises in political warfare the modern world has seen. There are several volumes published about the abortive negotiations under the Johnson Administration (of which Chester Cooper's *The Lost Crusade* is by far the best), but, alas, none of them makes the point that for years Ho Chi Minh and his colleagues were playing us like salmon. We were interested in negotiations to end the war on essentially a Korean or "stalemate" basis; they employed negotiations as a weapons' system in the effort to destroy our will to maintain our Southeast Asian commitment.

Anyone who is optimistic about the outcome of present developments should learn caution, recalling that in 1954 Ho Chi

Reprinted by permission of the American Enterprise Institute for Public Policy Research. (This essay originally appeared as part of the Rational Debate Series, *Vietnam Settlement: Why 1973, Not 1969?*)

Minh, bitterly resenting his treatment, was forced by Moscow and Peking (then in tandem) to accept what was *de facto* a "two Vietnams" solution. The basis for this decision to downgrade Southeast Asia was a Soviet trade-off with France involving the latter's rejection of the European Defense Community. (Both the Soviets and the United States had their central focus on Europe; indeed, American involvement with the French in Indochina originated from what were seen as NATO imperatives.)

At any rate, despite the Final Declaration, which everybody quotes but nobody signed, all that emerged from Geneva was bad news for the Viet Minh. Verbally unification of Vietnam was affirmed by the Communist powers, but the agreements actually signed at Geneva provided for regroupment of Viet Minh from the South to the North and conversely for regroupment of anti-Communists from North to South. Now patently regroupment and unification do not fit in the same logical universe: In effect, a "temporary" cold war boundary, like that between East and West Germany or North and South Korea, was drawn along the 17th parallel. (Subsequently the USSR nominated both Vietnams for UN membership!)

To revert to the main theme, optimists should recall that Ho Chi Minh, dismayed as he was by his betrayal by his "socialist brothers," simply went back to the drawing board. Ten years later Vietnam was back in the news. Today Pham Van Dong (who was at Geneva in 1954) probably views the cease-fire as Ho did the Geneva accord—as a tactical retreat forced upon Hanoi by its self-centered Communist allies. What remains to be seen is whether Hanoi's resources and commitment to "unification" are adequate for another "liberation" scenario.

It is difficult to get the American people to realize that although negotiations have been in the air for a decade, the recent Paris accord was the first time we have crossed the substantive threshold. To put it another way, up to now we have constantly been dealing with negotiations about negotiations. And the Paris arrangements are anything but a settlement, although *sub silentio* they incorporate certain principles and reject others. It is clear to anyone who has followed the ballet that Hanoi has backed down at certain crucial points. It is thus preposterous to say that the same terms could have been achieved in 1968 or 1969. We are dealing with a set of familiar pieces: a cease-fire (proposed by President Johnson in his 1968 State of the Union Address), the "leopardskin map" (a modern adaptation of the feudal technique that, for example, in the Edict of Nantes gave the Huguenots 100 fortified cities in Catholic France), coalition government and the like. What was distinctive about the Kissinger-Tho accord was the arrangement of the pieces.

As I said, the United States was subjected to a superb Communist agit-prop campaign on the subject of negotiations. The governing maxim was set out candidly by Pham Van Dong to the late Bernard Fall as early as 1962: "Americans," Pham said, "do not like long inconclusive wars—and this is going to be a long inconclusive war." Then, in 1965–67, we made a tragic strategic blunder which played into Ho Chi Minh's hand: We Americanized the war. Robert S. McNamara and his assorted "games" experts decided that it was a waste of time and energy to train the South Vietnamese Army (ARVN). After all, it took almost two years to train the first competent Republic of Korean divisions, and in that time we could win the war all by ourselves. The United States, with its massive technological assets, would directly force Hanoi to desist from aggression; bombing would "punish" them. Once Ho and Vo Nguyen Giap, his military chief, knew that they were up against *real* Americans, they would cooperate with the chess players in the Pentagon and concede "mate in eight moves." I was personally convinced in the spring of 1965 that there were men of eminence in the administration who were certain that the first time an American jet flew over Hanoi, Ho would come running out with a white flag. (Those who at this point suspect me of 20/20 hindsight are referred to the essay on p. 42.)

The "McNamara Shortcut" seemingly had two admirable arguments in its favor: First, we could effectively ignore the condition of the Saigon government; second, we could employ our air assets with a relatively light loss of American lives. The unfortunate consequence was the ARVN was treated as an orphan and given essentially a spectator's role in the U.S.-Hanoi competition. (The order for M-16's, automatic rifles, for ARVN was not placed until the spring of 1968!)

My friend Amrom Katz of RAND tells me that in California

pedestrians have an absolute right-of-way over drivers, but that before you start across the street you had better be certain that the car bearing down on you has California plates. In this sense, the McNamara Shortcut (which of course was approved by President Johnson) required the cooperation of Ho Chi Minh. In the recently published *Cairo Documents*, Mohamed Heikal relates that in 1959 the Syrians and the Jordanians wanted Nasser to launch a limited war against Israel. Nasser's reply was succinct: "I am willing to carry out a limited war," the Egyptian President said, "but only if one of you gets me Ben Gurion's assurance that he too will limit it. For a war to be limited depends on the other side."

Unfortunately Ho and Giap were never programmed by the Pentagon's game-theorists. They were determined to prevent the United States from fighting a cut-rate war. Down the Ho Chi Minh trail came the trained regiments of the North Vietnamese Army (PAVN) with the mission, not of defeating the United States on the ground, but of forcing the Americans to fight a ground war in full, costly visibility. To a considerable degree these troops were on a suicide mission, but when one appreciates that their goal was *political* rather than military the "kill-ratio" loses much of its impact. We were measuring one thing—they were calculating on a different system.

Perhaps at this point it would not be out of place to insert a memorandum I wrote to President Johnson on March 27, 1967. It was occasioned by Ho Chi Minh's release of the letters between Johnson and himself, an act which puzzled the late President (who was born without an ideological bone in his body) and led him to ask me what I thought lay behind it. (I have not edited the memo except to delete references to some materials included as appendices.)

March 27, 1967

MEMORANDUM FOR
    The President

I have been following the negotiation sequence very closely and have reached the conclusion that we are no longer fighting a "war" in Vietnam—we are fighting a "negotiation."

This is not intended as a cute play on words—on the contrary, it has serious consequences for American policy.

At the risk of boring you, let me set out the assumptions on which this is based:

1. Ho Chi Minh is not just a radical nationalist like Touré, Castro or Sukarno. He is a dedicated Leninist, the last of the first generation of the Communist International.

2. He is therefore not a simple-minded Vietnamese chauvinist who, for example, will "not negotiate under pressure." I was in the Air Force too long to believe all I read about the effectiveness of bombing. But the view that Ho will not negotiate until we stop bombing is nonsense.

—it might be true of Castro, who is basically a romantic Latin fascist, a "petty-bourgeois sentimentalist" in Communist jargon;

—but Ho—like Lenin at the time of Brest-Litovsk—would negotiate in cold blood for whatever goals he considers realistic— even if bombs were coming down his chimney.

3. The behavior of a dedicated, intelligent Leninist is highly predictable. I never doubted that Khrushchev would pull the missiles out of Cuba in October 1962.

4. A good Leninist looks on the use of force as merely a variety of politics. He never adopts an inflexible "unconditional surrender" position, but is always ready to alter the timetable if the costs of overt aggression become too high.

5. On the basis of various statements that have been emerging from Hanoi over the past six months, as well as articles in *Hoc Tap*, and other Communist organs in Hanoi, I am convinced that Ho knows that the road to victory in South Vietnam *by overt aggression* is closed.

6. He is therefore willing to shift from overt war to negotiations, with the latter in no way compromising his determination to someday "unify" Vietnam. Negotiations are a weapons system at which Ho is an expert (see his performance between the French and the Chinats [Chinese Nationalists] from 1946–49 or his 1949–53 moves with the French).

7. This willingness to shift gears created trouble for Lenin and has undoubtedly created internal difficulties for Ho. My guess is that he released the exchange of letters to show the hard-liners he is still tough. There is probably a "negotiate-now" faction in Hanoi and he rhetorically disassociated himself from them.

8. But the real issue is Ho's authority: his capacity to free himself from factional control and be completely "opportunist"—in Lenin's use of the word, i.e., maintain the right to seize and utilize any opportunity that arises.

9. Assuming that Ho has adopted a tactic of negotiation (no Leninist looks on negotiations as valuable in themselves), but does not think *now* is the time to move, the release of the exchange of letters makes sense in terms of maintaining his freedom of maneuver.

10. Under what circumstances can we expect him to actually implement this tactic of negotiation?

At the worst possible time in terms of American internal unity —say on September 1, 1968. Recall that in dealing with the French in 1953, Ho waited until France was in a state of almost total political chaos over the European Defense Community to float his offer to negotiate.

11. What this comes down to is a rejection of the newspaper view that Hanoi is full of parochial primitives who do not "understand the United States."

Let us rather assume:

1) That they know exactly what they are doing;

2) That they are now out to win a negotiation;

3) That they recall both Panmunjon and two Genevas;

4) That they believe their maximum retrieval can be accomplished when the American people are really hurting and have a chance to bring real pressure directly on the presidential election;

5) That their present "insane" military operations are designed not to "win" the war, or to cut I Corps off from the rest of Vietnam, but simply to kill more Americans at *whatever cost* in North Vietnamese. To a dedicated old Bolshevik a weekly headline in the *Times* "U. S. Deaths Reach New All Time High" is worth 5,000 dead peasants from the PAVN.

6) That, in short, Ho is not counting on the peaceniks but on the isolationists in the United States and believes (correctly) that coffins are more significant propaganda than leaflets. And he also believes that we will not invade, really destroy, or try to liberate the DRV, so he can outwait us in his political sanctuary.

12. This is getting too long, and it may be fantasy, but I think we have to be prepared for such a contingency. In practice, it is not enough to have Governor Harriman ready to sit down anywhere, any time. The key question is "What is he going to say?"

Suppose, sometime next year, Ho surfaces with a "Laotion solution"? Are we prepared to go for the principle of tripartite rule in SVN? Tripartism was a phony in Laos from the moment the 1962 agreement was signed, but it covered a *de facto* military partition which we and the Communists were prepared to live with.

When we say, therefore, that we are willing to go back to the 1962 Geneva agreement, we *mean* neutralization under great power guarantees, a stabilization.

But suppose Ho says, in the middle of a presidential campaign: "Fine, let's apply the 1962 Geneva principle to South Vietnam." The pressure to accept would be enormous, but acceptance would mean "coalition government" in Saigon, legitimation of the NLF and break the back of our moral/military commitment.

Which, finally, accounts for the Saigon reaction to Ambassador Bunker. The South Vietnamese leaders are no dumber than those in Hanoi and they have good memories. They have seen the gallows (to paraphrase Dr. Johnson) and it has most wonderfully clarified their thought.

If you put yourself in Ky's shoes, and listened to some of your advisors relate matters of recent history in Asia, Ellsworth Bunker *could* easily be seen as the man who implemented Bobby Kennedy's policy of "appeasement" of Sukarno.

You would then probably ask the question: "Bobby Kennedy has come out for 'coalition,' Harriman was the architect of Laos, 1962, where does Bunker stand?"

And you might well lie awake nights worrying about the "inscrutable Americans."

John P. Roche

This memorandum has been included because it establishes, I submit, my credentials as a critic of the negotiations process. (It is also revealing, I fear, as an index of the horrendous extent to which I fall under the bulls of excommunication recently pronounced on the Kennedy and Johnson administrations by Popes Henry Fairlie and David Halberstam).

From the very outset, then, Hanoi was always eager to negotiate on their own terms, but between 1964 and 1973 the North Vietnamese posture changed radically. In 1964, in an episode blown out of all proportions by the press when it came to light after Adlai Stevenson's death, Ho Chi Minh informed us through the United Nations that he would be pleased to meet our negotiator in Rangoon. Everything, he assured U Thant, could be worked out so simply: The United States would agree to withdraw, accept the position of the North Vietnamese, the Program of the National Liberation Front of South Vietnam (the Vietcong) and—presto—the war would be over.

He set no precondition for negotiations except the acceptance of "The Four & the Five," as they came to be known after full formulation in the spring of 1965. In blunt terms he agreed to accept our capitulation as a precondition for negotiating the modalities of surrender. Since "The Four & the Five" remained constants in the negotiating equation for some time, it might be well to set them out here.

HANOI'S FOUR POINTS

April 8, 1965

APRIL 8: SPEECH BY MR. PHAM VAN DONG (THE FOUR POINTS) IN NORTH VIET-NAM (EXTRACTS)[1]

It is the unswerving policy of the Government of the Democratic Republic of Vietnam to strictly respect the 1954 Geneva Agreements on Vietnam, and to correctly implement their provisions as embodied in the following points:

1. Recognition of the basic national rights of the Vietnamese people: peace, independence, sovereignty, unity and territorial integrity. According to the Geneva Agreements, the U.S. Government must withdraw from South Vietnam all U.S. troops, military personnel and weapons of all kinds, dismantle all U.S. military bases there, cancel its "military alliance" with South Vietnam. It must end its policy of intervention and aggression in South Vietnam. According to the Geneva Agreements, the U.S. government must stop its acts of war against North Vietnam, completely cease all encroachments on the territory and sovereignty of the Democratic Republic of Vietnam.

[1] As reported by the Vietnamese News Agency.

2. Pending the peaceful reunification of Vietnam, while Vietnam is still temporarily divided into two zones the military provisions of the 1954 Geneva Agreements on Vietnam must be strictly respected: the two zones must refrain from joining any military alliance with foreign countries, there must be no foreign military bases, troops and military personnel in their respective territory.

3. The internal affairs of South Vietnam must be settled by the South Vietnamese people themselves, in accordance with the programme of the South Vietnam National Front for Liberation, without any foreign interference.

4. The peaceful reunification of Vietnam must be settled by the Vietnamese people in both zones, without any foreign interference.

This stand unquestionably enjoys the approval and support of all peace and justice-loving Governments and peoples in the world.

The Government of the Democratic Republic of Vietnam is of the view that the above-expounded stand is the basis for the soundest political settlement of the Vietnam problem. If this basis is recognized, favourable conditions will be created for the peaceful settlement of the Vietnam problem and it will be possible to consider the reconvening of an international conference along the pattern of the 1954 Geneva Conference on Vietnam.

The Government of the Democratic Republic of Vietnam declares that any approach contrary to the above stand is inappropriate; any approach tending to secure a U. N. intervention in the Vietnam situation is also inappropriate because such approaches are basically at variance with the 1954 Geneva Agreements on Vietnam.

THE LIBERATION FRONT'S FIVE POINTS

March 22, 1965

MARCH 23: FIVE POINTS CONTAINED IN A STATEMENT BY THE
CENTRAL COMMITTEE OF THE SOUTH VIET-NAMESE LIBERATION
FRONT[2]

1. The United States imperialists are the saboteurs of the Geneva Agreements, the most brazen warmonger and aggressor and the sworn enemy of the Viet-Namese people.

2. The heroic South Viet-Namese people are resolved to drive out the U.S. imperialists in order to liberate South Viet-Nam,

2 Extracted from a report by the Viet Nam News Agency.

achieve an independent, democratic, peaceful and neutral South Viet-Nam, with a view to national reunification.

3. The valiant South Viet-Namese people and the South Viet-Nam Liberation Army are resolved to accomplish to the full their sacred duty to drive out the U.S. imperialists so as to liberate South Viet-Nam and defend North Vietnam.

4. The South Viet-Namese people express their profound gratitude to the wholehearted support of the peoples of the world who cherish peace and justice and declare their readiness to receive all assistance including weapons and all other war materials from their friends in the five continents.

5. To unite the whole people, to arm the whole people, continue to march forward heroically and be resolved to fight and to defeat the U.S. aggressors and the Viet-Namese traitors.

After we began sustained bombing of the North in February 1965, the Hanoi agit-prop division really moved into high gear. Now "Stop the Bombing!" became the worldwide *mot d'ordre,* President Johnson, at Johns Hopkins in April 1965, launched the only effective counter-attack of his Vietnam ordeal when he called for "unconditional negotiation." This sounded good, but unfortunately it was soon overpowered by the amazing orchestration of antibombing propaganda that spread throughout the world and began to make a dent in the United States, notably on the college campuses. Johnson, whose bombing policy was at least in part motivated by a belief that it gave us a chip to play in negotiations (i.e., you stop asking us to negotiate on the basis of the Four & the Five and we will stop bombing), found himself perplexingly confronted by a "world opinion" that seemed to make a moral distinction between high explosives delivered air mail and those sent parcel post. As far as Hanoi was concerned, it was money in the bank: They now added a bombing halt to their earlier negotiating preconditions.

At the risk of sounding cynical, I watched the American government's flailing efforts to launch negotiations with great skepticism. Walt Rostow's graphs were extremely persuasive in suggesting the degree to which we were "winning," but I wondered what Ho's graphs told him. Indeed, in a sardonic moment after a CINCPAC briefing in Hawaii, I sent a back-channel message to the White House suggesting that Ho Chi Minh was the man who should get the briefing so he would know enough to quit. Fortunately I was out of reach, but Harry McPherson later told me the President was not amused.

For several years the North Vietnamese political warfare experts had a marvelous time. Kites would be flown in the most unlikely places: a Hanoi actor performing in some African nation would pointedly tell the French (or British or Dutch or . . .) second secretary at a cocktail party that the Four & the Five were not inscribed in tablets of stone, that maybe there was some room for maneuver. First of course, the bombing must stop, but then . . . ? This would lead to a spasm in the Harriman office, a small unit in the State Department charged with following up all chances for negotiations. Cables would flow off to Ft. Lamy, or wherever, and inevitably, when the smoke cleared, there was nothing there. Except perhaps some headlines in the American press to the effect that we had thrown away another chance for peace by our rigidity.

In addition, North Vietnamese pronouncements were read with a textual passion worthy of a great Talmudist. I recall in the winter of 1967 the ubiquitous Pham Van Dong gave an interview to Harrison Salisbury of the New York *Times*. Salisbury quoted Pham as saying that the Four Points constituted *a* basis for settlement. Great excitement: obviously by the use of "a," Pham was opening up the field. (The Four Points had been previously dictated as *the* basis.) Just about the time the Talmudists had gotten their interpretive talents into motion, however, Pham issued a retraction, or a denial: He had said "the." "But comrade," to paraphrase one Talmudic whiz, "can it be a coincidence that the Hanoi censor cleared Salisbury's original dispatch complete with 'a'?" And on it went.

President Johnson and President Nixon were antipodal characters. Johnson, who needless to say hated the war, responded to criticism by frenzied activities designed to prove to the American people that he really did want peace. To employ the current vocabulary of politics, Johnson's motto was "when in doubt, punt." (Nixon, in contrast, operates on the maxim "when in doubt, fall on the ball.") He decided in the winter of 1965 that one way he could prove his bona fides to the people was to put on a peace extravaganza: He stopped the bombing on December 24, and immediately emissaries were practically shot out of cannons into the wide world to spread the tidings of American willingness to negotiate. The pause lasted thirty-seven days. In substantive terms, its effect was pithily summed up by the late President when he noted that everywhere the Hanoi reply was the same: "**** you, Lyndon Johnson."

To avoid misunderstanding, let me state that I would have been delighted to have seen genuine negotiations. My reservations (as indicated in the memo above) were founded on my reading of Hanoi's view of the situation. From their vantage point, by their graphs, they were *winning*. Thus they had absolutely no incentive to negotiate. While undoubtedly the bombing was doing a good deal of damage, it was tolerable and stimulated both the Soviets and Chinese Communists to substantial aid programs.

Sir Basil Liddell-Hart observed somewhere that if Stalin had modernized Russia's road network in the interwar period, the Nazis would have been in Moscow in six weeks. As it was, the very primitiveness of Soviet facilities bogged the Wehrmacht down. Bombing North Vietnam was analogous: provided we avoided saturation bombing and dike-busting, targets were soon in short supply. The notion that Hanoi's economy could be held "hostage" might make some sense in the case of, say, Japan, but it was in context absurd. Mining the harbors made a great deal of military sense, but Johnson outlawed it on the ground that it could trigger intervention by Peking or Moscow. (The fact that Mr. Nixon got away with it in 1972, by the way, is no proof that Johnson was wrong in 1965–68: the dynamics of international relations today are radically different from those only eight years ago.)

This rambles a bit, but art does reflect life and Vietnamese reality was and remains nothing if not rambling. Without trying to write a précis of the war, let us ask the question: "Under what circumstances would Hanoi have felt it to be in its interest genuinely to negotiate?" The answer, of course, is if it felt threatened. Or, alternatively, if it appeared that a viable regime could emerge in the South, negotiations could forestall the consolidation of powar in Saigon. So long as the United States and Hanoi were fighting a private war under restricted ground-rules (no invasion of the North, of the Cambodian sanctuaries, no bombing of the dikes or city-busting, etc.), Ho Chi Minh had no reason to feel threatened. True, in 1967 the Republic of Vietnam had adopted a constitution, held elections and generally moved toward a representative form of government. But President Thieu's army was still an orphan and realists in Hanoi had no reason to suppose that, once the Americans went home, the Saigon government could last a week under sustained military assault.

Right on into 1968, then, Hanoi played negotiating games. As American casualties mounted, and particularly with the Tet Offensive being billed as a big Communist victory, it seemed only a matter of time before the Americans, like the French before them, would "lose the war at home" and vanish across the seas. One intelligence report quoted a high North Vietnamese official as cheerfully announcing at a diplomatic function that he would be delighted to negotiate with the Americans—on what music would be played for their retreat. Obviously in a jovial mood, he offered to provide the bands and a red carpet strewn with rosepetals. After President Johnson's dramatic announcement of March 31, 1968, Hanoi was shrewd enough to pick up the offer to meet—and suggested Phnom Penh as the locus!

As usual we came out of the episode looking like clumsy clowns: In an expansive mood Johnson had said he would go anywhere, anytime to negotiate. Now we were forced, for perfectly sensible reasons, to turn down a series of cities, to rush around looking for counter-proposals to prove our sincerity and eventually to settle for the inevitable Paris (which the Vietnamese had probably decided on in the first place—they like Paris.) Delegations were appointed and set forth upon their labors, but the Hanoi team insisted that no substantive talks could occur until a total bombing halt had been declared. At this point Johnson dug in his heels and, despite the sometimes tearful pleas of Democratic politicans working for the candidacy of Vice President Humphrey, refused to budge until the other side came up with some specific pay-offs on their side of the hill.

Richard Whalen, in *Catch the Falling Flag* casts his paranoidal eye on Johnson's decision to stop all bombing virtually on election eve and declares it an "ambush." This is an insult to the late President—not just to his sense of obligation to the nation, but to his superb talent as an ambusher. When LBJ set out to ambush somebody, they stayed ambushed. The actual sequence of events was quite different. The President had instructed Harriman and Vance in Paris that the bombing would not stop until North Vietnam made a flat commitment to: 1) respect the Demilitarized Zone; 2) stop shelling and rocketing the cities of the South; and 3) ignore U.S. aerial reconnaissance of the North. The Hanoi representatives circled the bush, but began to make more friendly noises. These impressed Ambassador Harriman, who wanted to move ahead rapidly in the early fall, but the President by that time suspected that Harriman's top priority was Humphrey's election. "I want it carved in concrete," the President told me, and Hanoi was not about to comply.

Meanwhile some other players got into the action. First of all, the Soviets, who took a very dim view of Richard Nixon as President of the United States. Second, the Saigon government, which after Humphrey's Salt Lake City speech reached the perfectly understandable conclusion that "Nixon is the One." Although on its face the Salt Lake City speech adhered to the Johnson parameters on Vietnam, it was accompanied by extensive press backgrounding to the effect that Humphrey, if elected, would abandon the "rigidities" of the Johnson years. (The role of Anna Chennault as an intermediary between the GOP and Saigon has been played up, but in terms of their own self-interest the Thieu government would have been moronic not to back Nixon—and the Thieu government happened to include some extremely intelligent men.)

In the end, these late arrivals cancelled each other out. The Soviets obtained from Hanoi solid assurances about the three-point "understanding," on October 31 the President announced a total bombing halt and the beginning of substantive talks, and in the next few days Saigon blew the whole package sky-high. Recall again that—contrary to common belief—Hanoi had not at this point agreed to peace. It had simply agreed to stop negotiating about negotiating and go on to substantive talks. The only thing that was "blown" at this point was an opportunity to get to the merits; in January, after the shape of the table and other arcane matters had been arranged, the "two sides, four parties" finally held their first formal meeting.

To summarize, then, as Richard Nixon entered the White House, Hanoi's *substantive* negotiating position was essentially unchanged. "The Four & the Five" points had over the years been refined to two starkly simple demands: 1) get all American forces out of Indochina and 2) bust the government of the Republic of Vietnam, i.e., destroy the fragile legitimacy of President's Thieu's administration. The technique for achieving 2 was the patented Communist formula for a takeover: a "coalition government." Not even a coalition including Thieu (as the Soviets used in Poland in 1945 when they permitted the London Polish government-in-exile to participate in a brief coalition), but one from which the elected president was specifically excluded.

The key to what has happened in the four subsequent years lies in one concept: "Vietnamization." Actually Secretary of Defense Clark Clifford was the initiator of this policy, which amounted to de-Americanizing the war, in the last year of the Johnson Administration. There were some of us who had been struggling for it under the rug for years, though without perceptible impact. On May 1, 1967 for example, I sent the President a memo (known to a few insiders as the "pneumonia memo"). Since my memos seem to be among the few unpublished items in the literature on Vietnam, I trust I may be excused for partially remedying that gap.

May 1, 1967

MEMORANDUM FOR
    The President

I don't know whether it makes me a hawk, a dove, or a penguin, but for a year or more I have had very serious doubts about our Vietnamese strategy.

I don't think we have taken a "hard" enough line on what is really required to achieve our objectives.

—I have no objection to bombing North or South so long as we realize that air power, in anything short of a nuclear context, is merely *mobile artillery.*

—What has distressed me is the notion—(expressed time and again by the Air Force boys)—that air power would provide a *strategic* route to victory;

—And the parallel assumption that by bombing the North we could get a cut-rate solution in the South and escape from the problems of building a South Vietnamese army.

I raised the question of the rebuilding of ARVN in several memos to you last fall. Regrettably, I could write the same memos today. There are about 650,000 South Vietnamese under arms (in various categories), but we have still not done the job we did in Korea. Or even started to do it.

And the lead-time remains the same—stretched into the future—and the same argument seems to be employed against reforming ARVN—namely, that it will require too much lead-time.

As you know by now (I hope), I am not intellectually or temperamentally inclined to play "Rover Boy with the Joint Chiefs." But I do know that if I were a professional military man, I would be making demands upon you that would be contrary to the political strategy you have laid down for Vietnam.

Essentially the very concept of "limited war" runs against the grain of a dedicated military professional.

—And I don't *blame* him for this in the slightest. He is not trained, or paid, to think about political considerations.

(In this connection, I had a very interesting talk with General Clay in Bad Godesberg. I asked him why we had not insisted on land access to Berlin in 1945. He said that FDR had not so instructed Ike, and that anyone who blamed Ike for the decision (me among others) was a "dumb son of a bitch." Ike, he said, was paid to make military decisions—and made one. Those of us who didn't like the decision, should blame FDR and Truman. I am not in the habit of admitting that I am a "dumb son of a bitch," but in fact Clay was absolutely right.)

The simple military answer to the war in Vietnam is "destroy the enemy," and they could do a very good job of it if you turned them loose, doubled or tripled our commitment, authorized nuclear weapons, etc., etc.

In essence, they are like doctors who have a cure for pneumonia but not for a common cold—they therefore have a vested interest in the patient *getting* pneumonia.

To all of this you can correctly say "So what?" So let me try to set out what seems to me the outline of an effective strategy.

1. Our problems in the South, while sponsored and buttressed from the North, cannot be solved *in* the North unless we are prepared to abandon the strategy of limited war.

2. Specifically, we must win the war on the ground *in* the South. Ky and others have advocated an "Inchon landing" around Dong Hoi. Perhaps they should meditate on Anzio rather than Inchon—the analogy, in my judgment, is far more exact. Even by MACV's figures (which I profoundly mistrust—see my note to Walt at Tab 1), only a small percentage of the PAVN is in the panhandle.

3. At the risk of sounding banal, the war *in* the South can be won either by one to two million United States troops or by 500–750,000 United States troops and a *well-trained ARVN*.

4. The key to "pacification" is *not* "winning the hearts and minds of the peasantry." All they want is peace and quiet. The key to pacification is the capacity to pacify, i.e., to beat the hell out of the guerrillas and thereby convince the peasants that the VC is a loser. Like others in the world, peasants love a winner, and are much too smart to pick a winner by reading one of Zorthian's seven billion leaflets.

5. The decision to win the war in the South does not necessarily involve cessation of bombing. But I would suggest that a utility study of bombing should accompany it. When I was in Saigon, I asked a high ranking Air Force officer who was two sheets to the wind why they had flown 350 sorties the day before. He said: "We have to fly 1.2 sorties per plane per day—weather permitting. Last week we were down to 1.16, but yesterday brought it up. The goddamned Navy was up to 2.25 last week."

There may be something to this, but more fundamentally the problem is that the Air Force does not *want* to do the job that needs doing. For example, in South Vietnam the most useful *mobile artillery* are helicopters and prop aircraft (the A-1 for example). Every time an Air Force General sees a prop-plane, he has an aesthetic shudder: he wants jets—*beautiful jets*. Jets are beautiful, but they are lousy mobile artillery in terms of close ground support.

6. Finally, the constant pressure to *do something* must be resisted. Sometimes the only thing on the shelf worth buying is *time*. Assuming as I do that nothing in the limited war range will force Hanoi to negotiate (and that total war is out of the question), we have a force in Vietnam that can buy time and hopefully do something with it, namely, make ARVN into an army.

John P. Roche

This sort of ego trip has its gratifications, but the fact is that until Clark Clifford became Secretary of Defense (March 1, 1968) nobody in a position to implement policy paid the slightest attention to Vietnamization. Perhaps I should exclude Secretary of State Dean Rusk, to whom—at the President's request—I sent a copy of this memo. The result was a long private conversation in which it became clear to me that Rusk shared my misgivings but, always meticulous in these matters, felt that the question was in McNamara's jurisdiction. The President, who made no substantive comment at the time, mentioned the memo once later: In December, when he told me "maybe I'm going to do something that will make you happy. All they want is more of the same and I'm not going to give it to them. They're going to have to live with what they got—that common cold—and waste some of their valuable time training Viets." By the time I had figured out that "they" was the Joint Chiefs of Staff and the subject was training ARVN, he had changed the subject.

No, it was the Nixon Administration which finally reversed the tide, and did so in one of the most daring gambles in military history. The new President, realizing fully that the source of our Vietnam malaise was American casualties, not an upsurge of pacifism, decided to pull out the "teeth," that is, the American combat troops, and compensate for their relief by overpowering employment of tactical air power. And he decided to make an army out of ARVN, or at least do everything in our power to give Saigon the capability of self-defense.

He also decided, when the appropriate moment appeared, to hit the Cambodian sanctuaries and, more important, cut off the Communist supply line from Sihanoukville. Those opposing this action had always downplayed the significance of the Cambodian port, yet when the balance was finally figured, it appeared that even supporters of action had drastically underestimated the logistical importance of the "Sihanouk Trail." (The Department of Defense, for example, was low by over 50 percent!) Cambodia was in fact, not a state, but a gun-running syndicate which issued postage stamps.

The temptation to make this into a history of the Vietnam war must be resisted. Our concern is narrower: the effect of Vietnamization on negotiations.

Unlike Jane Fonda and other similarly equipped authorities on Indochina, the leaders of the Lao Dong—the North Vietnamese Communist party—are not under the illusion that 95 percent of the population of South Vietnam dreams of "liberation" from the alleged "police state" in Saigon. True, the South Vietnamese are war-weary, but they know the difference between a somewhat corrupt, somewhat authoritarian, somewhat inefficient government struggling up the ladder towards representative government and the ideological deep-freezer in the North. Thus Vietnamization, in the eyes of the Hanoi politburo, must have seemed like much more of a long-term threat than half a million American soldiers. This sent them back to the drawing board and what emerged was a new version of the classic "talk-fight" strategy.

The theory was that Vietnamization had to be utterly discredited in American and South Vietnamese eyes. The method was, of all things, a conventional invasion of the South complete with tanks and heavy artillery. (In the view of some friends who follow these matters closely, it was at this point that the Chinese Communists signed off, suggesting that the invasion was a species of lunacy. "No land wars in Asia" with the Americans [at least in the conventional-war context] was a lesson the Peoples' Liberation Army drew from Korea, where their fatalities approximated a *million* men.) Once the shock of surprise was over, the enormity of Giap's error became apparent: A T-54 is a formidable hunk of armor, but deploying tanks without air cover is another way of giving them away. A conventional invasion, to put it differently, was the one thing we could easily handle. Had Giap deployed his manpower in Phase II guerrilla operations, there would have been real problems, but apparently he has a fixation on set-piece battles, "a Dienbienphu Complex" as a Chinese Communist leader reportedly snorted.

The invasion did tear things up, but An Loc held, Quang Tri was retaken, and ARVN fought. In another era the American media would have treated the defenders of An Loc, who were taking 5,000 artillery and rocket rounds a day at the peak of the siege, as heroic figures. As it was, the siege was handled in a rather rancid fashion with heavy emphasis on the destruction of the town and the implication that if ARVN would stop defending it so stubbornly, there would be a lot less damage to innocent civilians. However, to those who were watching the important index, ARVN's performance indicated that our training program was working.

Also Mr. Nixon took some initiatives of his own in the "talk-fight" scenario. First, he accused the North Vietnamese of violating the 1968 "understandings" and cancelled the bombing halt, and second, he mined the harbors of North Vietnam. This was done against a background of visits to Peking and Moscow, where the President was greeted with far more warmth than would have been the case on the average American campus. (As a Secret Service friend once told me, "We always like state visits to Communist countries. They really turn the crowds out and you don't have to worry about a thing: Nobody gets shot there except on orders.") The net result of this combination of actions was that Hanoi must have begun to feel quite lonely. Furthermore, as American troop strength dropped the Communist demand for American withdrawal lost more and more of its utility. Le Duc Tho's task now centered on one objective: The United States must be forced somehow to break the back of the Thieu government.

On the surface, Le Duc Tho had some things going for him. 1972 was supposed to be an election year in the United States, the American people were sick and tired of the war, and with a little additional help from antiwar forces Thieu could be billed as the "obstacle to peace" who was single-handedly keeping the war going. (It got a bit confusing: Thieu, long featured as a U.S. "puppet" now turned up with Nixon on strings.) However, the Democratic Party waived its right seriously to contest the presidency, and Le Duc Tho had to continue his dialogue with Henry Kissinger.

Without rehashing historical detail, it appears that Hanoi—under pressure from both Peking and Moscow—broke the ice on October 9 when the demand for Thieu's removal and replacement by a coalition government was dropped. As a fig-leaf the frustrated PRG (whose leaders in Paris were openly accusing Hanoi, Moscow and Peking of selling them down the Mekong) was offered membership in a tri-partite National Council for Reconciliation and Concord. To Saigon this "administrative structure" (as it was originally called) still smacked of coalition government (in Vietnamese the phrases are very similar) and eventually that term was dropped.

The real sticking points, once Le Duc Tho had accepted "two Vietnams" *en principe* were the modalities of the cease-fire and the prisoner issue. Hanoi's proposal for a 250-man peace-keeping force was patently a bad joke, particularly given the operation in South Vietnam of perhaps 150,000 North Vietnamese troops. Saigon was justifiably unsettled by the fact that the cease-fire left them in place, but Thieu's concerns could be offset by an effective policing mechanism (to say nothing of the continued presence of U.S. airpower in Thailand and the Seventh Fleet in the Tonkin Gulf—in effect, the fleet consitutes an island we hold off the North Vietnamese coast.)

As far as prisoners were involved (American POW's aside), the issue was one of definition. Was the friendly neighborhood Communist who had chucked a grenade into a restaurant a "political prisoner"? Or a common murderer? (This question is going to plague us for some time. In that spirit I would suggest to the antiwar militants that their Vietnamese definition is fungible, that is, if the friendly neighborhood Vietcong guerrilla is a "poitical prisoner" so is the Arab terrorist in Israel or, for that matter, the black Muslims who recently killed members of a rival sect in Washington.) Le Duc Tho's strategy in October was clearly one of leaving everything as vague as possible and getting the Americans to sign on the dotted line.

At this point, late October, I suspect that an understandably jubilant Henry Kissinger went beyond his brief when, on the twenty-sixth, he announced that "we believe peace is at hand."

Although he hedged his bet by noting that there were some unresolved details, the Communist instantly began an orchestration demanding instant signature. It depends on what you mean by an unresolved detail: the difference between a 250-man force and one of 3,300? The existence or non-existence of the DMZ? The definition of terrorists as POW's?

In any event, perhaps in the belief that the President would be forced by American opinion to leave such details unresolved, Le Duc Tho began stone-walling and accusing the United States of reneging on prior agreements. Mr. Nixon in return flatly announced that we would not play, that he would not "allow an election deadline or any other kind of deadline to force us into an agreement which would be only a temporary peace and not a lasting peace." The election passed quietly and Kissinger returned to Paris on November 20 to iron out the details. Meanwhile, to prepare the Thieu government for the day it would have to handle its own defense, the United States rushed equipment to Saigon.

There are those who claim that Hanoi's hardening posture in November and December arose from an internal fight between the politburo's hawks and doves, with the hawks temporarily gaining ascendancy. Lacking second sight, I am not competent to evaluate that contention, but the fact is that Le Duc Tho proved extremely obdurate about details, particularly the question of the DMZ. Symbolically, he had a point—as did Saigon, which had the DMZ very much on its mind: The DMZ is the clearest overt concession of the existence of two Vietnams. After all, unless Korea is the model, one does not carve a demilitarized zone across the middle of a nation which is abstractly on the road to unification. And Korea is not the model Hanoi had in mind.

It is, I think, fair to say that over the past quarter of a century I have not been known as an admirer of Richard M. Nixon. However, I never made the error of underestimating his intelligence or of overlooking his renown as a poker player. Indeed, I date the demoralization of the antiwar movement to January 25, 1972, when—after being denounced far and wide throughout the media for his rigidity and unwillingness to negotiate—on nationwide television he flashed his hole card: the fact that he was negotiating secretly with Hanoi and had, in fact, submitted to Le

Duc Tho *via* Henry Kissinger an eight-point peace program. Even Anthony Lewis was slowed down a bit—though only momentarily.

In December 1972, the President obviously decided that enough was enough and on the eighteenth the planes took off again for the North. Probably the B-52 strikes on Hanoi and Haiphong performed a useful military function, but my hunch is that their purpose went far beyond that. What the bombing campaign did was vividly demonstrate to Hanoi that 1) the antiwar movement in the United States was dead; and 2) the Soviets and Chinese Communists had left them to their fate. To my knowledge, no top Soviet official made any comment (*Tass* issued a low-level condemnation), and Chou En-lai merely observed to an American reporter that the bombing would "adversely affect" U.S.-Peking relationships. Hanoi, in short, learned the hard way that it was cold out there. On the thirtieth the President was able to announce that bombing above the 20th parallel had stopped and that the Kissinger-Tho meetings would resume on January 8, 1973. We all know the outcome.

As I suggested earlier, anyone who is optimistic about Vietnam should be instantly sent off for psychiatric observation. Yet, it is apparent that the terms of the cease-fire of 1973 are a quantum jump beyond any accord that could have been reached in 1968 or '69. What President Nixon did was develop a "talk-fight" strategy of his own and pursue it with single-minded dedication. Like President Eisenhower, who threatened to use nuclear weapons to end the Korean War, Nixon realized that the Hanoi politburo was not a branch of the Fellowship of Reconciliation. But unlike Eisenhower, whose immense prestige protected him from hostile domestic opinion, President Nixon had to manage his "talk-fight" campaign against a background of public and congressional enmity.

The cold-blooded use of military power to obtain political objectives is never a pleasant thing to watch. For understandable, indeed admirable reasons the citizens of a free society (and their elected representatives in Congress) find "carpet bombing" repugnant, particularly in a twilight war against a small nation. What they fail to take into consideration is that the Hanoi regime (a "grotesque dwarf" in Reinhold Niebuhr's vivid phrase) has been dominated by as brilliantly ruthless an elite as the Communist movement has produced. What the President had to do was convince them that their national interest required serious negotiations. Once that was accomplished, as I noted in my memo to President Johnson, they would negotiate "with bombs coming down their chimneys." They did.

Achieving the cease-fire was, as the Duke of Wellington would put it, "a close run thing" what with Congress and the media constantly mounting pressure for virtually any means of extrication. What the future holds, God only knows, but as a primitive, liberal cold warrior I personally am glad that—like John F. Kennedy and Lyndon B. Johnson before him—Richard Nixon does not consider American honor to be a bargain-basement commodity. The Paris accords, *if successfully implemented,* do constitute the fundaments of "peace with honor."

EDUCATION

The Rebellion
of the Clerks

I WANT TO TRY to escape from the trap of subjectivism and discuss as dispassionately as I can the sources, thrust and probable consequences of present student unrest. This is, I confess, a bit difficult—my office library will smell to the end of time because some unidentified arsonist tried to burn the building down. Yet if we are to emerge successfully from the present "era of confrontation," it is essential that we push our emotional responses into the background and attempt to place the current disorders in rational perspective.

To begin with let us consider the statistics. Everyone agrees that student disorders are the work of a tiny minority—the highest figure I have seen is 2 percent. In gross terms, with over 6.5 million college students, this means we have roughly 120,000 activists scattered throughout the United States. Then we must add the nonstudent contingent: the permanent group of lumpen-intellectuals who hang around universities, many of them drop-outs, and seem to live on indefinitely as students emeritus. Still,

Reprinted, with permission, from *The New Leader,* June 23, 1969.

we are dealing with a statistically trivial minority. The militant Negroes, it should perhaps be noted here, not only constitute a minute proportion of the 6.5 million but are in an entirely separate category that I shall explore later.

I want to concentrate first on the so-called "SDS types," though in fact SDS probably has no more than 5,000 dues-paying members and meets only to split. Who are these young people, and what do they want?

Survey techniques have not proved very helpful, so my suggestions are admittedly impressionistic. But I might add, for whatever it may indicate, that over the past fifteen years a singular number of my best students have belonged to this ambiance. And since Herbert Marcuse, the grandfather figure of the New Left, was a colleague in the Brandeis Politics Department for a decade, I had ample opportunity to see at close range the source of his appeal. During my years in Washington as Special Consultant to President Johnson, too, I had infinite exposure to the views of both the New Left and its juvenile group: Adults for a Student Society.

On the basis of these experiences, I submit that the main demands of the student activists are not directed at the war in Vietnam, the "military-industrial complex," the universities or even directly at their parents. Their indictment runs against the very nature of our society, and not because it is "racist" or "militarist." At root they object to egalitarianism, to the institutions of a mass society in which they are not accorded the status they believe their intelligence, sensitivity and sincerity merit. In short, we are faced with a new medievalism—a demand that students be given special status resembling that of "clerks" in fourteenth-century Europe.

Take as a random example the activists' attitude toward crime and punishment. They bitterly reject the notion that they are subject to civil and criminal law, denounce the whole theory of *in loco parentis,* and when apprehended for clear violations of the law (as at Harvard) plead "benefit of clergy." In other words, they insist on exclusion from the normal jurisdiction of constituted authority and demand judgment by their self-ordained peers.

Now this is completely different from the tradition of protest against "illegal laws" as employed, for instance, by the civil rights movement in the South. There, the men and women who violated segregation statutes never denied their guilt, but claimed the law invoked was unconstitutional. (Or compare the behavior of Leon Trotsky after the Revolution of 1905 with that of Dr. Benjamin Spock. Trotsky, on trial for his life, announced his total commitment to revolution; Spock, accused of conspiring to muster resistance to the draft, pleaded innocent and demanded proof that he had stimulated any overt act. Spock had every right to take this position—but like the Harvard students who demanded amnesty, this was the response of a picador, not a matador.)

Thus, what we have is a number of extremely unhappy, intelligent young people who for various reasons have been taking out their grievances against our mass egalitarian society by attacking its most defenseless institutions, the colleges and universities. "We do not want to be computer cards," "We will resist the faceless bureaucracy," "We want relevant, meaningful education" are the key battle cries. Alas, they are Luddite slogans. As Zbigniew Brzezinski suggested in a harsh but cogent analysis, the counterrevolution has disguised itself in the vestments of radicalism.

I must admit, however, that on the existential level I have deep sympathy with the activists' anguish. Emotionally, I am an educational Luddite who loves small classes and seminars, intellectual give-and-take in a relaxed atmosphere. I know the educational theorists have satisfied themselves that the lecture system is as effective a pedagogical device as the seminar, that class size is irrelevant to the learning process. This may be true in broad terms, but nothing puts this eccentric professor of politics into despair the way a large lecture class does—it destroys my sense of empathy, my pride of craftsmanship. I want to know my students by name and grade their papers.

I share the sense of deprivation that suffuses a bright freshman who walks into a course in the history of political theory or physics or whatever, and finds several hundred others present, waiting to be addressed by what is for all intents and purposes an animated tape recorder (or in some situations, literally a lecturer on closed-circuit television). I can understand clinically why a number of the brightest students—usually from permissive backgrounds where, in David Riesman's phrase, "every time they cried, they were picked up"—become primordial rebels lashing out at all the institutions which, as they see it, keep them in collective bondage.

But to understand is not to pardon or approve. For the harsh fact is that the very forces "enslaving" them have made it possible for more than a third of all young Americans to attend college. (Interestingly, after major efforts at reform, there are now roughly 400,000 in British institutions of higher learning—on a population base of roughly 50 million. Already, loud voices are raised demanding an end to this watering of the educational whisky, to this absurd egalitarian program.) Mass education obviously requires bureaucracy. When I taught at Haverford in the early 1950s, there was a student body of perhaps 500, a president, a dean of students, a director of admission and a nice lady who handled all the work of the registrar's office. This was idyllic, but just think of the complications and costs of educating 6.5 million students at Haverford.

When I came to Brandeis in 1956, we had about 800 students; we now have about 1,800 undergraduates alone. At every step along the way of enlargement, the "radical" students were up in protest. While I was dean of faculty we went to 1,200, and I was hanged in effigy for "destroying the old, intimate Brandeis." I happened to like the old, intimate Brandeis; but I was also quite aware of the impossible financial burden—what I once called "the curse of smallness"—that intimacy demanded.

As anyone familiar with the ways of faculty knows, every department must have coverage of certain major fields if it is going to be first rate. And good departments are good black-mailers. Annually at budget time, I would receive a letter from the chairman of mathematics submitting the resignations of the whole faculty if they could not make a new appointment in homological algebra, topology or whatever happened to be the field of the year. Unfortunately, they meant it. This same process occurs throughout the feudal realm that we call a university.

The long and the short of it was that we were absurdly over-staffed for the size of our student body; I recall the ratio as 4–1. We had to increase our student body to remain respectably insolvent. Yet no matter how much explaining we did, the chorus came back, "You are destroying Brandeis." This year we have reached the appallingly impersonal ratio of 7–1, though this average is deceptive. In net terms we are losing over $4,000 per undergraduate, which means a student pays only about one-third of his freight. It would be absurd to charge $6,000 tuition and fees, but still the clamor goes on for more "relevant" courses (there is one on witchcraft this year), more tutorials, more individual reading programs—that is, more faculty. (Some departments have experimented with student-taught courses, resulting in the facile leading the docile. But a number of the faculty, while having no objection to academic bull sessions, feel that to assign such powwows academic credit is to engage in anti-intellectualism.)

It is amazing how most discussions of high theory in the end come down to problems of finance. To put it bluntly: Right or wrong, the American people are not prepared to subsidize, through taxes or private benefaction, 6.5 million youngsters "doing their own thing." As a result, those who come to the average American university or college with lofty aspirations of self-fulfillment are going to be frustrated and enraged. They want to become "intellectuals"; they want to join the élite; they want intimacy with their teachers—in brief, they want to enter clerical orders, to be admitted to an exclusive community. Instead, they find themselvs with the *hoi polloi,* taught by graduate students and young instructors (who often share their antiegalitarian malaise), citizens of the multiversity, not the City of God. They react as the "primitive rebels" that E. J. Hobsbawm has so brilliantly chronicled in his book of that name.

Although the source of their frustration is the mass society that refuses to single them out for the tonsure, the university is the convenient symbol of their status deprivation. And the average college or university is a sitting duck for what Bruno Bettelheim has called "id discharges." The huge expansion of American higher education has led to the breakdown of the time-honored authoritarian organization and the *in loco parentis* tradition, but no new forms have emerged. Fifty years ago, because of the small number of college students (roughly 4 in 100 of the age category) and the homogeneous class structure, disciplinary rules of the most ridiculous character were automatically enforced, and family sanctions buttressed those of the institutions. To be "rusticated" by Harvard was hardly a badge of honor among Brahmins.

Suddenly in recent years, student activists have realized that the emperor has no clothes, that the liberalization of customs in American society has left the dean of students and the president out on a very shaky limb. Could Haverford in 1969 expel a student for violating the ban on campus drinking? Could Cornell expel a student (as it did when I was a graduate student) for having unlicensed sexual relations in private, off-campus housing? In sum, the colleges and universities claimed the right to discipline as surrogate parents well after the real parents had abandoned the battlefield.

As we all know, most university administrations have given up active enforcement of parietal rules and save their ammunition of extreme, exemplary cases. In terms of actual freedom, I doubt if there are any institutions in the world that compare with large American universities. But to the alienated activists, this very freedom was the instrument for revenge. They set out to test its limits, realizing that generational solidarity would bring a large number of noncommitted students to their defense in a show-down.

Worse, perhaps, is the fact that few people are willing to defend wholeheartedly the existing structure of universities and colleges. Take the "publish or perish" issue. Any statistical examination will reveal that the great majority of American professors neither publish nor perish, but that hides the fact that failure to publish is often the only objective, self-evident way a faculty tenure committee can handle a man with whom it does not want to be sentenced to life imprisonment. If you say he is a deficient teacher, he pops up with a petition signed by 1,000 students declaring he is the greatest since Socrates (I recall one with the names in alphabetical order). If you say that his support of Lysenko's genetic theories is preposterous, he announces he is a victim of political persecution. (Indeed, things have gotten to the point where I suspect some nervous assistant professors take out insurance by urging draft evasion and denouncing the war in Vietnam.)

True, a tenure committee can go wrong. Nevertheless, from a

cold-blooded, long-run institutional view, it is best to err on the side of severity. A good man turned down will surely land on his feet; a bad decision may well block a departmental slot for thirty years. Yet who can build a formidable logical case for tenure procedures when the young Manichees start howling? The system is simply the best one that has been devised so far, and all suggested modifications seem to me to be deficient. Directly involving students on the committees has the inexorable impact of starting a popularity contest among assistant professors. And if students, why not alumni? (Those interested in the case for alumni participation are referred to William F. Buckley's *God and Man at Yale.*)

When the activists attack, then, there is a natural reaction among rationalists of goodwill. "Certainly the university needs reform" they say, "and we welcome the challenge of these concerned young people." The only difficulty is that the activists are not interested in university reform—they want to destroy the "corrupt institution," not improve it. If you instantly conceded their first ten "non-negotiable demands," they would simply invent ten more. Their demands are purely tactics in a strategy of nihilism. And so unfortunately the rationalists of goodwill, who keep searching for a compromise, will not receive their cooperation.

We are faced with a situation analagous to that in the 1930s, when liberals reacted to Hitler by talking about the Treaty of Versailles and "legitimate German demands." The Germans did indeed have legitimate demands, but they were irrelevant to the threat of Nazism. Students, too, have legitimate demands, but SDS has no right to make them. For fundamentally, as extremists they have rejected the very concept of legitimacy.

So much for the white militants. What about the Negroes (or "blacks," as we are ordered to call them by the dissenting academy)? Here, as many perceptive commentators have noted, we have an entirely different set of principles operating. The Negro student is not interested in becoming an alienated clerk; he wants that ticket of admission to the meritocracy, a college degree. The behavior of Negro militants has been completely functional: Recognizing the educational disadvantages they have suffered, they want to establish a sanctuary on campus that will make it possible for them to compete with better-trained whites. The idea of a school or department of "black studies" run by them exactly fills the bill, since it could presumably grant degrees without interference from "white cultural imperialism." It is, in fact, a brilliant improvisation, and the man who thought it up deserves an honorary degree in politics.

The substantive curricula that I have seen for black studies strike me as consisting largely of intellectualized, xenophobic inventions. Parochial school textbooks in math used to have problems like, "If seven nuns are walking down the street, and two leave to make a novena, how many nuns are still walking?" A course in "black statistics" could inquire, "If fifteen panthers are busted by the Man and three escape, what percentage got away?" Maybe this would enliven the course and make it relevant, but I doubt it. On the other hand, when I look around at all the nonsense that is currently taught on American campuses, I really cannot get worked up over a fractional increase.

I recall hearing how in my grandfather's time the Holy Name Society went on a campaign in Brooklyn to get the Bible out of public school classrooms. "Better no Bible than the King James" was the motto. (Few people today realize that in many industrial states the original impetus to get religion out of the public schools was Catholic in origin.) In other words, coming as I do from a militant ghetto culture, I am prepared to live with a department of Afro and Afro-American studies and with a considerable amount of what I consider chauvinist nonsense on the part of Negroes—after all, they couldn't be as bad as the Irish!

I insist at the same time, however, that this department be a regular academic organization, run by the rules governing the university faculty, not an independent black barony. Whatever our collective historical debt to the Negro may be, a university should not try to pay it off by undermining the educational integrity of the institution in sponsoring what amounts to an ethnic insurgency training center. Its function is education, not service—though service is hopefully a by-product of education. In the same sense that a university is not a federal arsenal (I am opposed to classified research on the campus) or a basic training center (I am opposed to academic credit for ROTC, even when voluntary), it cannot be a settlement house.

Higher education must of course be concerned with the problems of our society, but its overriding obligation is to maintain certain pedagogical values. To say, for example, that a student comes from a broken family, or is suffering from an Oedipus complex, or can only study what "turns him on" is no answer to the academic question, "Why did he flunk?" It is the answer to the question, "What is his problem?" He flunked because he could not or did not do the work. And it is no argument against the need for academic standards to say that some departments or institutions do not have them; that is an argument for improving those institutions or departments.

Let me turn now to the question of how the university is to cope with the current campus unrest. Here the point of departure has to be the clear fact that it must not become an armed camp with riot police at the ready. This can only sap the intellectual life of the school, erode faculty and student morale, and possibly lead administrators to volunteer for the Marines, where at least you get medals for valor.

An administration confronted with violence has three options: It can call the police; it can encourage counter-insurgency activities among those students and faculty opposed to violence; or it can simply close down. I have excluded capitulation as an alternative, because in my judgment it merely encourages the extremists to start a new round. (There is a story about a dean negotiating with a group of extremists, who went over their "non-negotiable" list and finally said: "Look, we can improve the food, we can build more parking lots, we can admit more Negroes, we can sell our South African stocks, but how can we liberate Greece, save Biafra and end the war in Vietnam?")

Since students who seize a campus building, throw out its occupants, break into desks and files, and steal (or is the word "liberate"?) whatever is lying around loose are patently committing trespass *vi et armis* and larceny, the logical case for calling the cops is compelling. Unfortunately, in this world logic is often a poor guide to tactics; as any politician will tell you, a straight line in tense community problems is usually the shortest route to disaster.

Calling the cops, sensible as it might seem, looses irrational demons among the intelligentsia and the students. Every faculty that ever existed has been certain in its heart that it could run the school better than the administration, and most professors cherish at least one grievance against the president or the dean. A police bust provides a perfect occasion for the academics to vent their aggressions, which characteristically takes the form of an Olympian resolution stating "a plague on both your houses." The Harvard faculty statement reminded me of the advice President Johnson constantly got from the academy on Vietnam: "Don't pull out, but stop fighting." To students, calling the police, with their inevitably well-publicized "brutality," seems like an invasion of their generational sovereignty. (There was one front-page photo of a boy at Harvard protecting an injured girl, apparently from further police savagery: She was a Brandeis student who broke her leg jumping out of a window.)

The use of the police power, while unavoidable in certain situations, thus tends to fracture the university community, generate escalation and leave psychological scars that will be a long time in healing. Closing the school, another ultimate weapon, in effect amounts to a strike by the Establishment. If the president says to a group holding a building, "You have eight hours to get out or the university will close down," the burden of guilt is automatically shifted to the extremists. The great majority of students, who are interested in trivial things like course credits and degrees, will put the heat on the troublemakers. (Such student pressure can also be employed as a deterrent in advance of any violent acts.) But a university exists to be open, and the closure may turn out to delight the extremists who dream of bringing down Goliath.

As for self-policing—that is, vigilantism—it is a very tricky affair. It has been put to use at the University of London, where the medical school rugger team dribbled a group of demonstrators out of the student union. And recently at Princeton, a stalwart group defended Nassau Hall from SDS. Because it has strong overtones of the American past, of the direct democracy the majority applied to minorities, such counter-insurgency makes those of us who have worked over the years to replace direct democracy with due process of law rather nervous.

Nonetheless, this tactic does meet the disruptors squarely on their own terms: "participatory democracy" and "confrontation."

An extremist who claims he has the right to eject a dean from his own office by force clearly has no theoretical ground for complaint if somebody stronger bounces him down the stairs. He has named the weapons. Moreover, self-policing does not involve the dreaded cops—unless they were to be called in to protect the SDS from an unduly militant majority.

None of these alternatives has much appeal to me, and I hope that somebody can devise another. Whatever solution is found for the problem, one thing has to be kept in mind: There can be no vacuum in authority on the campus or anywhere else; if the constituted bodies do not act, someone else will.

This brings me to my final proposition, which relates to the broad societal consequences of student disorder. I doubt if anything has served to strengthen the Right side of the American political spectrum as much as the various campus riots. An overwhelming majority of the people is not just concerned—it is infuriated (the Gallup poll is enough to scare you to death). The students involved go merrily on their way in the conviction that they are going to destroy American society. Yet they are dabbling in catastrophe politics, and the catastrophe is likely not only to engulf them but to seriously damage the foundations of higher education in this country. I am not talking about "fascism" or a police state. All that is required are cutbacks in state and federal educational funding, the provisions now under discussion in several state legislatures to bar out-of-state students from state universities, and a drying up of philanthropic funds available in the private sector.

Beyond this, I suspect that the activists' effect on their own generation of students will be to create millions of conservatives. As it is, Hubert Humphrey got only 37 percent of the college-educated electorate, and many in college today are privately enraged at their radical colleagues. At this point, the generational conflict paralyzes them: They are extremely reluctant to side with the "old" men against their peers. But that paralysis is transitional. Soon they will discover that they have been sentenced to life, and the aggressions they have suppressed against the crazies, the hippies and the miscellaneous long-hairs who unsettled their college experience will come to the fore.

Ironically then, the attempts by young extremists to radicalize the campus and use it as a launching pad for destroying American society will probably have precisely the reverse impact. If we liberals are to head this off, we must stop mumbling such incantations as "They are trying to tell us something," and stop flagellating overselves for sins we never committed—"We all killed Martin Luther King." We have to remember that liberalism stands for rational authority, not anarchy, and that while rationality is vital, authority is no less essential. If we do not police our own area, someone else will certainly do it for us, and we will have nobody to blame but ourselves.

The Retreat
of the Faculty

THE TREMENDOUS post-World War II expansion of higher education has had its impact not only on student attitudes, but upon the nature of the professoriate as well. When I began my teaching career in 1949 at Haverford College—admittedly not wholly typical of big universities, yet not a deviant case either—the senior faculty was essentially immobile. In seven years, as I recall, we lost to other institutions no more than two or three tenured professors.

The unadventurous majority were not untalented (a number subsequently left); rather, I believe, they were institutionally oriented. Mostly veterans of the Depression, these men had an entrenched "Alamo complex." Deep down inside they constantly anticipated the sudden collapse of prosperity and the academic seller's market. Haverford had proved a safe haven in times of economic chaos, and they were extremely reluctant to pull up the anchor and go wandering out after what might prove to be fool's gold.

Reprinted, with permission, from *The New Leader*, November 10, 1969.

This sense of permanent institutional commitment gave them a feeling of responsibility for the school, and not because they "ran it"—in fact, Haverford had one of the ablest, strongest presidents I have ever known, a man whose administrative specialty was letting the faculty and students have his way. For better or worse, despite the usual grumbling, the general attitude of the faculty was paternal.

We took *in loco parentis* for granted, and students rarely complained because they knew the doctrine worked in their favor; it gave them the kind of *de facto* protection no elaborate bureaucratic guarantees could match. One year, for instance, my top student, who had written a brilliant honors paper, went catatonic in the oral. The honors committee soothed him, sent him off and voted to grant him *summa*. When this had to be justified at a full faculty meeting, I explained the circumstances, discussed the student's record and asked for approval. There was a bit of a stir about the poor oral, but it was abruptly terminated when the doyen of the staff, a magnificent old classicist, rapped out, "The purpose of a grading system is to give 'A' students 'A.' Next case?"

In short, it was our school, and these were our kids. And from my experience as a graduate instructor at Cornell in 1946–49, I would say this was not unrepresentative of general faculty attitudes in the premultiversity era.

Then came the student explosion and the seller's market (I was happy to get $3,200 when I started at Haverford), and all sorts of strange things happened. Now, I am the last man to complain about earning a decent living; indeed, anyone who thinks that poverty generates virtue and that affluence corrupts, can turn over his worldly goods to me and I will find him a tenement to gratify his spiritual needs. Nevertheless, the growth of the affluent professoriate had several unfortunate consequences. To cite one, the academy now attracts characters who would never have dreamed of college teaching in 1949. Secretary of Health, Education and Welfare Robert Finch recently observed that a tenured professor has the softest life in the world—an unkind cut, but true for those seeking a vacation, rather than a vocation.

To put it another way, for anyone with a real entrepreneurial bent the academy is a drunk to be rolled. Any dean who empirically explores the faculty teaching load and compares it with the optimistic claims of the catalog is likely to send for the grand jury. I once caught a department that had folded three discrete courses into one room with the same curriculum, with none of the three listed instructors teaching. When I gently raised the matter this was described to me as a dynamic new innovation: The students taught themselves. When I suggested distributing half of the salaries of the three nonteaching innovators to the students, the department threatened to call the American Association of University Professors and accused me of political persecution.

But this is marginal. Most academicians, I am convinced, are not trying to beat the system and actually work considerably harder than many high federal officials—to say nothing of the members of various government commissions, such as the Subversive Activities Control Board (at $36,000 per annum). The problem is not that professors are disloyal to their institutions, but that they have gained a new superinstitutional loyalty to their academic specialty which takes precedence. As Seymour Martin Lipset has noted, these new professional subcultures have evolved to the point where a Brandeis historian has more in common with a Nebraska historian than with a Brandeis colleague in philosophy.

Those birds of passage, the men who bounce from one university to another, create the ethos for the nonmobile. The latter, usually acutely aware of their position and envious of the upper caste, take out their frustrations by rejecting university commitments and behaving as if they, too, were in demand; they are often *plus royalist que le roi*, adding a dimension of alienated bitterness to campus discussions.

A natural, though paradoxical concomitant of the seller's market is that as faculties become less and less interested in assuming institutional responsibilities, they become more and more greedy for institutional power. Unwilling to do the work of running a school, they are powerful enough to prevent anyone else from doing the job, producing a form of paralysis known as participatory bureaucracy. Let me provide an example.

In 1967–68, the Brandeis faculty set up a committee to plan a concentration in Afro and Afro-American studies. Because of schedule conflicts and similar obstructions the committee did not meet for six months and, of course, nothing happened. Suddenly, last fall "black studies" became an issue. Student extremists denounced the *administration* for stalling, "racist provocations," etc. Needless to say, the real offenders did not march out and do penance; they became invisible and let the president carry the can. Presidents are paid to carry the can, but when they cannot act without prior faculty approval on academic matters, they are really in a corner. And what would the average professor think of the sporting instincts of a president who stood up before a tv camera and said, "I can not tell a lie. My incompetent faculty created this mess."

In addition to obfuscating power relationships, the new super-institutional loyalties have undermined several old campus verities, including the traditional distrust between administrators and professors. This still exists, but today it manifests itself unpredictably, and over issues many faculty members seem to feel first developed when their particular schools were hit by disruption. Some of these issues, such as defense research and ROTC, are political; others concern the allocation of power within the university (or restructuring, as it is sometimes called); still others, like black studies, have elements of both. Since the power of administrators has been crippled by the faculty, and the power of the faculty has been weakened by lack of commitment, the situation is wide open.

In my own Department of Politics at Brandeis, we assume we know what we are doing and have made it perfectly clear to our students that, while we love them, we do not consider them competent to administer, design curriculum, help choose faculty and so on. They know that if they want a course on "Ghetto Watching," they will be told to major in sociology—we are not interested in teaching middle-class kids to be poverty-peepers. In this way everyone saves an immense amount of time that would otherwise be used to convert education into a futile game of "Who's in charge here?"—where everybody loses.

One interesting result of the breakdown of "community" has been the desperate effort of some students, particularly post-graduates, to somehow bureaucratize "trust" and institutionalize "intimacy." My colleagues in American History put three graduate students on the Graduate Committee (with limited functions), and we recently had a long, fascinating "dialogue." The gist of their complaint was that Life is Hard. They seemed to consider graduate work an adversary proceeding in which they will inevitably get sandbagged, and proposed protections that would require every student to keep a lawyer in permanent reserve. When I noted that if the faculty were really so hostile, no procedural device in the world could save them, they were appalled. But alas it is true—you cannot build a community with erector sets.

Whether we like it or not, graduate students are almost completely at the mercy of their professors. They must adapt to the whims and values of their masters, but without any of the security that accrues to the latter. This helps to explain the appeal of political extremism among postgraduates. To take just one example, a former student of mine went to a distinguished university to get a doctorate with three top historians. Before he had been there a year, two left, and the third departed the following year. Today there is no one in that department who either knows him (he has been away writing his dissertation) or is qualified in his field. He is an apprentice without a master and only his wife has kept him from dynamiting the place.

Legitimate complaints of this kind naturally generate resentment. For years administrators have essentially fulfilled the role of the eighteenth-century marines: protecting the officers from the crew. Now professors are being confronted with the consequences of their own rhetoric. Having claimed sovereignty, they are being asked to exercise it; the scorned deans and provosts have stopped running interference. In other words, the faculty's function has changed from free-floating criticism to decision-making and, as any observer-participant could predict, the results are appalling.

Many commentators have accused faculties of cowardice in the recent confrontations. This is unfair. They are accustomed to living in an infinitely manipulatable universe, where ideas about the nature of reality determine the shape reality takes. There is nothing more infuriating to those accustomed to playing with malleable abstractions than the suggestion that they must choose between two options, "yes" or "no," "fight" or "run" or whatever.

Anyone who so much as hints the world is this simple will probably be denounced as a vulgar boor. Unfortunately, in the real world most hard questions do demand a yes/no response. And every so often, the real world impinges upon academia.

Back in 1960, for instance, the faculties of many institutions were asked to establish a policy on the loyalty affidavit then attached to National Defense Education Act funds. The administrations concerned clearly had the right to expect these master rationalists to provide an answer to the relatively simple question, "Should we take the money?" The Harvard faculty, however, voted down five successive motions, ranging from acceptance to rejection—no resolution passed. At Brandeis, the faculty voted not to permit students to take the contaminated lucre, but was silent on the subject of faculty participation in the largesse. Anybody who expects a straight answer from a meeting of scholars is a real utopian.

Lyndon B. Johnson made countless enemies among academic critics of the Vietnam war who visited the White House by handing them the options. Invariably, they arrived with a program of "Stop fighting, but don't pull out." The President thanked them for this pearl and then asked, "Suppose Hanoi won't cooperate? Should I fight or quit?" After a good deal of toing and froing, they usually said, "Try not to get in that position"—and went home to denounce LBJ for bullying.

In the last couple of years universities have been faced with a parallel situation, and the "Stop fighting, but don't pull out" advice is being taken seriously. The result is chaos because SDS, like Hanoi, has no intention of cooperating. And meanwhile, faculties are desperately trying to somehow force reality into the procrustean bed of theory, or more frequently, pretending that the difficulties arise from poor communications or remote historical circumstances.

This takes the form of asking "Why did it happen?" instead of "What shall we do?" It is a marvelous detour from reality, and with a little stimulation you can get as far back as the Dark Ages in the search for historical causes. It is also partly an outgrowth of ethical relativism, of the assumption that all values are equal. (This reached its classic formulation when the anthropologist, while being marinated by cannibals, observed "Well, they think it's right.") A faculty does not like to condemn anyone for "doing his thing." It violates ecumenical traditions and makes one seem bigoted. In addition, these days it may get one's classes raided, office burned and family threatened.

Thus if a faculty is reluctant to get into a fight—and we are hardly professional soldiers—it can find an infinite number of reasons why the present situation, however objectionable, is the inexorable consequence of the African slave trade, the Protestant Reformation, the Treaty of Aix-la-Chapelle or sexual deprivation in Western society. Obviously, none of these factors can be altered in 1969, so the faculty retires from the field satisfied that since nothing can be done, it has properly done nothing. I cannot resist quoting here A. J. P. Taylor's classic exposition of the historicist dodge in the June 6, 1968, *New York Review of Books.*

"Germans were no more wicked in aspiring to dominate Europe, or even the world, than others were in resolving to stop them. The Germans were in a sense less wicked. For their domination of Europe was achieved with little physical destruction and comparatively few casualties, whereas the effort to resist them produced general devastation."

Now when a leading historian like Taylor can manage to get the Nazis off the hook, is it any surprise that lesser historians can justify violence on a campus? After all, more violence was used by the cops at Harvard to clear the building than by SDS in occupying it.

A variation on the preceding is the assertion that one has no moral standing or right to act unless one is pure. No university is pure, of course, therefore no university can act against disruption. (This is a variation on what I call the Kitty Genovese gambit: When asked why she did nothing to help Kitty, who was being publicly murdered in Queens and screamed for help, a neighbor said: "Why should I help her? She had no morals.")

I have watched colleagues at Brandeis and elsewhere, alleged intellectuals, wail like medieval penitents. At one faculty meeting, men who could not hit a barn door at six paces with a shotgun announced that they had "killed Martin Luther King." The place was knee-deep in guilt. Exhibitionists who want to confess to sins they never committed can take their place in the great American tradition of evangelism. But I object to the point of all this angst: the moral incompetence of the faculty to reject "black militant" demands.

I am imperfect and impure—though I don't want to make a psychodrama out of it—but I fail to see the relevance of my state of grace to the imperatives of living in the real world. The rain falls on the just and unjust alike. With a full admission of human imperfection, we have to choose, and a failure or refusal to choose is itself a choice.

Another cause of faculty paralysis is the cult of sincerity. Perhaps because I accept a secularized version of the doctrine of original sin, drawn from the Niebuhrian notion that human selfishness is the snake in the Garden of Eden, I find the emphasis on the sincerity of the militants essentially irrelevant. Every time the balloon goes up in a college or university, out trots the chorus defending the innocence and good intentions of the disrupters. First of all, I doubt the factual assessment; with George Orwell I believe that "saints must be presumed guilty until proved innocent."

But more important, assuming for purposes of argument the sincerity of whoever tried to burn down the History and Politics building at Brandeis, so what? While on the moral level sincerity is a great virtue, in any political universe (in the broad Aristotelian sense) it is meaningless. Will anyone, for example, argue that a sincere white supremacist is a better *citizen* than an insincere egalitarian? (Theologians and existentialists can decide whether he is a better *man*.) On the campuses we are dealing with a crisis in social behavior, not measuring abstract moral worth.

Let me make it clear that I would prefer to have as associates people who are right for the right reasons. But I am also prepared to bear with those who are right for the wrong reasons. The sincerely wrong are still wrong and have to face the objective consequences of their wrong acts. If a faculty concentrates on motives and ignores acts, it is hiding from the world of responsibility. Faculties must recognize that in the present conflict, they are not invisible men, that in fact they are prime targets. Unless they are prepared to fight for the integrity of the academy, the ballgame is over.

It is fitting to end with a text from Saint Matthew: "That every idle word that men shall speak, they shall give account thereof in the day of judgment. For by thy words thou shalt be justified, and by thy words thou shalt be condemned." For those of us who live by words, the day of judgment has come; we should examine carefully the consequences of our rhetoric. The ivory tower has regrettably become the ivory fox-hole.

On Being
an Unfashionable
Professor

THE HELL of being a historian who has spent a good deal of time over the past quarter-century rummaging around in political theory is that one is never really surprised at contemporary follies. Thus the events on American campuses last spring gave me an acute sense of *déjà vu*—all one has to do is turn to the late Ronald Knox's brilliant study of enthusiasm as a recurring religious phenomenon.

With loving care, Monsignor Knox chronicled the activities of those groups in the Catholic Church which had—over the centuries—denounced the Establishment in the name of their private visions of truth, which rejected the rationally disciplined concept of a Christian community, postulated by the Fathers, in favor of a perfervid revivalism. For these enthusiasts, reason and logic were always the Devil's instruments, inhibiting a total, spontaneous, unstructured response to the trumpet of righteousness. On their banners, one could invariably find some version or other of the precept: "Reason destroys Grace," a formal way of saying, "If you're not part of the solution, you're part of the problem."

Knox's book might usefully serve as a manual for charting events on many college and university campuses, as a metaphysical replacement for Dr. Spock. While the subject matter and the language have changed somewhat over the past 2,000 years—we no longer argue in Greek or Latin about the standing of mystics—the thrust of the rhetoric has changed little. What is distinctive about events in 1970 is not that Holy Rollers are loose in politics, but that the intellectual sector has been animated by this quintessential anti-intellectualism.

Examine closely the actions of college and university faculties last May. In the wake of President Nixon's Cambodian decision and the tragedy at Kent State, faculties all over the nation gathered to conduct elaborate rites of exorcism. The whole affair was completely stylized—it was rather like American Legion posts reacting to news that the United States was going to recognize Red China. The time allotted to the ceremony varied from place to place: our faculty took about eight hours (with a bomb scare providing intermission), but one institution went to eighteen hours before the final purgation.

Everywhere the same scenario unrolled. After the faculty had Gathered by the River, a seemingly endless stream of Pentecostal witnesses rose to affirm their guilt and their salvation—and to excommunicate the heretics who persisted in contending that a university is not an Anabaptist sect, that it is concerned with exploring alternate routes to truth, not with establishing Truth. In the background, like a Greek chorus, were the students chanting, "Close it up!," "Strike!," "Stop the war machine!," "End repression!," "Free Bobby Seale!" and similar intellectual slogans. An outsider who did not know these were faculty meetings might have seen in them an uncanny resemblance to lynch mobs.

While no sane man enjoys an atmosphere of intimidation, this aspect of the purification rites did not bother me particularly. I have been excommunicated by experts, and have been lambasted on occasion by two Presidents of the United States. After I wrote an article in October 1962, entitled "The Limits of Kennedy's Liberalism," I received a fifteen-minute call from the White

House in which the President told me more unpleasant things about myself than I learned in eight hours last May. And Lyndon Johnson could sometimes be a fairly vigorous critic of my views, though I must add that—unlike my colleagues—he never tried to tell me *what* to think.

In short, there was no impulse to take refuge in self-pity last May; this was *sub specie aeternitatis* minor-league attrition. But I confess I was deeply disturbed by this organized effort to impose a party line within the academy. I have been teaching college for twenty-three years, and this was the first time I ever saw my *peers* attempt to establish Truth by referendum.

Of course, there have always been pressures for "right-think" from outside the academy. In 1951, for example, the local American Legion urged the president of Haverford College to fire me. In the course of a campaign for, as I recall, a township school board, I had made the papers by referring to Senator Joseph McCarthy as "Stalin's secret weapon." President Gilbert White (who was the ablest and most unintimidatible administrator I have ever known) merely asked me, wryly, where I had picked up my talent for "nonviolent speech."

In 1965, former Senator Ernest Gruening of Alaska similarly suggested that my support for the war in Vietnam made me incompetent to teach at Brandeis. I doubt if President Abram Sachar, who had stood like a rock in the wild 1950s, even noticed it. After all, Yahoo attacks are par for the course, and good colleges and universities simply ignore them.

These were attacks from without, but now we are confronted with an entirely different situation. The faculty and students have taken to expounding "right-think." By a vote of 127–3, the Brandeis faculty announced its "fervent opposition to the United States involvement in the war in Southeast Asia and to the decision to send American troops into Cambodia." By 123–22, it voted "solidarity with our students as part of a nationwide demonstration against political repression in the United States, American military and paramilitary presence in Southeast Asia, and applied war research at universities." (These were the essentials—both resolutions were provided with elaborate rhetorical wrappers.) The student body passed similar, though more strident resolutions.

Now the first question to ask must be: What was the purpose of these formal, official decisions? Clearly they were not simply devised for informative reasons—a statement to the President of the United States signed by faculty in their individual capacities could have served that purpose. (Indeed, this suggestion was made and voted down.) As the sponsors unequivocally stated, these resolutions were designed to put the university as a *university* (as a "community," someone said) on record against imperialism, repression, etc.

Which brings us to the crucial point: As far as Brandeis and probably 300 institutions of higher learning in the United States (who went through the same drill) are concerned, it is Officially True that the United States is "repressive," that the Indochina war is an immoral, imperialist foray and that war-related research is wicked. Suppose, then, you are a professor or a student in one of these schools, and you happen to believe that the United States is one of the least repressive societies in human history, that the war in Indochina is not immoral and imperialist, and that war-related research is not necessarily wicked. What are you supposed to do? Shoot yourself? See a psychiatrist? Change your mind? Shut up? Perhaps the next thing to expect is a campus bumper-sticker: "The Panthers: Love Them or Leave!"

For me this is not an academic question. As I pointed out to my colleagues as politely as I know how, I not only disagree with everything they voted,[1] but I also object on fundamental principle to such dogmatic safaris—even when I happen to share the

---

[1] Strictly speaking, my views on American foreign policy are not relevant to the argument here. However, for the benefit of ornithologists, who keep tabs on the miraculous transformation of hawks into doves, I might note that the views I expressed when Vietnam was a tiny cloud on the horizon still make sense to me. I am still, as I was when I wrote for this magazine in November 1962, a liberal who agrees with President John Kennedy's November 16, 1961, formulation that "we are neither 'warmongers' nor 'appeasers,' neither 'hard' nor 'soft.' We are Americans, determined to defend the frontiers of freedom by an honorable peace, if peace is possible, but by arms if arms are used against us." If this makes me a hawk by contemporary standards, my flight pattern includes both the Middle East and Southeast Asia. Despite some battle fatigue, I am prepared to argue the merits of liberal interventionism against the isolationist alternatives—on both the Right and the Left—that currently dominate the American spirit.

substantive view of the majority. Though I am, for example, a militant supporter of Israel in the Middle East, I would repudiate any effort to put the university on record as pro-Israel. This kind of mechanical Truth-finding is a pervasive violation of academic freedom, designed to cultivate a conformist sect, not a community of free minds. We may find it most efficient to set up a bulletin board by the campus gate listing the local Truths and warning off dissenters—an intellectual version of the law of trespass.

When I put this to some of my colleagues who supported the resolutions, they accused me of paranoia, of being uptight on symbols. "Ignore it," said one distinguished intellectual. "After all, it is only a resolution." Curiously, this response depressed me even more. It suggested that (in the words of a League for Industrial Democracy study, "The State of the Student Movement—1970," a first-class analysis) "there is a strange rightness in the contempt a young Weatherman has for those liberals who, having convicted the American people en masse of incorrigible racism, a lust for imperial power and a total lack of any progressive impulses, are—so to speak—*afraid to pull the trigger.*"

But there is another vital dimension. The worst aspect of the whole sordid business is not the impact of Enacted Truth on dissenters. Dissenters (at least in my generation) had to be prepared to take some heat. What this attitude really imperils is the teaching function itself. If one believes—as I do—that teaching is the central mission of a college or university, he must reject any notion of Community Truth. By this I do not mean a teacher should be uncommitted—God forbid! Rather, I would hope that he would not (in a seventeenth-century formulation) "confuse the rumblings of his bowels with the workings of the Holy Spirit." And I would insist that he inhabit a pluralistic universe of *beliefs* in which deeply held truths can compete on the open market.

For a decade, Herbert Marcuse and I taught the same subject in the same department at Brandeis. Although—to engage in understatement—our political philosophies differ radically, we rarely differed in our evaluation of students. By and large, his "A" students got "A's" from me, and vice versa. The reason for this congruity was simple: we were, each in his own fashion, teaching political theory. We were not recruiting for the Marcuse, or Roche, Marching and Chowder Societies. Students were examined on, say, Rousseau or Marx—they were not examined on "What Roche thinks of Rousseau" or "What Marcuse thinks of Marx."

In this same period, Marcuse and I went to the mat on innumerable public issues. This began in 1956 when he supported the suppression of the Hungarian Revolution while I was pleading for United Nations intervention, and it lasted into the mid-sixties as he opposed American intervention in Southeast Asia while I endorsed the containment of Asian Communism. But these were our private views (and it might be worth noting that our disputes did not carry over into our personal relations, which were always cordial); neither of us ever dreamed of asking the university to give them its imprimatur—nor, what is most important, did we attempt to impose them on our students.

Since he left Brandeis in 1965, Marcuse has developed an amazing reputation as a revolutionary, as the purported Svengali of the New Left and, in recent weeks, as Angela Davis's alleged mentor in violence. Actually, Marcuse-the-Revolutionary is a media creation: I'm convinced that one of his speeches would disperse a revolutionary mass meeting faster than tear gas, and his fondness for violent abstractions conceals the fact that probably the most revolutionary act in his career was subscribing to *The Peking Review.*

Now various groups in Southern California are out to get Marcuse for inspiring Miss Davis, for providing ideological justification for her alleged gun-running. This is Moscow Trial logic—as usual the rightwingers are drawing on Stalinist jurisprudence for a Los Angeles version of *Darkness at Noon.* The notion of "objective guilt"—that a teacher is responsible for the use made of his ideas—is intolerable in a free society. The question that can be asked is, "Did Marcuse impose his views on his students?" And, to repeat, in my experience he did not.

Everyone's educational theory is, I guess, his autobiography. For deep personal reasons, I believe that it is an academic felony to force-feed students. Back in 1941, when I was in college, a Stalinist English teacher virtually murdered me because I refused to agree that Emerson was a "fascist" or that World War II became "moral" the day the Soviet Union was invaded by the Nazis. He announced that I was a "Nazi-Trotskyite-wrecker" (much to the bemusement of the local Trotskyites, who denounced me as a "rightwing Social Democrat") and flunked me. Other faculty members intervened and he quietly changed the grade, but this episode gave me a profound and lasting sense of a student's right *not* to be pressed into a professor's crew.

Since that time I have perhaps bent over backwards on occasion to be fair to a student who disagreed with me. Early in my teaching career, a couple of academic entrepreneurs (with that unnerving gift for spotting an Achilles heel that talented neurotics often possess) probably got higher grades than they deserved by engaging in conspicuous McCarthyism (old-style, that is—Joe, not Gene). By announcing in class and out that "supporters of Joe McCarthy would never get a fair break from that liberal Roche," these characters may have engaged in a little successful blackmail, though I doubt if my generosity significantly influenced their lives. But that was the price of an education and one I was cheerfully prepared to pay. I would far sooner have the reputation for being a patsy on this ground than be considered an academic *Gauleiter*, mobilizing his students behind his True Faith.

In any event, over the years I have had a remarkable group of students who have scattered all over the ideological spectrum. They include Bernadine Dohrn, the Weatherwoman, at one extreme; a couple of rightwing nuts at the other; and in between everything from democratic radicals to establishment liberals to austere and distinguished conservatives. I never asked whether they shared my views on contemporary national or international issues; my concern was their work in political theory and constitutional law. From time to time, one or another of my students has inveighed against my "cold-war liberalism" in the campus paper, but that is their privilege. Out of the formal classroom context—in an article such as this, or in discussion—I honor them with equal frankness. I operate on the premise that it would be a violation of their civil rights for me to invoke my university authority to set out a party line on Vietnam, or Israel, or the ABM. Similarly, while they are free to contest opinions with me in their private capacities, it is a violation of my civil rights for a student body as such to tell me what to think.

Which brings us to the current academic scene, where faculties and student bodies have conducted solemn referendums and proclaimed the Truth. Right or wrong, I hold strong positions to the contrary. I have no illusion of infallibility; if I had been endowed with the capacity for witless certainty possessed by some of my critics, life would be a lot simpler. Obviously I think I am right, but I am also fully aware that in this contingent universe one has to make 100 percent action decisions on the basis of imperfect information—so I'm never sure I'm right.

Unable to produce any Sign, pessimistically sensing with the Prophet that "no Sign shall be given," I find myself confronting a couple of hundred intelligent eighteen- and nineteen-year-olds, of whom perhaps 10 percent (secretly) share my positions on American policy. Naturally I am sorry they disagree with me; I am basically an affable soul who dislikes the stigma of nonconformity. But what precisely does the university, which has formally gone on record, expect me to do? Am I supposed to find out what I think from my students? If so, they should get their money back, and I should be fired for grand larceny—or, perhaps, if we need a lesser offense, for prostitution.

For if I changed my views because my colleagues or my students (or both) disliked them, I would be an intellectual whore, patently unfit to teach the young. What kind of respect could a teacher of this sort expect? Obviously I can't speak for the present student generation, but in my day we had nothing but contempt for sycophantic professors—even though they occasionally stimulated our egos. I recall vividly the feeling of disgust I had at eighteen for the middle-aged faculty member who tried to be "one of the boys." On the generational scene, as elsewhere, good fences make good neighbors; each generation has its sovereignty, its zone of privacy which should not be invaded by aging Ponce de Leóns.

Indeed, what is more insulting to the young than to have their elders fawning upon their wisdom, dedication and virtue? As I have watched the student generations pass, I have become convinced that the best we can hope for is that they will be no worse than my generation—which in itself would be no mean accomplishment. The cult of youth has its benefits for bored middle-aged intellectuals, terrified of the calendar, but it is a massive insult to the intelligence of the young.

A university, then, is not a temple of youth. The best definition of a good education I have ever encountered was that it involves growing up in an atmosphere of intellectual conflict, even chaos, where talented young people are constantly forced to structure their own minds and lives. There is no guaranteed curriculum; no master plan (whether dynamic and innovative or conservative and rigid) will do the job. The teacher's function in all this is catalytic—he has to keep his students focused on the key questions and challenge all major premises (including his own). A university is a strange locale, full of strong-minded eccentrics presenting a variety of heresies. And doing so zestfully because, by definition, in an intellectual community there can be no Revealed Truth on matters of content. There is only one loyalty oath demanded: to the principle of free inquiry itself. A university or college cannot be a church and a faculty cannot be a church council, imitating the Fathers at Nicaea or Chalcedon in the determination of True Dogma.

Thus, when any group—a legislative committee, a bunch of big donors, the Veterans of Foreign Wars or a posse of New Left militants—demands that a university fly its flag and pledge allegiance to its Truth, a teacher can have only one automatic, fighting reaction. It is, in the immortal words of e. e. cummings's Young Olaf, "I will not kiss your ——ing flag."

LAW

The Strange Case of
the "Revolutionary"
Establishment

$\mathbf{T}$HE KEY CONCEPT to be kept in mind in understanding the development of American governments after Independence is that at ground zero virtually nothing happened when the King's writ ceased to run. Since the seventeenth century, America had been a "do-it-yourself" enterprise. The British were far too busy fighting continental wars—and settling their own civil war —to involve themselves at the *operational* level in the government of these remote colonies. Except for protection from the French in Canada, all most Americans wanted was to be left alone. And they were largely left alone to create their own governmental institutions. (As Richard B. Morris pointed out forty years ago in his neglected classic, *Studies in the History of American Law,* law reforms not achieved in Britain until the 1830s were incorporated in the Massachusetts Body of Liberties [1641] and in colonial legislation which simply hacked away the

Reprinted with permission of James Ford Bell Library, University of Minnesota.

jungle of writs that provided the essence of common law litigation.)

Curiously enough John Calvin spotted this phenomenon incredibly early, presenting in his *Commentary on Deuteronomy* (c. 1535) the nub of what later became known as the "safety valve thesis." Justifying capital punishment for blasphemy, Calvin observed: "Some object that since the offense consists only in words, there is no need for such severity. But we muzzle dogs, and shall we leave men free to open their mouths as they please? Those who object are like dogs and swine. *They murmur that they will go to America where nobody will bother them.*" (Italics mine).

No commentator in his sense would argue that American institutions in the seventeenth and eighteenth centuries were "democratic" in the modern sense of the word. However, the level of citizen participation in the decisions of his governments was certainly greater here than anywhere else in the contemporary world. As I have pointed out elsewhere,[1] one found an open society with closed enclaves: The Anglican oppressed by the Bay Colony could move to Virginia and get his licks in against the local Puritans. To put it differently, there was a high level of consensual authoritarianism: It was hardly necessary to employ Dr. Gallup to find out how a Puritan felt about Quakers (it would be comparable to polling Israelis on their view of anti-Semites).

What these scattered communities along the coast of North America shared, then, was not a common ideology in substantive terms, but a complete conviction that it was their business to define whatever ideology might be relevant and applicable. As royal governor after royal governor (to say nothing of excisemen) learned the hard way, the Americans simply took for granted precisely the question allegedly at issue: Who ran the colonies? (Those interested in the colonists' talents at attrition are referred to the hilarious adventures of Edward Randolph in

---

[1] See my "American Liberty: An Analysis of the 'Tradition' of Freedom," in Milton Konvitz & Clinton Rossiter, eds., *Aspects of Liberty* (1958), pp. 129–162.

his efforts to enforce the customs laws against various provinces in the late seventeenth century.[2] And who but the Marx Brothers could master the political scenarios that the good citizens of Rhode Island later mounted?[3])

To put it in more scholarly terms, to an average American very little changed—except when British troops turned up to inconvenience him. The town meetings kept in business, the legislatures shifted ground (as from Boston to Salem under Gage's duress), the same justice of the peace with the same veniremen ran the "hundreds." In short, the social system retained its integrity.

A number of eccentrics opted for the Crown, either because they did not discern the strength of the American civic religion or—more frequently—because they were personal enemies of the local elite. But they were handled with an efficiency that Lenin might well have envied: They were outlawed under sentence of death and their goods and chattels confiscated by their "conservative" (or were they "radical"?) neighbors. While Robert R. Palmer's statistics[4] on refugees may be a bit existential, it is clear that any opposition to the American order would be located in England, Canada or the West Indies, not on its home ground.

What was the American rationale for this assumption of *de facto* sovereignty? Did a careful reading of John Locke lead to this universal upsurge of "radical Whiggery"? Obviously, as the Declaration of Independence evidences, John Locke's concepts were useful things to have on the shelf. But then there are some sticky precedents that have to be explained. Listen to Edward Winslow, writing in 1646: "If the Parliaments of *England* should impose Lawes upon us having no Burgesses in their house of

---

[2] See Michael G. Hall, *Edward Randolph and the American Colonies, 1676–1703* (1960).

[3] See David S. Lovejoy, *Rhode Island Politics and the American Revolution, 1760–1776* (1958).

[4] See Palmer's comparison of the emigré rate from the American and French Revolutions in *The Age of the Democratic Revolution* (1959), p. 188. Needless to say, I share Palmer's opinion that ours was a "real" revolution, but I would not want to take his admittedly rough estimates into a court of history.

Commons, nor capable of a summons by reason of the vast dis-
tance of the Ocean being three thousand miles from *London*,
then wee should lose the libertie and freedome I conceived of
English indeed."⁵ (Italics in original.)

This was not idle rhetoric. In 1661, when the Restoration of
Charles II threatened a wholesale reorganization of colonial
government, the Great and General Court of Massachusetts Bay
rejected the British right to reimpose the Navigation Acts, but
then—in as neat a legal ploy as one can imagine—the legislature
passed *in its own right* statutes enforcing the navigation mea-
sures.⁶ (An interesting reversal of the technique employed by the
British Parliament a century later when the Stamp Act was
repealed but accompanied by a Declaratory Act stating Parliament's rights in the premises.)

"No taxation without representation" was thus rattling around
in the American arsenal a century before it became a *mot d'ordre*.
There are other interesting coincidences which suggest that John
Locke was in some respects a codifier of the majoritarian view of
sovereignty rather than its author.⁷ For instance, in dealing with
the reach of colonial authority the 1648 Massachusetts *Laws and
Liberties* provided that anyone entering the province "doe(s)
tacitly submit to this Government and to all the wholesome laws
thereof." A third of a century later John Locke in his *Second
Treatise* (Section 119) presented a virtually identical difinition
of "tacit consent."

This is not the place to set out the innumerable techniques that
the various American assemblies devised to circumvent the day
to day jurisdiction of the Crown. (Or, for that matter, the way
the good Quakers of Pennsylvania dealt with their Proprietor
when the latter, deciding to collect his quit-rents, sent Captain

⁵ Cited in Perry Miller, *Orthodoxy in Massachusetts* (1958), p. 307.
⁶ See Perry Miller, *The New England Mind From Colony to Province*
(1953), pp. 125–6.
⁷ Those interested in the development of Locke's views are referred to
the invaluable introduction Peter Laslett wrote for his definitive edition of
the *Two Treatises of Government* (1960). Among other things, Laslett
proves conclusively that the *Second Treatise* was written *before* the Glorious
Revolution.

John Blackwell to Philadelphia to institute law and order.[8]) It was not that Americans were disloyal; they just insisted on defining for themselves the outward and visible manifestations of fealty. The latter, needless to say, did not include payment of taxes except those enacted by their provincial legislatures. Because of royal preoccupation with crises of a far higher order (the Second Hundred Years War, for example), and British administrative inefficiency, the Americans by and large got away with their autonomy.

Indeed, by 1765 I think it is legitimate to say that Americans were simply habituated to self-government. Again, to clarify, this did not mean that the majority of the population were actual participants, but there is no reason to suspect that the largest group of nonparticipants—women—held different views from their husbands. Indeed, there were those in the British government who favored leaving the French in Canada as a means of keeping the colonies attached to the homeland. On May 9, 1761, for example, the Duke of Bedford wrote that he wondered if "the neighborhood of the French to our Northern Colonies was not the greatest security of their dependence on the Mother Country who I fear will be slighted by them when their apprehensions of the French are removed."[9]

When you recall that there was no civil list for the American colonies, that the royal governors were dependent for their salaries on the provincial assemblies, and that a navy is hardly the ideal instrument for what we today call "pacification," it is immediately obvious the extent to which the British had in all but symbolic terms waived their rights to sovereignty. In each province the political class effectively ran public affairs. This political class could be elected on a quite broad franchise (in 1757 there was a bitterly contested election to the General Court in Watertown, Massachusetts: statistical microanalysis of the records indicates that there were 135 qualified voters and 131

[8] See Nicholas Wainwright, "Governor John Blackwell," 74 *Pennsylvania Magazine of History & Biography* (1950), pp. 457–72.

[9] Cited in Sir Lewis Namier, *England in the Age of the American Revolution,* 2nd ed. (1961), p. 276.

voted![10]), on a narrow one, or could simply hold its position by deference. But there it was in place assuming without argument the legitimacy of its authority.

Of course, the pamphleteers were out in force arguing all sorts of Talmudic questions ("When is a tax not a tax? When it's a regulation," etc.) but this was icing on the cake. As Mary Beth Norton has recently suggested,[11] the poor Loyalists never understood what hit them. They thought they were loyal, only to discover as they were dispossessed and exiled that, properly understood, they were "rebels."

These poor folks had plenty of time in the wilds of Canada to meditate on the problem, but they never did grasp the difference between loyalty to a symbol and loyalty to a social system. Concededly, the political class (or "Establishment," if you prefer) had some unique definitions: in March 1775, for example, the Newport, Rhode Island Committee of Inspection demanded the banning of a newspaper in the name of freedom of the press—which it defined as "the diffusion of liberal sentiments on the administration of Government."[12] Equally unnerving was the political class' views on law and order on which Lieutenant Governor Thomas Hutchison of Massachusetts was something of an authority: After a 1768 "tumult," he had the Attorney General lay the facts before the Grand Jury, but to no avail since, as he caustically noted to the Lords of Trade, the foreman of the Grand Jury had been the instigator of the affair.[13]

Civil libertarians who look back to a "Golden Age" of American

[10] For these figures I am indebted to an unpublished honors thesis by Susan Naomi Greene, a former Brandeis student. To fill out the statistical base, the census of 1763 indicated there were 179 polls in Watertown, of whom 25 percent were between 16–21 and thus ineligible to vote. There may have been a minor variation in this base figure between 1757–63, but it hardly affects the generalization. Americans apparently began taking the suffrage for granted at a remarkably early stage: "A Committee of the [Massachusetts] General Court protested in 1655 that everyone including 'scotch servants, Irish [, ?] negars and persons under one and twenty years' was voting." Darrett B. Rutman, *Winthrop's Boston* (1965), p. 162.

[11] Mary Beth Norton, *The British-Americans* (1972).

[12] Cited in Roche, *op. cit.,* p. 139.

[13] This was among Hutchison's letters leaked to the *Pennsylvania Chronicle* by Benjamin Franklin. It appeared on July 5, 1773.

liberty which—in their view—has been replaced by an era of "repression" might meditate briefly on the "chilling effect" of the following Resolution of the Continental Congress, passed in October 1775:

"Resolved, That it be recommended to the several provincial Assemblies or Conventions, and councils or committees of safety, to arrest and secure every person in their respective colonies, whose going at large may, in their opinion endanger the safety of the colony, or the liberties of America."[14]

What this adds up to is the hardly novel thesis that (as John Adams later wrote Mercy Warren) "the Revolution was over before the War began." But beyond that I would contend that far too much time and energy has been expended by scholars on taxonomic exercises in the realm of political theory.[15] The Americans did not inch their way towards a theory of autonomy: They took autonomy for granted and turned the high theorists loose to make the brief. ("No taxation without representation," for example, sounded pretty good until a canny anonymous critic, "F.L.," in the *Pennsylvania Journal*, March 13, 1766, spotted the joker—suppose the royal authorities got clever and passed out some seats? The Americans would be sawed off at the knees: "represented" but outvoted.[16] So it was back to the drawing board with the ultimate design of a federal theory of the British Empire.) As Jack Greene has shown in his fine *Quest for Power,* the colonial elite was constantly on the alert for ways of moving in on the prerogative, and once some commanding height or other had been effectively seized, a scribe could be found to prove that, in fact, the action was fully justified by Section 31 of *Magna Carta,* or the Assize of Clarendon, or both.

Which is not to say that the debate was not sharp and interesting. John Dickinson, for example, was a grand master of the art

---

[14] Worthington C. Ford et al., *Journals of the Continental Congress,* (Washington, 1904–37), vol. III, p. 280.

[15] See, e.g., H. Trevor Colbourn, *The Lamp of Experience* (1965) or Pauline Maier, *From Resistance to Revolution* (1972) which is, in other respects, an excellent work.

[16] John Adams later made the same point in ("Novanglus") *Letters Addressed to the Inhabitants of the Colony of Massachusetts Bay,* letter of March 6, 1775.

of circular reasoning: Conceding the Parliament could regulate trade but not lay internal taxes, he set himself the question, "When is a regulation actually a disguised tax?" Answer: "When it has the impact of a tax." Q.E.D.

On the other side of the hill Soame Jenyns was a superb dialectician—indeed, at the risk of confiscation of goods and chattels and exile to Nova Scotia, I think his *The Objections to the Taxation of Our American Colonies . . . briefly consider'd* merits first prize in the trans-Atlantic dispute. But this exchange of polemics was at the fundamental level trivial because it burked the real issue, namely, who has the ultimate authority to draw the boundary lines between conflicting claims to sovereignty? Each side took for granted its right to define its own rights leaving an "Appeal to Heaven" (Locke's euphemism for war) as the inexorable solution.

The theoretical model perfectly designed for American use was that provided in John Locke's *Second Treatise* which combined legislative supremacy with majority rule. However, crucial to the employment of Locke's design was the determination that the provinces were the *units of sovereignty*. To turn the proposition around, before one proclaimed the sovereignty of the legislature, Parliament had to be expelled from the premises and replaced by the provincial assemblies. Once this feat was accomplished, the rest was easy: The King had betrayed his trusteeship and, *ipso facto*, destroyed his own claim to jurisdiction. George III, in short, was in revolt against the good people of Massachusetts, New York, et al., as represented in their sovereign legislatures. Note carefully the superbly functional character of this logic: It left the fabric of the community intact. Everything was distinctly *not* up for grabs.

Take New Hampshire, for example, where the colonial legislature in December 21, 1775, regretted that the Royal Governor John Wentworth had let them down by departing and promptly went on to write a constitution. They wasted no time establishing their jurisdiction: "We, the members of the Congress of New Hampshire, chosen and appointed by the free suffrages of the people of said colony, and authorized and empowered by them to meet together and use such means and pursue such measures as we should judge best for the public good; and in particular *to establish some form of government. . . ."*[17] (Italics added.)

But the application of Locke which doubtless had that worthy spinning in his grave was the Declaration of Independence. (Locke it might be recalled took a very dim view of the application of his doctrines against British parliamentary authority: When his disciple Thomas Molyneux applied the logic to Ireland [*Case of Ireland*, 1698], Locke disowned the argument completely.) The Declaration of Independence was a masterpiece of political warfare. An innocent observer reading its indictment of royal abuses would understandably tuck George III into the same category as Henry VIII or Elizabeth I—a Tudor monarch ravaging the rights of Englishmen. The authors of the Declaration were quite aware, of course, that the source of their discontent was not George III engaged in tyrannical use of the prerogative but the British Parliament. Yet Parliament *qua* Parliament was egregiously downgraded.

What we find are two references: 1) "He [George III] has combined with others to subject us to a jurisdiction foreign to *our constitution* (italics added), and unacknowledged by our laws; giving his assent to their acts of pretended legislation." And 2) "We have warned [our British brethren], from time to time, of attempts by their legislature to extend an unwarrantable jurisdiction over us." The implication of 1 is that Parliament was a kind of Star Chamber working in tandem with the King; the implication of 2 is that Parliament was simply the British equivalent of the Massachusetts Great and General Court, i.e., an "internal legislature."

This was a breath-taking application of the technique of *petitio principi,* of assuming one's conclusions in his premises and moving on from there. For once it was settled that George III stood in precisely the same relationship to the General Court in his capacity as King of Massachusetts Bay as he did to Parliament in his role as King of England, the ideological battle was won. All one now had to do was turn to Locke and find the appropriate citations for coping with a usurping executive; Sec-

[17] This and other citations can be found in the standard source, Francis N. Thorpe, ed. *The Federal and State Constitutions, Colonial Charters, and other Organic Laws of the United States of America* (Washington, 1907).

tion 238 of the *Second Treatise* was made to order. Asking himself in Section 237 when the people can resist a king, Locke replies that "The People therefore can never come by a Power over him, unless he does something that makes him cease to be a King." In Section 238 he elaborates an example: "When a King makes himself the dependent of another, and subjects his kingdom . . . and the People put free into his hands, to the Dominion of another." Thus when George III turned his American "kingdoms" over to "a jurisdiction foreign to our constitution," he automatically *unkinged himself*.

When I was young, and historians learned Latin tags instead of calculus, there were great controversies over the "legality" of these various American scenarios. The followers of Charles McIlwain were at daggers drawn with the acolytes of Robert Livingston Schuyler on whether the American Revolution was based on a correct or incorrect reading of various esoteric precedents—I recall wrestling for a week with the arcane intricacies of *Poyning's Case*. A quarter of a century later I look back on this exercise with some amusement for it is crystal clear that—with the exception of a few ill-fated skeptics—the Americans took the legality of their actions as a given in the equation.

In the formal sense, just about everything that happened from the Stamp Act Congress, the First and Second Continental Congresses onwards to the Federal Constitution was "illegal." Provincial legislatures converted themselves into state legislatures and constitutional conventions, or called for separate constitutional conventions, or (as in Connecticut and Rhode Island) simply made minor amendments in their colonial charters. As far as law enforcement was concerned, the various states provided that the common and statutory law of England should remain in force as altered by the legislature. Judges and juries—purged of course of Tories—continued their business. Fundamentally the definition of legality hinged on the outcome of the War: *inter arma leges silent*.

As was noted above, each of the newly independent states took action to provide formal legitimation for its jurisdiction. Since Gordon S. Wood has in *The Creation of the American Republic* provided us with a fascinating exploration of this period in what might be called the history of ideas metier, I will concentrate more on what the "Fathers" did than what they said. As anyone who has closely compared the work of the Constitutional Convention in Philadelphia with its *a posteriori* justification in *The Federalist* will suspect, there is no necessary connection between rhetoric and reality.

Putting aside for the time being the question of a "national" government, let us turn to the states—where until at least the mid-1780s lay the locus of action.[18] Since executive despotism had been the rationale for independence, it is hardly surprising that the states in their new constitutions virtually demolished executive power. The casual reader may be disconcerted by a recurring statement to the effect that "the legislative, executive and judiciary departments, shall be separate and distinct, so that neither exercises the powers that properly belong to the other" (Virginia, 1776). Similar formulations appeared elsewhere (e.g., Georgia, North Carolina) and it was finally cast in concrete by John Adams in the Massachusetts Constitution of 1780 (Section I, Article 30).

The "separation of powers" thus became enshrined as one of the fundaments of American constitutionalism, that is, until you take a closer look at those documents themselves. Then you realize with a shock that (with a few exceptions to be noted later) the new governments were built around a radical version of Locke's supreme legislative. True, as in Maryland, some checking and balancing could be introduced by the creation of a second *legislative* chamber. But these two houses elected the governor, denied him a veto, supervised his appointments, and the like. In short, we are dealing here with a parliamentary model. The so-called "radical" Pennsylvania Constitution of 1776 went even further: the executive was a body of twelve elected from various counties who, in conjunction with the unicameral legislature, chose a president from their number. Since the legislature retained the right to appoint all important officials, and the president had no veto, he was simply a figurehead.

[18] At this point let me note my indebtedness to my friend and former student, Fred L. Richardson, presently on the Political Science faculty at Ohio Wesleyan University. His unpublished doctoral dissertation, *Early American Political Authority* (1973) is the source of most of the specific material on state constitutions incorporated herein.

This catalogue could be continued at some length, but the crux of the matter is that except in Massachusetts and New York, there was nothing resembling an executive veto power (and in New York the governor's power was limited by a Council of Revision). Where the governors or presidents had appointing power, it was hedged about with legislative checks: in New York a Council of Appointments; in Massachusetts, the Governor's Council of nine "annually chosen . . . by the joint ballot of the Senators and Representatives assembled . . ." Only in Massachusetts, Rhode Island, Connecticut and New York was the governor publicly elected, which in political terms meant that he could develop an independent constituency. (New Hampshire revised its constitution in 1784 to include an elected "president," but circumscribed his authority far more strictly than that of his legislatively selected predecessor!) Most judges were chosen by legislative ballot, a purposeful break with British tradition which included them (as, indeed, did John Locke) in the executive category.

So much for the "separation of powers." It was a precept much honored but virtually ignored. It is interesting in this context to anticipate by noting that the Randolph Plan presented by James Madison to the Philadelphia Convention as the preliminary model for the new federal government was built around the total supremacy of the legislature.[19] (The Articles of Confederation created a legislative supremacist pseudogovernment, but its problems were of a different order: it had no power.)

The second major characteristic of the new state governments was their dedication to the principle of "power to the people." Again recall that the legitimacy of the legislative power in Locke rested on its representative character (Section 140, *Second Treatise*) and on the application of the majority principle (Section 96). Here the trick question had always been the majority of *whom?* That is, the extent of the political class to which the majority rule proposition was applied. Writing of the English electorate in the 1640s J. H. Plumb observed that "the situation in the counties as well as the boroughs had changed out of all

[19] See my "Founding Fathers," 55 *American Political Science Review* 799–816 (1961), pp. 804–5.

recognition from Elizabethan times, and we witness the birth of a political nation, small, partially controlled, but no longer coextensive with the will of the gentry."[20]

It is my contention that the Revolution legitimized the birth of a "political nation," that throughout the colonies-turned-states there was a great awakening of political consciousness. Indeed, in 1777 the Constitution of Georgia not only awarded the franchise to virtually every freeman but included a mandatory voting provision: "Every person absenting himself from an election, and shall neglect to give in his or their ballot at such election, shall be brought to a penalty not exceeding five pounds."!

Ultimate power lay in the "people" and every state constitution contained a more or less elaborate "Bill of Rights" or declaration of the residual jurisdiction of the populace. Plus certain procedural guarantees against arbitrary exercises of power. But, and this is vital, the underlying assumption was that these rights were to be protected from an arbitrary executive—few precautions were taken against what Tocqueville later described as the "tyranny of the majority," or more specifically, the tyranny of a representative legislature. Indeed, the bills of rights in a number of these early constitutions darkly warned against speaking "slanderously" of the government, i.e., the legislature!

The legislature was supreme and was kept on a very tight leash through the mechanism of short terms "to the End that those who are unfit for their Posts may be easily dropped, and such as are Worthy as they come on the stage Elected."[21] One almost visualizes the Rousseauistic ideal of the annual session of the community as a whole deciding whether or not to retain its governors. In point of fact this ideal had existed for over a century in the New England town meetings.

Moreover, the concept of instructions to legislators was common; that is, in its paradigmatic form, the town meeting of Barnstable or Belchertown, Massachusetts, had no reservations

[20] J. H. Plumb, "The Growth of the Electorate in England from 1600 to 1715," *Past and Present* (November 1969), pp. 90–116.

[21] Cited in Oscar and Mary Handlin, *The Popular Sources of Political Authority* (1966), p. 47. This is a fascinating collection of the materials that were published in the long controversy over the Massachusetts Constitution.

about telling its representatives in the General Court what to do,[22] and the same practice applied in other states. The Burkean view of the conscientious autonomy of the legislator was considered part and parcel of the "aristocratic" order. (It was perhaps on this ground that most constitutions barred clergymen from office-holding: There were real risks that men of the cloth would refuse to confuse *vox populi* with *vox Dei.*) State delegates to the Congress under the Articles of Confederation were, except in Rhode Island, Connecticut, and New Hampshire, chosen by the legislatures, and expected to get instructions from home: In essence, they were ambassadors.

On the eve of the Constitutional Convention, then, we can summarize the governmental situation in the United States in the following terms: The fiercely independent states had created governments on the unitary, parliamentary model with a supreme legislative and subordinate executive and judicial branches. That is, they implemented (with partial deviations here and there, notably in New York and Massachusetts) John Locke's ideal. Paradoxically, the American response to the growth of parliamentary power in Britain was to create in miniature precisely the system they saw as the source of their woes. At the "national" level, there was the United States government under the Articles which substantively had no power and procedurally also followed the parliamentary model: The Chairman of the Committee on Foreign Affairs was *de facto* Secretary of State.

I have elsewhere explored in considerable, even excruciating detail the political and social forces that led to the Federal Convention.[23] Suffice it for our purposes to say that the leading reformer, James Madison, wanted to enact a constitution that would incorporate the Lockian model. If anybody can find a trace of the "separation of powers" in the "Randolph Plan," he has second-sight. Not only did Madison's model establish a supreme legislative in the federal government, but it conferred decisive powers over the states. To make a long story short, what later emerged as the great American doctrine of "Federalism" was a set of improvisations, compromises between those dele-

[22] *Ibid.*
[23] Roche, "Founding Fathers."

gates who wanted to strengthen the center and those who felt that if they took Madison's plan home, they would probably be lynched.[24]

Eventually things worked out, the compromise was adopted by the popularly elected conventions, and Madison, Hamilton and Jay provided one of the great works of American political fiction, *The Federalist*. While all this was taking place, while the states were writing their constitutions and the war was winding along in its desultory fashion, what was the reaction of the "average" American? This is a lovely question because it is subject neither to proof, nor disproof, but my hunch is that—to revert to my original theme—he just went about his business (more accurately, his farming) with the unarticulated assumption that there was no great crisis. The elite (with few defectors) remained incredibly stable over a quarter of a century. Were they "radicals"? Were they "conservatives"? This strikes me as a foolish question, one based on the supposition that they had extensive access to the writings of Karl Marx and V. I. Lenin. Their sole concern was to maintain the social system: Their didactic descendants could figure out the appropriate labels.

[24] See my discussion of this and related matters in "Constitutional Law: Distribution of Powers" in the *International Encyclopedia of the Social Sciences* (1968).

John Marshall:
Major Opinions
and Other Writings

John Marshall's public career began in May 1775, when at age twenty he was appointed a lieutenant in the Virginia Militia. It ended sixty years later on July 6, 1835, when the Chief Justice of the United States slipped off peacefully to rejoin his generation. Between these dates there stretched a life of service unmatched, even in the remarkable elite which dominated the political destiny of the early Republic. Indeed, with the exception of John Quincy Adams of the next generation, it is difficult to find any American who has ever approximated Marshall's incredibly long and versatile performance as a public figure.

It is obviously impossible in a short essay to attempt more than the necessary minimum of biography. This is particularly true since Albert J. Beveridge published, with loving and monumental detail, his immense *Life of John Marshall*—a work which, despite its filiopietistic compulsions, remains a landmark in

From *John Marshall: Major Opinions and Other Writings*, edited by John P. Roche, copyright © 1967, by the Bobbs-Merrill Company, Inc., reprinted by permission of the publisher.

American biography.[1] Moreover, I have not thought it necessary to intrude into Marshall's private life, though in some respects his tenderness towards his clearly disturbed (if not psychotic) wife gives him greater stature as a man than his contributions to his country.

Indeed, reading his deeply moving letter to Justice Joseph Story describing the death of a child, and his efforts to shield his wife from the terrible shock, one suddenly realizes the depth and intensity of his private burdens. The letter also deserves extensive quotation for the light it throws on the anguish involved in raising children in the early years of the Republic.

"You ask me," he wrote Story[2]—who had just lost his ten year old daughter,

> if Mrs. Marshall and myself have ever lost a child. We have lost four, three of them bidding fairer for health and life than any that have survived them. One, a daughter about six or seven, was brought fresh to our minds by what you say of yours. She was one of the most fascinating children I ever saw. She was followed within a fortnight by a brother whose death was attended by a circumstance we can never forget. When the child was supposed to be dying I tore the distracted mother from the bedside. We soon afterwards heard a voice in the room which we considered as indicating the death of the infant [but he was] still breathing. . . . I concealed his being alive and prevailed upon [his mother] to take refuge with her mother. . . . The child lived two days, during which I was agonized with its condition and with the occasional hope . . . that I might enrapture his mother with the intelligence of his restoration to us.

When Mrs. Marshall refused to return to the house, Marshall wrote her a letter "in verse" with "a pressing invitation to return to me and her children." He tried to find a copy for Story, but it was "lost." His deep concern for his wife's precarious sanity was expressed time and again in his letters from France in 1798–99 to

---

[1] Albert J. Beveridge, *The Life of John Marshall,* 4 vols. (Boston and New York 1916–1920). The detail in this essay, unless otherwise cited, is drawn from Beveridge.

[2] See Marshall to Story, June 26, 1831, in Charles Warren, "The Story-Marshall Correspondence (1819–1831)," *William and Mary Quarterly,* Second Series, vol. XXI (1941), pp. 21–22.

his relatives in Richmond who were looking out for "Polly." John Marshall—to borrow Walton Hamilton's fine phrase—clearly deserves promotion from immortality to mortality.

THE FORMATIVE YEARS

John Marshall was born into Virginia politics. His father Thomas Marshall was a leading political figure in western Virginia, a member of the House of Burgesses from Fauquier County, sheriff of the county, principal vestryman of Leeds Parish, clerk of Dunmore County and captain of the militia. In a word, he was a magnate—a paradigm of the self-made frontier leader who rose to eminence on the implicit or explicit support of his neighbors, a member of the homemade elite which dominated the American countryside from Massachusetts to Georgia. Like his friends George Washington and Patrick Henry, Thomas Marshall responded automatically to British efforts to assert sovereignty over the colonies as usurpations of prescriptive rights; like Washington and Henry, it never entered his head that this was a "radical" response. He simply defined the "rights of Englishmen" as the status quo in Virginia—and drilled his militia company.

John Marshall, born on September 24, 1755, was the oldest of a family of fifteen children. Even the diligent Beveridge could discover little to say about his first twenty years except that he had a happy childhood and no significant formal education. Then the American Revolution began and Lieutenant Marshall went off to war with the Culpeper Minute Men—a march which for him was not to end until four years and many battles later. For when, in 1776, the Culpeper Minute Men were disbanded, John Marshall joined his father in the Third Virginia Regiment of the Continental Line. During the next three years he was with Washington's army, not—as in the state lines—on a temporary, come and go basis, but on a permanent footing. He spent the winter of 1777–78 at Valley Forge starving and freezing rather than retiring to his home for the winter, as did the state soldiers.

It is interesting to speculate on the impact of Continental service on Marshall, and on others who shared the fearful deprivations of Washington's standing army. Indeed, a fascinating study for statistical analysis would be the differences in political attitudes of Revolutionary veterans in terms of the forms their service took. It would be worthwhile, in particular, to see if there was any correlation in the 1780s between strong nationalism and service in the Continental Line. These soldiers bore the brunt of a war managed by ineffectual committees of an impotent Congress, and it would hardly be surprising if they had become, in every state, the carriers of a strong nationalist virus. In any case, this was clearly a strong formative influence on Captain John Marshall.

Discharged from the army, Marshall immediately determined upon a legal career and entered the College of William and Mary. He was to stay there only six weeks—long enough to get elected to the parent chapter of Phi Beta Kappa (presumably for academic potential!), do a little debating and a great deal of reflecting on the merits of marriage. With that talent for direct action which was to characterize his work on the bench, he went to Richmond and was granted a license to practice law, signed by his cousin Thomas Jefferson, the governor. On August 28, 1780 he was admitted to the Richmond bar.

Then, as now, law was the supreme access route to politics. Marshall apparently did not spend much time on his briefs, but he made up for it by winning election to the Virginia House of Delegates in the fall of 1782. The following January he married seventeen-year-old Mary Ambler, a marriage which, as Beveridge said, "was inspired exclusively by an all-absorbing love,"[3] but which had the adventitious benefit of an alliance with one of Virginia's wealthiest families. By 1785 Marshall had accumulated a substantial practice and, moving up the magnate's ladder, accumulated his second public office: city recorder of Richmond. His status was reinforced in 1786 when Edmund Randolph, upon election as governor, eliminated any conflict-of-interest problems by conveying his legal practice to the rising young attorney.[4]

From this point on, until he joined the Supreme Court, Marshall was a permanent fixture in Virginia politics. By all accounts he was a handsome, personable man with enormous charm. In addition, he had an invaluable political capacity (sorely lacking,

[3] Beveridge, *op. cit.*, vol. I, p. 170.
[4] *Ibid.*, p. 190.

for example, in Thomas Jefferson, John Adams and Alexander Hamilton): he was a magnificent listener. He rarely clashed head-on with opponents (his correspondence on political matters is notable for his tendency to agree in ambiguous terms with his correspondents, whatever their positions) and always moved to blur lines of clear confrontation. An efficient vote-getter on his own (particularly among veterans), he had also inherited his father's accumulated political capital when the latter moved to Kentucky, and in addition, he picked up some from his father-in-law, the state treasurer. This was a formidable aggregation and it was not surprising that eleven days after he entered the Virginia legislature, he was elected by joint ballot of the Senate and House to the Executive Council—a body with extensive executive powers, particularly over appointments to office. However, in accepting this position he seems to have overextended his political lines by moving too far too fast; he shortly was attacked by some of the old magnates (notably Edmund Pendleton) for his lack of experience, and he resigned. He immediately was re-elected to his seat in the House, even though he no longer lived in the county, and he settled in as a legislator.

The Marshall who emerged from the 1780s was a figure who would have been easily recognizable to the late Sir Lewis Namier, or to any who have read Namier's great studies of the structure of British politics in the eighteenth century.[5] In 1785, for example, Marshall decided not to run for the legislature; in 1786 he chose to re-enter the General Assembly and was elected from a different county. In the legislature, he was a firm national-ist who fought consistently against Virginia laws contravening the Treaty of Paris—notably those which, in effect, made it impossible for private British creditors to collect their pre-Revolutionary debts. He was, of course, a strong supporter of all efforts to invigorate the central government, that infirm, impotent creation of the Articles of Confederation.

Because he was not addicted to political metaphysics, Marshall never prepared for posterity a precise justification of his variety

[5] See Sir Lewis Namier, *The Structure of Politics at the Accession of George III,* 2nd ed. (London, 1957): and *England in the Age of the American Revolution,* 2nd ed. (London, 1961).

of nationalism. It has been suggested that he was basically a spokesman for the mercantile interests—the Richmond "capitalists" and land speculators to whom he was related both by family connections and economic interest. This, however, is of little analytical value: if the Richmond "capitalists" wanted a strong national market and credit structure, they had no economic interest in the enforcement of that part of the Treaty of Paris which validated their pre-Revolutionary debts to British merchants. Marshall was squarely for both.

Normally in politics—as William of Ockham suggested centuries ago—the simplest explanation of behavior is the most likely to be correct. In this spirit, it would appear that the decisive basis of Marshall's nationalism was his military experience and his worship of Washington. Like the General (whose life he would later write in the best "lives of the saints" tradition), Marshall felt that American international impotence was a standing invitation to aggression and perhaps division. Only a strong central government could assert and defend America's sovereignty in the Hobbesian international forum.

Marshall was a vigorous nationalist, but he had that singular political talent which makes it possible for a man to be strong-willed without being provocative. A case in point was his role in passing the resolution by which the Virginia legislature in the fall of 1787 summoned a state convention to deal with the newly written Constitution of the United States. Virginia was a key state and at the Constitutional Convention the Virginia delegation had ended up in total disarray: George Mason had flatly refused to sign alleging that to do so would be an act of treason; James Madison, who had wanted a stronger frame of government, signed and organized support; the influential governor, Edmund Randolph, also refused to put his name on the document and explained his action in Delphic terms. Back in Virginia, Patrick Henry, who had "smelt a rat" and refused to attend the convention in the first place (he appears to have believed that his archenemy Thomas Jefferson was behind the project!), was organizing his forces to defeat ratification. Before the decision was finally made one way or the other, there was obviously to be some rough play in Virginia.

The legislative resolution creating the state ratifying convention was the first stage, and the legislators immediately began to polarize in terms of their substantive views on the new Constitution. The proconstitutionalists introduced a resolution calling on the ratifying convention to say either "yes" or "no" without qualifications. Henry and his allies, who were trying to stall, hoped to have the state convention equivocate, offer amendments as a prerequisite for endorsement, perhaps call for a second Constitutional Convention. After the debate had waxed hot and heavy, Marshall rose and performed a masterpiece of political magic: he agreed with everybody who had spoken—to some extent—and disagreed somewhat with the opinions on both sides—to some extent. He then proposed a compromise resolution of his own, "that a Convention should be called and that the new Constitution should be laid before them for their free and ample discussion."[6] There was a great sigh of relief (neither side seems to have felt confident of clear victory) and Marshall's resolution passed "unanimously."

The battlefield was now shifted from the legislature to the ratifying convention itself, and the proconstitutional forces organized energetically and effectively. The delegates to this convention were elected by the people, but one should not assume that the electorate polarized on the same basis as the magnates. Indeed, each side picked as candidates its leading figures, whom the people were accustomed to designating as their political surrogates; and each side used its most distinguished prospects in districts that were doubtful. As Beveridge said, "the people simply would not vote against such men as Pendleton, Wythe, and Carrington."[7] Marshall was handed the particularly difficult task of contesting Henrico County (Richmond) where anticonstitutional opinion was allegedly very strong. The people voted him in, along with Governor Randolph (still believed to be opposed to the Constitution) and the militantly anticonstitutional George Mason! The populace seems to have operated on a quite sensible, division-of-labor principle: send the best men to the Convention and let them fight it out among themselves.

The proceedings of the Virginia Convention remain today a

[6] Beveridge, *ibid.*, pp. 246–247.
[7] Beveridge, *ibid.*, p. 359.

fascinating document. Except for Washington and Jefferson, all the notables were there, operating in an intimate political universe. Each had a political history, a few running back twenty-five years, and the others were fully aware of all of the details and quite prepared to point out inconsistencies in behavior. Patrick Henry completed a sonorous discourse on the evils of arbitrary government, for example, and was promptly asked to explain his dictatorial behavior in the case of Josiah Philips, an alleged Tory bandit whom Governor Henry, in 1778, had moved against by a bill of attainder. (The bill of attainder itself was drafted by a member of the legislature named Thomas Jefferson!)[8]

This is hardly the place for an extensive analysis of the Virginia Convention; suffice it to say that the constitutionalists clearly outmaneuvered their opponents, forced them into impossible political positions, and won narrowly.[9] The Virginia Convention could serve as a classic study in effective floor management: Patrick Henry had to be contained, and a reading of the debates discloses a standard two-stage technique. Henry would give a four- or five-hour speech denouncing some section of the Constitution on every conceivable ground. (The federal district, he averred at one point, would become a haven for convicts escaping from state authority!) When Henry had subsided, "Mr. Lee of Westmoreland" would rise and literally poleaxe him with sardonic invective. When Henry complained about the militia power, "Lighthorse Harry" really punched below the belt, observing that while the former governor had been sitting in Richmond during the Revolution, *he* had been out in the trenches with the troops and thus felt better qualified to discuss military affairs. "It was my fortune to be a soldier of my country. . . . I saw what the honorable gentleman did not see—our men fighting. . . ."[10]

[8] See Leonard W. Levy, *Jefferson and Civil Liberties: The Darker Side* (Cambridge, Mass., 1963), p. 33.

[9] The discussion of the Virginia Ratifying Convention here is adopted from "The Founding Fathers: A Reform Caucus in Action," in John P. Roche, *Shadow and Substance: Studies in the Theory and Structure of Politics* (New York, 1964).

[10] See Jonathan Elliot, *The Debates in the Several State Conventions on the Adoption of the Federal Constitution*, vol. III, p. 178 (Washington, 1836).

Then the gentlemanly constitutionalists (Madison, Pendleton and Marshall) would pick up the matters at issue and examine them in the light of reason.

Marshall had performed nobly in the convention and, once the new national government was established, President Washington moved to reward him for his labors. He was offered the post of United States Attorney for Virginia immediately after the Judiciary Act, creating the structure of federal law enforcement, was passed. Inexplicably Marshall rejected the office and, after another year's absence, chose to run again for the Virginia legislature. Without detailing his record, it is clear that any time Marshall ran for anything in Henrico County, he was safely elected. If he chose not to run—perhaps in the interest of building his private practice—the Richmond electorate kept the spot warm for his next appearance.

This personal political stature was quite remarkable, particularly as Virginia politics became riven by ferocious factionalism with the antinationalists clearly in command. Part of it arose simply from his personality which made it possible for George Mason to refer to Marshall as "an intimate friend of mine" at a time when he was bitterly fighting Marshall's views on the constitutionality of Hamilton's assumption of state debts.[11] But part of it also derived from Marshall's astute political posture, comparable in our time to that of New York Republicans such as Jacob Javits. While holding his strategic position firmly, Marshall's political tactic was always to roll with the punches: he never became an isolated nationalist ideologue.

When the Virginia legislature, led by Henry, took up a resolution denouncing the assumption of state debts, for example, Marshall did not enter an unconditional defense of assumption. Denying Henry's contention that assumption was unconstitutional, Marshall and his nationalist colleagues introduced an amendment decrying assumption as unjust to Virginia and inexpedient for the nation. (He was to employ this same tactic later on with respect to the Sedition Act of 1798.) This might not have been music to the ears of Alexander Hamilton in New York, but Marshall's constituency was in Virginia. A letter from Jefferson to

11 Beveridge, *op. cit.*, vol. II, p. 78.

Madison in 1792 suggests that Hamilton understood the realities of Virginia politics and provides an insight into Jefferson's *modus operandi*. Noting that Hamilton hoped Marshall would run for Congress in Richmond, Jefferson wrote: "I am told that Marshall has expressed half a mind to come. Hence I conclude that Hamilton has played him well with flattery and solicitation, and I think that nothing better could be done than to make him a judge."[12] Although Jefferson was referring to a state judgeship, there is—in the light of later events—a certain historical irony in the proposal.

By 1796 "General" Marshall (of the Virginia militia) was clearly the leading proadministration spokesman in Virginia. American politics was dominated by the struggle between the emergent Jeffersonians and Federalists which had been precipitated, though not caused, by the arguments over foreign relations centering on the Jay Treaty. Washington had unsuccessfully tried to bring Marshall into the Cabinet as Attorney General in 1795, and in 1796 he offered him the ticklish post of Minister to France. But Marshall showed great reluctance about leaving Richmond and his most successful legal career. He did, however, carry the burden of defending Washington and his policies in the hostile environment of the Virginia legislature, though—in the best tradition of the legal profession—he did not permit his public position on the treaty power to deter him from acting as counsel for a group of debtors who challenged the supremacy of the Treaty of Paris over Virginia legislation which had relieved them of their private obligations to British merchants. Marshall lost in the Supreme Court—*Ware* v. *Hylton*, 1796[13]—and, unfortunately, we do not know whether he rejoiced in his public capacity or grieved in his professional role.

Marshall's long-delayed entrance to national political life occurred in 1797 when President Adams named him one of the three envoys to negotiate a détente with the French Republic. French leaders had been infuriated by the Jay Treaty and had retaliated by authorizing privateers to prey on American shipping and by insulting the new American Minister, Charles Cotesworth

[12] Beveridge, *ibid.,* p. 80.
[13] 3 Dallas 199.

Pinckney. With Marshall in the delegation were Pinckney and the unpredictable Elbridge Gerry of Massachusetts (inventor of the "Gerrymander"), a Jeffersonian by persuasion but a personal friend of Adams who had cast his electoral vote for the latter.

The negotiations, which lasted into the spring of 1798, were a shambles with overtones of *opera bouffe*. The French Directory, whose general Napoleon Bonaparte was unrivalled in the field of battle, was itself unrivalled in political corruption. The Americans found themselves in a Kafkaesque environment: in and out of their lodging flitted the three incredible agents of Talleyrand the French Foreign Minister, who have lived on in history as "X, Y and Z." It was suggested that France could be bribed to end its depredations on American commerce; but before the Americans could get the opportunity to consent to this bribe, they had to pay antecedent bribes to get the French in the right mood. Marshall and Pinckney carried the burden of these non-negotiations, and the former patiently recorded their travail in dispatches to President Adams. They flatly refused to pay the antecedent bribes and told the French that they had no authority to make a "loan" (the form of the major bribe was the purchase by the United States of worthless Dutch securities at par value— a fraudulent "loan"). After interminable discussions with X, Y and Z and utterly inconclusive, brief talks with Talleyrand, capped by threats of further French hostility, Marshall and Pinckney decided to terminate the farce. The French cooperated by ordering them out of the country, keeping the more pliable Gerry around in the hope of dividing the mission. Pinckney's daughter was ill, and he was permitted to take her to southern France for recuperation. On April 24, 1798 Marshall sailed home alone.

On June 18, 1798 he arrived in Philadelphia a national hero. The background for this was the greatest political miscalculation of Thomas Jefferson's career. Convinced that Adams was pro-British and that the negotiations in Paris were a masquerade, aimed in no way at reaching an understanding with the French, the Jeffersonians denounced the President as a warmonger. They drummed up pro-French and anti-British feeling. In March, Adams, having received Marshall's first dispatches, suddenly informed Congress that the nation should prepare for war with

France, and his opponents went into a frenzy: Vice President Jefferson referred to his chief's message as "insane."[14] Amazingly sure of their ground, the Jeffersonians demanded the full publication of the dispatches; after some delay, Adams transmitted them in full to Congress (disguising the French agents as X, Y and Z).

As the stunned Jeffersonians—caught in a paradigmatic self-gambit—took cover, public opinion rose in a tidal wave of anti-French sentiment. James Morton Smith has given us a superb description of this period and of Alexander Hamilton's program for using the surge of chauvinism to dispose of the Jeffersonian party and fortify the Federalists in power.[15] Marshall's tumultuous welcome was from a political viewpoint completely justified: he had provided the instrument with which it seemed the growing Republican movement could be annihilated. President Adams promptly offered him a position on the Supreme Court vacated by the death of James Wilson, but Marshall, who was in financial difficulties arising from his land speculation, felt he could not afford to leave his practice.

He could, however, run for the House of Representatives without what we today would call conflict-of-interest problems, and the Virginia Federalists implored him to make the race in Richmond. A Marshall victory in the Jeffersonian heartland would be a real Federalist accomplishment—and no one else could possibly achieve it. Marshall agreed and promptly had the Alien and Sedition Laws (passed in the summer of 1798) as a political albatross draped around his neck. Madison, with Jefferson's urging, returned from Congress to the Virginia legislature to lead the struggle against the Federalist repressive statutes. The outcome was, of course, the Virginia Resolutions declaring the federal laws unconstitutional (and the similar Kentucky Resolutions secretly penned by Jefferson).

Marshall, as was his custom, avoided a total confrontation with Jeffersonian power. Much to the chagrin of New England Federalist ideologues, the Federalist candidate in Richmond engaged in some intricate broken-field running. In the Virginia legislature

---

[14] Beveridge, *ibid.*, p. 336.

[15] See his *Freedoms' Fetters: The Alien and Sedition Laws and American Civil Liberties* (Ithaca, N.Y., 1956).

(apparently aided by his close friend and ally General Henry Lee) he drafted the "Address of the Minority" which—at tedious length—dealt with the Virginia Resolutions[16]; in his congressional fight he answered a series of questions put to him by "Freeholder."[17] The gist of his views was that while the Alien and Sedition Laws were constitutional, they were unnecessary—a strategic affirmation of federal power, yet it enabled him to avoid defending the specific, and in Virginia highly unpopular, statutes. Fisher Ames fumed and called Marshall "the meanest of cowards"[18]; Theodore Sedgwick said he had "degraded himself by a mean and paltry electioneering trick"[19]—but they were writing in Massachusetts. The important consideration in Virginia was that in April 1799, when the congressional election was held in Richmond, John Marshall won by 108 votes. This was a bad year for the Jeffersonians in Virginia—they won only eleven of the nineteen seats in the House of Representatives. Anticipating trouble in the presidential election of 1800, Madison hastily pushed through the Virginia legislature a statute shifting from the "district" to the "at-large" system of choosing presidential electors.

The Sixth Congress met on December 2, 1799, and Marshall was soon launched on his abbreviated congressional career; it was to last barely six months. Marshall followed the habits of a lifetime in politics: strategically a good Federalist, he reserved the right to tactical independence. He refused to endorse the Sedition Act and played a vital role in destroying the prize creation of the high Federalists: the Disputed Elections Bill. This was a measure, passed by the Senate, establishing a Grand Committee to determine all contests in presidential elections (it resembled the commission established after the election of 1876 and doubtless would have fulfilled the same partisan function). It was particularly designed with an eye to the tight Pennsylvania situation, where a legislature in which each party held one house would have the task of choosing the electors. Marshall proposed a substitute which converted the commission, in es-

16 See Document 4, *infra*.
17 See Document 3, *infra*.
18 Beveridge, *ibid.*, p. 391.
19 *Ibid.*

sence, into an investigating committee without final jurisdiction, and his views were endorsed by the House. When Senate and House could not reach agreement, the measure vanished into limbo. The disgusted Speaker of the House, Sedgwick (who had never trusted Marshall's ideological credentials) accused Marshall of "dissipating our majority" which "never could again be compacted."[20]

The Federalists, temporarily triumphant, were in fact sitting on a time bomb, John Adams by name; by profession, President of the United States. In the spring of 1800, Adams discovered that Alexander Hamilton had been quietly running his administration, caucusing privately with his Cabinet and playing *deus ex machina* for the Federalist leadership in Congress. The bomb went off in May: Adams summarily fired Secretary of War James McHenry and Secretary of State Timothy Pickering and offered Marshall first the war department (which he refused) and then the state department. After some meditation, Marshall accepted in June the Secretaryship of State and entered Adams' Cabinet. Marshall had always been interested in foreign policy; his most enduring speech in the House of Representatives had dealt with the Robins/Nash case and had been a masterful presentation of the role of the President in the conduct of foreign relations.

The Federalist *gotterdämmerung*—which enlivened the election year 1800—has been analyzed in detail by Manning J. Dauer and we need not linger on the details.[21] Suffice it for our purposes to say that Marshall managed to retain simultaneously the confidence of John Adams and Alexander Hamilton; as Secretary of State he went his own way, performed his hardly burdensome functions admirably, and (as far as one can discover) avoided the savage civil war which was racking the Federalists. As a result, on January 20, 1801, when Adams nominated Marshall Chief Justice of the United States, there was no controversy among the Federalists: he formally took office on February 4, but agreed to stay on as Secretary of State for the remainder of Adams' term. While he accepted only the salary of the Chief Justice ($4,000), his work that last month was exclusively in the

[20] Beveridge, *ibid.*, p. 457.
[22] See *The Adams Federalists* (Baltimore, 1953).

partisan, political sphere—he was industriously sealing the commissions of lame-duck Federalist appointees including, of course, the famous "midnight judges."

THE CHIEF JUSTICE

On March 4, 1801, the new Chief Justice performed his first official act in that capacity: He administered the oath of office to Thomas Jefferson as President of the United States. It was an ironic confrontation for in Henry Adams' words Marshall ". . . nourished one weakness. Pure in life; broad in mind, and the despair of bench and bar for the unswerving certainty of his legal method; almost idolized by those who stood nearest him, and loving warmly in return,—this excellent and amiable man clung to one rooted prejudice: he detested Thomas Jefferson. He regarded with quiet, unspoken, but immovable antipathy the character and doings of the philosopher standing before him, about to take the oath to preserve, protect, and defend the Constitution. No argument or entreaty affected his conviction that Jefferson was not an honest man."[22] It need hardly be added that Jefferson reciprocated these sentiments in full.

It would be superfluous here to enlarge on Marshall's career as Chief Justice, at least in its legal dimensions. However, a few things might be highlighted to throw his accomplishments into sharper perspective. First of all, it should be noted how the strategy of his opinions was derived from his political posture: He invariably seized the high ground with unnerving aplomb, and then he became extremely wary and flexible in his tactics.

The case of *United States* v. *Judge Peters*[23] is a good example of this technique and, since it is often cited as an early demolition of the states'-rights concept of "interposition" and is impossible to edit meaningfully, let us examine Marshall in action.

The Court was confronted by a particularly vitriolic clash between Pennsylvania and the federal judiciary which arose when Richard Peters, United States District Judge in Philadelphia, set aside a decision of the Pennsylvania admiralty court.

[22] Henry Adams, *History of the United States of America During the Administration of Thomas Jefferson,* vol. I, p. 194 (New York, 1889).
[23] 6 Cranch 114 (1809).

The State tribunal had in 1778 awarded a prize to one set of litigants, but its decision then was overruled in favor of Gideon Olmstead by the Court of Commissioners of Appeals in Prize cases—the only national court established under the Articles of Confederation.

Pennsylvania simply ignored the appellate decision asserting that the Court of Commissioners had exceeded its statutory *vires* when it overturned a jury determination in the Pennsylvania court. The problem vanished into limbo for the next fifteen years.

The circumstances under which this litigation again surfaced between 1803 and 1809 defy brief analysis. They are fully described in the introduction to the Supreme Court decision and by Charles Warren.[24] The net outcome was that in 1803 Judge Peters reaffirmed the validity of the earlier appellate holding, favoring Olmstead, which brought the federal court into a head-on collision with the militantly Jeffersonian state authorities.[25]

Governor McKean of Pennsylvania immediately mobilized state power to frustrate Peters' judgment, with the state legislature passing a law (designed to inject the Eleventh Amendment as a barrier to federal jurisdiction) vesting the funds at issue in the state treasurer, David Rittenhouse. Olmstead then went to the Supreme Court for a *mandamus* requiring Peters to execute his judgment—that cautious jurist had been stalling with the obvious hope that a compromise could be effected—and in 1808 the writ was granted. Peters then informed the high court that "an act of the legislature of Pennsylvania had commanded the governor . . . to call out an armed force to prevent the execution of any process."

In 1809, the Supreme Court had to meet the issue squarely. Marshall drew upon his resources and wrote an opinion which, first, asserted the supremacy of national law; second, held that —properly understood—there was no conflict between the federal government and Pennsylvania because; third, David Rittenhouse was holding the funds in dispute in his *private*, not public, capacity.

Despite the actual ground of the holding, Marshall's opinion

[24] Charles Warren, *The Supreme Court in United States History*, rev. ed., vol I (Boston, 1947), pp. 374–387.
[25] *Op. cit.*, fn. 23.

has been cited ever since for one majestic (and decisionally irrelevant) paragraph:

> If the legislatures of the several states may, at will, annul the judgments of the Courts of the United States, and destroy the rights acquired under those judgments, the Constitution itself becomes a solemn mockery, and the nation is deprived of the means of enforcing its laws. . . .

The *Cohens* case[26] is another model of this technique, and *Marbury* v. *Madison*[27] ranks close to it. (Chief Justice Earl Warren has been criticized for the ambiguity of some of his constitutional holdings, but compared to Marshall, Warren is a model of precision.) It must be remembered that Marshall spent the years 1801–1835 on the Court with no hope of reinforcement from the ranks of the Federalists—and he dissented in only nine decisions![28]

Which is not to say that he always concurred with his brethren; in 1827 he noted in one of his rare dissents (*Bank of United States* v. *Dandridge*)[29] that it was his normal policy when in disagreement to "acquiesce silently" in the Court's opinion. Concerned as he was with the Court's role and status in American life, he was apparently convinced that unanimity helped to maintain the standing of the Justices among the people. Moreover, as one might suspect, he was characterologically disinclined to lead quixotic charges on a lost battlefield. He saved his energy and logic for more favorable occasions, and—in personal terms—he banked a certain amount of credit with fellow Justices who appreciated his silence.

The secret of Marshall's success was his remarkable talent as a committee chairman, a small-group manager. One new Justice after another was appointed to the Court by the Virginia dynasty, and each seemed to vanish into Marshall's sector of influence. In 1822, Thomas Jefferson irately pointed this out to his first appointee, Justice William Johnson, denouncing the practice of unanimous opinions as "convenient for the lazy, the

---

[26] 6 Wheaton 264 (1821).
[27] 1 Cranch 137 (1803).
[28] Warren, *op. cit.*, vol. I, p. 813, fn. 2.
[29] 12 Wheaton 64, 90.

modest and the incompetent."[30] To a Virginia friend, the ex-President wrote on the same theme: "An opinion is huddled up in conclave, perhaps by a majority of one, delivered as if unanimous, and with the silent acquiescence of lazy or timid associates, by a crafty chief judge, who sophisticates the law to his mind, by the turn of his own reasoning."[31] Johnson, in reply, gave a very frank explanation of Marshall's influence. Explaining that he had not found the Court a "bed of roses," Johnson recounted his experience when he joined the bench in 1804:

> Some case soon occurred in which I differed from my brethren, and I thought it a thing of course to deliver my opinion. But, during the rest of the session I heard nothing but lectures on the indecency of judges cutting at each other, and the loss of reputation which the Virginia appellate court had sustained by pursuing such a course. At length I found that I must either submit to circumstances or become such a cypher in our consultations as to effect no good at all. I therefore bent to the current. . . .[32]

In a small room with his six (five until 1807) colleagues, Marshall's personal charm was most effective. Moreover, in that era—with Washington still a primitive administration capital—the Justices of the Supreme Court tended to live an almost monastic existence, sharing rooms in a boarding house, eating together, attending the same social functions. Moreover, in this close and familiar context, Marshall moved as the dominant figure for that greatest of all reasons, the timeless foundation of committee leadership: he was willing to do most of the work. Various studies have yielded slightly different figures, but Charles Warren's computation was that "between 1801 and 1835, there were 62 decisions involving constitutional questions in 36 of which Marshall wrote the opinion; . . . Of a total of 1215 cases during that period, in 94, no opinions were filed; in 15 the decision was by the court; and in the remaining 1106 Marshall

[30] Jefferson to Johnson, October 27, 1822, cited in Donald G. Morgan, *Justice William Johnson* (Columbia, S.C., 1954), p. 169.

[31] Jefferson to Thomas Ritchie, December 25, 1820, cited by Morgan, *ibid.*, p. 172.

[32] Johnson to Jefferson, December 10, 1882, cited by Morgon, *ibid.*, p. 181.

delivered the opinion in 519. . . . In the same period there were 195 cases involving questions of international law or in some way affecting international relations. In 80 of these, the opinion was delivered by Marshall. . . ."[33] In short, the Chief Justice was a prodigious worker whose personal virtues and willingness to carry the burden of writing opinions probably played a greater role in his dominance than the logic of his views.

In any event, he found a Supreme Court which in 1801 existed on the margin of American political consciousness. One Chief Justice had used the position as a launching pad in his candidacy for governor of New York—John Jay ran and lost in 1792; in 1795, he was successful and resigned from the Court. Jay's successor, John Rutledge, was refused confirmation by the Senate, apparently on the ground that he was mentally deranged; and Washington's next two nominees, Patrick Henry and William Cushing (the latter an Associate Justice), refused the honor. Marshall's immediate predecessor, Oliver Ellsworth, followed another of Jay's precedents in accepting a concurrent diplomatic assignment abroad, and while in France as Minister resigned both positions on grounds of health.[34] President Adams then offered Jay his old post—and the latter was in fact approved by the Senate—but Jay rejected it because, as he put it, "I left the Bench perfectly convinced that under a system so defective, it would not obtain the energy, weight, and dignity which are essential to its affording due support to the National Government, nor acquire the public confidence and respect which, as the last resort of the justice of the nation, it should possess."[35]

Marshall thus moved into a judicial vacuum and in thirty-five years converted the Supreme Court from an object of derision, even contempt, to a major coordinate agency of the national government. He did not—as both admirers and critics have maintained—run the country, and he was quite capable of cutting his losses and liquidating his liabilities when the political pressure became too heavy. Indeed, one has the distinct impression that the Chief Justice put a considerable amount of energy and ingenuity into skirting the most explosive constitutional issue

[33] Warren, *op. cit.*, p. 813, fn. 2.
[34] *Ibid.*, pp. 124–172.
[35] *Ibid.*, p. 173.

of the era: the status of the slave and the legal position of slavery in American law. He had no reluctance to assault the states' rights doctrine, and in his *Cohens* opinion (written against a background of the congressional debates over slavery in the territories) Marshall deprecated "sections." But on slavery itself, the root of so much constitutional controversy, the Chief Justice refused to be drawn:

> It appears that he regretted the existence of slavery, feared the result of it, saw no way of getting rid of it, but hoped to lessen the evil by colonizing in Africa such free black people as were willing to go there. . . . He was far more concerned that the Union should be strengthened, and dissension in Virginia quieted, than he was over the problem of human bondage, of which he saw no solution.[36]

In this connection, Marshall's circumspect handling of the Virginia law barring free Negroes from entering the state[37] should be compared with Justice Johnson's head-on collision with the South Carolina authorities over a similar statute, which the Justice (also on Circuit) declared to be an unconstitutional intrusion on interstate and foreign commerce (*Elkison* v. *Deliesseline*, 1823).[38]

As the years went by, the Supreme Court became more and more established as a principal instrument of the national government. Partly this arose from the singular stability of Court membership. During Marshall's tenure as Chief Justice, four other members of the bench served for more than twenty years: Todd, Duval, Story and Washington. And a fifth, Livingston, served for seventeen years. In the fifteen-year period 1811–1826, only *one* vacancy occurred, and that in 1823. After 1827 this pattern of continuity was disrupted, but the Court had taken full advantage of its homogeneity and had become a "traditional" entity in its own right.

So had the Chief Justice, who was in his person something of a historical monument. As we have seen, Marshall was always a political "loner," and once elevated to the Court he largely dis-

---

[36] Beveridge, *op. cit.*, vol. IV, pp. 478–479.
[37] Brig Wilson v. U.S. (1820).
[38] 8 Fed. Cas. 493, No. 4366.

engaged himself from Virginia politics and from the fortunes of the dispirited and declining Federalists. His closest friends were, however, drawn from the ranks of hard-core Federalism, and it appears that in the period 1807–1812—when the embargo and related enforcement measures brought sections of New England into open insurrection against federal authority—these friends cherished the hope that Marshall would run against Madison for President.[39] The Chief Justice was strongly opposed to the foreign policy of the Virginia dynasty and doubtless considered himself adequately equipped for the presidency, but his characteristic caution led him to express his critical views only in correspondence. In fact, Marshall was so closed-mouthed that his long-time friend James Monroe, Secretary of State when war was declared in 1812, communicated with him on the apparent assumption that the Chief Justice was a supporter of administration policy vis-à-vis Great Britain![40] The presidential boomlet that Pickering and others were promoting never gained any headway.

In terms of judicial politics—and Marshall was incapable of thinking in other than political terms—this policy of nonintervention was soundly conceived. The ambitious dabbling of early Chief Justices had undoubtedly contributed to the low opinion of the Court which prevailed throughout the first decade. A Supreme Court that was prepared to confront state power in Virginia, Pennsylvania, Maryland, Ohio and Kentucky on basic substantive issues had to imitate Caesar's wife. Any partisan political activities on the part of the Justices would merely arm the enemies of their doctrines. In fact, Marshall—like an old-fashioned, regular army officer—did not vote in presidential elections after 1804 (with the possible exception of 1828).[41] He apparently regretted his one venture into public controversy: a series of three articles in the Philadelphia *Union* in April 1819 (by "A Friend of the Union") defending his *McCulloch* holding against the savage attack of Chief Justice Spencer Roane of Virginia.[42] (At least he refused to send a copy of the series—it

[39] Beveridge, *op. cit.*, pp. 30–35.
[40] *Ibid.*, p. 41.
[41] *Ibid.*, pp. 462, 464.
[42] *Ibid.*, pp. 318–320.

was "mangled" by the editor, he said—to Justice Story and refused the latter's request that it be republished in Boston.[43])

While not playing any active political role in Virginia, Marshall did on occasion undertake various assignments: In 1812, for example, he vanished into the wilderness of western Virginia as the head of a body of commissioners to survey a route through the mountains. (The Chesapeake and Ohio Railroad later followed roughly the path he surveyed.[44]) In 1829, he participated (with former Presidents James Madison and James Monroe) in the Virginia Constitutional Convention, where—joined interestingly enough by Madison on most substantive issues!—he played an active and thoroughly conservative role.[45]

Toward the end of his career, with Jacksonian Justices driving him even to dissent, Marshall became somewhat despondent; but he never relaxed his efforts to assert the supremacy of the Constitution as he read it, whether over contumacious states or an arrogant President. There was poignant symbolism in the three dissents "from the grave" that his old friend and ideological twin, Joseph Story, registered in 1837 on behalf of his dead chief (*New York* v. *Miln,*[46] *Charles River Bridge* v. *Warren Bridge,*[47] *Briscoe* v. *Bank of Kentucky*[48]). John Marshall was no longer merely a judge; he was an incarnation of American constitutionalism, one whose views on public law should be enshrined (Story believed) despite his departure from the bench.

In the immediate sense, Story failed, but in the long view the shade of John Marshall has hovered over the growth of judicial power in the United States. Whatever his opinions on the merits of anti-New Deal decisions might have been, Marshall would surely have chuckled as that brilliant judicial politician, Charles Evans Hughes, demolished Franklin D. Roosevelt's "court pack-

---

[43] *Ibid.,* p. 322. (Since this was written, Professor Gerald Gunther, a superb historical detective, has uncovered the original Marshall articles. See 21 *Stanford Law Review* 449 [1969].)

[44] *Ibid.,* pp. 42–45.

[45] *Ibid.,* pp. 467–507.

[46] 11 Peters 102.

[47] 11 Peters 420.

[48] 11 Peters 257.

ing" plan. American constitutional law, he recognized, was in some of its aspects more a body-contact sport than a jurisprudential exercise; and Hughes alone among subsequent Chief Justices has approximated Marshall's tactical skill.

Finally, what Justice would not agree with the ironic Virginian that the "acme of judicial distinction means the ability to look a lawyer straight in the eyes for two hours and not hear a damned word he says?"[49]

[49] Beveridge, *op. cit.*, pp. 82–83.

Entrepreneurial Liberty and the Fourteenth Amendment

IN THE LAST QUARTER of the nineteenth century and well on into the twentieth, so the legend runs, the United States was dominated by a "conservative," "individualist," *laissez-faire* elite which succeeded in rewriting the Constitution and notably the Fourteenth Amendment to impose its ideology upon the nation. This notion has a certain superficial persuasiveness, but regrettably it is hardly sustained by a close analysis of the history of the period. There was clearly an elite of businessmen, but it was neither ruggedly individualistic, in terms of classic liberal economic thought, nor "conservative," in any acceptable definition of that much-abused term. On the contrary, this elite lived at the public trough, was nourished by state protection and devoted most of its time and energies to evading Adam Smith's individualistic injunctions. In ideological terms, it was totally opportunistic: It demanded and applauded vigorous state action in

Reprinted, with permission, from *Labor History*, IV (1963), 3–31 (University of Massachusetts).

behalf of its key values, and denounced state intervention in behalf of its enemies. The Constitution was not, in short, adapted to the needs of *laissez-faire* "conservatism"—which is a respectable, internally consistent system of political economy—but to the exigent needs of the great private governments. The "Robber Barons" had no ideology, they had interests. They had no theory of the state, but they knew what they wanted from it. Their key value, entrepreneurial liberty, might require a strong state one day (to combat trade unions) and a weak state the next (which would not pass wage and hour legislation), and this inconsistency troubled them not. If some scribe wanted to make them into "industrial statesmen," or "pillars of conservatism," that was merely one of the eccentricities of the division of labor.

Nowhere does this opportunism, this absence of theoretical consistency or of any concern for consistency, appear more clearly than in the adaptation of the Fourteenth Amendment, especially the due process clause, to the needs of private government. Central to the power of private governments in the American "Age of Enterprise" was the doctrine that private agreements between parties attained a sacred status, that such contracts were on a higher level of legitimacy than the police power of the state. To put it another way, the sanctity of contract put inter-"personal" (corporations, it should be noted, qualified as "persons") relationships largely beyond the authority of the political sovereign. From a different perspective the question was, to what extent is the authority of the community limited by private arrangements among its citizens; that is, by "liberty of contract"?

The argument began early in the history of the Republic. The framers of the Constitution included, without discussion, a proviso that no state could "impair the obligation of a contract." It is impossible to know what they had in mind, but in all probability the stipulation was aimed at state legal tender laws, such as that in Rhode Island, which had required creditors to accept depreciated paper currency in payment of debts incurred in specie. While on its face the limitation was absolute, it is inconceivable that the authors of the Constitution intended to put private agreements wholly beyond the reach of the state's police power.

Like many other provisions of the Constitution, it was agreed to in haste to be interpreted by later generations in leisure.[1]

In the early Supreme Court cases, the Justices established the basic positions which, in differing contexts, have survived to our own time. John Marshall on one side asserted the vested rights view that contracts are made in heaven; that is, they have their roots in the natural law and are superior to the civil law. Marshall was far too shrewd to claim that all interpersonal agreements were inviolable contracts; by employing his favorite device—circular logic—he explained that a law forbidding usury did not impair contractual obligations because an arrangement to pay excessive interest was not, in the first place properly speaking, a "contract." Q.E.D. The opposing view, that contracts are conceived in the womb of positive law rather than in a natural law Never-Never Land, was vigorously asserted by Justice William Johnson. Contracts, he argued, were always formulated and executed within the jurisdiction of the state police power. True the legislature did not have unlimited authority to modify or abrogate agreements, but it could establish rules and standards binding on private parties. These rules and regulations could even be applied retrospectively—to contracts made before they were enounced—if it could be shown that the contracting parties *should have known* that the legislature had reserved power in this area.

This is an extremely complex, even metaphysical doctrine. If, for example, X, a brewer, signed a twenty-year contract to supply Y, an innkeeper, with beer and after five years the state instituted prohibition, was the contract voided? From the natural-law viewpoint, the contract cannot be impaired by such a statute, and as the prohibition movement swept across the United States in the mid-nineteenth century many liquor manufacturers hopefully fortified themselves with long-term contracts with a view to putting their business beyond the reach of the police power. But from the positive law position, no private arrangements can bind the sovereign; therefore when X and Y made their contract, they did so with the knowledge tht it was subject to later legislative

[1] See John P. Roche, "The Founding Fathers," *American Political Science Review*, vol. LV (1961), pp. 814 ff.

modification. To put it another way, all contracts are enacted in a contingent universe, and this contingency is an implicit premise in the private agreement. Once the Taney Court added to this proposition the corollary that all doubts are resolved in favor of the public, the Contract Clause of the Constitution (Article I, Section 10) went into hibernation as a significant limit on public policy.[2]

With this hasty summary in mind, let us direct our attention to the revival of the concept of contract which in the last years of the nineteenth and first quarter of the twentieth centuries became the fundamental buttress of private government. This resurgence took place under two main headings. First, the concept of contract was broadened to include the substantive right to pursue a calling, both on an individual and on a corporate level. Second, the right to make contractual arrangements to exercise one's calling became a "property" right protected from state infringement by the due process clause of the Fourteenth Amendment. As Justice Field argued in a classic formulation of this position, his dissent in the *Slaughterhouse* cases,[3] a butcher has a natural right to exercise his trade—contract for his services—and a state law which deprives him of his freedom to make his own arrangements (contracts) has expropriated his property rights in his enterprise. Field was even prepared to argue that such a statute constituted slavery in violation of the Thirteenth Amendment!

In effect, the old Marshallian interpretation of the contract appeared in a new guise, a far broader and more sophisticated one than the Chief Justice had ever envisioned. Instead of giving natural law attributes to contracts only, Field and his followers widened the protection to encompass the *right to enter into contracts,* that is, to the prerogative of doing business on one's own terms, which I have designated entrepreneurial liberty. And on his own West Coast Circuit, where he was boss, Justice Field implemented his convictions in what was known as "Ninth Circuit Law." Relying on a technicality which prevented Supreme Court review of *habeas corpus* decisions, Field and his judicial

---

[2] See generally Benjamin F. Wright, *The Contract Clause in the Constitution* (Cambridge, Mass., 1938).

[3] 16 Wall. 36 (1873).

associates established as constitutional law in the Ninth Circuit the proposition that the rights to pursue legitimate callings, to make and enforce contracts, and to do business free from extraordinary legislative control were incorporated in the due process and equal protection clauses of the Fourteenth Amendment. In this backdoor fashion, natural entrepreneurial rights obtained constitutional leverage.[4]

While Field never denied the existence of the police power, his whole position was based on the proposition that in any conflict between private *economic* rights and public authority the burden of proof rested on the state. The state, in other words, had to demonstrate to the satisfaction of the Court that its regulations were justified. In the absence of strong historical or contextual proof of legitimacy, Field almost automatically voted "No!," but it was possible on occasion—e.g., *Barbier* v. *Connolly, Soon Hing* v. *Crowley*[5]—to convince him that the police power had been legitimately exercised. Yet in the area of noneconomic rights (rights of Negroes, for example, to equal political treatment) he gave the police power its head.

This is not the place for a discussion of the rapid spread of Justice Field's—and Justice Bradley's—dissenting views in the *Slaughterhouse* cases. Needless to say, the conception that there was constitutional protection for the right to follow one's calling—and that the contractual arrangements made in pursuing business goals were largely immune to public authority—became the ideological *point d'appui* for the corporations in their struggle against regulation. State judges were particularly susceptible to this line of argument, and in New York, Pennsylvania, West Virginia and many other states the divine right of contract supplied the rationale for voiding state regulatory legislation.[6] Contracts were the instruments by which men asserted and implemented their property rights in their economic capacities; thus legislatively to prohibit paying miners in company script, when they had agreed to this form of remuneration in their employment

---

[4] See Howard Jay Graham, "Justice Field and the Fourteenth Amendment," *Yale Law Journal*, vol. LII (1943), pp. 851–889.

[5] 113 U.S. 27 (1885); 113 U.S. 703 (1885).

[6] See generally Clyde E. Jacobs, *Law Writers and the Courts* (Berkeley, 1954); Benjamin R. Twiss, *Lawyers and the Constitution* (Princeton, 1942).

contracts, was to deprive the *miners* of their "property right" to make their own economic decisions. The average miner never really appreciated this judicial concern for his integrity; from his worm's-eye view a contract with the coal company was hardly the outcome of bargaining between equals. But the judges persisted in protecting him from his own base instincts, which would have led him to become a "ward of the state"—a fate worse than death.

This judicial altruism deserves emphasis. There is no necessity to believe that the judges were insincere when they protected the furious farmers from "serfdom" by striking down legislative enactments designed to curb railroad shipping practices, or when they rescued the industrial worker from "slavery" by asserting freedom of contract in his behalf. Just as in the *Income Tax* cases (1895) communism was seen as the logical consequence of a graduated tax, so serfdom and slavery were seen as the natural end results of dependence on the state. This was the era when, under the Social Darwinist aegis, that evil abstraction the State was first loosed in the land. The conflict of the age was seen as one between the Individual and the State, and the consequences of Statism (the triumph of the weak over the strong in Spencerian terms) would be decadence and dictatorship.

The logic of this position was absurd in its own terms. As a contemporary critic like Lester F. Ward pointed out (to an empty house), if the weak succeeded in beating the strong by ganging up against them, according to the syllogism of Social Darwinism, they became the "fittest." In other words, if one argues that Nature awards the prize to the "fittest" and that the "fittest" are those who emerge on top of the pile, then the workers or farmers who successfully club down the industrial magnates with the state as their weapon deserve the Darwinian accolade. The logic of Social Darwinism was that the winner takes all; no ground rules were prescribed. What the state, and later the federal judges, did in the name of impartiality was strip the weak of their capacity for collective action. In the event that the workers did persuade the state legislature to act in their behalf, a judge would hastily blow the whistle, cancel the victory, and in the name of fair play return power to the opposition. Or, to change the analogy, the courts effectively sent the workers and the farmers into the boxing ring with the injunction that if they used their best punch on the corporations, it would be ruled a foul.[7]

Moreover, this judicial posture completely overlooked the extent to which the great private governments were in point of fact "wards of the state." Hothouse conditions were established for industrial growth by the protective tariff which in essence gave these tariff-protected industries the power to tax the American consumer. On a different level, state and federal judges were always ready to rush to the aid of a corporation which was having difficulties with a labor union—even if it was necessary, as in the *Debs* case, to improvise a legal foundation for such intervention. Indeed, the Debs imprisonment and the Pullman Strike which led to it provide an excellent example of the extent to which the federal government would aid a private government in distress.

In May 1894, trouble broke out in the feudal demesne of George Pullman, the company town of Pullman on the outskirts of Chicago. Workers who protested against wage cuts were thrown out of their "homes"; Pullman refused even to discuss the matter, and his employees *en masse* joined Eugene Debs' American Railway Union (ARU) and struck. Debs, who had led the ARU to a sensational victory over the Great Northern Railroad in 1893, realized that the strike had to be handled with great care—any violence or disorder would provide the federal government with an excuse to intervene as it had in 1877. With great care and tactical brilliance, Debs masterminded a spectacular "functional revolution" against the private government of George Pullman: On June 26 the word went out along the lines to boycott the "Palace Cars" without interrupting other rail transportation. Suddenly, all over the West Pullman cars appeared quietly resting on sidings—the workers simply shunted them out of trains and left them behind.[8]

This tactic unsettled the railroads, who could hardly claim that shunting Pullman cars out of trains was "revolutionary violence," and they hastily devised a counter-tactic: They attached the

[7] See Richard C. Hofstadter, *Social Darwinism in American Thought* (Philadelphia, 1945), especially Chapter 4.

[8] Ray Ginger, *The Bending Cross* (New Brunswick, 1949), p. 121.

United States' mail cars to the Pullmans. This hardly deterred the workers, who cut the Palace Cars out of any location in the train, so the managers took the next step: *They* refused to run any trains not made up to *their* specifications, i.e., they declared war on the "public" and tied up the railroads. Knowing the close connection between the General Managers' Association and Attorney General Richard Olney, Debs had been particularly careful not to interrupt mail service; now it was stopped by the Managers themselves, though of course they assigned the blame to the ARU.

The national government moved into action on July 2, 1894, when at Olney's instruction an injunction was requested from the United States District Court in Chicago forbidding any interference with rail traffic into that city. Although there was no federal statute governing the matter, the Court took jurisdiction on the grounds that the strike was holding up the mails and was an unlawful restraint on interstate commerce. At this point, violence did break out—aimed at preventing the enforcement of the decree—and the next day, over the objections of the Governor of Illinois, John P. Altgeld, federal troops were moved into Chicago to break the strike. Concurrently Debs and other leaders of the ARU were arrested on a shotgun indictment charging them with violations of the Sherman Anti-Trust Law and contempt of court.[9]

We can not linger with the details, which have been chronicled at length by several historians. The important point for our purposes here is the flimsy legal basis on which federal intervention was founded. There simply was no federal law authorizing the Debs injunction, and it supposedly had been determined as far back as 1812 (*United States* v. *Hudson and Goodwin*)[10] that the national government had no common-law jurisdiction; that is, that the federal authorities could not exercise punitive sanctions without statutory authority. But the Supreme Court was equal to the occasion: Justice Brewer for a unanimous Court held that the absence of specific authority was inconsequential since the "obligations which [the federal government] is under to promote the

[9] *Ibid.*, Chapters 6–7; See generally, Almont Lindsay, *The Pullman Strike* (Chicago, 1942).
[10] 7 Cranch 32.

interest of all, and to prevent the wrongdoing of one resulting in injury to the general welfare, is often of itself sufficient to give it standing in court. . . ." *In re Debs.*[11] The implication of this startling and revolutionary holding was that the federal government had an inherent power to protect the "general welfare"—a view which conservatives would later denounce as unconstitutional and communistic, but which they welcomed in 1895 when it justified the imprisonment of "Dictator Debs."

Mr. George Pullman and the General Managers' Association were obviously "wards of the state." Their right to engage in business on their own terms, allegedly founded in higher law, rested in fact on the coercive power of the government: on the injunction, which the Managers' Association significantly called a "gatling gun on paper"; and on the actual gatling guns of United States troops. But while we can, armed with the clarity of hindsight, make this assertion, the fact remains that the myth of rugged individualism dominated the constitutional ethos, seemingly unharmed, even untouched, by the corrosion of contrary data. Let us now turn to an examination of the Supreme Court's application of this dogma of entrepreneurial liberty to three areas of political economy: labor relations, rate regulation and social legislation.

The trade union movement in both the United States and Great Britain began life with a common-law bar sinister emblazoned on its shield; it was considered as a conspiracy in restraint of trade liable to criminal prosecution, civil suit for damages, or both. While by the end of the nineteenth century trade unions in the United States were no longer automatically illegal conspiracies, in any attempt to exercise economic power they were subject to an almost infinite number of legal harassments. The long-range goal of union organizations has always been job control; that is, the power to require union membership as a condition of employment. With this, of course, goes the right of the union to recognition by management as the bargaining agent (or agents, there can be more than one union involved) for the employees. Few nineteenth century employers were willing to accept unionization, and when the unions attempted to attain

[11] 158 U.S. 564 (1895).

their ends by striking, they found the weight of legal precedent an almost insuperable barrier to success. I have mentioned above the fiction of equilibrium which was important in trade union litigation; here let us concentrate on a few Supreme Court decisions which exemplified the judicial approach towards industrial relations. These cases, it should be noted, are those which used "liberty of contract" as the rationale of decision—rather than those resting on the commerce power and Sherman Act.

In the wake of the Pullman strike, President Cleveland appointed a special commission to investigate railroad problems. When this body reported to the President in November 1894, it recommended, *inter alia,* that Congress take action to protect the railway workers' right to organize unions, and a bill was subsequently introduced by Congressman Erdman of Pennsylvania which included such a provision. A ferocious legislative battle ensued—the Senate killed two House versions in 1895 and 1897 —but finally in 1898 President McKinley signed the Railway Labor Act establishing the Railway Labor Board, mediation machinery and a provision (Section 10) banning the "yellow dog" contract, the blacklist and dismissal for union membership.[12] All this enactment accomplished was the legitimatizing of unionism on interstate railroads—essentially it superseded the feudal law of the private railroad government which had made union activity a capital offense in economic terms. In other words, it gave the railroad unions *rights of access,* but no more.

It was one thing to have such a law on the books, quite another to get it enforced. Despite widespread violations, it was not until 1907 that the first test case reached the Supreme Court (two others had aborted *en route*). William Adair, the chief of operations of the Louisville and Nashville Railroad, had been indicted for firing O. B. Coppage on the ground that the latter had, in violation of his contract, joined the Brotherhood of Locomotive Firemen. The railroad claimed that Section 10 of the Erdman Act was unconstitutional: first, it was not properly within Congressional authority under the commerce power to regulate labor relations; and, second, assuming it could be founded on the

[12] See Elias Lieberman, *Unions Before the Bar* (New York, 1950), pp. 44–45.

commerce power, the provision was a violation of the due process clause of the Fifth Amendment as an infringement of "liberty of contract." Our concern here is with the second of these allegations.

In *Adair* v. *United States*[13] the Supreme Court sustained the railroad view by a vote of six to two. Writing for the majority, Justice Harlan first of all declared Section 10 to be a violation of the Fifth Amendment, and then for good measure he added that the power to regulate labor contracts was *not* encompassed in the commerce power. Section 10, Harland held, was "an invasion of the personal liberty, as well as of the right of property, guaranteed by" the due process clause of the Fifth Amendment. The Louisville and Nashville Railroad thus had the right "to prescribe the terms upon which the services of Coppage would be accepted, and it was the right of Coppage to become or not, as he chose, an employee of the railroad company upon the terms offered to him." In other words, the Louisville and Nashville Railroad and Coppage "have equality of right, and any legislation that disturbs that equality is an arbitrary interference with the liberty of contract which no government can legally justify in a free land."[14]

Justice Oliver Wendell Holmes, Jr., who as we shall see shortly was himself anything but flexible in his approach to the mythology of the common law, dissented on the ground that the Erdman Act was a legitimate exercise of the commerce power and that "the section [10] is, in substance, a very limited interference with freedom of contract" well within the power of Congress.[15] Justice McKenna also dissented, confining himself almost wholly to the question of the commerce clause.

If the due process clause of the Fifth Amendment could be construed as banning legislative efforts to end the "yellow dog" contract on the national level, it logically followed that the equivalent provision of the Fourteenth Amendment could similarly undermine state efforts to the same end. And so the Court

---

[13] 208 U.S. 161 (1908).

[14] *Ibid.* at 172–5.

[15] *Ibid.*, 191. For an example of Holmes at his ritualistic worst see his dissent in the peonage case, Bailey v. Alabama, 219 U.S. 219 (1911).

held in 1915 by a six to three division (*Coppage* v. *Kansas*).[16] Justice Pitney, who replaced Harlan in 1912, continued Harlan's views but added to them a pious patina which the bluff old Kentucky Unionist never employed. In some ways the Pitney opinion in *Coppage* v. *Kansas* sounds like a caricature of the "rugged individualist" viewpoint written by an enemy. The right freely to enter into contracts, said the Justice, "is as essential to the laborer as to the capitalist, to the poor as to the rich." Unfortunately perhaps "wherever the right of private property exists, there must and will be inequalities of fortune; and thus it naturally happens that parties negotiating about a contract are not equally hampered by circumstances."[17] Translated into English, Pitney's cloudy legalese amounts to the statement that the poor man's right to negotiate from weakness is as essential to him as the rich man's right to negotiate from strength.

To ensure that his point was appreciated on the appropriate philosophical level, Pitney then turned to cosmology for what might be called the ontological proof of the validity of the "yellow dog" contract:

> And, since *it is self-evident* that, unless all things are held in common, some persons must have more property than others, *it is from the nature of things* impossible to uphold freedom of contract and the right of private property without at the same time recognizing as legitimate those inequalities of fortune that are the necessary result of the exercise of those rights. (Italics added.)[18]

Holmes dissented tersely; one suspects that he may have been slightly nauseated. The old warrior believed firmly that the first law of life was struggle, but he despised metaphysical efforts to demonstrate that the winners in the battle of life had received some devine afflatus.[19] Justice Day, joined by Hughes, also dissented, pointing out at some length that the Kansas statute under attack was "intended to promote the same liberty of action for the employee as the employer confessedly [through employer

16 236 U.S. 1.
17 *Ibid.*, 14, 17.
18 *Ibid.*, 17.
19 *Ibid.*, 26.

groups such as the General Managers' Association] enjoys. The law should be as zealous to protect the constitutional liberty of the employee as it is to guard that of the employer."[20]

The third, and last, case for discussion here took the principles enounced in *Adair* and *Coppage* to their logical conclusion. The long legal struggle began in 1906 when the United Mine Workers of America (UMW) struck the Hitchman Coal and Coke Company in the West Virginia panhandle. The strike was defeated and in its aftermath the company set up its own "union" which required as a condition of employment that the miners sign a "disloyalty oath" to the UMW in which they promised, under penalty of dismissal, never to affiliate with that union. In 1907 the UMW began its campaign to recapture the allegiance of the miners, and the company went to court. Without going into the intricate legal details, the company asked for and received an injunction prohibiting the UMW from attempting to organize its workers—such an effort, even though it was peaceful, amounted to a conspiracy to induce breach of contract. Indeed, Judge Dayton forbade the union from employing "argument, reason and persuasion" with the Hitchman workers; he actually barred union organizers from "talking to" the men.

This "temporary" injunction was in effect until 1912, when Judge Dayton finally got around to a decision on the merits. (In injunctive proceedings, there are various stages: in the first, a preliminary injunction can be issued on an *ex parte* basis—that is, one party threatened by immediate damage, can get a freeze order; in the second, which is an adversary proceeding, both parties present argument and the judge decides whether or not there is an adequate case for continuing the freeze; in the third, if the preliminary injunction has been made temporary at the second state, the judge holds a full trial on the merits and reaches a final determination.) To the surprise of no one, Judge Dayton made the injunction permanent—which meant that any efforts to unionize Hitchman would be punishable as contempt of court. However, the union was pleased and startled when, two years later (the organizers had now been barred from the mines for seven years), the Court of Appeals overruled Judge Dayton at

[20] *Ibid.*, 40.

every point. Hitchman promptly appealed to the Supreme Court.[21]

The Supreme Court, in 1917 (*Hitchman Coal & Coke Co.* v. *Mitchell*),[22] split six to three in favor of the company. Justice Pitney for the Court had no difficulty fitting the Hitchman situation into his cosmology: If the "yellow dog" contract had divine sanction, then it was self-evident in the nature of things that the union's efforts were sacrilegious. The injunction was sustained and the labor movement was effectively barred from ever attempting to organize workers who had signed "yellow dog" contracts—any effort to this end would automatically fall into the category of a conspiracy to achieve an illegal end, breach of contract. The right of union organizers even to freedom of speech was held to be subordinate to the sanctity of contractual obligations.

Justice Brandeis wrote a sharp dissent for himself, Justice Holmes and Justice Clarke. In essence, Brandeis denied every contention of the majority: The UMW was a legal body employing legal means to achieve a legal end. While he did not question the validity of the "yellow dog" contract, Brandeis pointed out that dismissal was a consequence of joining a union, not of talking about or preparing to join the union. Brandeis' views were warmly greeted by the unions as well as by progressives generally, but the employers had the majority and set to work with it.[23]

In tactical terms, the opinion of the Court enshrined the injunction as the primary weapon against unionization. And it was a devastating weapon. In the first place, as we have seen in *Hitchman,* the procedures were such that, once a temporary injunction had been granted, years might pass before final determination of the issues. Throughout this period the injunction remained in force undermining any sustained organizing campaign. If the union organizers decided to ignore the injunction and go ahead with their drive (even today, with all the conveniences of the National Labor Relations Acts, a unionization campaign calls for sustained, continuous effort), they were

[21] Lieberman, *op. cit.*, pp. 84–95.
[22] 245 U.S. 229.
[23] *Ibid.*, 263.

promptly arrested for contempt of court. Under the Clayton Act of 1914, they had the right to a jury trial; but jury or no jury, they went out of circulation in the sense that their work for the union ceased. In managerial circles the injunction was rated higher than a regiment of national guardsmen. In psychological terms, the onus for "breaking the law" was always on the unions; a refusal to obey even the most openly bitter antilabor judge left the unionists under these circumstances in "defiance of the Constitution."

When the Supreme Court incorporated what I have called the dogma of entrepreneurial freedom into the Fourteenth Amendment, it crippled the efforts of the trade unions to organize. In a different sector of the economy this potent concept was at work undermining the efforts of state and local governments to regulate the rates charged by utilities, railroads and similar corporations. Probably no area of public law is more complex than that concerned with the determination of "reasonable" rates, and we shall not get involved in the substantive problems. Our concern is rather with the antecedent question: Who shall have the power to evaluate the "reasonableness" of rates? What might be called the administrative school of thought, which was on the rise in the years we are discussing, asserted that the determination of rates was a legislative-administrative problem, one which could be handled intelligently only by a body of experts acting under state authority. In this tradition various states established railroad or public utility commissions with rate-fixing powers. The other school of thought asserted that only a judicial body could exercise jurisdiction over "reasonableness," that historically the concept of a "reasonable return" was a common law derivative, that for the legislature to meddle in the area was a violation of the separation of powers, and of due process of law.

All utilities are inherently quasi-public in character, and under the old rules of the common law they were subjected to a special degree of control by the sovereign. A railroad, for example, was given a public charter, trolleys operated on the streets by franchise, gas companies ran their pipes with public assent. No one has a natural or civil right to build a railroad any more than he can convert his suburban backyard into a stone quarry or an airport. Throughout the middle years of the nineteenth century the police power was dominant over the assertion of vested rights, and in 1877 the Supreme Court in the so-called *Granger* cases,[24] appeared to give the states the green light for vigorous regulation of "businesses affected with a public interest." The *Granger* cases are fascinating reading; the first, *Munn* v. *Illinois,* is characteristically quoted in case books, but there were eight cases decided *en masse* (with Justice Field in bitter opposition) which effectively undercut every line of attack that corporations could launch against the police power, at least in the constitutional sense. In the leading case, Illinois was permitted to establish maximum storage rates for grain elevators; in the remaining cases a wide range of legislative railroad regulation was approved, including freight and passenger rates. Chief Justice Waite flatly and virtually without discussion rejected the contention that the states could not regulate interstate railroads; he suggested that if various citizens did not like the substance of the regulations, they should go into politics and get the legislature to change its laws. These decisions, barked Field in dissent, "practically destroy all the guarantees of the Constitution and of the common law . . . for the protection of the railroad companies." The nub of the controversy was the locus of authority to define "reasonable" rates: The corporations asserted that only by a judicial proceeding could this be done—a judge, or a judge and jury, would then decide in a specific case whether the company had overcharged. The states, with the Court's agreement, felt that the evaluation of fair and reasonable rate structures was within the jurisdiction of the legislature—either directly or through delegation to a commission.

From the corporate viewpoint, there were several lines of possible assault on the *Granger* decisions. For the railroads, in particular, the claim could be made that state regulation was an intrusion into Congress' power over interstate commerce. In the absence of any commerce power issue, the corporations could keep chewing away at the police power on several grounds and hope that one or another Justice would be converted, or that new judges coming on the bench would accept their views. There was always hope that the contract clause could be revived; Justice

[24] 94 U.S. 113 (1877).

Field was constantly recommending the useful potentialities of the Fourteenth Amendment; and there were even odd-ball decisions such as Justice Miller's in *Loan Association* v. *Topeka*[25] which suggested that the Court could find a basis in natural law for frustrating "robbery" carried on under the auspices of the police power. Moreover, the vital statistics of the Court were morbidly reassuring: In the decade following the *Granger* cases (1877), five new Justices were appointed to the Court, all from legal and professional backgrounds, which suggested they would take seriously the threat to property rights.

With this transformation of the Court in mind, let us turn to the famous case of *Chicago, Milwaukee & St. Paul Railway Co.* v. *Minnesota*[26] in which the Supreme Court began the retreat from the *Granger* cases. Minnesota had set up a railroad commission charged by the legislature with ensuring that the roads exacted only "equal and reasonable rates," and this commission had ordered the Chicago, Milwaukee & St. Paul to lower its charges for hauling milk. Writing for the six-judge majority, Justice Blatchford neatly sidestepped *Munn* v. *Illinois*, holding that the determination of a "reasonable" rate could not be delegated to a nonjudicial body such as a commission. "The question of the reasonableness of a rate of charge for transportation [he asserted] is eminently a question for judicial decision."[27] In essence, Blatchford announced that no administrative (and by implication, legislative—legislatures do not operate "under the forms" supplied "by the wisdom of successive ages for the investigation judicially" of controversial issues) determination of a rate schedule could never be final. He issued an invitation to any railroad or utility grieved by legal rate schedules to take the issue of "reasonableness" to court. Perhaps caught up by the spirit of the age, the Justice declared a judicial corner on "reasonableness," and would permit no unsanctified legislative body to infringe the monopoly.

Four years later Justice Brewer—Field's nephew, and if possible a stronger supporter of entrepreneurial freedom than his

[25] 20 Wall. 655 (1875). It should be noted that Miller used this improvisation to strike down, not support "privilege."

[26] 134 U.S. 418 (1890).

[27] *Ibid.*, 461.

uncle—filled in the gaps in Blatchford's argument. Under review was a schedule of rates prepared, *after notice and hearings*, by the Texas Railroad Commission which were challenged as "unreasonable" by a railroad bondholder. Conceding that the Court could not itself go into the rate-making business, Brewer made it perfectly clear that the Justices knew "unreasonable" rates when they saw them. A railroad had a constitutional right to charge enough to defray its expenses and make some return to its investors: "Justice demands that every one should receive some compensation for the use of his money or property, if it be possible without prejudice to the rights of others." Brewer was a bit vague on the constitutional basis of this right to make a profit, but he seems to have tucked it into the Equal Protection clause of the Fourteenth Amendment: "The equal protection of the laws—the spirit of common justice—forbids that one class [railroad bondholders] should by law be compelled to suffer loss that others [shippers] may make gain."[28]

If one recalls the fantastic financial operations of the railways in the nineteenth and early twentieth century, the problem comes into better focus. The common prank of the financiers was overcapitalization—a railroad with a cash value of $1 million would be capitalized at $2 million, bonds would be issued calling for 4 or 5 percent return, and rates would be fixed at a level which would, hopefully, bring this or better. In California in the 1870s, the Southern Pacific Railroad was bitterly contesting its valuation for tax purposes at $16,500 per mile as confiscatory, but was capitalized at $43,500 per mile![29] Now the question arises: Which figure should be used to compute a "reasonable" rate? If the railroad commission employs the net value of the property, the rates necessary to provide a "fair return" will be considerably below those which would be derived from using the capitalized value of the property. Assuming that a 5 percent return is considered "reasonable," and we continue the fictitious example above of the $1 million railroad capitalized at 2 millions, a fair rate in the first instance would bring in $50,000 a year, in the second, $100,000. In practical terms, freight and passenger

[28] Reagan v. Farmer's Loan & Trust Co., 154 U.S. 362, 412, 410 (1894).
[29] Cited in Howard Jay Graham, "An Innocent Abroad: The Constitutional Corporate 'Person'," *U.C.L.A. Law Review*, vol. ii (1955), p. 191.

charges would have to be doubled to sustain the two million rate-base.

Turn this proposition around and another dimension, basic to the cases under discussion, becomes obvious. A railroad, over-capitalized let us say by 50 percent—a $15 million indebtedness on a $10 million cash outlay—in order to stay solvent must pay its bondholders a total of $600,000 a year, assuming a 4 percent coupon. But a state railroad commission, after careful assessment of the net value of the actual assets of the line, fixes a rate schedule which cannot earn more than $450,000 in profits. Has the commission acted "unreasonably"? The answer to this question is not founded on legal doctrine, but on economic and political presuppositions. If a judge adopts the ruthless view of classic *laissez-faire* economics, he will doubtless hold that the investor has the job of anticipating future risks and acting accordingly, that it is not the task of the judiciary to rescue bondholders from the penalties of economic stupidity. If the judge believes that it is the function of the state to protect the public from extortion, he will unquestionably accept the decision of the railroad commission as binding on the corporation.

However, to return to the main line of the argument, if the judge believes that the well-being of the investor and the liberty of action of the entrepreneur are the key social and economic values, he will defend the corporation's inflated rate-base against both economic rationality and the police power. It was this course which the Supreme Court took in the 1890s and early decades of this century. As time went by, the judicial weapon became more precise: Indeed, in 1930 the Court was able to state, *ex cathedra,* that a Baltimore trolley company had a constitutional right to a return of 7.44 percent on the value of its property![30] Presumably 7.43 percent might have been a deprivation of due process.

What is important to note is that the Court assumed, without any justification, that the restrictions of due process on the state's police power were identical with the restrictions on its power of eminent domain.[31] Once this analogy was established, the fight

---

[30] United R'ways & Electric Co. of Baltimore v. West, 280 U.S. 234.

[31] See Robert L. Hale, *Freedom Through Law* (New York, 1952), pp. 461–73.

was over—the conclusions were subsumed in the premises. Now it is quite clear that the state acting under its power of eminent domain must reimburse the citizen fair value for his property. If a house is condemned to make room for a superhighway, its owner is entitled to full reimbursement of his investment. *But the police power does not proceed on the same basis.* One may have paid a thousand dollars for an ounce of the best heroin, but if it is seized by the state there will be no compensation. Nor do prohibition laws respect a man's property right in alcoholic beverages. The only due process a heroin pusher or a bootlegger can expect is procedural: He has the right to a fair trial in criminal court. He has no right to a 7.44 percent return on his investment.

Thus if one begins with the assumption that the state of Texas, or Minnesota, in establishing regulations governing railroad rates, was limiting the corrupt endeavors of corporate officials and protecting the public from institutionalized embezzlement and extortion, the Supreme Court's decisions amounted to a protection of criminal behavior. Indeed, this was the way many agrarian radicals and urban progressives interpreted the work of the Court. However, from the viewpoint of Justice Field, Justice Brewer or the seven other Justices who *unanimously* concurred in the Texas holding discussed above (*Reagan* v. *Farmers' Loan and Trust Co.*, 1894), this criticism was a form of blasphemy. And it should be reiterated that they were honest, dedicated men—dedicated to the proposition that entrepreneurial rights were a mundane manifestation of natural law, and to its siamese twin which holds that those who would lay profane hands on corporate prerogatives were the harbingers of socialistic serfdom.

Before the Court could with confidence invoke a precise fraction such as 7.44 percent, there had to be a formula. As Robert L. Hale pointed out many years ago,[32] the process of formulation was rather peculiar. The Court in fact began with the "right" answer, and then had to work backwards to the "right" question. The answer as we have seen was that a utility had the right to a "fair return" or a "reasonable return" on its investment. But what was to be the rate-base, the foundation on which any hypotheti-

[32] *Ibid.*, Chapter 15 *passim*.

cal "fair return" would be computed? In 1898 the question for this answer was formulated by Justice Harlan in *Smythe* v. *Ames*.[33]

This is not the place to investigate the chaos which for half a century developed in the wake of the "rule of *Smythe* v. *Ames*"; nor are we here concerned with the circular logic which sustained it (earning power is a key consideration in "value"; thus to diminish the earning power by rate restrictions is automatically to reduce the "value").[34] Its importance lay in the enormous freedom it gave to public utilities and the almost infinite number of roadblocks it put in the way of effective state regulation. No matter how much work a group of utility experts had put into the determination of a rate-scale based on a "fair value," once this schedule had been promulgated by a regulatory commission, an inevitable trip was taken to the federal court. There the whole question was argued *de novo* with the Supreme Court reserving the right to throw out any set of regulations that did not insure a "reasonable" return on "fair value" as violative of the due process clause of the Fourteenth Amendment. And while this argument was, of course, conducted in precise legal terminology, it was in essence an elaborate exercise in constitutional mysticism. As Justice Stone, discussing one component of Harlan's formula, observed many years later: "In assuming the task of determining judicially the present fair replacement value of the vast properties of public utilities, courts have been projected into the most speculative undertaking imposed upon them in the entire history of English jurisprudence."[35]

The constitutional dogma of entrepreneurial liberty thus simultaneously crippled the power of the trade unions to achieve recognition and bargaining status and undermined the authority of the state over public utilities. In both instances, the natural right to conduct business on one's own terms was incorporated into the Fourteenth Amendment. Let us now turn to the third dogmatic manifestation: the employment of "liberty of contract" as a weapon against social legislation. It would be wise at this

[33] 169 U.S. 466, 546–7 (1898).

[34] See Hale, *op. cit.*, pp. 416 ff.

[35] Cited *ibid.* p. 478 (from West v. Chesapeake & Potomac Tel. Co., 295 U.S. 662, 689 [1935]).

point to re-emphasize a definitional matter which is relevant here, serving to distinguish this category of legislative interference from the one just examined. No public utility could ever, even in the view of a judge as committed to entrepreneurial liberty as Stephen J. Field, justify in legal terms full freedom from special regulation. These "quasi-public" enterprises—railroads, turnpikes, traction companies, gas and water distributors—were designated as businesses "affected with a public interest" and were theoretically far more subordinate to the police power than "private" undertakings. The category of businesses "affected with a public interest" was, however, not simple to define. In the *Granger* cases, Chief Justice Waite ducked the definitional issue by suggesting that it lay within the jurisdiction of the state legislature; Field retorted that to do so would leave the entire business would at the mercy of meddling legislation, that it would permit legislative interference on a self-validating basis and effectively destroy the line between "quasi-public" and private enterprise.

In his dissent in the *Munn* case, Field argued that the state of Illinois had no right to regulate the charges of an admittedly monopolistic combine of grain elevator operators. This monopoly, he indicated, was an outgrowth of their entrepreneurial talent, not of state action; therefore there was nothing "quasi-public" about their actions. He was infuriated by the Chief Justice's statement that property "becomes clothed with a public interest when it is used in such a manner as to be of public consequence and affect the community at large." Logically Field's argument was sound (Waite's definition was circular) but for the time being he had to bide his time and merely register his protests in choleric dissents. And it should be added, just to maintain the right atmosphere of ambiguity, that the Chief Justice was forced to hedge his bet: in 1886 (*Stone* v. *Farmers' Loan & Trust Co.*) while sustaining the actions of Mississippi's railroad commission, he added by way of dictum that "it is not to be inferred that this [regulatory power] is itself without limit. This power to regulate is not a power to destroy, and limitation is not the equivalent of confiscation."[36] In

[36] 116 U.S. 307, 331 (1886). Professor C. Peter Magrath has been good enough to supply me with material from the Waite Papers which indicate that the Chief Justice inserted this dictum to hold Justice Stanley Matthews

short, Waite too had to admit that there were situations where the legislative power could be checked by judicial application of the Fourteenth Amendment.

While the Court was undergoing the personnel shift discussed earlier, the drums of reform were beating throughout the land. Under pressure from populists and urban progressives, state legislatures began to enact social legislation designed to ameliorate some of the worst evils of corporate power and industrial squalor. In most instances these statutes had to run the gauntlet of due process in the state courts before they entered the federal forum. While I have not, for reasons of space, devoted coverage to decisions of the inferior federal or state courts, it would be wise at this point to note that the precepts of entrepreneurial liberty gained support on the state judicial level before they did in the federal jurisdiction. The vehicle for this judicial offensive was the due process clause of state constitutions. The courts of Illinois, New York and Pennsylvania were particularly vigorous in their exposition of the Bradley gloss on due process as set out in the *Slaughterhouse* cases (1873).[37]

Let us examine one extremely significant New York decision, *In re Jacobs*,[38] for the path that it broke, a path which the United States Supreme Court took in several later decisions. The *Tenement House Cigar* case, as it was called, arose from a New York statute of 1884. Trimmed to the essentials, this law prohibited the manufacture of cigars or other tobacco products on the dwelling floors of tenements (four or more family habitations) in cities of more than 500,000 population (Brooklyn and New York). Like many other pieces of social legislation then and now, it was passed on an *ad hoc* basis, by cigar-smoking legislators, and a cigar-smoking governor, Grover Cleveland, after a newspaper exposé of the filthy conditions of cigar manufacture. Cigars were then made by hand and the wrapper was sealed by the

---

in the majority. The decision was 5–3; had Matthews swung the other way, the decision below in favor of the *railroads* would have been sustained by an equally divided Court (4–4). In short, Waite's abstract genuflection to entrepreneurial liberty did not symbolize a change of heart, but rather a tactical compromise, on his part.

[37] Jacobs, *op. cit.*, Chapter 3 *passim*.

[38] 98 N.Y. 98 (N.Y., Ct. of Appeals, 1885).

cigarmaker in a primitive and unhygienic fashion—he licked it with his tongue. As the legislators learned of the squalid environment and the high disease rate of tenement dwellers (tuberculosis was endemic), they rushed to protect the public health from this menace.

An obscure cigarmaker named Peter Jacobs violated the law, was arrested and convicted, appealed, and then vanished from history.[39] At this point in the process, the poverty-stricken defendant turned the matter over to the highest-priced lawyer in New York, William M. Evarts. Evarts took his responsibilities to the cigarmakers seriously, and presented to the New York Supreme Court a brief arguing that the state law violated the due process clause of the New York Constitution by arbitrarily depriving tenement-house cigarmakers of their livelihood. The Supreme Court agreed with Evarts, and the State appealed to the Court of Appeals (New York's highest tribunal). Here Evarts rang all the changes on entrepreneurial freedom, invoking due process, freedom of contract and even natural law. He denied that the statute was a health measure; on the contrary, it was a discriminatory piece of class legislation *disguised as a health measure*. Carried away by his compassion for the small entrepreneur, Evarts even saw the evil hand of monopolistic capital behind the bill: it would place "the whole industry under the domination of organized capital and combination on the one hand, and lays it open on the other to unrestrained domination of trade unions."[40]

Not only did the Court of Appeals accept Evarts' contentions, but Judge Earl virtually wrote his decision from Evarts' brief—which in turn plagiarized extensively from the earlier dissents of Justices Field and Bradley. Speaking for a unanimous court, Earl agreed that the law arbitrarily deprived the cigarmakers of their property rights in their calling and of liberty as well. The court gave short shrift to the allegation that this was a health measure —there was no evidence that manufacturing cigars was bad for the health—and added:

> Under the mere guise of police regulations, personal rights and private property cannot be arbitrarily invaded, and the deter-

[39] See Twiss, *op. cit.*, pp. 93–109.
[40] *Ibid.*, p. 103.

mination of the legislature is not final or conclusive. If it passes an act ostensibly for the public health, and thereby destroys or takes away the property of the citizen, or interferes with his personal liberty, then it is for the courts to scrutinize the act and see whether it really relates to and is convenient and appropriate to promote the public health.[41]

To show that it meant business, the same court six months later uncovered another arbitrary interference with property rights disguised as a health measure—this time an act prohibiting the manufacture of butter substitutes.[42]

Both the late Benjamin R. Twiss and Clyde E. Jacobs have discussed at length the spread of the dogma of entrepreneurial liberty and there is no need, or room, here to recapitulate their findings. It is an index of the extent of this phenomenon in the state jurisdiction that when the first important case came before the United States Supreme Court in 1898 (*Holden* v. *Hardy*) those opposing the statute involved pointed out that in fourteen states similar enactments had been declared unconstitutional! *In re Jacobs* became one of the most extensively cited cases in legal history.

In 1897, in a case of little substantive significance here (*Allgeyer* v. *Louisiana*),[43] the Supreme Court squarely affirmed the doctrine of liberty of contract and voided a state insurance regulation which impinged on this "property" right. Then in 1898 came the first big test in the area of "social legislation," *Holden* v. *Hardy*.[44] A Utah statute of 1896 penalized any employer who required more than an eight-hour day of underground miners or smelter workers. Holden violated the law and upon arrest filed a petition for *habeas corpus*. He claimed that since the statute was unconstitutional, he was illegally imprisoned and, getting no succor from the Utah courts, appealed to the Supreme Court. The Utah enactment, he asserted, was a regulation of hours of employment disguised as a health measure; it was an

[41] 98 N.Y. 98, 110 (1885).

[42] People v. Marx, 99 N.Y. 377 (N.Y., Ct. of Appeals, 1885). Cited in Jacobs, *op. cit.*, p. 55. See generally, Roscoe Pound, "Liberty of Contract," *Yale Law Journal*, vol. xviii (1909), p. 454.

[43] 165 U.S. 578.

[44] 169 U.S. 366.

arbitrary infringement on entrepreneurial liberty which hid under the cloak of the police power. But, despite the pressure which had built up in the state and lower federal courts, the Supreme Court sustained the eight-hour law, though on a very narrow basis. Writing for the seven Justice majority, Justice Brown held that traditionally the states had special police jurisdiction over dangerous employment and that the Utah law fell into this category. The problem, Brown suggested, was at root factual; that is, the Court had the task of examining the facts in any specific case and determining whether "there are reasonable grounds for believing that [special health regulation for an industry] is supported by the facts . . . or whether [legislative] action be a mere excuse for an unjust discrimination, or the oppression, or spoliation of a particular class."[45] In short, Justice Brown accepted the premise of *In re Jacobs*, but denied its applicability to the matter *sub judice*.

Justice Rufus Wheeler Peckham and David Brewer dissented without opinion, but it is not difficult to project their views. Brewer we have already identified as Stephen Field's nephew and a fanatical fighter for entrepreneurial freedom of action; Peckham was a graduate of the reactionary New York Court of Appeals. And although the Court's opinion in *Holden* v. *Hardy* had rejected their view of the merits, it had endorsed their presuppositions. Underground miners were a hard test of their principle; they had to accept Holmes' view that hard cases make bad law and await a better opportunity. One was shortly forthcoming.

In 1897, following another series of newspaper articles exposing the foul conditions in bakeries, the New York legislature passed a statute which was designed to deal comprehensively with the problems of the baking industry. Although a health measure in form, in substance it was more; after the success of the Utah eight-hour law (which had been promoted by the Western Federation of Miners), the trade unions decided to press for regulation of working hours as part of the "health" package—similarly the Cigarmakers Union had supported the statute voided in *In re Jacobs*. In addition to requiring bakeries

[45] *Ibid.* at 398.

to install sanitary equipment and follow (from our view in the middle of the twentieth century) minimal health standards— "Every such bakery shall be provided with a proper wash room and water closet . . . apart from the bakeroom"[46]—the enactment stated that "no employee shall be required or permitted to work . . . more than sixty hours in one week, or more than ten hours in any one day."

The New York courts sustained the act as a valid exercise of the state's power and Lochner appealed to the Supreme Court. The decks were cleared and the Court was confronted with the one key issue: Was the New York statute a "health" law? In the light of Justice Brown's remarks in *Holden* v. *Hardy,* both sides presented briefs designed to base their cases on the "facts." Indeed Julius Mayer, for the State, submitted what later became known as a "Brandeis Brief": an elaborate study of the vital statistics of bakers to demonstrate that special measures were justified to protect the health of this category of workers. Bakers, he urged, were like underground miners or smelter operators, engaged in a "dangerous trade"; thus *Holden* v. *Hardy* was binding.

Justice Peckham wrote the opinion of the Court for the five judge majority. Precisely speaking, he held that the New York law was not a "health" measure but an unconstitutional violation of liberty of contract. Broadly construed, and his language was such as to encourage broad construction, he denounced all efforts to limit entrepreneurial freedom in the name of the public health and welfare. His opinion, in fact, was little less than a tirade against "social legislation"; he was determined not to permit the camel's nose under the tent:

> If this statute be valid, and if, therefore, a proper case is made out in which to deny the right of an individual, *sui juris* [legally competent], as employer or employee, to make contracts for the labor of the latter . . . there would seem to be no length to which legislation of this nature might not go.[47]

Disregarding statistics to the contrary, Peckham then announced that there could be "fair doubt that the trade of the

---

[46] The statute is cited in Lochner v. New York, 198 U.S. 45, 110 (1905).
[47] *Ibid.* at 58.

baker" was particularly unhealthy—it was healthier than some, and less healthy than others. With some sardonic cruelty he pointed out that "very likely physicians would not recommend the exercise of that or of any other trade as a remedy for ill health," and that "it might safely be affirmed that almost all occupations more or less affect the health . . . labor, even in any department, may possibly carry with it the seeds of unhealthiness." Thus if the state law was upheld, "No trade, no occupation, no mode of earning one's living could escape this all pervading power, and the acts of the legislative in limiting the hours of labor in all employments would be valid, although such limitations might seriously cripple the ability of the laborer to support himself and his family."[48]

It is a great temptation to quote at length from this incredible holding—which almost reads like a Marxist parody of capitalist principles—but the tone, the temper and the law have all been conveyed by these excerpts. One final matter deserving notice is Peckham's general bull of excommunication; after listing a number of state court decisions invalidating "social legislation," he concluded: "It is impossible for us to shut our eyes to the fact that many of the laws of this character, while passed under what is claimed to be the police power for the purpose of protecting the public health or welfare, are, in reality, passed from other [and by implication unconstitutional] motives."[49] This was nothing less than an invitation to aggrieved entrepreneurs to bring their legislative woes to the Supreme Court for principled redress.

Justice Harlan wrote a dissent which was joined by White and Day in which, drawing from the New York brief, he argued that the facts indicated that baking was a dangerous trade and consequently the rule of *Holden* v. *Hardy* should be determining. Separately dissenting, Oliver Wendell Holmes wrote one of his classic little *feuilletons* in which he seemingly rejected the judicial function as viewed by *both* Peckham and Harlan. "The Fourteenth Amendment," he noted caustically, "does not enact Mr. Herbert Spencer's Social Statics" and the job of the Court

---

[48] *Ibid.* at 59, 64.
[49] *Ibid.* at 65.

was not to prescribe a political economy for the people, one way or the other: "I strongly believe that my agreement or disagreement [with the principles of "social legislation"] has nothing to do with the right of a majority to embody their opinions in law." Holmes succinctly, with his usual flair for epigrammatic prose, concluded:

> [A Constitution] is made for people of fundamentally differing views, and the accident of our finding certain opinions natural and familiar, or novel, and even shocking, ought not to conclude our judgment upon the question whether statutes embodying them conflict with the Constitution of the United States.

> "General propositions [e.g., liberty of contract] do not decide concrete cases. The decisions will depend on a judgment or intuition more subtle than any articulate major premise. . . ." Every opinion tends to become a law. I think that the word "liberty," in the 14th Amendment, is perverted when it is held to prevent the natural outcome of a dominant opinion, *unless it can be said that a rational and fair man necessarily would admit that the statute proposed would infringe fundamental principles as they have been understood by the traditions of our people and our law.* (Italics added.)[50]

This dissent has been widely hailed as a rejection of the theory that the Court should intervene to substitute its views on economic, or political policy for those of a state legislature, or Congress. Careful reading of the section I have italicized indicates, however, that Holmes too hedged his bet. He did not deny that there might be circumstances when the Court should reject state regulations as violative of due process. In fact, in Holmes' thirty years on the Court, the Justices declared state action to be in violation of the Fourteenth Amendment 174 times, and Holmes only dissented in forty-three.[51] In other words, Holmes was not opposed to judicial oversight *per se*, but he was ready to give the wisdom of the legislature far greater weight than most of his colleagues. To some extent he identified legal theory with autobiography: Who is his "rational and fair man" if not a wise

---

[50] *Ibid.* at 75–6.
[51] My computation from data presented in Felix Frankfurter, *Mr. Justice Holmes and the Supreme Court* (Cambridge, 1938), Appendix I.

and sceptical old historian of the common law who has looked death in the face in battle, and recognizes with the Preacher that "all is Vanity"?

For years populists, progressives and socialists had been demanding that the Supreme Court's authority be circumscribed—William Jennings Bryan had made a campaign issue of the Court's power in 1896[52]—but the *Lochner* case also led enlightened conservatives into the ranks of the critics. Even Charles Warren, a constitutional scholar as eminent for his vehement endorsement of judicial review as for his meticulous historical work, was unable to find a good word for Peckham's holding,[53] and the latter was denounced in season and out by the ever-swelling group of distinguished intellectuals, lawyers and social workers who were spearheading the drive for social legislation.

However, *Lochner* was law and Peckham's views went forth as an authoritative pronouncement on the meaning of due process—even though the shift of one judge could lead to a different determination of similar matters in later litigation. The New York Court of Appeals, in particular, took the words of its alumnus seriously: if *Lochner* was a caricature of myopic entrepreneurial principles, the New York decisions in *People* v. *Williams*[54] and *Ives* v. *South Buffalo Railway Co.*[55] were caricatures of a caricature. In the former case, a New York law prescribing a ten-hour day and prohibiting night work for women *only* was voided, and in the latter, a very moderate (by later standards) Workmen's Compensation Law was invalidated; both enactments were unconstitutional limitations on entrepreneurial freedom. Whatever may have been the legal niceties (*Holden* v. *Hardy* was, of course, still good law for relevant categories of employment), *Lochner* appeared to be a virtually impregnable barrier to the enactment of effective factory legislation.

There was one hopeful sign, but it was hard to know its

[52] See Alan F. Westin, "The Supreme Court, the Populist Movement, and the Election of 1896," *Journal of Politics,* vol. xv (1953), p. 3.

[53] See his curt observation in *Congress, the Constitution, and the Supreme Court* (Boston, 1925), p. 236, and in "The Progressiveness of the Supreme Court," *Columbia Law Review,* vol. xiii (1913), p. 294.

[54] 189 N.Y. 131 (N.Y., Ct. of Appeals, 1907).

[55] 201 N.Y. 271 (N.Y., Ct. of Appeals, 1911).

portent. In 1908 (*Muller* v. *Oregon*),[56] the Supreme Court unexpectedly sustained an Oregon statute which forbade employers to contract for more than a ten-hour day with women factory workers. The unanimous Court, without in any way undermining or challenging the validity of *Lochner* v. *New York*, revived *Holden* v. *Hardy* and held it applicable. Women, said Justice Brewer, are different—as everyone knows—and the Court takes "judicial cognizance of all matters of general knowledge."[57] In the brief presented for Oregon, Louis D. Brandeis had set forth at elaborate length historical and contemporary evidence that women were entitled to special protection (the first "Brandeis Brief"): since there were two perfectly good precedents, one (*Holden* v. *Hardy*) which would validate the statute, and the other (*Lochner* v. *New York*) which would invalidate it, Brandeis concentrated on a factual presentation to lead the Court into the right category. The extent of his success can be gauged by the unanimity of the Justices and by the fact that Brewer wrote the opinion—though Paul Freund has suggested that Brewer always exhibited "marked sympathy for womenkind," which may have provided a special feature in this case.[58] At any rate, for whatever it may be worth, the Supreme Court did assert as a constitutional principle that women were different, thus providing some foothold for social legislation.

To conclude this analysis, we can summarize by stating that in the period from roughly 1890 to World War I a new principle became entrenched in American constitutional law: the doctrine of entrepreneurial liberty. Essentially this doctrine was a break with the common law and the common-law premise of the overriding interest of the community, or police power. The right to use one's property, to exercise one's calling, was given a natural law foundation—in a philosophically vulgar fashion—over and above the authority of the society to enforce the common weal. The consequence of this doctrine was not a *laissez-faire* universe, but one dominated by private governments which demanded (and to a great extent received) freedom for their activities and

---

[56] 208 U.S. 412.

[57] *Ibid.* at 421.

[58] Paul A. Freund, *On Understanding the Supreme Court* (Boston, 1951), p. 126.

restraints on the actions of their competitors, e.g., trade unions, regulatory commissions or reform legislatures. In historical terms, "free enterprise" thus involved two concomitant propositions: freedom of the entrepreneur to follow his calling, and a governmental, constitutional protection of the entrepreneur from his institutional enemies, public and private. We can get the full flavor of the *zeitgeist* by concluding with the entrepreneurial benediction pronounced in July 1902, by George F. Baer, president of the Reading Railroad:

> The rights and interests of the laboring man will be protected and cared for—not by the labor agitators, but by the Christian men to whom God in His infinite wisdom has given the control of the property interests of the country, . . .[59]

[59] Cited in Samuel Yellen, *American Labor Struggles* (New York, 1956), p. 160.

Entrepreneurial Liberty and the Commerce Power: Expansion, Contraction and Casuistry in the Age of Enterprise

THE HALF-CENTURY that separated 1870 from 1920 was the Age of Enterprise, the era in which the Industrial Revolution took the United States by storm, an era in which the terrific pressures of a new economic and social order were confronted, and largely contained, by the authority of the entrepreneurial elite. Only later, in the throes of the Depression, would the legitimacy of this "old order" come under serious attack. (Ironically, it was overturned by the New Deal electorate more as a penalty for failure than for any moral shortcomings implicit or explicit in its philosophy.) The key dogma of the "old order" was the concept of entrepreneurial liberty.[1] Put in its starkest terms, it amounted to the notion that what was good for business was good for the nation—more broadly, that the values of the business elite determined the political theory of the community as a whole. Aristotle pointed out long before Karl Marx that the

Reprinted, with permission, from *The University of Chicago Law Review,* Volume 30, Summer 1963, Number 4, pages 680–703.

[1] See the essay on p. 205.

character of the "political class" (*politeuma*) would establish the core values of the community (*polis*), and without any recourse to the Hegelian mystifications of Marxism one can assert that the entrepreneurs of the Age of Enterprise constituted the political class.

Moreover, and here the divergence from Marxist and progressive critics of the "Robber Barons" becomes decisive, the authority of the entrepreneurial elite rested, I submit, on the foundation of public approval. There was no conspiracy—there was no need for one: Until they demonstrated their incompetence to govern, and to provide the rationale for government in the shambles of the Depression, the entrepreneurial elite and its political spokesmen had the confidence of a clear majority of the American people. Since I have elaborated this proposition at some length in a forthcoming work,[2] I will pass over it here except to emphasize in specific terms what I take to be a simple fact: That even in the heavily industrialized states of the Northeast a majority of the population looked with suspicion on the work of trade unions. Indeed, I am not even convinced that trade union sentiments dominated among the "proletariat" itself—Horatio Alger was an ideal type with almost universal appeal.

Thus the critic in 1963 must face the hard reality that the behavior he condemns in terms of his own liberal standards was the outgrowth of a whole social pattern, not the work of a few insidious, capitalist plotters. And if he is to understand the workings of the Age of Enterprise, he must transport himself into a different universe of discourse, into a time when socialist leader Eugene Victor Debs could write John D. Rockefeller a letter requesting the oil baron's financial help in establishing a cooperative commonwealth.[3] Perhaps the *reductio ad absurdam* of the Age was reached when the Negro graduating class at Tuskegee in 1886 chose as its motto: "There's Always Room at the Top."[4]

The thesis here is that the interests of the entrepreneurial elite provided the warp and woof of American political and legal

[2] Roche, *The Quest for the Dream—Civil Liberties in Modern America* (New York, 1963).

[3] Ray Ginger, *The Bending Cross* 201 (1949).

[4] C. Vann Woodward, *Origins of the New South* 218 (1951).

theory in the Age of Enterprise—indeed, well on into the 1930s so far as certain crucial aspects of public law were concerned. There is a persistent legend that throughout this period the country was dominated by "conservatism," "rugged individualism" and *laissez-faire;* this seems to me to fly squarely into the face of the facts. As I have put it elsewhere, in an examination of "entrepreneurial liberty and the Fourteenth Amendment":

> There was clearly an elite of businessmen, but it was neither ruggedly individualistic, in terms of classic liberal economic thought, nor "conservative," in any acceptable definition of that much-abused term. On the contrary, this "elite lived at the public trough, was nourished by state protection and devoted most of its time and energies to evading Adam Smith's individualistic injunctions. In ideological terms, it was totally opportunistic: It demanded and applauded vigorous state action in behalf of its key values, and denounced state intervention in behalf of its enemies.[5]

In discussing the Supreme Court's interpretation of the police powers of the states, I argued that the "Constitution was not . . . adapted to the needs of *laissez-faire* 'conservatism' . . . but to the exigent needs of the great private governments."[6] It is my contention in this article that the same analysis can be rewardingly applied to the Court's interpretations of the commerce clause, indeed that only this set of interests can provide a framework of rationality to the contradictions that drive the logical analyst to despair. There is no master key to constitutional law, but this one seems to open more doors than most, and, in the tradition of William of Ockham, suggests an analytical proposition which eliminates both elaborate ideological and legal rationalizations and the need for villainous capitalists and meretricious judges. Honest and sincere men, like the dishonest and insincere, simply applied the dominant values of the epoch in their own fashions to the world around them.

When the Supreme Court in the 1870s and 1880s was forced to come to grips with the commerce clause, it discovered that the

[5] Roche, *supra* note 1, at 3.
[6] *Ibid.*

ambiguities of the Constitution and of constitutional interpretation by prior Courts provided little guidance for coping with novel situations, particularly those arising from the conflicts and disruptions of the new industrial order. Precedents gave little succor.

The framers of the Constitution had been characteristically Delphic: Article I, Section 8 gave Congress power over "Commerce with foreign Nations, and among the several States." This sounds simple and adequate, but upon reflection several difficulties emerge. First of all, what is "commerce"? Second, assuming we know the answer to that one, is the federal power to regulate interstate commerce exclusive? Or do the states also have jurisdiction? If so, when?

John Marshall, whose talent for avoiding constitutional clarity was positively unnerving, laid down a broad definition of "commerce" in the famous "steamboat case," *Gibbons* v. *Ogden*,[7] but flatly refused to divulge the broad basis of his opinion that New York had no right to regulate (in this case, grant a steamboat monopoly) Hudson River traffic. It had been argued—as Justice William Johnson contended in his separate concurrence—that congressional power over interstate commerce was complete and exclusive even if Congress took no action to implement its jurisdiction. That is, the very existence of this power in Congress excluded the states from the area. Marshall, however, was unwilling to go out on this limb. As he put it, "whether this power . . . is surrendered by the mere grant to Congress, or is retained until Congress shall exercise the power [was a problem that needed no exploration] because [the power] has been exercised. . . . The sole question is, can a State regulate commerce . . . while Congress is regulating it?"[8] "No" was his reply, but to justify it he put on an intricate legal morris dance and terminated with a sardonic denunciation of that "refined and metaphysical reasoning" which led men away from commonsense principles of constitutional interpretation. It was patent, he observed, that a national statute of 1793 licensing coastal vessels deprived the states of authority over interstate shipping.[9]

[7] 22 U.S. 9 Wheat. 1 (1824).
[8] *Idem.* at 200.
[9] 1 Stat. 305 (1793) (now 46 U.S.C. §§ 251–336 [1958]).

This is not said to denigrate the "Great Chief Justice." On the contrary, his capacity for broken-field running—approached only by Chief Justice Hughes in the 1930s—deserves the admiration of those who appreciate the political function of the Supreme Court. The point is that Marshall's opinion in *Gibbons* v. *Ogden*,[10] like his masterly and elusive holdings in *Dartmouth College* v. *Woodward*,[11] *Fletcher* v. *Peck*,[12] and *Cohens* v. *Virginia*,[13] were better politics than they were precedent. In each case, state power was checked in precise terms, but the grounds of decision were set out by Marshall in such a fashion that a seemingly broad rule of law was in fact hung on a very narrow holding.

An example can be found in the interpretation of the commerce clause. Marshall founded his extensive rhetorical foray against state power over interstate shipping on the coasting statute of 1793, but five years after the New York "steamboat case," he endorsed a different, and contradictory, construction of state jurisdiction over commerce. Delaware had authorized a dam across Black-Bird Creek—a navigable stream—and a shipowner knocked the dam down as an illegal obstruction to interstate commerce. *Willson* v. *Black-Bird Creek Marsh Co.*[14] reached the Supreme Court in 1829 on what appeared to be a simple variation of the facts of *Gibbons*: The shipowner had a license from the federal government under the act of 1793, and a state had impeded his right to conduct interstate commerce on an admittedly navigable stream. But this time John Marshall was not having any broad constructions. In a brief opinion, which reads as though he was rather annoyed at being bothered with such trivia, he suggests that the Middle and Southern states were full of small navigable creeks and that "under all circumstances of the case" the state was within its rights in authorizing a dam.[15] Presumably Willson should have picked a creek without a dam for the exercise of his commerce activities. The Chief

[10] 22 U.S. 9 Wheat. 1 (1824).
[11] 17 U.S. 4 Wheat. 518 (1819).
[12] 10 U.S. 6 Cranch. 87 (1810).
[13] 19 U.S. 6 Wheat. 264 (1821).
[14] 27 U.S. 2 Pet. 245 (1829).
[15] *Idem.* at 251.

Justice simply ignored the principle involved: Unlike a monopoly on the Hudson River, a dam on Black-Bird Creek was hardly worth the Court's concern. Metaphysicians could worry about matters of this sort; Marshall merely applied the maxim *de minimis*.

Marshall, in short, left the commerce clause strengthened as to content, but open-ended as to jurisdiction. Commerce was interpreted to include the process of transportation as well as the "stuff" transported, that is, Marshall set out a functional rather than a static definition of commerce.[16] But when it came to the problem of the relationship between federal and state control of interstate commerce, Marshall's precedents worked both ways. One defending a state limitation on interstate commerce could cite the *Black-Bird Creek* case, while his opponent could quote *Gibbons* v. *Ogden*. Both these precedental traditions marched on through the Taney years when because of the explosive problems of slavery and its states' rights buttress, the commerce clause of the Constitution became a controversial issue.[17] The Taney Court reflected this national dissension: Its interpretations of the commerce clause were literally a shambles of constitutional construction.[18]

Among the opinions, dissents, partial concurrences and partial dissents that litter the battlefield where the Taney Court met the commerce clause, one decision stands out: *Cooley* v. *Board of Wardens of Philadelphia*.[19] Without going into the details of the case, we can summarize by stating that in his opinion Justice Benjamin Curtis attempted to delineate the extent of state authority over interstate commerce. Congressional power over commerce, Curtis said, was only exclusive when the subject matter required exclusive congressional control. "Now the power to regulate commerce, embraces a vast field, containing not only many, but exceedingly various subjects, quite unlike in their

---

[16] *Cf*. Frankfurter, *The Commerce Clause*, chapter 1 (1937).

[17] If slaves were "property," could Congress exercise jurisdiction over interstate slave transactions? In 1803, Congress had prohibited the importation of slaves into states whose laws prohibited slavery. 2 Stat. 205. The Southerners wanted no more statutes on this model.

[18] Frankfurter, *op. cit.*, chapter 2.

[19] 53 U.S. 12 How. 929 (1851).

nature; some imperatively demanding a single uniform rule, operating equally on the commerce of the United States in every port; and some, like the subject now in question [pilot regulation in the Delaware River], as imperatively demanding that diversity, which alone can meet the local necessities of navigation."[20]

Curtis went on to imply that some sectors of commerce were beyond regulation even if Congress had not acted. (The so-called theory of "dormant exclusion" which postulates that the *latent* power of Congress *ex proprio vigore* bars the states from exercising jurisdiction even though the national government has not exercised its authority.) "Whatever subjects of this power are in their nature national, or admit only of one uniform system, or plan of regulation, may justly be said to be such a nature as to require exclusive regulation by Congress."[21] This has a fine solid ring about it—only Congress can regulate those aspects of commerce which require a national rule—but a moment's meditation will indicate that this formulation opens up a series of problems that would probably disconcert a master theologian. How, precisely, does one determine whether some aspect "imperatively" demands national uniformity? If Curtis knew, he was not telling; his opinion, he noted, was limited to the facts of the case at bar; it did not "extend to the question what other subjects . . . are within the exclusive control of Congress, or may be regulated by the states in the absence of all congressional legislation; nor to the general question how far any regulation of a subject by Congress may be deemed to operate as an exclusion of all legislation by the states upon the same subject."[22]

With this as background, let us move ahead to the 1870s and 1880s and the specific issue of railroad regulation. In *Munn* v. *Illinois*,[23] one of the lines of attack on the Granger laws which subjected railroads to state regulation was that they invaded a sector of interstate commerce which imperatively demanded a uniform national rule, that is, they intruded on the "dormant" commerce power. Chief Justice Waite refused to be drawn into

[20] *Idem.* at 319.
[21] *Ibid.*
[22] *Idem.* at 320.
[23] 94 U.S. 113 (1876). *Munn* was concerned with grain elevators; the other seven cases in the group dealt with state railroad regulations.

Curtis' theological web. State railroad regulation, he asserted, was simply a regulation of railroad activities *in* a state; it did not attempt to regulate matters in another state, but stopped at the state line. Quietly deserting Marshall's functional definition of commerce, Waite took his stand on geography: When Wisconsin, Minnesota, Iowa or Illinois clamped restrictions on railroads operating in their geographical jurisdiction, they were not impinging on commerce among the states. As in *Willson* v. *Black-Bird Creek Marsh Co.*, the state laws were not concerned with commerce; they were police regulations.

Munn v. *Illinois* was decided in the same year that the great railroad insurrection swept across the North and West, an episode that strongly attached the railroad managers to the federal government which had so decisively intervened in their behalf. The protection of the national government had demonstrated potency in yet another area: Federal judges were willing to defend railroads that were in federal receivership from the damage that strikes involved. Indeed, this seems to have been the first trying-ground for the antistrike injunction enforced in federal court by contempt proceedings, the "paper gatling gun" that later became the major corporate weapon in the anti-union struggle. In short, farsighted railroad leaders worked throughout the late 1870s and early 1880s to bring their enterprises within the scope of the *Cooley* rule of "dormant exclusion."

In 1886, the Supreme Court in the *Wabash* case[24] changed its position, despite a denial of change. Actually, said Mr. Justice Miller, *Munn* v. *Illinois* was still good law so far as the narrow facts presented in the Granger cases were concerned. But in the broader picture presented by Illinois' attempt to regulate freight rate abuse it was apparent that the jurisdiction of the national government had been invaded: "We must, therefore, hold that it is not, and never has been, the deliberate opinion of a majority of this Court that a statute of a State which attempts to regulate the fares and charges by railroad companies within its limits for a transportation which constitutes a part of commerce among the States, is a valid law."[25]

[24] Wabash, St. L. & Pac. Ry. v. Illinois, 118 U.S. 557 (1886).
[25] *Idem.* at 575.

Justices Bradley and Gray, and Chief Justice Waite, the latter the author of the *Granger* opinions, dissented with some vigor.[26] They took their position squarely on the *Munn* case and denounced the Court for undermining precedent in so devious a manner; essentially they concluded that if Congress chose to regulate interstate rates, the states would be superseded, but until such positive regulation was enacted, the states were surely within their rights under the police power.[27]

The impact of the *Wabash* decision was to withdraw the interstate activities of railroads from the jurisdiction of the states, thus leaving the corporations subject only to potential congressional regulation. Congress, however, took immediate action: Four months later, in February 1887, it created the Interstate Commerce Commission, the first national regulatory agency.[28] The ICC was assigned a broad jurisdiction in the area of rates, but was given virtually no armament; President Cleveland signed the bill with "reservations" about its constitutionality and wisdom, stating that "the cure might be worse than the disease."[29] Whatever curative powers it might have had were exorcised by the courts, which soon held that the ICC had no rate-fixing powers of its own and tied it up in a procedural strait-jacket.[30] Some railroad leaders attacked the Commission, but wiser heads prevailed. As Richard Olney, Cleveland's Attorney General, wrote one railroad president who had urged the abolition of the ICC:

[26] Bradley and Waite were perhaps a bit miffed by Miller's calm observation that when they had upheld the state rate laws in 1877, they were unaware of what they were doing—Miller and Bradley were the two strong minds on the Court and they often clashed. Miller, in addition, had been an active candidate for the Chief Justiceship in 1874, and was understandably aggrieved when Waite received the post. See Fairman, *Mr. Justice Miller and the Supreme Court, 1862–1890* (1939), especially Chapter 11. He also suspected that Bradley, who had ambitions of his own, had helped to block his nomination. See generally Magrath, *Morrison R. Waite: The Triumph of Character* (1963).

[27] Wabash, St. L. & Pac. Ry. v. Illinois, 118 U.S. 557, 577 (1886) (dissenting opinion).

[28] 24 Stat. 379 (1887), 49 U.S.C. §§ 1–27 (1958).

[29] Cited by Josephson, *The Politicos, 1865–1896*, at 389 (1938).

[30] See Cushman, *The Independent Regulatory Commissions* (1941), especially pp. 65–68.

The attempt [at abolition] would not be likely to succeed; if it did not succeed, and were made on the ground of the inefficiency and uselessness of the Commission, the result would very probably be giving it the power it now lacks. The Commission, as its functions have now been limited by the courts, is, or can be made, of great use to the railroads. It satisfies the popular clamor for a government supervision of railroads, at the same time that such supervision is almost entirely nominal. Further, the older such a commission gets to be, the more inclined it will be found to take the business and railroad view of things. It thus becomes a sort of barrier between the railroad corporations and the people and a sort of protection against hasty and crude legislation hostile to railroad interests . . . . The part of wisdom is not to destroy the Commission, but to utilize it.[31]

Many close students of American government would argue that Olney here predicted in uncanny terms the history of the ICC; we shall take the opportunity at a later point in the narrative to pay tribute again to his dialectical insight.

Three years after the Interstate Commerce Act, Congress again utilized the commerce clause for regulatory purposes, this time to strike at the "trusts" which had aroused a considerable amount of bad publicity by their total disinterest in the common weal. The Sherman Anti-Trust Act, passed in July 1890, on a wave of congressional apathy, was in institutional terms what the Chinese call a "paper dragon." Among other things it provided that "every contract, combination in the form of trust or otherwise, or conspiracy, in restraint of trade or commerce among the several States, or with foreign nations, is hereby declared to be illegal;"[32] and that "every person who shall monopolize, or attempt to monopolize any part of the trade or commerce among the several States . . . shall be deemed guilty of a misdemeanor."[33] Enforcement was to be by action in federal courts; no agency was established.

In commonsense terms, this statute probably made a criminal out of almost every businessman in the United States. In legal terms, it was hardly worth the paper it was inscribed on. What

[31] Cited by Josephson, *op. cit.*, at 526.
[32] 26 Stat. 209, 15 U.S.C. § 1 (1958).
[33] *Ibid.*

exactly was a "trust"? Or a "monopoly"? Or a "restraint of trade"? The Sherman Act was not so much an antitrust measure as it was a legal full-employment bill. Every one of these ambiguities had to be glossed in court. Antitrust law in the United States thus resembled nothing so much as the Jewish Talmud in which a few obscure texts were the basis of an enormous body of exegesis—with the Supreme Court as the *Sanhedrin*. Congress did not again concern itself with the problem for a quarter of a century.

Before we examine intensively what the Court and the inferior courts did with the commerce clause as an instrument of regulation, let us specify the dimensions of the problem. First, the Court had to determine the *reach* of the commerce power. Take for instance insurance contracts. In *Paul* v. *Virginia*[34] the Court had tersely held that insurance contracts were local in nature and thus 1) within state regulatory jurisdiction; and 2) by implication not subject to national control under the commerce clause. The Sherman Act, however, outlawed "every contract" in restraint of interstate commerce. Could a contract which was not itself *in* interstate commerce yet be a restraint *on* interstate commerce within the purview of the antitrust law? In other words, was it possible for something to be within the scope of the commerce power for one purpose, and not for another?

As a second dimension of the problem the Court had to determine the *limits* or *checks*, if any, on the exercise of congressional jurisdiction. Were some substantive areas, such as agriculture, manufacturing, mining, completely within the police power of the respective states? Or could Congress regulate certain aspects of enterprises essentially local in character? Finally, were there any procedural checks on Congress? Were any techniques of regulation *ultra vires*? On all of these matters the Constitution was obscure, the precedents were open-ended, and the Supreme Court was on its own.

Now a study of this sort cannot go into the intricate aspects of judicial construction of the commerce clause for obvious reasons. There are many volumes dedicated to the analysis of railroad regulation, antitrust and other ramifications of that one ambiguous constitutional pronouncement. Here we are concerned with

[34] 75 U.S. 8 Wall. 168 (1868).

the broader issues with full recognition of the fact that when a wide brush is used, details are often blurred. The important proposition is that there was no road map for the Court to follow: Every constitutional route forked before the Justices, and no matter which fork they took, there were adequate precedents to supply legal rationalization. In applying the antique commerce clause to an unforeseen industrial universe, the Court was rewriting the Constitution in terms of its own dominant value patterns.

Let us begin the analysis with the growth of the "national police power," an area which leads naturally to the more complex sectors of judicial improvisation. By its terms, the Constitution did not grant to the federal government plenary authority to legislate for the health, safety, morals and welfare of the people —the so-called "police power." The national government was to exercise authority only in those areas specifically designated in the Constitution, largely those specified in Article I, Section 8. From the outset, as we have seen, congressional authority naturally came into conflict with the police power of the states—both *Gibbons* v. *Ogden* and *Willson* v. *Black-Bird Creek Marsh Co.* were instances of this confrontation—and the Court always made explicit the point that, properly understood, there was no overlap. The powers of the federal government ended where the police power of the states began and vice versa.[35] The law is the nesting-place par excellence of circular definition, of propositions that are mutually validating when stripped to their essentials. National and state jurisdiction have always been in an uneasy, definitional equilibrium in which state authority is authority which is not national.

The framers of the Constitution were an extremely shrewd group of professional politicians and were quite aware of this central ambiguity. At certain points they took special measures to guarantee the police power of the states against *indirect* federal encroachment. After all, one of the big issues in the struggle with Britain had been the parliamentary employment of trade regulations for taxation purposes and in *Letters from a Farmer in Pennsylvania,* John Dickinson, later a member of the Constitu-

---

[35] See Powell, "Child Labor, Congress, and the Constitution," in 3 *Selected Essays on Constitutional Law* 527 (1938).

tional Convention, had made an ingenious and rather disingenuous distinction between parliamentary regulations of trade (which were legitimate) and taxes (which were illegitimate).[36]

The framers, then, were not babes in the woods. They were quite aware that such powers as the taxation and commerce clauses bestowed were capable of employment to achieve social goals or political purposes seemingly unrelated to raising revenue or establishing interstate commercial rationality. This can be verified by turning to Article I, Section 9, of the Constitution, a section that represented institutionalized suspicion. The slavery interests at the convention, led by the South Carolinians, were concerned lest the commerce and taxation powers be used for antislavery purposes.[37] They demanded guarantees, and one of the resulting compromises provided that "the Migration or Importation of such Persons as any of the States now existing shall think proper to admit, shall not be prohibited by the Congress prior to the Year 1808, but a Tax or duty may be imposed on such Importation, not exceeding ten dollars for each Person." Later in the same section, the mercantile interests got some protection they felt necessary: "No preference shall be given in any Regulation of Commerce or Taxation to the Ports of one State over those of another."

Almost immediately the commerce power was put to work as

[36] See Dickinson's Letter II (1767–68) cited in Mason, *Free Government in the Making* (1949), pp. 102–04. Dickinson's logic is worth brief mention: He anticipated fully the logomachy of the Supreme Court a century and a half later when the judges came to grips with regulatory problems. There were two categories—one legal: trade regulation; the other illegal: taxation for revenue—and the question was how to identify a specific parliamentary act that *appeared* to be a trade regulation, but could also be a tax. The answer, said Dickinson was simple: The *intention* of the enactment determined its category. So far, so good—but how did one ascertain the intention of the legislation? Different men have supported it for different reasons and a clever draftsman may in his preamble have announced an innocent purpose for a sinister act (parliamentary debates were still secret). Again, Dickinson urged, the answer was plain: The intention was evaluated by the *consequences*. In short, an act was "illegal" if founded on "illegal" motives, and "illegal" motives were established on the basis of "illegal" consequences.

[37] See Roche, "The Founding Fathers: A Reform Caucus in Action," 55 *Am. Pol. Sci. Rev.* 799, 811 (1961).

an instrument of foreign policy. In 1794, President Washington put a temporary embargo on shipments to Britain and France, which were seizing American shipping, and asked Congress to enact a strong measure. Senator Aaron Burr prepared a bill which was directed against England; it lost in the House, and a subsequent anti-French proposal failed in the Senate. The power to regulate foreign commerce had become an instrument for attaining a pro-British or pro-French foreign policy.[38] Later President Jefferson was to employ the same embargo device in a utopian quest for American disengagement from European problems. The Embargo of 1807 was a massive exercise of national power; it forbade Americans to engage in commerce with the belligerents.[39] In other words, the congressional power over foreign commerce was employed to prohibit it. The Federalists, hastily abandoning national power in the interests of New England shipping, denounced the bill as unconstitutional—the power over commerce, they claimed, was not the power to destroy it—but in the United States District Court for Massachusetts, Judge John David delivered a resounding defense of national authority.[40] No case reached the Supreme Court.

There were other instances of "police" regulations being enacted under the commerce and taxing powers. In 1803, for example, Congress passed an act[41] that made it a federal offense to import slaves into a state whose laws banned importation. This enactment was an early example of a so-called "divesting statute," an enactment which delegated federal authority to the states in specific areas as a buttress for state law. And in 1866, Congress imposed a 10 percent tax on state banknotes, designed to drive this erratic currency out of existence, and despite great howls that it was a violation of states' rights disguised as a tax, the statute was sustained by the Court in 1869.[42] Henceforth the

---

[38] Schachner, *Aaron Burr* (1961), pp. 134–35.

[39] See 2 Adams, *History of the United States of America During the Administration of Thomas Jefferson* (1930), pp. 249–71.

[40] United States v. The William, 28 Fed. Cas. 614 (No. 16,700) (D. Mass. 1808).

[41] See fn 17 *supra*.

[42] Veazie Bank v. Fenno, 75 U.S. 8 Wall. 333 (1869).

discussion will be confined to the development of a national police power with regard to the commerce clause only—the taxing power underwent a parallel development.[43]

There is an inherent paradox in the concept of interstate commerce: Everything that happens in interstate commerce simultaneously happens in a state (or territory). Consequently, every regulation based on the commerce clause directly affects goods, people or transactions that are within the geographical jurisdiction of a local legislature. From a logical perspective, the big problem has always been to specify the point at which this invisible entity called commerce among the states begins or ends. But logic, as usual, supplies no answer—or rather, supplies several, depending on the premise adopted. If, for example, a farmer refuses to grow corn in Iowa for sale in Illinois, it can be argued that he is hindering interstate commerce. If a group of radicals tell farmers not to grow Iowa corn for "exploiters" in Illinois, it can be urged that they are conspiring to hinder interstate commerce. If a newspaper urges a group of radicals . . . and so it goes to infinity. Another syllogism begins with an assertion that the regulation of morals is a matter exclusively within state jurisdiction[44] and thence argues *ex hypothesi* that the federal government can have no authority over private morality; thus a federal law prohibiting interstate shipment of, say, poker chips would be an unconstitutional and unwarranted extension of the commerce power. Put differently, the courts had the task of identifying the external manifestations of an intangible process— it was rather like designing a suit for a poltergeist.

By 1890 certain broad propositions seemed to be taken for granted; both the Interstate Commerce Act and the Sherman Act were in principle affirmations of Congress' power to police certain categories of interstate business. Moreover, beginning about 1890, a succession of statutes were enacted which were designed to prevent "the arteries of interstate commerce from being employed as conduits for articles hurtful to the public health, safety,

[43] See Cushman, "Social and Economic Control Through Federal Taxation," 18 *Minn. L. Rev.* (1934), p. 759.
[44] This argument is based upon the Tenth Amendment.

or morals."[45] Leading the procession here were the prohibitionists. (John Marshall had ruled in *Brown* v. *Maryland*,[46] that state jurisdiction over articles in interstate commerce began only when the "original package" had been broken and in 1890, the Supreme Court had manipulated the "original package" doctrine to make a shambles of state prohibition laws by applying this rule to interstate liquor shipments.)[47] The prohibition lobby succeeded in 1890 by gaining congressional enactment of the Wilson Act which gave the states control over interstate shipments of liquor upon arrival in the state.[48] While the Supreme Court subsequently sustained the act, it crushed the prohibitionist ambition of stopping liquor at the state line by holding that "arrival in the state" meant arrival at the address of the consignee.[49] Instead of succeeding in blocking the border and holding the carriers liable for violations—the key to effective enforcement—the drys were again forced to pursue each shipment to its destination before applying sanctions. Back they went to Congress for redress and eventually, in the Webb-Kenyon Act of 1913,[50] the technique was perfected: Liquor was simply defined out of interstate commerce! That is, liquor shipped across state lines was by definition *not* interstate commerce, but instead was subject to the plenary authority of the states.

While the prohibitionists led the way with amazing legal creativity, others were not far behind. It is often forgotten that the Sherman Act contained a provision (Section 6) that barred the products made by "trusts" from using the facilities of interstate commerce. The legislative antechambers in Washington seemed full of lobbyists proposing that Congress should use its control over commerce to eliminate lotteries, obscene literature,

[45] The phrase is Senator Knox's, cited in Cushman, "The National Police Power Under the Commerce Clause of the Constitution," 3 *Selected Essays on Constitutional Law* (1938), pp. 36, 64.

[46] 25 U.S. 12 Wheat. 419 (1827).

[47] Leisy v. Hardin, 135 U.S. 100 (1890).

[48] 26 Stat. 313 (1890), 27 U.S.C. § 121 (1958); see Cushman, *op. cit.*, at 81–84.

[49] See *In re* Rahrer, 140 U.S. 545 (1891) (sustaining statute); Rhodes v. Iowa, 170 U.S. 412 (1898) ("Arrival in the state" means arrival at address of consignee.)

[50] 37 Stat. 699 (1913), 27 U.S.C. § 122 (1958).

contraceptives, oleomargarine, prostitution, impure food and drugs, and a number of other items adjudged evil for one reason or another.[51] The opponents of this sort of regulation knew they had a bad case with liquor, which had been traditionally subjected to extraordinary regulations and which was in poor repute, in theory at least, among the better elements of the community. But in 1895 a better instance for legal defense emerged when Congress passed an antilottery statute forbidding the shipment of lottery tickets either through the mails or in interstate commerce.

The lottery was a fine old American institution that had fallen on evil days. In colonial America it had been a fundraising technique for charities[52] and later a standard method for raising revenue in many states but, by the turn of the century, had apparently become a racket with many citizens protesting that they could not collect on winning tickets. Modern techniques of communication had made it possible for a crook in Louisiana (a big lottery state) to bilk investors 1500 miles away. When the aggregations of the bilked got their own state legislatures to act, they found that, while local lotteries could be suppressed, nothing could be done about those in other states who solicited by mail or express. So Congress was wheeled into action, and the mails and express channels were closed.[53]

A Texas lottery promoter, appropriately named Champion, provided the test case. Indicted for conspiring to ship lottery tickets to California by express, he sought release by *habeas corpus* claiming the statute to be unconstitutional and void. A tremendous legal battle developed: The Supreme Court twice asked for reargument and was seriously divided in the final decision which downed Champion 5–4. The opinion in *Champion v. Ames*,[54] delivered by Mr. Justice Harlan, deserves close atten-

---

[51] During the same period, the taxing power was moving in an identical direction: The dairy interests, for example, managed to get a commerce bill barring colored oleo from shipment into states which forbade it, *and* a special excise tax on colored oleo: one-quarter cent per pound on uncolored margarine and ten cents per pound on oleo colored to resemble butter. Cushman, *supra*, at 774.

[52] The founders of Princeton University, good Calvinists all, ran a lottery. Schachner, *op. cit*, at 12.

[53] 18 U.S.C. § 1302 (1958).

[54] 188 U.S. 321 (1903).

tion, for it supplied the constitutional foundations of what will be referred to here (in Robert E. Cushman's phrase) as the commerce-police power. What Harlan had to do was provide a rationale for this exercise of congressional power that would not automatically open the door for legislative regulation of anything that struck its whimsy. To repeat, the precedent of liquor was not too useful since the argument there was that alcoholic beverages were things harmful in themselves—Bad Things. But a lottery ticket was not intrinsically evil—it could not even harm a small child who found it, a characteristic test of Bad Things.

Justice Harlan was not daunted by this difficulty: He knew an immoral enterprise when he saw one. Once he had asked himself the question in the form he used—"[W]hy may not Congress, invested with the power to regulate commerce among the several States, provide that such commerce *shall not be polluted* by . . . lottery tickets . . . ?"[55]—the reply was obvious. A lottery ticket was symbolic of a Bad Thing; thus, while not harmful in itself, it represented what Harlan referred to as the "widespread pestilence of lotteries" and was an essential component in a process "confessedly injurious to the public morals." The Chief Justice (Fuller) dissented with strong support from Justices Brewer, Peckham and Shiras on the ground that Congress was invading the reserved powers of the states.[56]

After *Champion* v. *Ames,* the road to regulation seemed clear; it appeared as though Congress had extensive authority to employ the commerce power for social, political, health and moral purposes. Naturally enough, Justice Harlan had engaged in the usual judicial fudging about potential limitations: "[T]he power of Congress to regulate commerce among the States," he noted darkly, "although plenary, cannot be deemed arbitrary, since it is subject to such limitations or restrictions as are prescribed by the Constitution."[57] However, he also suggested that the Constitution offered little protection to a Bad Thing, or a Bad Man doing a Bad Thing. Referring to the Fifth Amendment's guarantee of entrepreneurial liberty he excluded Champion's lottery business from its protection—like liquor distillers, lottery managers were

[55] *Idem* at 356. (Emphasis added.)
[56] *Idem* at 364 (dissenting opinion).
[57] *Idem* at 362–63.

under the entrepreneurial ban of excommunication.[58] The laws, and the decisions sustaining them, came thick and fast after 1900, and it would be tedious to enumerate them here. What would be useful is a classification from the other end of the problem; that is, an examination of the character of the things regulated and the legal justifications for the regulations.

Initially, the answers are easy. The first group of things barred from interstate commerce were clearly *bad in themselves:* poorly packed explosives, opium, diseased animals, infected food products, poisonous patent medicines. Next was the category of items that could be harmful, but hardly ranked with poisons—notably alcoholic beverages and narcotics. However, this second group still retained a tangible quality—one could get drunk or narcotized. With the third category, one entered the realm of legal metaphysics—a realm no less real for being repudiated by its very progenitors—and was confronted by things *harmless in themselves* which involved or symbolized bad and immoral activities. At the risk of boring the reader with classification, this third group can be roughly subdivided into two further classes: Those things which symbolized Evil because of the way they were manufactured (goods produced by "trusts" or by child labor are fine examples), and those which were corrupted by the purpose to which they were destined (prostitutes under the terms of the Mann Act, for instance, could be transported interstate to visit their grandmothers but not their customers).

Little more need be said about the things (a clumsy word, perhaps, but the only one that takes in the whole genus) which were patently or potentially harmful in themselves; the crux of the problem of the federal police power lay in identifying things properly in the third category. Let us examine a few cases which exemplify the two suggested subclassifications. Congress, disturbed by the fact that some railroads owned coal mines and other industrial holdings, provided in 1906—in the so-called "commodities clause" of the Hepburn Act—that a carrier could

---

[58] See Roche, *supra* note 1, for an examination of the interesting question: When was property not property? I have there suggested that the real problems of the Fifth and Fourteenth Amendments in this connection are not so much in defining "due process" as in defining "property." See also Mugler v. Kansas, 123 U.S. 623 (1887).

not haul its own commodities.[59] The purpose was to prevent rate discrimination in favor of the road's own products. Now coal is coal; there is no intrinsic difference between coal owned by a railroad and that owned by some other party—*ownership* was the basis of classification. From the viewpoint of the commerce-police power, coal owned by a carrier was Bad Coal, barred from interstate commerce. In 1909, this proposition was sustained by the Supreme Court in *United States* v. *Delaware & Hudson Co.*[60] Section 6 of the Sherman Act, which prohibited the shipment of "trust"-made items in interstate commerce was similarly upheld in *United States* v. *American Tobacco Co.*[61]

A somewhat different application of the same technique was employed in 1900 in the Lacey Act.[62] Under great pressure from conservationists to protect egrets and other birds that were being mercilessly butchered to feed the millinery market—no woman was complete without a plumed hat—and recognizing the inadequacy of state conservation laws to cope with the problem, Congress made it unlawful to ship in interstate commerce any birds or animals (or components thereof) killed in violation of state law. Yet the legality or illegality of the shooting in no way affected the character of an egret's plume. The Lacey Act was the ancestor to many laws today which penalize criminal acts committed in a state on the basis of subsequent utilization of the channels of interstate commerce—the federal kidnapping statute, the "Lindbergh Law,"[63] is the most famous, but another widely employed law, the Dwyer Act, makes it a federal offense to take a stolen car across a state line.[64] One wonders how the police could possibly deal with crime in our day—when a criminal may be at the other end of the continent in five hours—if this particular technique had not been devised. It made nationwide law enforcement possible.

In the same way that a lump of railroad-owned coal looks like

---

[59] Lumber was excepted. 34 Stat. 584 (1906), 49 U.S.C. §§ 1, 6, 14, 15, 16, 16(a), 18, 20, 41 (1958).

[60] 213 U.S. 366 (1909).

[61] 221 U.S. 106 (1911).

[62] 31 Stat. 187 (1900), as amended, 16 U.S.C. §§ 668(d), 701 (1958).

[63] 18 U.S.C. §§ 10, 1201 (1958).

[64] 18 U.S.C. § 2312 (1958).

any other lump of coal, a woman bound across a state line for immoral purposes looks about like any other woman. But for a man to escort her is a crime against the United States. The Mann Act, passed in 1910 after the newspapers and magazines had discovered and publicized the "White Slave Trade" or organized prostitution, was based on the theoretical principle that a man who took a woman from one state to another for a lascivious purpose, converted her into a Bad Thing. Originally aimed at organized vice, the Mann Act was later extended by the Court to cover interstate movement for sheer, unorganized, unpaid concupiscence.[65] The evil purpose alone was sufficient to bring the national government's police power into action. The Mann Act may have harassed the white slavers, but unfortunately it has also supplied a fertile basis for blackmail against rich young men in fast cars who have not kept adequate track of either the state lines or of the legal education of their companions.

Each of these commerce-police statutes was passed, in the usual American fashion, to deal with a specific problem over which the public was momentarily up in arms. After the muckrakers got through with the patent medicine industry, for example, millions of Americans purged their bathroom cabinets, fearfully consulted their doctors, and wrote outraged letters to their congressmen. The latter, who had probably undergone a similar sequence themselves, rushed to enact the Pure Food and Drug Act of 1906.[66] The Supreme Court, whose members also read the horror stories of the "poison-squad" experiments in the *Ladies' Home Journal* (Dr. Harvey W. Wiley, the driving force behind the pure food and drug movement, had fed food preservatives and similar material to guinea pigs with horrifying results) and Mark Sullivan's blasts against the patent medicine quacks in *Collier's*,[67] upheld the statute without a murmur in 1911.[68]

[65] 36 Stat. 825 (1910) (now 18 U.S.C. §§ 1421–24 [1958]) upheld in Hoke v. United States, 227 U.S. 308 (1913), and extended by the Court to outlaw mistresses in Caminetti v. United States, 242 U.S. 470 (1917).

[66] 34 Stat. 768 (1906) (repealed in 1938) (now 52 Stat. 1059 [1938], 21 U.S.C. §§ 1–5, 7–15 [1958]).

[67] Cited by Filler, *Crusaders for American Liberalism*, rev. ed. (1950), pp. 144–156.

[68] Hipolite Egg Co. v. United States, 220 U.S. 45 (1911).

Or take the regulation of meat packing. When, during the Spanish-American War, troops had been sickened and killed by "embalmed meat," the nation had been horrified, but little good came of it. Then, topping several articles about the filthy conditions in the packinghouses presented in muckraking journals, came Upton Sinclair's literally nauseating blockbuster—*The Jungle*.[69] Like the patent-medicine industry, the meat packers fought vigorously against federal regulation. Both were successful in the sense that they prevented legislation with real teeth from being enacted.[70] But still, public revulsion against the packers forced through a meat inspection statute in 1906[71] which provided the wedge for later effective regulation. The public demanded action and Congress turned to the commerce power for the peg on which to hang an inspection law and a set of regulations governing the "manufacture" of canned and preserved meat. No one worried much about the country's Constitution; they were concerned wholly with their own constitutions.

From this narrative, one might get the impression that there was no opposition to the expansion of the commerce power or that the judiciary simply and invariably endorsed congressional action—an erroneous assumption. While it is true that after the close decision in *Champion* v. *Ames* the other commerce-police cases fell into line and that in none of the instances of legislation mentioned here did the Court hold an act of Congress unconstitutional, in most of these areas judicial opinion merely coincided with public opinion. No one particularly wanted to be poisoned by cough medicine or eat hams prepared in *The Jungle*. Nor was there much sympathy for prostitution among the judges. Yet the fight against the widening of the national police power went on and in certain sectors was extremely successful. These cases have been retained for analysis after the main lines of the argument have been established, for they provide startling contrasts with the decisions we have been examining. It will hardly come as a surprise to learn that the two sectors in which the Court refused

[69] Upton Sinclair, *The Jungle* (1906).

[70] See Filler, *op. cit.* at 168–70.

[71] 34 Stat. 674 (1906); see 34 Stat. 1260 (1907), 21 U.S.C. §§ 71–91 (1958).

to permit the Congress a wide range of authority were those intimately associated with entrepreneurial liberty; the regulation of big business and corrective labor legislation.

When in the early 1890s, the American Sugar Refining Company, popularly known as the Sugar Trust, bought out its last big competitors and achieved control of roughly 98 percent of the nation's production of refined sugar, the United States government invoked the Sherman Act. The Department of Justice claimed that the contracts eliminating the competition constituted a conspiracy in restraint of trade as they were designed to monopolize interstate commerce in sugar. In 1895 the Supreme Court blasted the government's hopes, ruling 8–1 that "commerce succeeds to manufacture, and is not a part of it."[72] The Sherman Act was thus judicially emasculated so far as its primary purpose, "trust-busting," was concerned. Chief Justice Fuller, who two years earlier had dissented in the lottery case, this time carried the day with only Mr. Justice Harlan dissenting. He effectively defined commerce and the concomitant federal police power as beginning after the production process is complete—"trade and commerce [only] served manufacture to fulfill its function," and were not part of one continuous entity.[73] Moreover, he revived the doctrine of *Paul* v. *Virginia*[74] that contracts were matters of local concern, and simply ignored the conspiracy aspects of the indictment. Thus the agreements signed in Philadelphia which brought 98 percent of the sugar production in the country under one corporate roof were not subject to national regulation—even though in commonsense economic terms they determined, on a nationwide basis, the price of sugar.

What must be kept in mind here is the curious fact that the Court limited the scope of the commerce power here without in any direct way intruding on the precedental value of *Champion* v. *Ames* or any of the other subsequent decisions putting a wide construction on the commerce clause. In the *Knight* case, the Court initiated the two-track approach to the commerce clause which became so distinctive in later years. Indeed, in the same year of 1895, the Court speaking through Mr. Justice Brewer interpreted

---

[72] United States v. E. C. Knight Co., 156 U.S. 1, 12 (1895).
[73] *Idem* at 17.
[74] 75 U.S. 8 Wall. 168 (1868); see text at fn. 34 *supra*.

the commerce authority broadly enough to justify the imprisonment of Eugene V. Debs,[75] who in one view of his activities with the American Railway Union had merely been influencing workers not to fulfil their (local) labor contracts—that is, to strike. Apparently the commerce-police power was broad enough to enforce labor contracts, but too weak to inhibit business agreements. And Mr. Justice Harlan, who disliked trade unions about as much as he despised "trusts," concurred in the *Debs* opinion.

Justice Harlan returned to the fray in 1904 summarily to dispose, for a minority of the Court,[76] of the contention that an agreement to form a holding company was not in interstate commerce. In *Northern Securities Co.* v. *United States,* Harlan set forth the decisions on the Sherman Act, including the *Sugar Trust* case, and announced that they fully supported the following propositions;

> That although . . . [the antitrust act] has no reference to the mere manufacture or production of articles or commodities within the limits of the several States, it does embrace and declare to be illegal every contract, combination, or conspiracy, in whatever form, of whatever nature, and whoever may be parties to it, which directly or necessarily operates in restraint of . . . [interstate and foreign commerce];
>
> That the act is not limited to restraints of interstate and international commerce that are unreasonable in their nature, but embraces all direct restraints imposed by any combination, conspiracy or monopoly upon such trade or commerce;
>
> That combinations even among private manufacturers or dealers whereby interstate or international commerce is restrained are equally embraced by the act. . . .[77]

It is impossible to reconcile Harlan's summary of the antitrust law with the decision in the *Sugar Trust* case, and not unexpectedly Chief Justice Fuller joined the dissent. Harlan's remark

[75] *In re* Debs, 158 U.S. 564 (1895).

[76] Northern Securities Co. v. United States, 193 U.S. 197 (1904). Brown, McKenna and Day, J.J., joined in the opinion. Fuller, C.J., and Holmes, White and Peckham, J.J., dissented while Brewer, J., concurred on narrow grounds.

[77] *Idem* at 331.

that *all* restraints of trade, not merely "unreasonable" ones, were comprehended in the statutory ban was directed at Mr. Justice Brewer, who was plugging for the "Rule of Reason"—a judicial amendment to the Sherman Act that will be discussed subsequently. It is noteworthy that the conspiracy provisions were crucially emphasized by Harlan—and burked in Fuller's dissent.

Some "local" contracts were thus Bad Things from the perspective of the commerce-police power; both the *Debs* and the *Northern Securities* decisions suggested that railroad contracts in particular were within the national jurisdiction. Then came the first *Employer's Liability* cases[78] and *Adair* v. *United States*[79] in which Justice Harlan put on a spectacular display of judicial existentialism in considering each case as an original matter, with no connection or continuity. Although the Government contended that the Federal Employers Liability Act of 1906[80] could be considered to fall under the general heading of a safety measure, it was radically different from previous enactments of the sort which had prescribed safety regulations for railroads engaged in interstate commerce. Instead of prescribing automatic coupling devices, adequate lights or reasonable speeds, this statute altered the traditional master-servant relationship in liability actions. Without going into the details of the common law of liability, suffice it to say that this federal act undermined the carriers' legal defenses against damage suits. It applied to all railroad employees, not just to those engaged in interstate railroad operations. The Supreme Court, over Harlan's semi-dissent,[81] held the statute to be unconstitutional because it applied to employers of workers in intrastate as well as interstate commerce[82] (though three years later the Safety Appliance Act of 1903 was sustained in its application to equipment used only in intrastate commerce[83]). Harlan insisted that the statute was

[78] 207 U.S. 463 (1908).

[79] 208 U.S. 161 (1908).

[80] 34 Stat. 23 (now Employers' Liability Act [Railroads] of 1908, 34 Stat. 65, as amended, 45 U.S.C. §§ 51–60 [1958]).

[81] 207 U.S. at 540.

[82] *Idem* at 504.

[83] Southern Ry. v. United States, 222 U.S. 20 (1911), upholding 32 Stat. 943 (1903), 45 U.S.C. § 8 (1958).

constitutional in its application to workers in *interstate* commerce and felt that the Court had misconstrued the law.

However, in the *Adair* case Justice Harlan went wild. He declared that the congressional attempt to bar "yellow dog" contracts in the railroad industry violated the due process clause of the fifth amendment as an impairment of entrepreneurial liberty. Then he proceeded to proclaim further, in a totally unnecessary judicial safari, that the commerce power did not reach labor relations! Not only did Harlan cite with seeming approval the opinion of the Court in the first *Employers' Liability* cases, but he proceeded to set out the view that labor contracts (unlike liability rules) were *not* subject to regulation: "[W]hat possible legal or logical connection is there here," he asked, "between an employee's membership in a labor organization and the carrying on of interstate commerce?" His answer? "Such relation to a labor organization cannot have, in itself and in the eye of the law, any bearing upon the commerce with which the employee is connected by his labor and services."[84]

Now this was a two-edged sword. If it forbade federal government intervention on the worker's behalf, it also implied that federal action to enforce labor contracts, that is, break strikes, would be *ultra vires* the commerce power. In other words, if railway labor relations were beyond the reach of the national government, the *Debs* case would silently be overruled. Not unexpectedly, Richard Olney, whose ruthless intervention as Attorney General had broken the Pullman strike and accompanying boycott, picked this intimation up from the decision and hastened to write an article criticizing this aspect of the opinion in the *American Law Review*.[85] However, as the *Danbury Hatters* case[86] later demonstrated, Olney was needlessly distressed: The Supreme Court was only excluding from the commerce-police power prolabor legislation.

Before examining the legal legerdemain that characterized the

---

[84] 208 U.S. at 178. The commerce clause, in his view, could thus reach the liability aspects of a labor contract but not the conditions of employment presumably encompassed in the same agreement!

[85] Olney, "Discrimination Against Union Labor—Legal?," *42 Am. L. Rev.* 11 (1908); see Lieberman, *Unions Before the Bar* (1950), p. 54.

[86] Loewe v. Lawlor, 208 U.S. 274 (1908).

Danbury Hatters case, it might be well to reiterate the line of argument so far. Contemporaneously with a series of decisions sustaining the commerce-police power of Congress over a broad congeries of national problems, the Supreme Court was marching up the hill and down again on the subject of contracts in restraint of trade. A lot of loose logic went into the discussion on both sides of the argument, but the law might be summarized as declaring that 1) production and manufacture and contracts relating to them were local in character *except* 2) when they were part of a process that restrained interstate or foreign commerce or "directly affected" it. To point up the paradoxes involved in the *Danbury Hatters* case, it should be emphasized that control of 98 percent of the nation's sugar production did not deprive the American Sugar Refining Company of its "local" character, and that the labor contracts even of interstate railroad workers appeared to be outside the range of federal control.

In 1901, the United Hatters of North America, AFL, began a campaign to unionize the Danbury hat shop of Loewe and Fuchs and in 1902 they called a strike. When Loewe and Fuchs continued to produce hats with nonunion labor, the union began a nationwide campaign to bring the firm into disrepute. Merchants were requested not to handle Loewe's hats, and the union asked the public to refuse to buy hats made in nonunion premises. The American Federation of Labor put the firm on its "boycott" list.[87] Loewe, with a war chest supplied by the American Anti-Boycott Association, then went into the United States District Court and brought a civil action for conspiracy in restraint of trade under the provisions of the Sherman Act claiming $240,000 in treble damages.[88] The only jurisdictional basis for this suit was that indirect interference with the production and sale of Loewe's hats was an illegal restraint on interstate commerce. Leaving aside the problem of statutory construction as to whether the Sherman Act was intended to include trade union activities,

---

[87] Technically this was a "secondary boycott," a "Do Not Patronize" list appealing to individuals not involved in the strike, rather than a "primary boycott" in which union members refuse to work or to handle, ship, or process their own employer's goods.

[88] Lieberman, *op. cit.* at 59.

which is highly improbable,[89] the courts had to determine if the litigation fell legitimately within the purview of the commerce clause. If they were to rule that an embroglio between labor and management in Danbury was local in character, thus following the trail cut in the *Sugar Trust* and *Adair* cases, no federal court could entertain jurisdiction over the suit. It would be a problem for the Connecticut courts to settle under applicable state law.

The district judge denied jurisdiction, the court of appeals was uncertain and passed the question to the Supreme Court, and in 1908—still the same confused year—Chief Justice Fuller ruled for a unanimous Court that there was sufficient cause for jurisdiction under the Sherman Act.[90] The case went back for trial on the merits; the union lost a long legal battle in November 1912, and treble damages plus costs were assessed against its members at $252,000—a decision sustained by Justice Oliver Wendell Holmes for a unanimous Supreme Court in January 1915.[91] At this point, had the Clayton Act not been injected into the statute books, there was good reason to believe that any trade union action hindering production or distribution of goods would have been a conspiracy in restraint of trade under the antitrust law. Loewe and Fuchs was a small firm with a small proportion of the market. (The strike and boycott had in fact had an insignificant impact on the national hat market.) But in contrast with the American Sugar Refining Company, Loewe and Fuchs' status had a *direct* effect on interstate commerce and a "local" squabble over labor contracts fell under the jurisdiction of the federal commerce-police power. The Clayton Act theoretically put an end to this sort of litigation by providing that unions were not per se conspiracies in restraint of trade, but the Court later rewrote the Clayton Act to minimize this immunity.

While the Supreme Court was applying the dogma of entrepreneurial liberty to the commerce power in a fashion which effectively made successful or militant union activity a conspiracy in violation of the antitrust laws, it was moving toward vitiation of the provisions relating to "trusts" themselves. In the *Danbury Hatters* case Chief Justice Fuller went to some length to point

[89] See Gregory, *Labor and the Law*, 1st ed. (1946), pp. 205–17.
[90] Loewe v. Lawlor, 208 U.S. 278, 309 (1908).
[91] Lawlor v. Loewe, 235 U.S. 522 (1915).

out that the Sherman Act interdicted *any combination what-soever* in restraint of trade—its ban was complete.[92] Mr. Justice Brewer, who had argued for the "Rule of Reason" in his separate concurrence in the *Northern Securities* case, issued no complaint in the instance of the hatters. But the judicial concern that Congress could not have meant what it said continued and in 1911 reached fruition. In the *Standard Oil*[93] and *American Tobacco Co.*[94] cases, while sustaining the government's demand that these two great "trusts" be dissolved, Chief Justice White inserted the "Rule of Reason" into the Sherman Act. He announced that the language of the statute should be construed in the tradition of the common law as barring only "unreasonable" restraints of trade, not all.

In the light of history, this was a poignant day for the Court—it featured John Marshall Harlan's last great dissent. Appointed in 1877, the "massive, organ voiced Kentuckian"[95] had become a fixture in the Court. He appears at his worst in the labor decisions we have examined, but in the field of civil rights, it will be seen[96] that he was the conscience of the Court with respect to the Negro and a vigorous proponent of enforcing federal standards of criminal due process on the states. Moreover, he hated monopolies in the best Populist tradition. Harlan was always troubled by what he once called "dissent-ary."[97] After White had delivered the opinion of the Court in the *Standard Oil* Case Harlan, "His tongue loosened by whiskey," rose to dissent in bitter terms against the "Rule of Reason": He "bellowed bitter invectives that caused his brethren to blush with shame" and "rattled the benches of the staid old courtroom." Charles Evans Hughes, newly appointed to the bench, later observed that it

[92] Loewe v. Lawlor, 208 U.S. 278, 292–93 (1908). His *Knight* opinion was no barrier to this conclusion because the contracts in that case related *to manufacture* and were thus, by definition, not efforts to restrain trade. Q.E.D.

[93] Standard Oil Co. v. United States, 221 U.S. 1 (1911).

[94] United States v. American Tobacco Co., 221 U.S. 106 (1911).

[95] 1 Pusey, *Charles Evans Hughes* (1951), pp. 283.

[96] See Roche, "Civil Rights in the Age of Enterprise," Vol. 31, No. 1, *U. Chi. L. Rev.* (1963).

[97] See Westin, "Stephen J. Field and the Headnote to O'Neil v. Vermont: A Snapshot of the Fuller Court," 67 *Yale L.J.* 361, 376 (1958).

"was not a swan song, but the roar of an angry lion."[98] Shortly Harlan was dead and President Taft appointed his sixth new Justice; the Court had been virtually reconstituted in the space of four years.

The consequence of the judicial amendment of the Sherman Act to incorporate the "Rule of Reason" was that thenceforth every antitrust case was *wholly* at the mercy of the courts—who according to the mythology of American jurisprudence were the sole oracles of reasonableness. In practice this came down to a definition which stated that a reasonable restraint of trade was one which appeared reasonable to five Justices of the Supreme Court. Given the political and economic convictions of the members of the Court, and their intense dedication to the doctrine of entrepreneurial liberty, it is not surprising that for the next quarter of a century the antitrust laws became a laughing-stock— except among trade unionists.

To conclude, in the years that we have examined the Supreme Court spent a good deal of time and energy construing the commerce clause of the Constitution. In doing so, it established two streams of precedent which would go on into the 1920s and 1930s to provide the constitutional bases for either upholding or rejecting new exercises of national power. At times the Court expanded the commerce power to such a point that it appeared ready to permit Congress to regulate matters which were traditionally within the police power of the states. In two cases not discussed here, *Swift & Co.* v. *United States*[99] and the *Shreveport* case,[100] the Justices had devised the "stream of commerce" doctrine to justify regulating local enterprises (stockyards) which were necessary intermediary stops in a flow of commerce, and the "Shreveport doctrine" that activities admittedly in intrastate commerce which directly affected interstate commerce (railroad lines in this instance) were subject to federal regulation. The door seemed to be open—at least in logical terms—for federal oversight of most significant industrial endeavors in the nation as well as for a mass of ancillary regulations arising from

[98] 1 Pusey, *op. cit.* at 283.

[99] 196 U.S. 375 (1905).

[100] Houston E. & W. Tex. Ry. v. United States, 234 U.S. 342 (1914).

the new police problems created by rapid communications and transportation.

At the same time, and without admitted contradictions, the Court had also narrowly construed the commerce clause on certain occasions and asserted that the reserved powers of the states constituted a check on the reach of the commerce-police power. For example, in *Hammer* v. *Dagenhart*[101] the Court declared unconstitutional the Child Labor Act of 1916,[102] which had barred from interstate commerce goods produced by children. Congress, Mr. Justice Day asserted, could not legitimately achieve an illegitimate goal by employing the commerce power to regulate local manufacture. Yet the Court had earlier sustained Section 6 of the Sherman Act which operated on the identical principle by closing interstate commerce to "trust-made" goods. And it might be added that, despite the pieties of the Clayton Act, it would continue to find local conditions of employment within the ambit of the antitrust laws with respect to labor relations.[103]

The commerce clause was thus capable of almost infinite adjustment to the needs of a Court majority: In accordion-like fashion it could be expanded or contracted as the imperatives of a factual situation dictated. The fundamental problem for liberals and New Dealers in the 1930s was not therefore any absence of adequate precedents for their labor and welfare legislation—all New Deal measures could be justified on one authoritative interpretation of the commerce power or another—but rather that the dominant judicial philosophy militated against their particular precedents. (Cardozo's dissent in *Carter* v. *Carter Coal Co.*[104] rested, for example, on a perfectly valid body of precedent—one no less encompassed by *stare decisis* than that which supported the opinion of the Court.) In short, the determination that one body of precedent would be invoked (to sustain) rather than another, equally valid (to overturn), was not a *legal* problem. Every Justice came equipped with a double-barreled shotgun—the question was, *which* barrel would he fire?

[101] 247 U.S. 251 (1918).
[102] 39 Stat. 675.
[103] *Cf.* Coronado Coal Co. v. United Mine Workers, 268 U.S. 295 (1925).
[104] 298 U.S. 238, 324 (1936).

And this in turn rested, at base, on the extent to which he took for granted the legitimacy of the fundamental dogmas of entrepreneurial liberty. The tragedy of the New Deal Court was thus not rooted in Platonic irresponsibility or simple arrogance—on the contrary, the "Nine Old Men" were desperately responsible and faithful to the value system which had permeated their political and legal careers and which they, with good empirical reason, believed to express the "will of the people." When they chose the "wrong" precedents and lambasted the New Deal experiments, the Court majority was simply unaware, and probably incapable of learning, that the era of entrepreneurial liberty was over. Still living in an era where their economic views coincided with the election returns, they refused to believe that the American people had abandoned the creed of the "old order." Thus, at base, it was their political insensitivity rather than their jurisprudence which betrayed them.[105]

[105] From this analytical viewpoint, it was the election of 1936 rather than the "Court packing" plan which led, in Reed Powell's immortal phrase, to the "switch in time that saved nine." It also helps to explain the eccentric behavior of Chief Justice Hughes. Hughes, surely one of the most intelligent American politicians of this century, seems to have labored desperately to escape from the constitutional *culs-de-sac* so beloved by Justices Butler, VanDeventer, McReynolds and Sutherland. (See, for example, his extraordinary dissent in Morehead v. New York *ex rel.* Tipaldo, 298 U.S. 587 [1936].) See generally, Roche, "Executive Power and Domestic Emergency," 4 *Western Political Quarterly* 592 (1952).

Civil Liberty in the
Age of Enterprise

IN THE HALF-CENTURY which separated 1870 from
1920—which has been styled the "Age of Enterprise"—American
society was put through the wringer of the Industrial Revolution.
American constitutional law, like all other institutions, was trans-
formed to meet the exigencies of the new society, though some of
the transformations were delayed until virtually the eve of World
War II. Elsewhere I have examined the impact of the Age of
Enterprise on the interpretation of the police power and the
commerce power.[1] Here we turn to the examination of the place
of civil liberties in the constitutional firmament of the Age of
Enterprise.

There are continuities that can be traced, and discontinuities
that can be identified, in the interpretation of the police power
and the commerce power. The constitutional lawyer who in 1963
dilates on these topics is speaking essentially the same language

Reprinted, with permission, from *The University of Chicago Law Review*,
Volume 31, Autumn 1963, Number 1, pages 103–135.

[1] See the essays on p. 205 and p. 237.

as his predecessors in 1880 or 1920. But in the area of civil liberties there has been a qualitative jump between the views of our legal ancestors and those of our contemporaries. We can no more inquire how the Court in 1880 felt about civil liberties than we can ask how the physicists of that era responded to the theory of relativity. As I have argued at length in my recent study of civil liberties in modern America,[2] the whole notion of individual rights *enforceable against the community,* while traceable to abolitionist political theory, is a twentieth-century legal innovation.

This is not to say that American political thought in the eighteenth and nineteenth centuries did not endorse "civil rights." It did, but these rights were defined in a very special, essentially majoritarian fashion as safeguards against oppressive *governmental* action, i.e., legislative or executive "usurpations." Americans had, of course, fought the British for their "civil rights" on precisely this ground: They demanded the right to define their own rights. But nowhere except among the persecuted abolitionists have I discovered any theoretical justification for minority rights per se, and, as far as I can discover, state bills of rights extended no protection to the individual nonconformist confronted by the wrath and retribution of his neighbors. Although there must be some decisions of this sort somewhere in the state reports, I have yet to find an early case in which a state appellate court reversed a conviction below on the basis of a state bill of rights. Typical, I suspect, was the 1838 decision of the Massachusetts Supreme Judicial Court in the appeal of Abner Kneeland,[3] who asserted that his conviction for blasphemy violated the religious freedom guaranteed by Article II of the Massachusetts Bill of Rights. Kneeland, who had denied the doctrine of the Virgin Birth, was told by Chief Justice Lemuel Shaw for the court that the blasphemy statute was no limitation on his religious liberty—it merely punished acts which had "a tendency to disturb the public peace." Article II, in Shaw's view,

[2] Roche, *The Quest for the Dream: The Development of Civil Liberties in Modern America* (1963).

[3] Commonwealth v. Kneeland, 37 Mass. 206 (1838). See also Levy, *The Law of the Commonwealth and Chief Justice Shaw* (1957), pp. 43–58.

gave full protection to "honest" religious dissenters but none to those with "bad" motivation.[4]

Liberty, in short, was a condition conferred by the community at its discretion, usually only to "good" people who had earned their prerogatives. John Stuart Mill gave this philosophy its classic nineteenth-century formulation in his essay *On Liberty* when, after extolling the individual's absolute sovereignty over "his own body and mind," he hastened to add:

> It is, perhaps, hardly necessary to say that this doctrine is meant to apply only to human beings in the maturity of their faculties. We are not speaking of children or of young persons below the age which the law may fix as that of manhood or womanhood. . . . For the same reason we may leave out of consideration those backward states of society in which the race itself may be considered as in its nonage. The early difficulties in the way of spontaneous progress are so great that there is seldom any choice of means for overcoming them; and a ruler full of the spirit of improvement is warranted in the use of any expedients that will attain an end perhaps otherwise unattainable. *Despotism is a legitimate mode of government in dealing with barbarians, provided the end be their improvement* and the means justified by actually effecting that end. *Liberty, as a principle, has no application to any state of things exterior to the time when mankind have become capable of being improved by free and equal discussion.* Until then, there is nothing for them but implicit obedience . . . .[5]

Implicit in this statement—which those who praise Mill as the tribune of the "open society" have curiously ignored—is a jurisdictional grant: It is obviously the right of those who exercise liberty to determine when others shall graduate from despotism to this blissful state. To put it in the American context, it was the right of the community to decide when the Irish, the Jews, the Negroes, the industrial workers, the Mormons or whatever deviant group, should be admitted to membership. To return for a moment to the blasphemous Abner Kneeland, Chief Justice Shaw did point out that the blasphemy statute had no relevance to a

[4] 37 Mass. at 220.

[5] Mill, *On Liberty* (Library of Liberal Arts ed., 1956), pp. 13–14. (Emphasis added.)

"simple and sincere avowal of a disbelief in the existence and attributes of God"[6]—it constrained only the activities of *insincere* dissenters, i.e., Bad Men. When the American Legion argues today that Communists should be excluded from the coverage of the Bill of Rights because the party does not believe in civil rights, it is simply formulating in a contemporary context the standard eighteenth- and nineteenth-century maxim: "Bad Men Have No Rights." It was Jefferson, anticipating Joseph R. McCarthy, who announced in connection with the illegal arrest of the "Burr Conspirators" that, whatever the constitutional niceties, Burr had it coming, and that the public wanted no mercy shown to "traitors."[7]

This is the background which must be appreciated if one is to understand the Supreme Court's attitude toward civil liberties in the period under analysis. Perhaps a few words are also in order on the character of the Court and the general ideological position which it supported, particularly in view of the fact that my views differ rather sharply from many standard formulations.

A number of commentators on American constitutional law have, in their explorations of this period, discovered a "conservative" bias in the Supreme Court.[8] If this elusive designation is used in a rough and ready, essentially pejorative fashion to describe judicial favoritism toward the business elite and dedication to the theology of entrepreneurial liberty, there is no point in stirring up a terminological dispute. But if, on the other hand, the word "conservative" is employed in any meaningful ideological sense to suggest that the judiciary was inspired by a Burkean conception of history or a deep attachment to the principles of community, the usage is absurd. A perverse logician using the same set of facts could easily argue that the Court, and those who shared the judicial viewpoint, were engaged in a destructive

[6] 37 Mass. at 220.

[7] I am indebted to Leonard Levy for showing me his superb detailed study of Jefferson's handling of the Burr Conspiracy which became a chapter in his recent book, *Jefferson and Civil Liberties* (1963). See also Abernathy, *The Burr Conspiracy* (1954).

[8] See Jacobs, *Law Writers and the Courts* (1954); McCloskey, *American Conservatism in the Age of Enterprise* (1951); Paul, *Conservative Crisis and the Rule of Law* (1960); Twiss, *Lawyers and the Constitution* (1942).

and fundamentally "radical" assault on the underlying principles of American political theory. In the name of what Karl Marx called the "pig philosophy," they blasted away such antique notions as the obligation of the individual to the community (the Christian concept of "stewardship"), the subservience of entrepreneurial ambition to the police power, and the passion for equality. From this angle of vision, the defenders of the police power are converted into the "conservatives"—Burke's "little platoons"—in their unsuccessful attempt to hold back the disruptive forces of entrepreneurial aggrandizement.

On the abstract level, both positions can be defended indefinitely; this, indeed, is what gives abstract argument its charm. But in concrete terms, neither is viable, that is, supported by a coherent body of empirical data. The problem has arisen from the employment of such terms as "conservative," "radical," "liberal" or "progressive" in a sense fundamentally European: Categories which may have meaning in the analysis of European phenomena simply have not survived transplantation to the American scene. In fact, every attempt to utilize them in the American context has led to an ideological shambles in which analysts, hopelessly committed to their deductive categories, have saved the day for Theory by improvising such emergency rubrics as "conservative-liberal" or "moderate progressive." Nowhere has the empty character of these categories been more effectively demonstrated than in the investigation of judicial behavior.

Take Mr. Justice Harlan, for example: While Harlan was "progressive," if not "radical," in his dour view of monopolies and "trusts," his dissent in *Stone* v. *Farmers Loan & Trust Co.*[9] and his opinion of the Court in *Smythe* v. *Ames*[10] put him high on the list of "reactionary" enemies of the police power. But when two more variables are thrown in, identification in any ideological sense becomes impossible: How does one reconcile Harlan's solitary and magnificent defense of the deserted Negro with his bitter prejudice against trade unions and their members? There are, of course, explanations, but they have to be sought in

[9] 116 U.S. 307, 337 (1886).
[10] 169 U.S. 466 (1898).

Harlan's biography and in the personal scale of social, economic and political value priorities that he developed.[11] Mr. Justice Stephen Field was probably about as close to being an ideologue as any Justice has ever been, at least before Frank Murphy, but even Field knew when to rise above principle. The Justice, who insisted that the Fourteenth Amendment had been designed to nationalize liberty, and who could work himself into a frenzy over the plight of butchers deprived of their employment, was totally unmoved by efforts to enforce the equal protection clause on behalf of the Negroes[12] or the due process clause in aid of the convicted Haymarket anarchists.[13] In short, to employ such designations as "conservative" or "liberal" is completely misleading (unless one simply means by them "good" and "bad," in whichever order) in its pretension that there are coherent philosophical patterns. These terms have been outlawed from this analysis.

The modern reader may be startled by some of the material included in this essay—the *Income Tax* decisions, for example—and note the absence of much that he normally includes under the contemporary heading of civil liberty. Perhaps the point should be reemphasized that each epoch establishes its own definitions and the proper concern of the historian is to examine the constitutional status of civil liberties as the latter were defined in the legal and political lexicons of that time. As was noted earlier, what we today think of as civil liberties largely date from definitions adopted in the 1930s; the very absence of a civil rights tradition was a distinctive characteristic of the period before World War I. True, there were groups which fought for their own rights—radicals, suffragettes, trade unionists, Jews, Negroes, etc., but they did so on an *ad hoc* basis. The old abolitionist dream of basic natural rights guaranteed by national

[11] See Westin, "John Marshall Harlan and the Constitutional Rights of Negroes," *Yale L.J.* 637 (1957). Harlan's attitude toward trade unions suffuses his opinion Adair v. United States, 208 U.S. 161 (1908).

[12] See Mr. Justice Field's opinions in *Ex parte* Virginia, 100 U.S. 339, 349 (1879); Virginia v. Rives, 100 U.S. 313, 324 (1879); Strauder v. West Virginia, 100 U.S. 303, 312 (1879).

[13] Spies v. Illinois, 123 U.S. 131 (1887); David, *The History of the Haymarket Affair*, 2nd ed. (1958), pp. 375–88.

power collapsed among the debris of Reconstruction, and among civil libertarians, as elsewhere, the guiding maxim was *sauve qui peut*. Finally, for reasons which I have examined at length elsewhere,[14] I consider World War I to be the watershed between the "old America" and the "new" with respect to the development of a civil liberties jurisprudence; I have therefore excluded from this study the civil liberties problems that proliferated with American involvement in the First World War.

Let us begin with the evisceration of the Fourteenth Amendment and the Civil Rights Acts. We cannot take the time here to explore the logic of the *Civil Rights* cases[15] in which the Supreme Court delivered the *coup de grace* to the effort to protect the Negro from race discrimination. By giving an extremely narrow interpretation to the Fourteenth Amendment, Justice Bradley (with the former slaveholder Justice Harlan alone dissenting[16]) ruled that only formal state action of a discriminatory character fell within the amendment's interdict. Consequently, "private" racial discrimination by railroads, theaters, hotels and the like was held to be a matter within the sole jurisdiction of the states. Bradley suggested that to rule otherwise would make the Negroes favorites of the national government and would discriminate against white men, who presumably were in need of equal treatment.

The Bradley opinion has to be understood as a period piece. It was grossly unhistorical: The framers of the Fourteenth Amendment were attempting to provide constitutional certainty for the Civil Rights Act of 1866 which penalized racial discrimination by "custom" as well as by "law."[17] In an ironic sense, Bradley's opinion echoed President Johnson's veto of the Civil Rights Act, which was promptly overridden by two-thirds of both houses of Congress.[18] And it was Johnson's veto, and the fear that the good work might be undone by future Presidents and legislatures where two-thirds could not be mustered, that led to the passage

---

[14] Roche, *op. cit. supra* fn 2.

[15] 109 U.S. 3 (1883).

[16] *Idem* at 26.

[17] 14 Stat. 27 (1866).

[18] See Johnson's veto message of March 27, 1886, in 6 Richardson, *Messages and Papers* 405 (1897).

of the Fourteenth Amendment.[19] Fundamentally, Justice Bradley declared the Fourteenth Amendment, as originally conceived, to be unconstitutional.

It is worth noting that Bradley's decision here marked a sharp break with his earlier construction of the purpose of the Fourteenth Amendment and the reach of the civil rights statutes. In December 1870, Bradley's Circuit Judge (later Justice) William Woods wrote him at length on the constitutional problems involved in a suit by the United States under the Enforcement Act of May 31, 1870. An Alabama mob led by Hall, it was charged, "did unlawfully and feloniously band and conspire together with intent to injure, oppress, threaten and intimidate" a group of Negroes "with intent to prevent and hinder their free exercise and enjoyment of the right of freedom of speech" and "freedom of assembly," rights which were "granted and secured to them by the constitution of the United States." Hall filed a demurrer on constitutional grounds claiming that "the matters charged in said counts are not in violation of any right of privilege granted or secured" by the Constitution since neither the Fourteenth Amendment nor the Civil Rights Acts could legitimately penalize private action.

Woods described the situation to Bradley in detail in a letter dated December 24, 1870[20]: A peaceful Republican gathering of Negroes engaged in "political discussion" was broken up by a gang of armed whites who had killed two and wounded over fifty. The authority of the state of Alabama, however, had nowhere been involved, and Woods queried Bradley, in essence, whether jurisdiction existed over private action as distinct from state action. On January 3, 1871, Bradley replied that "viewed simply as a riot, it was an offense against the municipal law only; but viewed as a riot to intimidate persons and prevent them from exercising the right of suffrage, guaranteed to them by the Fifteenth Amendment to the Constitution, it was a violation [of

---

[19] McKitrick, *Andrew Johnson and Reconstruction* (1960), pp. 326–36.

[20] The following correspondence is among the Bradley Papers in the New Jersey Historical Society. I am indebted to C. Peter Magrath of Brown University for calling this material to my attention. See also Magrath, *Morrison R. Waite* (1963), pp. 119–23.

national law]."[21] Woods was not satisfied and again raised the subject with Bradley inquiring whether the riot was a federal offense "when committed simply for that purpose [to break up the Negro gathering], without any definite intent to prevent the exercise of the right of suffrage."[22]

Replying, Bradley came down vigorously in support of national jurisdiction. Writing on March 12, 1871, the Justice informed Woods that under the Fourteenth Amendment Congress could protect fundamental rights such as speech and assembly "against unfriendly or insufficient state legislation."[23] Treating these basic rights as privileges and immunities of national citizenship, Bradley continued:

> Therefore, to guard against this invasion of the citizen's fundamental rights, and to ensure their adequate protection, *as well against state legislation as state inaction or incompetency,* the amendment [Fourteenth] gives Congress power to enforce the amendment by appropriate legislation. And as it would be unseemly for Congress to interfere directly with state enactments, and as it cannot compel the activity of state officials, the only appropriate legislation it can make is that which will operate directly on offenders and offenses and protect the rights which the amendment secures. The extent to which Congress shall exercise this power must depend on its discretion in view of the circumstances of each case. If the exercise of it in any case should seem to interfere with the domestic affairs of a state, it must be remembered that it is for the purpose of protecting federal rights: and these *must be protected whether it interferes with domestic laws or domestic administration of laws.*[24]

In May 1871, Judge Woods issued his opinion in *United States v. Hall*,[25] overruling the demurrer and sustaining the jurisdiction of the federal government under the Fourteenth Amendment and the Enforcement Act of 1870. His views were practically identical

[21] Letter from Bradley to Woods (draft), Washington, D.C., January 3, 1871.

[22] Letter from Woods to Bradley, March, 1871.

[23] Letter from Bradley to Woods (draft), Washington, D.C., March 12, 1871.

[24] *Ibid.* (Emphasis added.)

[25] 26 Fed. Cas. 79 (No. 15,282) (C.C.S.D. Ala. 1871).

with the formulations in Bradley's letter. Freedom of speech and assembly were privileges and immunities of national citizenship and consequently:

> [C]ongress has the power, by appropriate legislation, to protect the fundamental rights of citizens of the United States against unfriendly or insufficient state legislation, for the fourteenth amendment not only prohibits the making or enforcement of laws which shall abridge the privileges of the citizen, but prohibits the states from denying . . . the equal protection of the laws. Denying includes inaction as well as action, and denying the equal protection of the laws includes the omission to protect, as well as the omission to pass laws for protection. The citizen of the United States is entitled to the enforcement of the laws for the protection of his fundamental rights, as well as the enactment of such laws. Therefore, to guard against the invasion of the citizen's fundamental rights, and to insure their adequate protection, as well against state legislation as state inaction, or incompetency, the amendment gives congress the power to enforce its provisions by appropriate legislation. And as it would be unseemly for congress . . . . [the remainder of Bradley's formulation quoted above follows].[26]

Although Bradley, in a different context, endorsed this nationalizing interpretation of the privileges and immunities clause by joining the Field dissent, and elaborated on the due process theme in his own dissent in the *Slaughterhouse* cases,[27] in the decade that followed he came about full circle. As he put it to a friend, he was *"seeking the truth"* rather than "dogmatically laying down opinions,"[28] and beginning with his circuit opinion in the *Cruikshank* case,[29] he moved perceptibly toward the position, incorporated in his decision in the *Civil Rights* cases,[30] that congressional power limited only formal state action. In a later comment on one of the letters cited here he noted retrospectively

---

[26] *Idem* at 81–82.

[27] 83 U.S. (16 Wall.) 36, 111 (1872).

[28] Letter from Bradley to Frederick Frelinghuysen (draft), Stowe, Vt., July 19, 1874.

[29] United States v. Cruikshank, 25 Fed. Cas. 707 (No. 14,897) (C.C.D. La. 1874).

[30] 109 U.S. 3 (1883).

that his views "were much modified by subsequent reflection, so far as relates to the power of Congress to pass laws for enforcing social equality between the races."[31]

"Social equality" was hardly a real issue in the 1870s; the fact of the matter was that by 1883, the Negro had been left to his fate by Congress, the President and the American (white) people.[32] All Justice Bradley did was incorporate the realities of the day into the Fourteenth Amendment. Moreover, echoes of "Black Reconstruction" can be heard in his opinion; indeed, right down to our own time the reputation of the Southern Reconstruction legislatures, in which the Negroes were often manipulated by rascally "carpetbaggers," has been one featuring egregious corruption. Though an objective historical observer might have difficulty deciding whether these governments were more corrupt than their "lily-white" successors, or than those in the Northern states at the same time,[33] Bradley shared the common view that the white man had been discriminated against by the civil rights laws with unfortunate results. He demanded fair play for the white population.

"Private acts" (though in fact they were enforced by the police power of the state) were thus eliminated from national jurisdiction. Even the action of a railroad, which Bradley in the *Granger* cases[34] had agreed was "affected with a public interest," being in effect a quasi-public corporation, was a "private" decision so far as racial discrimination was concerned. Thus a railroad became a schizophrenic entity: Some of its decisions were public (rates and schedules, for example) and some private (racial segregation). By these same paradoxical rules, a state law banning racial segregation on interstate carriers was unconstitutional as a burden on interstate commerce,[35] while a similar law requiring segregation was upheld as a legitimate police regulation.[36]

As it survived the *Civil Rights* cases, the Fourteenth Amend-

---

[31] Noted in letter to Frelinghuysen, *supra* fn 28.
[32] See Woodward, *Reunion and Reaction* (1951).
[33] See Josephson, *Robber Barons* (1934); Josephson, *The Politicos* (1938).
[34] Munn v. Illinois, 94 U.S. 113 (1876).
[35] Hall v. DeCuir, 95 U.S. 485 (1877).
[36] Chiles v. C. & O. Ry., 218 U.S. 71 (1910).

ment limited only state action depriving individuals of due process or equal protection of the laws. Occasionally the Court did find some state action, for example, a law barring Negroes from juries,[37] to be unconstitutional, but the characteristic pattern of racial discrimination was left undisturbed by the development of two subsidiary propositions. First, "state action" was generally defined in a very narrow legalistic fashion as action taken in pursuance of state law: The fact that no Negro had ever been called to jury duty was, for example, no proof as far as the Court was concerned that Negroes were being discriminated against providing no law forbade their serving on juries.[38] Moreover, if an official act of discrimination was technically in violation of a state constitution or statute, it was not considered "state action" on the ground that a state cannot be held responsible for the illegal actions of its agents.[39]

In the second case, the Court began in 1882 the process of redefining "equal protection" which culminated, with *Plessy* v. *Ferguson*,[40] in constitutional sanction for "Jim Crow" laws in 1896. Although seldom emphasized by commentators, the decision in *Pace* v. *Alabama*[41] was *in loco parentis* to the "separate but equal rule" of *Plessy*. At issue were two Alabama laws: The first punishing fornication or adultery between persons of the same race as a misdemeanor ($100 fine or six months in jail); the second essentially making it a felony for persons of different races to intermarry or live in adultery or fornication with each other (two to seven years in jail). A Negro man and a white woman, who had been sentenced to two years in prison, appealed their sentences on the ground that the differential treatment prescribed by statute for interracial sexual relations was state action denying them equal protection of the laws. Note that

[37] Neal v. Delaware, 103 U.S. 370 (1880). This was a Fifteenth Amendment case: Delaware required that jurors be voters and limited the vote to whites; Strauder v. West Virginia, 100 U.S. 303 (1880).

[38] Virginia v. Rives, 100 U.S. 313 (1880). But discrimination by a state judge, even in the absence of a statute, was held to be state action, *Ex parte* Virginia, 100 U.S. 339 (1880).

[39] See the discussion of this proposition by Frankfurter, J. dissenting in Monroe v. Pape, 365 U.S. 167, 202 (1961).

[40] 163 U.S. 537 (1896).

[41] 106 U.S. 583 (1883).

the law penalized intermarriage on the same basis as illicit relations.

Justice Field, for a unanimous Court, found no difficulty in sustaining the Alabama Code. A man may have had a natural right to follow his calling, in Field's view, but he had no equivalent right to choose his wife free from state control. The laws under attack did not discriminate against Negroes, observed Field, any more than they did against whites: "The two sections of the Code cited are entirely consistent. The one prescribes, generally, a punishment for an offense committed between persons of different sexes; the other prescribes a punishment for an offense which can only be committed when the two sexes are of different races. There is in neither section any discrimination against either race."[42] After all, Field concluded, both the Negro and the white woman received the same punishment. For some reason he did not seem to feel that the penalization of intermarriage violated "freedom of contract."

While Field's opinion was brief, its import for the future was enormous. In less than three pages, the Justice, his eight brethren concurring, effectively torpedoed the equal protection clause. Even Harlan could not dissent in this instance; miscegenation probably hit him at his weakest point: his fundamentally Southern social and religious convictions about the distinctiveness of the "races."[43] What *Pace* v. *Alabama* did was re-establish the *legal* category "Negro"—it now became legitimate for the states to differentiate formally between Negroes and whites as they did between men and women, or aliens and citizens. While the purpose of the equal protection clause had been to eliminate from American law the category "Negro"—its authors were infuriated by the "Black Codes"—the Court now told the states that race was a valid basis for differentiation among its citizens. Of course, there were potential limits. Under the equal protection clause every category had to be justified in terms of its purpose: A state would have no difficulty forbidding sale of intoxicants to minors, but would run into difficulties if sales were forbidden to blue-eyed citizens. There had to be, in other words, a reasonable

---

[42] *Idem* at 585.

[43] As pointed out in Westin, *op. cit.* at 673.

connection between the end and the means, and the category had to be discrete.

But in the case of the category "Negro" few limitations were discovered. Recall that in *Pace* v. *Alabama* the Court implicitly held that the state could, in the effort to maintain public morality, treat marriage between a white and a Negro as if it were adultery or fornication. In short, the race of one partner could convert a lawful relationship into a felony. Moreover, in defiance of the history of race relations in the South, "Negro" was treated as a homogeneous category; white supremacists apparently saw nothing illogical in defining as a Negro anyone with one Negro grandparent, or great-grandparent in some states, though when the odds get up to seven to one, some question arises as to which is the "master race." Even when, as in Alabama, one Negro grandparent was decisive, the category was a bit eccentric; it was rather as if a state legislature had defined a basket of apples as a basket containing at least 25 percent apples. This problem, however, never troubled either Southern politicians or the courts.

The Southern Negro, poor and landless, "knew very well that immediate, daily necessities came first—land, mules, plows, food, and clothes, all of which had to be got from a white man who oftener than not had too little himself."[44] Thus, in terms of the social system, the Negro, even at the zenith of "Radical Reconstruction," never achieved equality. From the viewpoint of the Southern white community, the Civil Rights Acts were a marginal harassment; Union troops were a problem, but the last blue contingent went North in 1877. With the outlawing of "Black Codes," informal measures of social control, which were no less effective because informal, were utilized to the same end. Then, in the late eighties and early nineties, began the flood of "Jim Crow" legislation, laws based on the principle enunciated in *Pace* v. *Alabama* that Negroes were different from whites and that this distinction justified differential treatment. Curiously, as Professor C. Vann Woodward has noted, "the barriers of racial discrimination mounted in direct ratio with the tide of political democracy among whites. In fact, an increase of Jim Crow laws upon the

[44] Woodward, *op. cit.* (1951), p. 209.

statute books of a state is almost an accurate index of the decline of the reactionary regimes of the Redeemers and triumph of white democratic movements."[45] The Redeemers had used the Negroes as pawns in their maintenance of political power; now the Negroes were to be punished for their cardinal sin—helplessness.

The classic Jim Crow law was an enactment requiring racial segregation in railroad and tram cars. In order to understand the importance of the Supreme Court's decision in *Plessy* v. *Ferguson*,[46] which provided the constitutional foundation for racial discrimination until 1954, let us review the principle involved. When a state required that railroads provide facilities for whites and Negroes on a separate basis, it was establishing a classification on the basis of race. For this classification to be sustained in the face of the equal protection clause, it had to be demonstrated that separation based on race was a reasonable method of attaining a legitimate legislative goal: the maintenance of public health, morals and welfare. Assuming for purposes of argument that some special "scientific" rationale could be introduced to justify laws against intermarriage, there would be no necessary carryover to transportation. One can require, for example, that men and women use different dressing rooms at the beach without insisting that they swim at different places. In short, the emotionally charged problem of sexual relations present in *Pace* v. *Alabama* was absent in *Plessy* v. *Ferguson*. If the Court sustained the statute, it would be hard to conceive of any social, economic or political relationship in which segregation could not be legally required.

In 1890, Louisiana passed a Jim Crow transportation law. One Homer Adolph Plessy was arrested for attempting to enter the coach reserved for whites and refusing to leave when ordered to do so. There is an air of unreality about the whole episode: Plessy was one-eighth Negro and insisted that he was "white." Like his French contemporary Captain Dreyfus, who was something of an anti-Semite, Plessy was hardly a fighter for the rights

---

[45] *Idem.* at 211.
[46] 163 U.S. 537 (1896).

of man. The Louisiana courts declared him a Negro and he challenged the constitutionality of the statute. Dividing seven to one, the Supreme Court upheld the Louisiana enactment.

Justice Henry B. Brown wrote the opinion of the Court. Early in his statement, he put the holding in a nutshell: "A statute which implies merely a legal distinction between the white and colored races . . . has no tendency to destroy the legal equality of the two races. . . ."[47] After examining precedents and noting that the state legislatures must be permitted a large area of reasonable discretion in their police power enactments—a latitude, it might be recalled, the Court was reluctant to grant in the economic sphere—Brown came to the heart of his opinion. The whole difficulty, he averred, arose from Negro hypersensitivity:

> We consider the underlying fallacy of [Plessy's] argument to consist in the assumption that the enforced separation of the two races stamps the colored race with a badge of inferiority. If this be so, it is not by reason of anything found in the act, but solely because the colored race chooses to put that construction upon it.[48]

As the clincher to this argument, Brown observed that if the Negroes controlled state legislatures and passed "precisely similar" enactments, white men would not feel they had been assigned an inferior position.

This brings us to Brown's sociology which needs to be set out at some length in his own words:

> The argument [against the segregation statute] also assumes that social prejudices may be overcome by legislation, and that equal rights cannot be secured to the negro except by an enforced commingling of the two races. We cannot accept this proposition. If the two races are to meet on terms of social equality, it must be the result of mutual affinities, a mutual appreciation of each other's merits and a voluntary consent of individuals. . . . *Legislation is powerless to eradicate racial instincts* or to abolish distinctions based upon physical differences. . . . If the civil and political rights of both races be equal, one cannot be inferior to

[47] *Idem* at 543.
[48] *Idem* at 551.

the other civilly or politically. If one race be inferior to the other socially, the Constitution of the United States cannot put them on the same plane.[49]

Although it might have come as a shock to Justice Brown, this opinion is an interesting theoretical statement; on a practical and somewhat foggy level, it was a combination of the leading scientific views of the time with Aristotle's conception of proportional equality.

It was in precisely this period that racial theories reached their apogee in the United States; among biologists, sociologists and social anthropologists as well as journalists and political commentators, the assumptions of Baron Gobineau and Houston Chamberlain—that races were discrete entities and that the white or Caucasian race was superior to the others—were taken for granted. The Southern politician, of course, needed no lofty theoretical justification for white supremacy—he knew what he wanted and really did not care how the scientists, journalists or Supreme Court Justices rationalized his attainment of racial segregation. But the better elements in the community needed a respectable intellectual base to justify discrimination, and the "social science" of the time supplied the requisite foundation.[50]

Negroes, then, were biologically different from whites, essentially members of a different species, set apart by their "racial instincts." Thus, in the same fashion that an intelligent zoo keeper separates the lions and the elephants in different compounds, the Supreme Court endorsed the proposition that biologically distinct Negroes and whites need not be given identical treatment. What was good for Negroes was not necessarily good for whites, any more than a lion would necessarily thrive on an elephant's diet. Fundamental to this view, though not explicit in Brown's opinion, was the further corollary that the whites were more advanced, more "civilized," than the Negroes, that they were several stages higher in the evolutionary scale. Incidently, this "science" also supplied a good genetic rationale for anti-

[49] *Idem* at 551–52. (Emphasis added.) Concretely, Brown thus held the statute to be a not unreasonable technique of foreclosing social conflict and maintaining the public peace.

[50] See Spitz, *Patterns of Anti-Democratic Thought* (1948), pp. 137–62.

miscegenation laws. As late as 1955 the Virginia Supreme Court justified an antimiscegenation statute as an effort to "preserve the racial integrity" of the state's inhabitants and to "regulate the marriage relation so that it will not have a mongrel breed of citizens."[51]

Once the proposition that Negroes were in essence a distinct biological category had been established (by *ipse dixit*), the principle of proportional equality could come into play. Equality, according to Aristotle and a steady stream of theorists since, is treatment according to merits or desserts. For Aristotle, however, a man's merits were a function of his potentialities, not of the color of his skin or the color of one great-grandparent's skin. Now merit became a function of membership in a racial category, and the "Negro Race" had no claim to treatment in the laws of the United States identical with that accorded members of the "Caucasian Race." While the analogy is perhaps banal, recall that the zoo keeper does not "discriminate" against the elephant when he feeds him hay instead of the red meat beloved by lions. On this basis, Justice Brown could blandly and quite sincerely state that segregated treatment for Negroes was only a consequence of their distinctiveness and was in no way a "badge of inferiority." Only a psychotic elephant would complain because he got no steak.

Justice Harlan wrote what many consider his finest dissent in *Plessy* v. *Ferguson*. It is an interesting opinion because Harlan subscribed completely to the "Negro Race" theory, but refused to admit the relevance of this "social science" to American constitutional law. "The white race," said Harlan, "deems itself to be the dominant race in this country. And so it is, in prestige, in achievements, in education, in wealth, and in power. So, I doubt not that it will continue to be for all time, if it remains true to its great heritage and holds fast to the principles of constitutional liberty."[52] The Constitution, Harlan thundered, "is color-blind"; the former colonel of Kentucky volunteers in Lincoln's army effectively charged the Court with overruling the verdict of

---

[51] Naim v. Naim, 197 Va. 80, 90, 87 S.E.2d 749, 756, *vacated and remanded*, 350 U.S. 891 (1955), *reaffirmed*, 197 Va. 734, 90 S.E.2d 849, *appeal denied*, 350 U.S. 985 (1956).

[52] 163 U.S. at 559.

Appomattox. He asserted bluntly that "the judgment this day rendered will, in time, prove to be quite as pernicious as the decision made by this tribunal in the *Dred Scott* case."[53] The nub of his position was that the Court had confused social with constitutional equality—the first was not at issue in the case, he said, since

> [S]ocial equality no more exists between two races when traveling in a passenger coach or a public highway than when members of the same race sit by each other in a street car . . . .
>
> There is a race so different from our own that we do not permit those belonging to it to become citizens of the United States. . . . But by the statute in question a Chinaman can ride in the same passenger coach with white citizens of the United States, while citizens of the black race in Louisiana, many of whom, perhaps, risked their lives for the preservation of the Union . . . are yet declared to be criminals, liable to imprisonment, if they ride in a public coach occupied by citizens of the white race.[54]

"Every true man has pride of race," observed the Justice, "but I deny that any legislative body or judicial tribunal may have regard to the race of citizens when the civil rights of those citizens are involved."[55]

Equal protection of the laws was in this fashion glossed by the Supreme Court to eliminate juridical equality of Negroes; essentially a state fulfilled the requirements of the Fourteenth Amendment if it treated all whites equally, all Negroes equally and granted "substantial equality" to Negroes vis-à-vis whites. The Court's holding unloosed a flood of Jim Crow lawmaking in all the Southern, and even some of the Northern, states, a flood which ended by submerging every aspect of day to day life under the protocol of segregation. As C. Vann Woodward has shown, some ingenious legislator in one state would devise a new law, providing segregation coverage for some area theretofore overlooked, and it would rapidly spread from state to state in a wave of mimicry.[56] It seems to have become a species of nasty game—and one totally lacking a logical rationale. The same

[53] *Ibid.*
[54] *Idem* at 561.
[55] *Idem* at 554.
[56] C. Vann Woodward, *The Strange Career of Jim Crow*, rev. ed. (1957).

Negro woman who prepared a white family's meals and all but raised its children would be compelled to use the "colored" drinking fountain, the "colored" wash rooms and sit in the back of the trolley to keep the white population uncontaminated. But few attempted to defend the system logically, and it did seem to keep the "red necks," or the "crackers"—the poor rural whites—happy and secure in a status *at least* one notch above the bottom.

The Negroes were in neither position nor mood to fight back. Their greatest leader, Booker T. Washington, the Negro prototype of Horatio Alger, was a conciliator who urged his fellows to accept the limitations established by the white community and work within them. Washington has been accused by later Negro leaders of being an "Uncle Tom," a cringing suppliant at the white man's table, but the more one studies those terrible years, the more he wonders what alternative Washington had if he wanted to stay in the South. There is a curious parallel here between Washington and Samuel Gompers of the American Federation of Labor, who was likewise condemned by impatient radicals as a "class collaborationist": When the odds against success reach a certain point, there is often a need for the courage to refuse to be drawn into a fight. So Washington accepted *apartheid* and set to work at Tuskegee Institute to develop a Negro elite, men who hopefully in the next generation could provide the anomic Negro community with leadership of a different sort than that supplied by preachers, who tended to be the foci of existing social organization. As Washington appraised the situation, the alternative to appeasement was the lynch mob and the race riot, and the events of those years should lead anyone to pause before pronouncing a malediction on the man and his message.

Indeed, a case can be made that from the viewpoint of the Negro, the picture got worse rather than better as the United States moved into the twentieth century. For one thing, perhaps under the impact of the racial dogmas which were so popular, the number of white men who were concerned about the cause of Negro rights went into decline after the Civil War. As the old radicals—Charles Sumner, Wendell Philips, George W. Julian, William Lloyd Garrison—died, there were no replacements. The *reductio ad absurdum* probably came in 1903 when the program of the Louisiana Socialist Party came out for "separation of the black and white races into separate communities, each race to have charge of its own affairs."[57] Eugene Victor Debs, the tribune of American socialism, rejected this leftwing version of *apartheid* in favor of full equality, but the socialists put little emphasis on race problems; the latter were merely manifestations of a fundamental social malaise and could be eliminated only at the source, by transforming the United States from a capitalist oligarchy into a socialist cooperative commonwealth.[58]

A second cause of Negro discouragement was the spread of Southern white racial mores into the North and West, a phenomenon which accelerated with World War I and the concomitant exodus of Negroes from Southern farms to Northern factories, or to service jobs in factory towns. The early years of the new century were racked by a series of savage race riots; significantly they took place in cities on both sides of the Mason-Dixon Line, the two worst being in Atlanta (1906) and Springfield, Illinois (1908). According to John Hope Franklin, more than 100 Negroes were lynched in the first year of the century and "before the outbreak of World War I the number . . . had soared to more than 1100."[59] Symptomatic of the rising pressure was the Kentucky legislature's assault in 1904 on Berea College and other unsegregated private schools in the state. The legislative instinct was probably sound. Berea, with its abolitionist heritage, was precisely the sort of school where able young Negroes could get the wrong ideas; and in an untheoretical way, the legislature moved to suppress a source of ideological infection in the Negro community. Let the colored youngsters go to agricultural schools on a segregated basis, but keep them out of a mixed intellectual atmosphere dedicated to Christian principles. The legislators may have reflected that Christianity had been subversive on occasions.

Berea College was fined $1000 for violating the 1904 statute, and in 1908 the case came before the United States Supreme Court for final determination. The right of the states to segregate public educational facilities had been covertly sustained by Har-

[57] Cited in Kipnis, *The American Socialist Movement, 1897–1912* (1952), p. 131.
[58] *Idem* at 131–36.
[59] John Hope Franklin, *From Slavery to Freedom* (1947), p. 432.

lan for the Court in 1899 in *Cumming* v. *Board of Education.*[60] In meticulous legal terms, Harlan ducked the substantive issue: The validity of "separate but equal" educational institutions, he observed lamely, was not raised in the pleadings and was therefore not before the Court.[61] In fact, it does not appear that Harlan considered integrated schools as part of the civil rights package. If he had, one can predict that he would have gotten to the merits over any number of technical, procedural hurdles.[62] The practical consequence of the *Cumming* case was a *de facto* validation of public school segregation. But in *Berea College* v. *Kentucky,*[63] the situation was different in Harlan's eyes, though not in the view of his judicial brethren, who disposed of the litigation on a narrow basis.

Berea College was a decision with interesting dimensions. In the first place, Berea argued that the Kentucky statute deprived it of the corporate right to do business on its own terms, that is, Berea invoked the blessing of the spirit of entrepreneurial liberty. Indeed, counsel for Berea relied heavily on both *In re Jacobs*[64] and *Lochner* v. *New York*[65] to support their contention that the Kentucky enactment was not *really* a police power action, but was an encroachment on contractual freedom disguised as a police measure. But while the lawyers did a noble job of trying to fit the case within the vested rights tradition—they even cited *Dartmouth College*[66]—Justice David Brewer suddenly developed a deep affection for the police power. He flatly refused to examine the constitutional issue of equal protection, ruling merely that Kentucky was within its rights in altering corporate charters.[67] Justice Holmes and Moody concurred in the judgment, Justice Day dissented without opinion, and Justice Harlan loosed his thunderbolts in a vivid, caustic dissent. This time

[60] 175 U.S. 528 (1899).

[61] *Idem* at 541.

[62] See Westin, "John Marshall Harlan and the Constitutional Rights of Negroes," 66 *Yale L.J.* 637, 689 (1957).

[63] 211 U.S. 45 (1908).

[64] 98 N.Y. 98 (1885).

[65] 198 U.S. 45 (1905).

[66] Dartmouth College v. Woodward, 17 U.S. (4 Wheat.) 518 (1819).

[67] 211 U.S. at 57.

Harlan brushed away the procedural difficulties as so much irrelevant fluff and struck at the heart of the matter.

The Kentucky law, said Harlan, deeply distressed and angered by this action in his beloved Commonwealth, was an unconstitutional infringement of the right of private association and of the equal protection clause. Moreover, Harlan, a deeply religious man (he objected to the Chicago World's Fair being open on Sunday),[68] felt that the decision of the Court would justify a state in laying "unholy hands on the religious faith of the people."[69] If a state could tamper in this fashion with the inner life of a religiously sponsored corporation, "white and colored children may even be forbidden to sit together in a house of worship or at a communion table in the same Christian church." "Have we became so inoculated with prejudice of race," he asked, "that an American government, professedly based on the principles of freedom, and charged with the protection of all citizens alike, can make [racial] distinctions in the matter of their voluntary meeting for innocent purposes?"[70] The answer given by his associates, and by the American people was clearly "Yes."

These decisions offer a good insight into the operation of the American constitutional process. Two Supreme Court holdings—*Pace* v. *Alabama* and *Plessy* v. *Ferguson*—dealt squarely with the merits of state segregation laws. Yet the Court's rulings in these cases, particularly in the *Plessy* case, were by extrapolation used to validate the whole structure of Jim Crow. The fundamental question—whether state enforced segregation violates the equal protection clause—was not (with one area of exception) re-examined by the Supreme Court until the 1940s and 1950s. Thus, while lawyers are technically within their guild prerogatives when they assert that a Supreme Court decision is only a determination of the case at bar, the Justices in one "limited" holding (enforced segregation in *transportation* does not violate the equal protection of the laws), *Plessy* v. *Ferguson*, in social and institutional terms gave their *imprimatur* to the whole structure of white supremacy. In other words, the *Plessy* opinion was a

[68] Westin, *op. cit.* fn. 62, at 639.
[69] 211 U.S. at 68.
[70] *Ibid.*

monumental piece of judicial legislation. In fact, the Supreme Court effectively amended the Constitution of the United States by rewriting the Fourteenth Amendment.

The problem of Negro suffrage arising under the Fifteenth Amendment was disposed of in parallel fashion; the Court in this period allowed the amendment, designed to guarantee the voting rights of the freedmen, to become virtually a dead letter. The states achieved Negro disfranchisement by a number of devices—literacy tests, payment of poll taxes, property qualifications, *inter alia*—but most effective of all was the "white primary." Political parties barred Negroes from membership and participation in primary elections, and the Court sustained this technique by holding parties to be "private" organizations beyond the reach of federal power.[71] Only in 1911[72] was a beginning made toward employing the Thirteenth Amendment to end the labor contract peonage system which held many rural Negroes in virtual slavery. As far as the Negro was concerned, the Civil War had altered his juridical status, but not his basic relationship to the power structure.

In only one area was the authority of the states circumscribed: when racial legislation flagrantly conflicted with the dogmas of entrepreneurial liberty. Justice Field set the precedent here when he and his associates on the Ninth Judicial Circuit in the 1880s declared war on the anti-Asian enactments of the West Coast states. The classic instance was the *Parrott* case[73] in which the federal circuit court in San Francisco declared unconstitutional a provision of the California Constitution of 1879 which forbade corporations to employ Chinese. While in this and similar instances, the net effect was to bestow protection on the helpless Chinese, the gravamen of the decision was clearly that the proviso in question violated entrepreneurial liberty, the employer's right to hire at his discretion. In 1886, in a decision anticipating *Lochner* v. *New York*,[74] Justice Matthews held that

[71] Grovey v. Townsend, 295 U.S. 45 (1935).

[72] Bailey v. Alabama, 219 U.S. 219. The antipeonage statute had earlier been sustained against charges of unconstitutionality, Clyatt v. United States, 197 U.S. 207 (1905).

[73] *In re* Tribucio Parrott, 1 Fed. 481 (C.C.D. Cal. 1880).

[74] 198 U.S. 45 (1905).

a San Francisco ordinance, allegedly a fire prevention measure, which eliminated wooden laundries was in fact designed to drive Chinese laundrymen out of business and thus violated the equal protection clause.[75] Justice Field, an intimate of the great corporate figures in California who had imported the Chinese to undercut the local (unionized) labor market, took these aliens under his personal protection. He and his loyal circuit and district judges struck down on one ground or another police power enactments which seemed to be part of the "Chinese Must GO!" campaign sponsored by the Union Labor Party and its "sandlot" allies.[76]

In the *Berea College* case, it will be recalled, counsel for the college attempted to call up the spirit of entrepreneurial liberty from the vasty deep. Their incantation, which included the magic words *Jacobs* and *Lochner*, was, however, a dismal failure. But in 1917, this formula did demonstrate its potency, and under its aegis certain property rights were excised from the sway of "separate but equal." In 1914 the city of Louisville, Kentucky, in order to "prevent conflict and ill-feeling between the white and colored races" zoned certain districts for Negro inhabitation and others for whites. By employing some quite complicated legal techniques which need not detain us here, a test case was brought to the Supreme Court which unanimously ruled that the municipal ordinance violated the due process clause of the Fourteenth Amendment.[77] Justice Day distinguished *Plessy* v. *Ferguson* and stated that the issue here was not the right of a state to classify legitimately its citizens by race. In his words:

> The case presented does not deal with an attempt to prohibit the amalgamation of the races. The right which the ordinance annulled was the civil right of a white man to dispose of his property if he saw fit to do so to a person of color, and of a colored person to make such disposition to a white person.
>
> . . .
>
> We think this attempt to prevent the alienation of the prop-

[75] Yick Wo v. Hopkins, 118 U.S. 356 (1886).

[76] See Graham, "Justice Field and the Fourteenth Amendment," 52 *Yale L.J.* 851, 881–88 (1943), for an account of Field's special dispensations for the Chinese.

[77] Buchanan v. Warley, 245 U.S. 60 (1917).

erty in question to a person of color was not a legitimate exercise of the police power of the State, and is in direct violation of the fundamental law . . . preventing state interference with property rights except by due process of law.[78]

In practical terms, this did not, of course, open up housing to Negroes in white districts; whites took recourse to restrictive covenants, private stipulations not to sell to Negroes or other "undesirable" ethnic groups which ran with property and were, until 1948, enforceable at law. What the decision did demonstrate was that in the event of clear conflict between ideologies, entrepreneurial liberty was even more sacrosanct than racism.

Let us turn now from the civil rights of racial minorities to the problems of the spokesmen for the economic and political underdogs, the socialists and the trade unionists. It should perhaps be emphasized that relatively few of the issues here ever reached the stratospheric level of Supreme Court adjudication. What we can attempt to convey is the atmosphere of the era and examine the few cases that did reach the top of the judicial pyramid. The first thing that has to be visualized is the tradition of direct action which played so striking a role in industrial relations. With effective legal techniques of unionization crippled by judicial roadblocks (particularly the inevitable injunction), it was not surprising that determined, militant unionists, usually of socialist persuasion, turned to violence to defend what they considered their rights. The employers, with their private armies, played rough, and in members of an organization like the Industrial Workers of the World (IWW) they found men who were ready to meet them on their own ground.

From roughly 1890 to the end of World War I an industrial civil war raged intermittently in the mining states of the West. On one side was the Western Federation of Miners, later to become a sponsor of the IWW, and on the other, the gradually consolidating mine owners, determined to break the power which the union had established in the early days.[79] The owners, mostly absentee, were exposed to problems in the West which they had seldom encountered in the Eastern mines. First, in

[78] *Idem* at 81–82.
[79] See Jensen, *Heritage of Conflict* (1950).

mining areas the population was almost totally committed to the union cause and characteristically elected pro-union men to local office—the sheriff and the town marshal were rarely "reliable" and elected judges too could create unforeseen problems. Second, there were few available strikebreakers in the isolated Western communities. Third, virtually everyone possessed arms and experts with high explosives were a dime a dozen; industrial conflict was punctuated with dynamite blasts: In 1899, at the famous "Battle of Bunker Hill & Sullivan" in the Coeur d'Alenes, ninety cases of dynamite (4,500 pounds) were used by the WFM to obliterate one of the largest ore concentrators in the country. ("It went up like an umbrella," one of the union leaders remarked.)[80]

Any campaign to break the union had to be prepared on military lines: Strikebreakers had to be imported, militia from nonmining sections of the states mobilized, and local judges and officials neutralized. And the WFM had its covert allies: At least one large shipment of "scabs" bound for southern Idaho was deposited in Oregon by railroad unionists. The injunction, that old standby in the East, was a complete flop. The Western equivalent was martial law. This is hardly the place to chronicle the thirty years' war which ended with the defeat and suppression of the WFM in its old strongholds; this story has been told with meticulous care by Vernon Jensen[81] and the dimensions of violence have been vividly etched by Stewart Holbrook.[82]

What is important here is the total absence of any tradition of civil rights, the willingness on both sides to utilize illegal techniques. The derailing of a trainload of "scabs," or the murder of a company "fink" by the WFM goonsquad, brought almost as much joy to the heart of a hard-rock miner as the deportation of 500 union stalwarts into the reaches of the desert did to a mine owner. Two quotations will reinforce this point. In 1904 the Cripple Creek district of Colorado exploded when the mine owners, who had advertised for labor as far away as Duluth, moved in strikebreakers and locked out the WFM. After various

[80] See Stewart Holbrook, *The Rocky Mountain Revolution* (1956), pp. 34–41.
[81] Vernon Jensen, *op. cit.*
[82] Holbrook, *op. cit.*

sanguinary events, Governor Peabody declared Teller County to be in rebellion and proclaimed martial law.

> The local police were deposed. National Guardsmen were set to patrolling all the towns. Citizens were ordered to bring in their arms. . . . The Western Federation hurriedly got out a handbill and distributed it throughout the district. It was a message from Federation President Moyer: "I strongly advise every member to provide himself with the latest improved rifle . . . so that in two years we can hear the inspiring music of the martial tread of 25,000 armed men in the ranks of labor."[83]
>
> All union leaders were hastily arrested by military authority and as promptly demanded their constitutional right to habeas corpus. "Habeas corpus be damned!" replied General Bell of the National Guard. "We'll give 'em post-mortems!"[84]

In the long run, the mine owners, with the federal army at their disposal in real crises, in other words, when the state militia were unreliable, could not lose. They were wards of the state, and if the state did not fulfill its obligations to entrepreneurial liberty, or wavered, they took direct action to guarantee their prerogatives. In 1904, when the liberal Democrat Alva Adams defeated Peabody in the gubernatorial election in Colorado, the mine owners immediately moved to block him from office and in 1905 convinced the legislature to install his defeated opponent![85]

The WFM was a well organized union and its men thought of themselves as "aristocrats of labor" and prided themselves on their courage and skill. By comparison the migratory agricultural workers of the West were a disorganized horde of peons, but it was this depressed constituency which the "Wobblies" (IWW) set out to organize. IWW organizers, or "job delegates" as they called themselves, were very bad insurance risks; if the private police of the "ranchers" did not catch up with them, the sheriff generally did. They lived their lives in the shadow of the noose, either private or public. As might be surmised, they were seldom models of gentlemanly decorum. A classic "Wobbly" handbill

---

[83] *Idem* at 104.

[84] *Idem* at 106. See the judicial fallout from this episode in Moyer v. Peabody, 212 U.S. 78 (1909), in which Holmes sustained the Governor's action.

[85] Jensen, *op. cit.*, at 155–59.

gives the atmosphere: "Don't put copper tacks in fruit trees! It kills them!" This was passed out in fruit country along with bags of copper tacks.[86]

The "Wheatland Riot" of 1913 is a good example of the impact of civil rights doctrines at the grassroots. Let us quote from Stuart Jamieson's authoritative study:

> Following a practice not unusual among large-scale growers, E. B. Durst, hop rancher, had advertised in newspapers throughout California and Nevada for some 2,700 workers. He subsequently admitted that he could provide employment for only about 1,500 and that living arrangements were inadequate even for that number. . . . A great number had no bedding and slept on piles of straw thrown on floors, in tents rented from Durst at 75 cents a week; many slept in the fields. There were no facilities for sanitation or garbage disposal and only 9 outdoor toilets for 2,800 people; dysentary became prevalent. . . . The water wells were insufficient . . . workers were forced to buy what supplies they could afford from a concession store on the ranch . . . [and Durst paid lower wages] because of the surplus labor he had recruited . . . [which] were further reduced by the requirement of extra "clean" picking.[87]

Into this appalling environment came a "Wobbly" organizer, Blackie Ford, who led a spontaneous demonstration against Durst demanding decent sanitary conditions and a fair wage. Durst, who attended the meeting, agreed to discuss issues with a grievance committee and promised to install adequate toilet facilities and supply water to the workers in the fields (whose only thirst quencher to that date had been lemonade at five cents a glass, sold by Durst's cousin). When Durst failed to fulfill his commitments, another meeting was called in a hired hall in Wheatland which was "invaded by a band of armed deputies who came to arrest Ford."[88] The meeting, which had been peaceable to that point, turned into a riot when one of the deputies fired an intimidating shot "to quiet the mob." Four were

---

[86] I am grateful to my colleague Professor Ray Ginger of Brandeis University for calling this item to my attention.

[87] Stuart Jamieson, *Labor Unionism in American Agriculture* (1945), pp. 61–62.

[88] *Idem* at 62.

killed and many injured in the melee, and then, in Jamieson's words:

> Hysteria apparently gripped the authorities. . . . Mass arrests of "wobblies" or sympathizers were carried out. Many of the arrested men were severely beaten or tortured, and many others were held incommunicado for weeks. Ford and Suhr, the two leading I.W.W. organizers in the camp, were convicted of murder and sentenced to life imprisonment.[89]

While this sort of open warfare was going on in the West, things were also going badly for the "conservative" wing of the labor movement, those in the organization dismissed by the IWW as the "American Fakeration of Labor." I have already examined in previous articles the devastating impact of the injunction on organizing campaigns and the problems of the Danbury Hatters.[90] Recall that in the *Hitchman* case[91] the district judge had forbidden union organizers even to *discuss* the case for the United Mine Workers with the employees of Hitchman Coal & Coke Company. This stringent limitation on freedom of speech was upheld by Justice Pitney with no apparent qualms. In *Gompers* v. *Bucks Stove & Range Co.*[92] and *Gompers v. United States*,[93] Samuel Gompers and the top leaders of the American Federation of Labor were found guilty of contempt of court essentially for acting like trade union leaders.

There must have been times when Gompers felt like wiring the Western Federation of Miners for some dynamite. In the *Bucks Stove* case, the AFL had responded to a plea for assistance from the Iron Molder's local in St. Louis by putting the company on its "We Don't Patronize" list, published in the monthly magazine, *The American Federationist*. The Bucks Stove Company, supported by the American Anti-Boycott Association which had financed Loewe and Fuchs' legal assault on the Danbury Hatters, asked a federal judge for an injunction against virtually the whole trade union movement and the nine members of the AFL

---

[89] *Ibid.*
[90] See the essays on p. 205 and p. 237.
[91] Hitchman Coal & Coke Co. v. Mitchell, 245 U.S. 229 (1917).
[92] 221 U.S. 418 (1911).
[93] 233 U.S. 604 (1914).

Executive Council to terminate the boycott. The judge promptly responded by enjoining the AFL from combining to injure the company's business and in particular from publishing any printed matter which listed Bucks Stove on an "Unfair" or "We Don't Patronize" list. The AFL appealed immediately.

The technical aspects of the case got very complex at this point. The injunction was not to go into effect for five days, and during that period the AFL leadership hastily rushed another issue of the *American Federalist*, featuring the Bucks Stove Company, into print. This brought a new lawsuit, this time for contempt of court; Bucks Stove charged that the rushed printing of the magazine and several public speeches by Gompers and others were in violation of the injunction. On December 23, 1908, Judge Wright agreed and sentenced Gompers to a year in jail, John Mitchell, President of the UMW, to six months and Frank Morrison, editor of the *American Federationist*, to nine months. This too was appealed, and thus there were two lawsuits moving up the appellate ladder.

It would be a labyrinthine task to trace the litigation fully. From a political viewpoint, it would appear that the Supreme Court was not overjoyed by Judge Wright's militance. It may be doubted whether the Justices wanted to see the top leadership of the AFL consigned to federal prison. Justice Lamar devised a splendid face-saver by upholding the substance of Judge Wright's action and voiding the procedures employed. Wright, who was thus given another chance, promptly—this time with appropriate legal rites—reimposed the sentences. Once again an appeal went up the line; the body was soon back on the Supreme Court's doorstep. This time Oliver Wendell Holmes, Jr., took charge of its disposal, and, by ingeniously inventing a statute of limitations applicable to contempt proceedings, sustained Judge Wright but freed the defendants.

Gompers did not go to jail, but the Court did sustain the injunction. To the argument that the injunction was an unconstitutional limitation on freedom of speech and a prior restraint of the press, the Justices were unresponsive. In concrete terms, this made possible injunctions which would prevent a trade unionist from saying or publishing anything of a derogatory character (which might hinder business) about a nonunion firm. Entrepreneurial liberty clearly ranked above the First Amendment on the Court's scale of constitutional priorities.

This somewhat mordant narrative may provoke the question: Were there any civil rights protected by the Constitution? Once the Fourteenth Amendment had been destroyed as an instrument for nationalizing basic "natural rights," the answer was that an individual's civil rights were those respected by a jury of his neighbors. There were some who argued that the due process clause of the Fourteenth Amendment was intended to enforce on the states the same procedural requirements—e.g., grand jury indictment, twelve-man petty jury with requirement of unanimity for conviction, privilege against self-incrimination, etc.—that the Bill of Rights imposed on the national government. It is historically doubtful whether the Committee of Fifteen which drafted the amendment had precisely this in mind, though one can assert with confidence that they intended to impose certain principles of "natural justice" on the states.

However, the intention of the Committee of Fifteen, whatever it may have been, became completely irrelevant when in a series of decisions the Supreme Court effectively eliminated the due process clause of the Fourteenth Amendment as a meaningful limitation on state procedures in criminal prosecutions. (The Justices were a bit more finicky about civil actions, in which valuable property was often involved.[94]) In *Hurtado* v. *California*,[95] the issue was California's right in a capital case to substitute indictment by information, a streamlined technique in which the state's attorney filed criminal indictments directly with a judge, for the traditional grand jury process. Hurtado claimed that California could not deny him a grand jury without violating the federal guarantee of due process. In reply, Justice Matthews lauded the dynamic flexibility of American law and its adaptability to new needs and announced that the Fourteenth Amendment could not be construed to put the states in a procedural strait-

---

[94] See e.g., Chicago, B. & Q. R.R. v. Chicago, 166 U.S. 226 (1897), where the Court held that the due process clause of the Fourteenth Amendment incorporated the Fifth Amendment's requirement of "just compensation."

[95] 110 U.S. 516 (1884).

jacket. He issued the customary malediction of unlimited state power:

> [I]t is not to be supposed that these legislative powers [to alter traditional legal procedures] are absolute and despotic, and that the amendment prescribing due process of law is too vague and indefinite to operate as a practical restraint.[96]

And he concluded by upholding the California procedure as a valid experiment well within the spirit of due process.

Subsequently the Court took the same position in a number of cases, holding for example, that Utah could cut the petty jury down to eight[97] and that New Jersey could impair the right against self-incrimination.[98] Justice Harlan invariably dissented in cases of this sort, asserting indomitably that the Fourteenth Amendment *had* been intended to impose precise procedural checks on state action.[99] It is interesting to note that whatever abstract potentialities Justice Matthews may have seen in the due process clause as a "practical restraint," no state criminal procedure was held to violate the Fourteenth Amendment in the period covered in this study.

In fairness to the Justices, one should make the effort to see the world through their eyes. From this vantage point, it is probable that the decisions endorsing "liberty of contract" were seen as major contributions to "civil rights." It also seems probable that the *Income Tax*[100] decision was considered by its authors to be a

---

[96] *Idem* at 535.

[97] Maxwell v. Dow, 176 U.S. 581 (1900).

[98] Twining v. New Jersey, 211 U.S. 78 (1908).

[99] See Harlan's dissents in Hurtado v. California, 110 U.S. 516, 538 (1884); Maxwell v. Dow, 176 U.S. 581, 605 (1900): Twining v. New Jersey, 211 U.S. 78, 114 (1908). There were two levels of argument which should be distinguished. One was that the due process clause of the Fourteenth Amendment imposed traditional common-law procedures on the states; the other that the due process and privileges and immunities clauses "incorporated" the Bill of Rights *in toto* as a check on the states. Justice Harlan began with the first position in Hurtado and switched to the far broader second view in Maxwell v. Dow. See Morrison, "Does the Fourteenth Amendment Incorporate the Bill of Rights? The Judicial Interpretation," 2 *Stan L. Rev.* 140, 146–57 (1949).

[100] Pollock v. Farmers' Loan & Trust Co., 157 U.S. 429, *affirmance upheld on rehearing*, 158 U.S. 601 (1895).

lasting blow in the eternal struggle to preserve liberty from tyrants. Briefly the background was this: In 1894 when the Democratic administration and Congress set out to lower tariffs, they agreed that the decrease anticipated in customs revenue should be compensated for by what amounted to a 2 percent tax on incomes over $4,000. While the tariff was not significantly dropped, the tax was enacted over bitter protests that it was a confiscatory, socialist piece of class legislation. Judge John F. Dillon, one of the outstanding leaders of the American bar, considered the tax:

> a forced contribution from the rich for the benefit of the poor . . . a means of distributing the rich man's property among the rest of the community . . . class legislation of the most pronounced and vicious type . . . violative of the constitutional rights of the property owner, subversive of the existing social polity, and essentially revolutionary.[101]

This subversive measure was, it should be recalled, a flat (not progressive) tax of 2 percent on most income, with all those who annually received less than $4,000 (roughly equivalent to $25,000 today) exempt; one can wonder what Judge Dillon would think of the annual communication that the American citizen today receives from the Internal Revenue Service. A minute proportion of the American people were affected by it; in 1891 a report of the United States Commissioner of Labor, based on 1890 census figures, indicated that the average annual money income of city wage and clerical workers in nine basic industries was $573; average monthly farm wages in 1894 were $12.50 with board, $18.50 without board, or sixty-five to eighty-five cents a day if that was the basis of computation.[102]

As Arnold M. Paul has chronicled,[103] the entrepreneurial community and its great legal sepoys became convinced that if the income tax were sustained by the courts, American liberty would be in dire peril and an almost unbelievably complex course of litigation was launched. The tax, in the view of its

---

[101] Cited in Arnold M. Paul, *Conservative Crisis and the Rule of Law* (1960), p. 164.

[102] *Historical Statistics of the United States* (1960), pp. 181, 281.

[103] Paul, *op. cit.* at 159–84.

enemies, was clearly unconstitutional, but the constitutional basis for this certainty was rather misty. Skilled lawyers set to work to demonstrate to the Supreme Court that when the answer is so obvious, there must be some good constitutional formulations which will evoke it. In a classic and much quoted summation before the Court, Joseph H. Choate called the tax by its rightful name: "communistic." Like Horatio and his stalwart Romans, the Justices had to hold the bridge against this "communistic march" and vindicate the rights of private property. To help the Court find a constitutional foothold, Choate and his associates elaborated some distinctions in the federal taxing power that would have turned a medieval scholastic green with envy. The essence of their argument was that the income tax was a "direct tax" in the constitutional meaning and therefore had to be apportioned among the states by population.

The Supreme Court took two formal hearings of the case in 1895 before it could reach a conclusive determination of all the issues involved. After the second, it decided by a 5–4 majority that the whole tax (which involved different provisions for various forms of income) was unconstitutional.[104] Although in historical terms the best definition of a "direct tax" was one either on polls (a capitation) or on land, and all others were "indirect" or excises, Chief Justice Fuller accepted Choate's line of reasoning: The tax *on the income* from real and personal property was ruled a tax *on the property itself,* hence "direct." Justice Harlan vented a furious dissent which led to his being accused of endorsing the "Marx gospel." Waving his finger under the Chief Justice's nose, Harlan accused the majority of participating in a "judicial revolution which may sow the seeds of hate and distrust among the people."[105] But the "communists" were short one Justice; the Constitution had to be amended before the income tax could again be instituted.

At any rate, the civil right not to pay an income tax was given a ringing endorsement; entrepreneurial liberty was preserved from the spoliation of the majority. As Justice Field, still ferocious though seventy-nine years old and close to retirement, remarked

---

[104] Pollock v. Farmers' Loan and Trust Co., 157 U.S. 429 (1895), *affirmance upheld on rehearing,* 158 U.S. 601 (1895).

[105] 158 U.S. at 665.

in his concurring opinion, the Constitution had to be protected from the masses. If this "usurpation" were upheld, Field said, the income tax would be the camel's nose under the tent:

> The present assault upon capital is but the beginning. It will be but the stepping-stone to others, larger and more sweeping, till our political contests will become a war of the poor against the rich; a war constantly growing in intensity and bitterness.[106]

The Income Tax Case, decided in the same year as *In re Debs*[107] and the *Sugar Trust* case,[108] contributed to precisely the eventuality that Field dreaded: In the presidential campaign of 1896, William Jennings Bryan, one of the congressional sponsors of the income tax, launched a bitter attack on the Court as a fortress of oligarchy, and demanded that judicial authority be curbed.[109]

Two other problems, which would be discussed today under the heading of "civil liberties," also came before the Court and deserve mention here. The first is important as showing how far Congress, the President and the courts were prepared to go in suppressing local practices which offended national morality. For this reason the rigorous employment of the mailed fist against the hapless Mormons provides an interesting contrast with the *laissez-faire* attitude toward Southern state governments. It is true that the Mormons involved were living in territories, not states, and might thus be considered more directly subject to national power than the white supremacists, but it is submitted that in the appropriate context of the Fourteenth Amendment this distinction is fictitious. State actions in the South enforcing racial discrimination were constitutional because they were quite "moral"; territorial actions in Utah condoning "plural marriage" were just plain Bad. The reasons that Mormon polygamy aroused such fierce antagonism must be left to the social psychiatrist; the fact is that no effort was spared to wipe out polygamous Mormonism. Indeed, in our own time, the polygamous underground

---

[106] 158 U.S. at 601.

[107] 158 U.S. 564 (1895).

[108] United States v. E. C. Knight Co., 156 U.S. 1 (1895).

[109] See Westin, "The Supreme Court, the Populist Movement and the Election of 1896," 15 *J. Politics* 3 (1953).

of primitive Mormons has been harassed under the Mann Act,[110] though no intelligent observer of this unorthodox remnant would accuse them of encouraging "vice."

The federal assault on the Mormons, as distinct from the lynch mobs under quasi-governmental auspices which drove them from Missouri and Illinois in the 1840s, began in the 1870s with indictments for bigamy.[111] The Mormons raised the issue of freedom of religion, claiming that their practices were protected from governmental infringement by the First Amendment. This argument got short shrift from the Supreme Court.[112] Chief Justice Waite agreed that Congress could not "pass a law for the government of Territories which shall prohibit the free exercise of religion," but promptly held for a unanimous Court that Mormonism was not a "religion."[113] But the federal government had its problems in Utah, particularly in finding juries which would indict and convict under this heading and in dealing with local officials elected by those of polygamous persuasion. As we have seen, when confronted with this sort of local resistance in the South, the national government had effectively said "boys will be boys" and dropped the matter. But with the "immoral" Mormons, a different line was taken: In 1882, Congress passed a statute which barred "bigamists," "polygamists" and "any person cohabiting with more than one woman" from voting or serving on juries. Again the Mormons took the matter to court; again the Supreme Court distinguished between bona fide and spurious religions and upheld the act.[114]

In 1890, the Court finally disposed of the issue in two cases. The territorial legislature of Idaho passed a drastic statute requiring a test oath from all voters: Before voting each had to swear that he was not a member of "any order, organization, or association which teaches, advises, counsels, or encourages" bigamy, polygamy or plural marriage. Note that this enactment was aimed at opinion—it did not merely penalize overt polygamous acts. Justice Field for a unanimous Court sustained this broad

---

[110] See Cleveland v. United States, 329 U.S. 14 (1946).
[111] See West, *Kingdom of the Saints*, chapter 15 (1957).
[112] Reynolds v. United States, 98 U.S. 145 (1879).
[113] *Idem* at 162.
[114] Murphy v. Ramsey, 114 U.S. 15 (1885).

interdiction, denouncing Mormonism in unrestrained fashion and asserting that "crime is not the less odious because sanctioned by what any particular sect may designate as religion."[115] Field dismissed the Mormon claim that the Idaho law infringed their rights under the First Amendment (territorial legislatures, it should be recalled, were congressional instruments) by stating in effect that Bad people have no rights.

Later in the year, Field had reason to modify this extreme view. In 1887, in a Draconic enactment, Congress repealed the federal charter to the Mormon Church, and confiscated all the nonecclesiastical property of the religious corporation! As one might imagine, Justice Field took a dim view of this. While Justice Bradley for the Court upheld the statute, on the grounds that Congress was *parens patriae* to all federal corporations with the sovereign's right of escheat, and found no religious issues whatsoever in the litigation,[116] Chief Justice Fuller with Field and Lamar dissented. The core of the dissent was that Congress could do anything it liked with Mormon opinion, but it could not "confiscate" Mormon property.[117]

The suppression of polygamous Mormonism has been examined at some length for two reasons: First, it is generally overlooked in studies of civil liberty; and second, it is a classic example of the exercise of vigorous congressional authority against people adjudged "Bad." No one seemed seriously distressed, except of course the Mormons, by this imposition of "stateways" on "folkways." Even those who seemed most convinced, with special reference to the South, that group custom was not an appropriate subject for social engineering, rushed to bludgeon the Mormons into conformity.

The last point to be examined in this essay is one which arose from the imperialist thrust of 1898, and the concomitant acquisition of possessions outside the continental United States. Up to that point, American expansion had been largely into a vacuum and the settlers took their law and their institutions with them. A few islands of French and Spanish culture existed in the Anglo-

[115] Davis v. Beason, 133 U.S. 333, 345 (1890).
[116] The Late Corp. of the Church of Jesus Christ of Latter-Day Saints v. United States, 136 U.S. 1 (1890).
[117] *Idem* at 66.

Saxon sea, but they were of little consequence in the overall fulfillment of "Manifest Destiny." However, with the acquisition of Puerto Rico, the Philippines and other miscellaneous pieces of foreign real estate after the Spanish-American War, a new problem emerged. Were the populations of these new territories, most of whom were non-English speaking, entitled to the full panoply of constitutional rights? In the current phrase, "Did the Constitution follow the Flag?"

To make a long story short, the Court in a series of *ad hoc* determinations over a period of twenty years held that parts of the Constitution followed the flag, while other parts did not. To supply a theoretical foundation for this improvisation, Chief Justice White invented two categories of territory: "incorporated" and "unincorporated"—the whole Constitution was applicable to a territory which Congress had incorporated *into* the United States, but only fundamental constitutional principles were resident in those territories not incorporated. This meant that in the Philippines, for example, which were held to be an "unincorporated" territory, the procedural requirements of the Bill of Rights (grand jury, right to counsel, etc.) were not enforced. In essence, the Court applied to the unincorporated territories roughly the same set of rules that it utilized vis-à-vis the states in procedural questions arising under the Fourteenth Amendment and refused, as it had in *Hurtado* v. *California*[118] or *Twining* v. *New Jersey*[119] to define the precise content of the "fundamental" constitutional provisions which *always* followed the flag. The so-called *Insular* cases[120] are above all interesting as remarkable examples of judicial legislation: Court holdings in this area were exercises in pure creativity.

To conclude, it is fair to say that the Constitution had no effective civil liberties content—in the contemporary sense of that category—throughout the period under analysis. The Fourteenth Amendment, I am convinced, was intended to nationalize fundamental individual rights—both personal and property—and put

[118] 110 U.S. 516 (1884).

[119] 211 U.S. 78 (1908).

[120] Rassmussen v. United States, 197 U.S. 516 (1905); Hawaii v. Mankichi, 190 U.S. 197 (1903); Downes v. Bidwell, 182 U.S. 244 (1901); De Lima v. Bidwell, 182 U.S. 1 (1901).

them under the umbrella of federal protection.[121] But within a decade after the Civil War the idealistic thrust of Abolitionist political and legal theory had vanished, leaving only a few lonely voices to maintain the tradition. Outstanding among them was that turbulent jurist, John Marshall Harlan who asserted in season and out, for a quarter of a century, that the framers of the Fourteenth Amendment had not been weighted down by concern about states rights, but had designed a strong instrument of national sovereignty over state and local instrumentalities. It is somehow most appropriate that today, as the Supreme Court restores the Fourteenth Amendment to its pristine power, Court decisions on Negro rights and criminal due process echo the embattled dissents of that grand old Kentucky Unionist.

[121] In saying this, I am not challenging Charles Fairman's massively documented case against full "incorporation" of the Bill of Rights, which has sometimes been interpreted as proving that the sponsors of the Fourteenth Amendment were simply killing time between important pieces of legislation. Fairman, "Does the Fourteenth Amendment Incorporate the Bill of Rights? The Original Understanding," 2 *Stan. L. Rev.* 5 (1949). I accept Howard Jay Graham's equally substantial arguments in favor of "selective incorporation," Graham, "Our 'Declaratory' Fourteenth Amendment," 7 *Stan. L. Rev.* 3 (1954), see particularly note 80 at 19–20. Graham's position escapes from the polemical overtones of Fairman's massacre of Justice Black and sets forth a view which Fairman indeed hints at in relaxed moments, e.g., *idem* at 81, 139.

Equality in America: The Expansion of a Concept

IF WE ARE GOING to understand the development of the concept of equality in the United States, we must first of all establish certain historical propositions, propositions which will provide the framework for the discussion to come later. At the risk of sounding un-American, I must insist that the most important fact in any analysis is the right theory—though theory alone can hardly carry the day. To paraphrase Justice Oliver Wendell Holmes, the status of equality in America cannot be solved by abstractions, nor without them.

Thus we must begin with what I have called "American exceptionalism," the remarkable fact that the conquest of liberty and equality in this country has been accomplished under unique historical circumstances. In every other free nation, the struggle for human liberation has been one of circumscribing the power of an irresponsible elite—a church, a monarch, an oligarchy, an aristocracy. In other words, freedom for the mass of the popula-

Reprinted from *All Men Are Created Equal* by Wattenberg (ed.), by permission of the Wayne State University Press.

tion has been attained by destroying the arbitrary jurisdiction of a small, self-anointed ruling class. In contrast, the problem in the United States has always been one of obtaining civil rights from the majority.

To put the matter differently, the society which emerged on this side of the Atlantic in the seventeenth and eighteenth centuries outran the authority mechanisms of Tudor-Stuart England. Despite certain rituals, the British provinces in North America were essentially "do-it-yourself" exercises in community building. And by the time the British—after the end of the Second Hundred Years War with France in 1763—got around to asserting their theoretical rights of sovereignty, these communities were deeply entrenched behind the barricades of local, responsible self-government.

It was John Adams—that brilliant, perverse and underrated social theorist—who noted all this and went on to point out that in terms of elite theory, i.e., who shall rule in America?, the American Revolution was over before the fighting began.[1] And it proved impossible for the British to cope with the colonists because the Redcoats were confronted not by a few malcontents, but by a thoroughly integrated society resting on a foundation of responsible self-government. To win the Revolution a few battlefield victories would not suffice: His Majesty's forces had to crack and destroy a whole social system.

The Americans fought the British for the right to define their own rights, the right they claimed from habit and prescription to run their own communities in their own fashions. And the truth-finding mechanism was majority rule. The sovereignty of the community—operating through the majority—was plenary. Everyone, of course, believed in "natural" and "inalienable" rights, but the crucial consideration was that the community had the authority to define the content of these abstractions. The "Peace of the Commonwealth" was substituted for the "King's Peace," and the result was that tyranny of the majority so brilliantly limned by Alexis de Tocqueville fifty years later:

> When an individual or a party is wronged in the United States, to whom can he apply for redress? If to public opinion, public

[1] 10 *The Works of John Adams* (Adams ed., 1856), pp. 282–83.

opinion constitutes the majority; if to the legislature, it represents the majority and implicitly obeys it; if to the executive power, it is appointed by the majority and serves as a passive tool in its hands. The public force consists of the majority under arms; the jury is the majority invested with the right of hearing judicial cases; and in certain states even the judges are elected by the majority. However iniquitous or absurd the measure of which you complain, you must submit to it as well as you can.[2]

The rights of man were thus accorded to the American as defined by his neighbors—a definitional process that could on occasion be a bit disconcerting. In 1794, for example, at the time of the discontent over the whiskey tax in western Pennsylvania, Albert Gallatin told some of his inflamed neighbors to stop acting like a "mob." They ominously referred him to a recent resolution which proclaimed "that if any one called the people a mob, he should be tarred and feathered."[3]

Or take the instance of Abner Kneeland, arrested and tried in Massachusetts in the 1830s for blasphemy on the basis of a tract denying the doctrine of the Virgin Birth. Kneeland asserted that the Massachusetts Bill of Rights guaranteed his religious freedom, but the Supreme Judicial Court held, in the words of Chief Justice Lemuel Shaw, that religious freedom was reserved for "honest" and "sincere" men—not for blasphemers who were, by definition insincere and dishonest disrupters of the peace.[4]

With this in mind, let us turn to the specific context of equality, specifically to Jefferson's majestic statement in the Declaration of Independence that "we hold these truths to be self-evident, that all men are created equal, that they are endowed by their Creator with certain inalienable rights, that among these are life, liberty and the pursuit of happiness."

A masterpiece of political warfare, the Declaration contained no qualifications, no reservations. Yet, if we are to consider it as more than pious propaganda for the American cause, we must immediately supply a number of unarticulated qualifications.

[2] Alexis de Tocqueville, *Democracy in America* (Vintage ed., 1954), p. 271.

[3] Brackenridge, *Incidents of the Insurrection* (1795), pp. 136–37.

[4] Commonwealth v. Kneeland, 37 Mass. 206 (1838). See Levy, *The Law of the Commonwealth and Chief Justice Shaw* (1957), pp. 43–58.

Negroes, Catholics and atheists (to say nothing of the female half of the population) could hardly view this as an act of emancipation. They were not accorded the status of equals in American society, and the men who voted for the Declaration did not rush home to remove their disabilities. A large proportion of the signees were, of course, slaveholders and apparently (and here Jefferson was an exception; at least he wrestled with his conscience on the slavery issue—but he won) saw nothing contradictory in affirming the equality of man one day and buying a slave the next. (This paradox was not unnoticed; the starkly logical Abigail Adams had written her husband on September 22, 1774: "It allways appeared a most iniquitious Scheme to me—fight ourselfs for what we are daily robbing and plundering from those who have as good a right to freedom as we have."[5])

If one were to have the temerity to translate this portion of the Declaration into operational political theory, a different proposition would emerge—the proposition which, I submit, is basic to an understanding of the development of equality in America over the past three centuries. It would run roughly as follows—*all those who have been admitted to membership by the political community are equal.* In other words, men achieve equality as a function of membership in the body politic—and this membership is not an inherent right, but a privilege which the majority accords on its own terms.

The myth of the libertarian past dies hard, but if we are going to grasp historical reality, we must once and for all lay to rest the notion that our forefathers built a pluralistic society around the principles of liberty and equality.[6] What throws many analysts off is the fact that restrictions on liberty, and inequalities, were unquestionably the consequence of "democratic procedures"— e.g., an overwhelmingly Protestant society unthinkingly limited the freedom of Catholics and atheists. Papists and atheists were not (in the spirit of the later Smith Act) spokesmen for "opinion," but were subversives, threats to public order. Which is not to say that the fathers did not believe in liberty and equality.

[5] 1 *The Adams Papers, Adams Family Correspondence, 1761–1776,* (Butterfield ed., 1963), p. 162.

[6] For an elaboration of this proposition, see Roche, *Shadow and Substance* (1964).

They believed completely in these great ideals *properly defined.*

Indeed, this proposition was at the heart of eighteenth- and nineteenth-century liberalism. Full membership in the political community, i.e., liberty and equality, was reserved to those who had—in the eyes of the Establishment—earned the right to exercise it. And in the United States the Establishment was majoritarian. It was John Stuart Mill who gave this collectivist notion of tutelage its classic statement.[7]

Mill was talking about India, which he ran with one hand while he wrote essays on "Liberty" with the other, but the basic theory applies equally well to the relationship within a society between those who "belong" and outsiders. Equality, like liberty, was a condition conferred by the community at its discretion, usually to "good" people who had earned their prerogatives.

The problem for discussion here is equality, but for obvious reasons I shall arbitrarily limit the analysis to the specific problem of the Negro. The question we are directing ourselves towards may be put as follows: What have been the historical stages that the Negro has passed through on his seemingly interminable journey towards full membership in the American community—i.e., toward acceptance by the majority in the category of "equals"?

This approach, I submit, throws new light on the dilemmas of the antislavery movement in the pre-Civil War period. Any individual or group which urged emancipation had perforce to come to terms with the free Negro, that is, include in his theory an answer to the question: What becomes of the Negroes after they have been released from slavery? The radical answer was full integration, social and political equality. But this ran head-on into the deep-rooted racial prejudices of the American majority— North and South.

Here again is de Tocqueville with his characteristic instinct for the jugular:

> As soon as it is admitted that the whites and the emancipated blacks are placed upon the same territory in the situation of two foreign communities, it will readily be understood that there are

[7] John Stuart Mill, *On Liberty* (Library of Liberal Arts ed., 1956), pp. 13–14. (Emphasis added.)

but two chances for the future: the Negroes and the whites must either wholly part or wholly mingle. I have already expressed my conviction as to the latter event. I do not believe that the white and black races will ever live in any country upon an equal footing. But I believe the difficulty to be still greater in the United States than elsewhere. An isolated individual may surmount the prejudices of religion, of his country, or of his race; and if this individual is a king, he may effect surprising changes in society; but a whole people cannot rise, as it were, above itself. A despot who should subject the Americans and their former slaves to the same yoke might perhaps succeed in commingling their races; but as long as the American democracy remains at the head of affairs, no one will undertake so difficult a task; *and it may be foreseen that the freer the white population of the United States becomes, the more isolated will it remain.*[8]

To hazard a historical generalization, I believe that outside of the South there was a clear majority of the white population opposed in principle to slavery—but equally convinced of the "natural inferiority" of the Negro. (The statute books in Northern states were littered with discriminatory provisions aimed at controlling the emigration of free Negroes and at preventing social, political and legal equality: the first adjudication of "separate but equal" was, after all, in Boston in 1850, and segregation was sustained.)[9]

Northerners, and Westerners, in other words, were not distressed by Negro inequality, per se, but were increasingly outraged by the savage social consequences of applied inequality: the slave system. Sincere and decent people (such as Abraham Lincoln) drew the moral line this side of chattel slavery, but on the other side of equality. Characteristically they attempted to formulate a solution which would simultaneously end slavery *and* terminate the Negro problem—and the one arrived at was "colonization," the establishment in Africa (on the model of Liberia and Sierra Leone), or the West Indies, or the American West (Texas was strongly favored for the location of the "Black Republic" at one time) of Negro communities. Thus slavery *and* the Negro would be banished from the white community in a

[8] de Tocqueville, *op. cit.*, pp. 388–89. (Emphasis added.)
[9] See Roberts v. City of Boston, 59 Mass. 5 Cush. 198 (1849).

fashion that should warm the heart of a contemporary Black Muslim. Except for a few dedicated abolitionists who argued for full equality, it seems clear that as far as the overwhelming preponderance of American opinion was concerned, there was no alternative to slavery as an institutional pattern of dealing with the Negro *within* the white community.

To say this is not to downgrade slavery as a cause of the Civil War; indeed, slavery was crucial. Not because Northerners and Westerners were committed to equality for the Negro, but because they were unwilling to allow the South to impose inequality on whites throughout the Union.[10] The necessary and logical consequences of the slave system were the suppression of civil rights, the Southern veto on all legislation which was seen as undermining the economic and political autonomy of the region, a proslavery foreign policy, civil wars in the territories—indeed, the "militant South" demanded that the whole thrust of national public policy be adjusted to the imperatives of the slave system. When the Southern states abandoned the Union in 1860–1861 because they had lost the presidential election, the evidence seemed conclusive: Slavery required a rule or ruin approach to American national interest, and it was obvious that the nation would live in dire jeopardy until this cancer was removed.

Ironically the majority in the states which sustained the Union was thus dedicated to freeing the Negroes, but not to making them equals. And this dichotomy was ominous because it signified that a Union victory in the Rebellion would only end human slavery; the future status of the Negro was wrapped in ambiguity and ambivalence. Lincoln's soldiers died in fearful numbers to "make men free," but the survivors did not have the foggiest notion of what to do with the freedmen once their chains had been removed.

If we examine (admittedly with 20/20 hindsight) the options that existed in 1865, it is immediately clear that two alternatives existed. (Colonization was patently out of the question: there were over 4 million slaves in 1860 and the establishment of even

[10] For an extraordinarily perceptive analysis of the general role of slavery in American political thought, see Elkins, *Slavery* (1959). I differ with Elkins on a number of points, but his synthesis is invaluable.

small colonies had proved inordinately expensive.) On the one hand, the slaves could simply be freed and left to fend for themselves; on the other, the national government could undertake a massive program of compensatory assistance for the freedmen, take them under its protection, and bring them under its tutelage to full membership in the American community. The problem was, however, that while the radical Republicans realized that the first alternative was disastrous, they lacked the conviction and the political base necessary to implement the second. Let us examine the situation as it developed in the Reconstruction period.

The Lincoln-Johnson program of Reconstruction contemplated freeing the slaves, establishing loyal state governments in the temporarily misled South, and then calling it a day. Anyone who appreciates Abraham Lincoln's sense of political reality may—admittedly on the basis of spectral evidence—question whether he would have followed this line to its logical conclusion. For one thing, the natural leaders of the Southern white community—though barred from politics for participation in the Rebellion—were hardly going to be eliminated from *influence;* and the marginal political credentials of Southern Unionists made them bad long-run political risks.[11] In short, the power structure of the Southern white community could never be cracked by marginal political figures, particularly those who had fought against the "Boys in Grey." (It is perhaps pure speculation, but I have always suspected that both Lincoln and Johnson—Southern poor whites in origin—held the illusion that if the planter magnates were excluded from the political process, the nonslaveholding whites would implement the principles of true democracy, i.e., they assumed the existence of a "class division" and refused to believe that the magnates *were* in fact the natural elite.)

It rapidly became apparent to the Republican leaders in Congress that the Lincoln-Johnson program of Reconstruction was a total failure; nothing was really reconstructed. The Negro, now free, was still at the mercy of the police power and was put into

[11] There is no finer study of the political dynamics of Reconstruction than McKitrick, *Andrew Johnson and Reconstruction* (1960).

what amounted to serfdom by the Black Codes and labor contract legislation. And the worst of it was that freeing the slaves *increased* Southern representation in the House of Representatives and the Electoral College. (In 1860, the slave states had seventeen members of Congress "representing" the three-fifths Compromise in the Constitution; with the freed Negroes counted per capita for representation purposes, they would pick up another dozen.[12]) Political self-interest, to say nothing of principle—or of the merger of the two that most of us silently manage—required guarantees for the future.

Thus began congressional Reconstruction which, from the viewpoint of social theory, had as its objective the demolition of the white power structure in the South. I can hardly take the time here to discuss Reconstruction in detail, but the key point for our purposes is that while the radicals knew precisely *what* they hoped to accomplish, they refused to accept the only theory which could provide consistency and justification to their actions, that of the full potential equality of the Negro. Some few did, but the great bulk of Republican congressmen and senators—and more important, their constituents—did not. The war had been fought to free the Negro, not to make an equal of him, and now that the fighting was over and slavery destroyed, the average Unionist wanted to go home and bask in the sunshine of peace. He was capable of getting quite angry at Southern efforts to reverse the verdict of Appomattox (see the congressional elections of 1866), but he was not willing to underwrite that sustained effort which alone could bring equality to the Negro.

Cracking a social system is not an exercise in rhetoric—it is a campaign which must be mounted with strong administrative instruments and backed by a full political commitment to change. Indeed, what has struck me as remarkable is the relative success of the much maligned Freedmen's Bureau. Sent out into hostile country with no conventional weapons for dealing with militant local majorities (only troops, the ultimate weapon in administration), and virtually no infrastructure to maintain day to day operations, the Bureau's many devoted agents were the

---

[12] *Idem* at 332.

unsung heroes of the one effort that could conceivably have broken the social pattern of the South.[13] One who today reads the statute[14] establishing the Bureau must marvel at the institutional genius of its authors: it was an extremely sound attempt at the most difficult accomplishment known to politics—elite building. And it failed not because of its conceptual weakness, but because it never obtained that massive commitment to its goals which made, for example, MacArthur's reconstruction of Japanese society possible.

To summarize, in the brief years of radical Reconstruction there was an effort in such measures as the Civil Rights Act of 1866,[15] the Freedmen's Bureau Acts,[16] the Fourteenth and Fifteenth Amendments, to establish a national definition of equality, one which looked to the incorporation of the freed Negro into the political community. But these measures were supported by different men for different reasons and, I am convinced, reflected in the bulk of their supporters a limited conviction that racial equality should be enforced *in the South* for political reasons. To say this is not for one moment to slur the memory of that noble band of true egalitarians who spearheaded both the struggle against slavery and against the reassertion of Southern racism under other forms in the post–Civil War period; it is simply to suggest that their idealism did not reflect the views of the majority in the North and West, whose immediate interest in eliminating Southern power was otherwise motivated. (It should be recalled that the Southern bloc in Congress had long barred the passage of a Homestead Act, a true protective tariff, railroad land-grants and a number of other measures near and dear to the hearts of the North and West.)

Every nation, it seems, had some national obsession; for the United States racism has been the plague which has undermined our strength and national purpose since the eighteenth century.

---

[13] There is no broad study of the Freedmen's Bureau which approaches it from the viewpoint I am suggesting. Bently, *History of the Freedmen's Bureau* (1955) is thorough—and thoroughly unsympathetic to the basic objectives of the Bureau.

[14] Freedmen's Bureau Act, chapter 90, 13 Stat. 507 (1865).

[15] Chapter 31, 14 Stat. 27.

[16] Chapter 90, 13 Stat. 507, *as amended,* chapter 200, 14 Stat. 173 (1866).

We cannot tarry here to recount the collapse of the Republican effort to nationalize liberty and equality—the political side of this has been told with sensitivity and perception by C. Vann Woodward in his *Reunion and Reaction*.[17] We should, however, examine the process by which the Fourteenth Amendment and its companion Civil Rights Act were converted into battle monuments. This evisceration began in the *Civil Rights* cases[18] in which the Supreme Court delivered the *coup de grâce* to national efforts to protect the Negro from the "customary" disabilities imposed by "private" action. By giving an extremely narrow interpretation to the Fourteenth Amendment Justice Joseph P. Bradley (with the former slaveholder Justice John Marshall Harlan alone dissenting) ruled that only formal state action of a discriminatory character fell within the amendment's interdict. Consequently, "private" racial discrimination by railroads, theaters, hotels and the like was held to be a matter within the sole jurisdiction of the states. Bradley suggested that to rule otherwise would make the Negroes favorites of the national government and would discriminate against white men, who presumably were in need of equal treatment.[19]

The Bradley opinion has to be understood as a period piece. It was grossly unhistorical: The framers of the Fourteenth Amendment were attempting to provide constitutional certainty for the Civil Rights Act of 1866 which penalized racial discrimination by "custom" as well as by "law."[20] In an ironic sense, Bradley's opinion echoed President Johnson's veto of the Civil Rights Act, which was promptly overridden by two-thirds of both houses of Congress.[21] Fundamentally, Justice Bradley declared the Fourteenth Amendment, as originally conceived, to be unconstitutional.

Significantly, Bradley noted in private correspondence that he

[17] Woodward, *Reunion and Reaction* (1951). Part of the remainder of this essay is adapted from the essay, "Civil Liberty in the Age of Enterprise," p. 269. A number of points alluded to here are there developed in detail.

[18] 109 U.S. 3 (1883).

[19] *Ibid.*

[20] Chapter 31, § 2, 14 Stat. 27.

[21] See Johnson's veto message of March 27, 1866, in 6 Richardson, *Messages and Papers of the Presidents* (1897), p. 405.

was very disturbed by the alleged "power of Congress to pass laws for enforcing social equality between the races."[22] In realistic terms "social equality" was hardly a real issue in the 1870s or 80s; the fact of the matter was that by 1883, the Negro had been left to his fate by Congress, the President and the American (white) people. All Justice Bradley did was incorporate the realities of the day into the Fourteenth Amendment. Bradley shared the common view that the white man had been discriminated against by the civil rights laws with unfortunate results. He demanded fair play for the white population.

I shall not attempt here to trace the story into the twentieth century (I have covered the matter in detail in my recent book, *The Quest for the Dream*).[23] Suffice it to say that it is quite clear to me that right up through World War II the Negro was excluded from the political community.

Indeed, we have lingered too long with the past—compulsive behavior in a historian, I suppose—and the time has come to show some respect for the constitutional injunction against cruel and unusual punishment. What I hope has emerged is the role of "American Exceptionalism" in the struggle for equality, that is, the fact that inequality for the Negro (and the Jew, the Irishman, the Asian, the Mexican) has been a consequence of the refusal on the part of the majority to accord equal status—which in turn has arisen from majority refusal to consider the Negro as a "man" among "men" at the same time that it affirmed vehemently that "all men are created equal."

The transformation of American attitudes towards equality has thus been an outgrowth of the tremendous war that has been waged in the United States over the past half-century against our ancient curse of racism, a campaign that began in private hands but has now been turned over to public authority. This has not been a passive affair, one based solely on education (that wonderful slogan for avoiding activism) because as we all know stateways *can* change folkways (to use Sumner's old categories) and the power of the state, notably of the national government,

---

[22] For an examination of Bradley's role in the undermining of the civil rights acts, see Roche, *op. cit.*, at 108–11.

[23] Roche, *The Quest for the Dream* (1963).

has been decisive in bringing real equality to the United States. Morality can be legislated—segregationists are currently fighting to *preserve* their huge body of morals legislation on the racial question—but it can only be legislated successfully when it is backed by strong national commitment. Legislation, however, cannot make the Negro equal—he has lived too long under the burdens of discrimination. It can and should provide him with the instruments by which to achieve his proper participating place in the American community and in particular it should be premised on the theory that only by giving this generation of Negroes special compensatory treatment can the next generation stand on its own.

Let us make one historical proposition perfectly clear: As a community we have, since the days when veterans of the American Revolution were given preference in western lands, applied the principles of compensatory treatment to many categories in the population. As a veteran of World War II, I have been compensated in many fashions: the G.I. Bill subsidized my Ph.D., a civil service point bonus awaits my use, and my home is mortgaged under highly favorable conditions. However, as an author I find myself without the benefits of a cotton farmer: Regrettably the government does not purchase and hold overstock of my books, nor pay me not to write more than one a year. The cotton farmer is given special preference because of the eccentricities of nature; the vagaries of book purchasers have yet to receive adequate historical standing.

Thus it is absurd to oppose special historical treatment for the Negro on principled grounds unless one is simultaneously urging the abolition of, *inter alia*, the Veterans Administration, the agricultural subsidy program, the "impacted areas" educational subventions, and the tariff. We can hardly argue that the Negro should be the first group in American history which must "stand on its own two feet."

The American people, led by their President, the courts, their churches and other private groups, have finally faced up to the fact that equality for the Negro is, in President Johnson's phrase, "a moral right." We have passed the Civil Rights Act of 1964,[24]

[24] Pub. L. 88–352, 78 Stat. 241.

the first meaningful civil rights act in our modern history, and this is only a beginning. As a political community we now have the obligation, the moral duty, to provide an existential as well as a formal content to equality: to display our remorse and our creativity by devising massive programs in the areas of housing, education, employment and the like which will indicate to the Negro that we are not merely paying lip-service to a slogan. (I support this for all deprived Americans, but the Negroes are clearly a priority case.)

Let me conclude by noting the significance of what I have been discussing. Without realizing it, most of us have lived through a truly remarkable episode in the development of a democratic society. By and large, we Americans are a historyless people—history begins the day we start a job—and we need on occasion to look backward and meditate on what we observe. What has happened in the course of the last quarter of a century in the area of equality is nothing less than spectacular: anti-Catholicism, anti-Semitism (once the common currency of our culture) have been driven to the paranoid littoral. And the Negro has been accepted as a *Man*.

No one living in the racial turmoil of 1964 can imagine for a minute that the war is over. Yet, as I look at American history, and the structure of politics in 1964, it appears that we have, on the crucial theoretical level, broken the back of racism. A lot of nasty mopping up remains to be done: The Negro has yet to receive his minimal rights in such citadels of racism as Alabama and Mississippi, and economic realities elsewhere, North and South, often make a mockery of his formal prerogatives. But, as the vote on the Civil Rights Act, the presidential election and polls indicate, the *consensus is there,* and the muscle will be provided.

In essence, we have had a "white Revolution" rather than a "Negro Revolution" (which would have been doomed in a society 90 percent white), a radical transformation in the attitudes of the majority. And as a majority "revolution" this trend has the inexorable crushing power of a glacier.

The American majority, in other words, has finally—in that violent, amorphous fashion which has always characterized our culture—determined to give full coverage to the Declaration of

Independence. And while we must feel shame at the intolerable delay, we can also find some pride in knowing that those of us who have fought for racial equality all our lives did not misjudge the vitality of the democratic process nor the latent decency of the American people.

Constitutional Law:
Distribution of Powers

DISTRIBUTION OF POWERS

From the beginnings of political speculation, much time and theoretical effort have been assigned to the demarcation and definition of jurisdictions between competing elites within various societies. While the bases of jurisdiction have shifted over the centuries, one can hear in contemporary Israel echoes of Old Testament disputes between kings and prophets, and in contemporary America the rhetoric of states' rights has archetypal resemblances to the polemical literature of the early modern struggle between royal centralists and feudal autonomists. And although the external form of modern disputes is radically different from earlier jurisdictional disputes, the key issue has not altered in 2,000 years, namely, where does the final jurisdiction to define jurisdictions rest?

This issue has always been, and remains today, the crux of the matter; in the vocabulary of modern politics it is known, of

Reprinted, with permission, from *The International Encyclopedia of the Social Sciences,* © 1968 by Macmillan Publishing Co., Inc.

course, as the question of sovereignty. Even the most ultra-montane Pope never denied the existence of the *imperium*, the Emperor's sector of jurisdiction. Nor did the most ambitious of the Holy Roman Emperors ever assert that the *sacerdotium*, the ecclesiastical jurisdiction, was nonexistent. But a struggle raged for centuries that, although seemingly centered on the scope of the respective judisdictions, was in fact directed to the antecedent problem of ultimate determination of the appropriate forum for settlement of jurisdictional disputes. Archbishop Thomas à Becket's argument in his confrontation with Henry II in 1164 over the question of the criminous clerk[1] was thus at base analogous to the logic of the Virginia and Kentucky resolutions of 1798–1799; like the archbishop, Thomas Jefferson and James Madison denied their opponents the right to define their own jurisdictions.

Every political community larger than the Greek *polis* has been faced with the problem of distributing power, at least in func-tional terms. Subgovernments—provinces, exarchates, shires, communes, etc.—have been established for purposes of adminis-trative convenience. Other varieties of subgovernment have origi-nated from more complex origins, for example, Huguenot auton-omy in France as a consequence of the Edict of Nantes, Scottish privileges under the Act of Union with England, Turkish com-munal rights as stipulated in the Cypriot Constitution. In this context, what problems arise do so as a result of ambiguity in the relationship of the peripheral units to the center. When sover-eignty, i.e., the final power to define jurisdictions, clearly resides in the center, we have what is commonly called a "unitary" system. In France, for example, the authority of *départements*, *arrondissements* and *communes*—the units of subgovernment—is clearly subject to determination by the central government. This does not prevent occasional conflicts: Communist-dominated *communes* from time to time invoked the wrath of the Minister of the Interior by banning hydrogen bombs from their territory, passing resolutions against the Algerian war, or renaming streets

[1] Frederick Pollack and Frederick W. Maitland, *The History of English Law Before the Time of Edward I* (1895), vol. I, 2nd ed. (Boston, 1952), pp. 447–457.

after Communist heroes, but the results contributed more in the way of publicity than jurisprudence. The offending local council, in such instances, is simply dissolved by order of the central government.

At the other end of the spectrum we find the confederation, which is characterized by the fact that the powers of the central government are subject to definition by the peripheral units. A classic instance of this type of government was the United States under the Articles of Confederation, a modern example is Switzerland, where residual power still—in theory if not always in practice—rests with the component cantons.

Between these two polar positions can be found a huge variety of intermediate forms of which the most significant for our purpose is American Federalism. For almost two centuries political theorists have been attempting to define "Federalism," and have had uniformly disastrous results because in analytical terms federalism is an institutionalized technique of question begging. It is, to put the matter differently, an effort to exorcise sovereignty from the political sector. Since definition is therefore understandably elusive, we shall have to settle for a description drawn from K. C. Wheare, which suggests that federalism is a system in which two levels of government operate within the same geographical limits and neither has the power to destroy the other.

However, before turning to a historical examination of the distribution of powers between the American national government and the states, it would be advantageous to define the other major dimension of the distribution of power: the relationship of various agencies of government to one another—or, in the American context, the issue of the separation of powers within the national government. Again, the problem is one that has been canvassed since the time of Aristotle (*Politics* 1298a40), although the form that the "separation of powers" took among political theorists through the eighteenth century was almost totally irrelevant to the American innovation. From Polybius and Cicero through Montesquieu, the "separation of powers" involved the allocation of governmental functions to orders of the realm or to estates, with the ideal result of a mixed government or "polity."

Thus, Thomas Aquinas (*Summa theologica, quaestio* cv), discussing the "right ordering of power in a principality," argued that the best form of constitution incorporated a "judicious admixture of the kingdom . . . of aristocracy . . . and of democracy."

This was the essence of medieval constitutionalism—the conciliar movement, indeed, attempted with ephemeral success symbolized in the *Frequens* decree, issued in 1417 by the Council of Constance, to apply this formula to the government of the church —and it provided the foundation for Montesquieu's famous chapter in *The Spirit of the Laws* (1748): "On the Constitution of England." To state the point differently, the tripartite division of the United States Constitution was not intended to balance the auhority of the "one, the few, and the many"; it was a functional differentiation between governmental organs. John Locke's notion of the "separation of powers" was founded on another premise, but one equally irrelevant to American constitutional law. It is true that Locke identified a threefold division of powers (*The Second Treatise of Government* 1690) but he never asserted the equivalence of his three branches: his "executive" was a thoroughly dependent figure (§152) and, so far as domestic jurisdiction was concerned, was little more than an agent of the "supreme" legislative power (§149). And his third division, the "federative," was indeed given wide authority and prerogative—but only for the purpose of conducting foreign relations (§147). The judiciary was attached to the executive.

What then are the origins of the American doctrine of the "separation of powers"? What did this doctrine involve in practice? By what means and to what degree has it been incorporated in American constitutional law? These are the issues that will concern us in the last section of this analysis. First, however, we shall examine the division of powers in the American federal system, that is, the relationship between the national government and the states.

THE DIVISION OF POWERS

The American federal system has been widely acclaimed as a great, even original, contribution to political science, and it has provided the model for many subsequent governments. Federalism has always appealed to spokesmen for vested minority interests—whether religious, ethnic or economic—who are seeking institutional guarantees against the power of a majority.[2] Nowhere has the connection between the integrity of the peripheral jurisdiction, i.e., the states, and the privileges and property of a national minority—slaveholders—been expressed more cogently than in John C. Calhoun's *A Disquisition on Government* (1851). Today we can discern variations on the Calhoun theme in the rhetoric of the Cypriot Turks, the French Canadians, the Ceylonese Tamils, the Fijis (outnumbered on their ancestral islands by Indians), the Nigerian Yoruba—to name only a few instances.

The theory that underpins this adulation is that federalism provides a viable framework for the reconciliation of majority power and minority rights. In terms of the distribution of power, the model rests on two assumptions: first, the central government has a plenary jurisdiction over certain sectors of policy making; second, certain other sectors of decision making are reserved in equally plenary fashion to the peripheral units (states, provinces, ethnic or religious communities). Obviously, such a system requires a written constitution, and for our purposes it is irrelevant whether residual power remains with the peripheral units (for example, U.S. Constitution, Article X of the Bill of Rights) or the center (for example, Canada under the provisions of the British North America Act of 1867).

In principle, then, an impenetrable wall is built between the jurisdiction of the center and the jurisdiction of the peripheral units. The nation as a whole exercises the necessary sovereignty to hold its place in the international community, while within the society the rights of minorities are protected from "nationalization." The character of the minorities may vary widely; in the United States—as in Australia—geographical prescription served as the justification for the establishment of the peripheral units: The previously self-governing units were integrated as the operating components of federalism. In Canada and the Union of

[2] William Riker, *Federalism: Origin, Operation, Significance* (Boston, 1964).

South Africa, geography mixed with ethnic considerations (the French in Quebec, the Afrikaners in the Transvaal and Orange River Colony) supplied the rationale.

It has been suggested[3] that when the framers of the United States Constitution met in Philadelphia in 1787, they found the theoretical and practical arguments for Federalism overwhelming, largely as an outgrowth of their colonial experience. In their struggle with the British over the status of the colonies, American spokesmen developed a wide-ranging theory of American rights. However, it is hard to assert that the colonial experience provided a formula for the new federal experiment; on the contrary, it supplied full support for precisely the form of association that the Constitutional Convention destroyed: the Articles of Confederation. The essence of the colonial position vis-à-vis the British was that the Americans had the right to define the jurisdiction of King and Parliament, i.e., the peripheral units defined the authority of the center, the very principle that later was incorporated into the Articles of Confederation. Curiously, then, when the framers set to work to limit the authority of the states (and the caprice of "Rogues Island"), the arguments they utilized were drawn from the British, not the American, arsenal. They were in search of sovereignty in the classic Hobbesian sense and, with few exceptions, took a dim theoretical view of states' rights.

This may seem to be an eccentric interpretation, flying as it does in the face of conventional wisdom. However, it has the great merit of being solidly grounded on the proceedings in the Constitutional Convention,[4] rather than on the *a posteriori* theoretical patina supplied by *The Federalist*. The views of "Publius" on the high merits of the Constitution were analogous to a man's eulogies of a wife he had secretly been forced to marry: both James Madison and Alexander Hamilton had supported the establishment of a unitary system at the convention, but debates were secret and no significant record was published until after Madison's death in 1836. What had occurred at the convention was that a strong unitary system—the "Randolph Plan," prepared

[3] Andrew C. McLaughlin, *Foundations of American Constitutionalism* (New York, 1961).

[4] John P. Roche, *Shadow and Substance* (New York, 1964), pp. 91–126.

by Madison—which put the states completely at the mercy of the nation, was modified into what later became known as federalism. The latter was an improvisation that only subsequently was promoted into a political theory. In practical terms, it was a compromise between the unitary convictions of the delegates and their sense of political reality: the leading opponents of the Randolph Plan endorsed its goals but argued that it would be an act of political suicide to return to their constituent states with such a radical innovation. Thus the scope of national power over the peripheral units was cut down, the sectors of national jurisdiction stipulated, and the states given equal representation in the Senate. In the course of ratification, proponents of the new government were forced to promise a bill of rights as a further safeguard to the jurisdiction of the states.

When the Constitution went into operation and the newly elected officials assembled in New York, there was nothing particularly lucid about Federalism. The Constitution was a model of studied ambiguity at certain key points, reflecting its authors' pragmatic notion that the best way to deal with sticky problems was to turn them over to the future unclarified. The institutions of the new republic were provided for, but even here a conflict in the convention had resulted in a semantic compromise; Congress was given the power to establish an independent federal judiciary (below the Supreme Court, which was explicitly created) but left with discretion to utilize inferior state judicial machinery for national purposes if it so chose. Yet the distribution of power within the national government was a model of clarity when compared with the relationship between the latter and the states.

An early dictionary, which Sir Ernest Barker was fond of quoting, defined a cello as a big violin and a violin as a small cello. The relationship between national and state powers under the Constitution was a similar exercise in logical circularity. In the body of that document there was no discussion whatever of the distribution of power between the center and the peripheral units; state objections led to the addition of the Ninth and Tenth Amendments in 1791, but these did little more than restate the central ambiguity. Article IX announced that "the enumeration in the Constitution, of certain rights, shall not be construed to deny or disparage others retained by the people." Article X provided that "the powers not delegated to the United States by the Constitution, nor prohibited by it to the States, are reserved to the States respectively, or to the people."

In other words, the Ninth and Tenth amendments, like the Constitution itself, ignored the crucial institutional question: How, and by whom, were jurisdictional conflicts between states and nation to be resolved? What was to be the truth-finding mechanism in this open-ended situation? The immediate answer is the United States Supreme Court, and although there is no direct evidence that the framers intended the Court to exercise this supervision over the distribution of powers (there was no recorded discussion of the problem in the Constitutional Convention), circumstantial evidence supports this contention. The Supreme Court's power to review both acts of Congress and state legislation was probably taken for granted; indeed, the notion of a written constitution containing limitations on states and nation carried with it a need for machinery of enforcement, and the Supreme Court seems to have been assigned this task *sub silentio*.

The Constitution was hardly ten years old before the question of states' rights shook the new republic to its foundations. In a desperate effort to hold their slipping popularity, the Federalists, marshaled by Alexander Hamilton, attempted in 1798–1799 to cripple the Jeffersonians by national legislation, primarily the Sedition Act of 1798, which was designed to muzzle the Jeffersonian press. The Jeffersonians lost the battle in Congress and then appealed to the courts to declare the Sedition Act unconstitutional as an intrusion on states' rights. The litigation never reached the Supreme Court, but at the circuit level the act was sustained as a legitimate exercise of congressional power. At this point, Jefferson and Madison realized that the rules had to be changed, that it was improper for an agency of the general government to have the right to assess the national jurisdiction, that, in Locke's phrase, "no one should be a judge in his own cause." The result was the Virginia and Kentucky resolutions of 1798–1799, the former prepared by Madison, the latter secretly drafted by Vice President Jefferson, which attempted to reopen the whole issue of distribution of powers. These resolutions have served ever since as the intellectual fountainhead for states' rights formulations.

Jefferson put the question concisely:

> . . . the several States composing the United States of America, are not united on the principle of unlimited submission to their general government; but that by compact . . . they constituted a general government for special purposes, delegated to that government certain definite powers, reserving each State to itself, the residuary mass of right to their own self-government; and that whensoever the general government assumes undelegated powers, its acts are unauthoritative, void, and of no force: . . . That the government created by this compact was not made the exclusive or final judge of the extent of the powers delegated to itself; . . . but that as in all other cases of compact among parties having no common Judge, *each party has an equal right to judge for itself, as well of infractions as of the mode and measure of redress.* (Kentucky Resolutions, Nov. 16, 1798)

Thus began the states' rights tradition. In characteristic American fashion, it was an *ad hoc* response to political peril by the losing faction in national politics; Jefferson and Madison took a very dim view indeed of the logic of the Virginia and Kentucky Resolutions when the latter were employed against the embargo of 1807 by Federalist state governments in New England.[5] Moreover, in a paradoxical fashion, Jefferson and Madison were engaged in precisely the behavior they were criticizing: Their concept of "compact" made the states the final judges of the extent of the powers of the general government, i.e., made the states judges in "their own cause." Each side engaged in *petitio principii* by silently incorporating their conclusions in their premises. On the one hand, the centralist view was founded on the assumption that the national government was founded by "the people"; on the other, the states' rights position rested on the notion that the states as integral units of sovereignty had made a "compact." And history was ransacked by all hands to "prove" the validity of the respective cases—with what a historian must report as inconclusive results.

[5] Leonard W. Levy, *Jefferson and Civil Liberties* (Cambridge, Mass., 1963), pp. 93–141.

But the problems of Jefferson and Madison fade into insignificance when compared with the definitional crisis that precipitated the Civil War. This is not the place to examine the constitutional turmoil over slavery except to note that the crucial question was not juridical, but moral, and was thus insoluble by legal mechanisms. If one took for granted that a Negro slave was "property," then the injunction of the Fifth Amendment that no person "shall be deprived of life, liberty, or property, without due process of law" stood as a massive barrier against national regulation of the South's "peculiar institution." If, in contrast, one assumed that a Negro slave was a "person," then slavery constituted an unconstitutional limitation on his life and liberty. *Pace* Chief Justice Taney's efforts in *Dred Scott* v. *Sanford*,[6] one does not settle this order of problem in a court of law.

The Union victory in the Civil War gave the compact theory its *coup de grâce*, and in *State of Texas* v. *White*,[7] the Supreme Court gave ideological approval to the work of Lincoln's armies. In constitutional terms, however, states' rights lived on and was from time to time extracted from the museum of antiquities as a device for limiting federal legislation deemed "radical" by a majority of the Supreme Court.[8] It is reasonable to argue that in the 1960s states' rights constituted no meaningful legal barrier to the exercise of national authority, and that the federal government operating in a national economy could reach any objective it wished through the exercise of the commerce power, the taxing power, or—as in the Civil Rights Act of 1964—a combination of the commerce power and the long-ignored jurisdiction provided by the Fourteenth Amendment.

Yet, curiously, to say this is not to assert that the United States has achieved a unitary form of government. Indeed, in net terms the substantive power of the states today is greater than it has ever been. What has occurred is a remarkable *de facto* distribution of power between states and nation (sometimes called "cooperative federalism"), in which the state governments exer-

---

[6] 60 U.S. 393 (1857).

[7] 74 U.S. 700 (1869).

[8] Edward S. Corwin, *The Commerce Power Versus States Rights* (Gloucester, Mass., 1936); *Court Over Constitution* (Gloucester, Mass., 1938); *Constitutional Revolution, Ltd.* (Claremont, Calif., 1941).

cise enormous autonomy. For many areas of public policy, for example, education, public welfare, urban renewal, road construction, federal funds are extensively provided to supplement local resources. In these areas the states are, in effect, "sovereign," provided they do not push their autonomy too hard or attempt to assert a theoretical basis for their jurisdiction. However, if state officials try to assert final power through gerrymanders, discriminatory practices in race relations, taxation of interstate commerce, the Supreme Court tends to reaffirm the principle of national supremacy. Moreover, since the states are the effective units of political party organization they often provide political obstacles to centralization that are far more effective than their constitutional position might indicate.

In short, the United States in a highly nontheoretical fashion has developed a relationship between the center and the peripheral units built around the operating principles of *de jure* national supremacy and *de facto* local autonomy. Most of the time this relationship works extremely well on the basis of a political consensus not to clarify issues of sovereignty but, rather, to get on with the business of governance.

THE SEPARATION OF POWERS

The doctrine of the separation of powers has occupied a distinguished position in the history of American constitutionalism. In its classic formulation the doctrine had two operating principles. The first was set forth by John Adams in Article XXX of of Massachusetts Constitution of 1780: "In the government of this commonwealth, the legislative department shall never exercise the executive and judicial powers, or either of them: the executive shall never exercise the legislative and judicial powers, or either of them: the judicial shall never exercise the legislative and executive powers, or either of them: to the end it may be a government of laws and not of men." The second, drawn from a maxim attributed to Bracton, announced that *delegata potestas non potest delegari,* that delegated powers could not be further delegated, for example, that authority delegated to Congress by Article I of the Constitution could not be passed on by the legislature to the President.

The difficulty with this doctrine, however, is that from the outset it was honored more in the breach than in the observance. The constitution of Massachusetts, which contained Adams' absolute interdict, also gave the governor a veto over legislation that could be overridden only by a two-thirds vote of the General Court. In other words, the governor of Massachusetts exercised immense "legislative" power. Elsewhere in the same document there was a provision that a number of "executive" officers (by our definition) would be "chosen annually by joint ballot of the senators and representatives in one room." All judicial appointments had to be approved by the Council, which was a curious hybrid of executive, legislative and judicial powers chosen by joint ballot of the two houses. In sum, the Massachusetts paradigm of the separation of powers on close examination is a shambles of interlocking powers and overlapping jurisdictions.

Yet, if we examine Adams' handiwork rather than his rhetoric, we discover a principle of separation founded on the proposition that the executive, legislative and judicial *institutions* should have autonomous constituencies. The governor was to be elected annually by the people as a whole, the legislature by geographical subdivisions of the commonwealth; and the judiciary was to hold tenure for life on good behavior. Adams was not, in other words, interested in separating powers in terms of their substantive content (executive, judicial, legislative) but divided authority among discrete agencies (governor, General Court, judiciary, Council), each of which exercised judicial, executive and legislative jurisdictions. Conflict among these quasi-autonomous power centers, he believed, would prevent the growth of any centralized autocracy. The separation of powers, then, rested on political physics, not metaphysics.

The original Madison draft of the Constitution, which served as the basis for discussion and modification at the convention, contained no trace of the separation of powers. All power was vested in a supreme legislature; the upper house was picked by the lower house; the President and judges were selected by both houses. Gradually over the summer of 1787 this centralist model was weakened, over the militant objections of Madison, Hamilton and James Wilson, and in an *ad hoc* fashion the "separation of powers" (like "Federalism") emerged from the compromises. Later, in the forty-seventh *Federalist,* Madison observed that "the accumulation of all powers legislative, executive and judiciary in the same hands, . . . may justly be pronounced the very definition of tyranny."[9] Later in the same essay he adopted John Adams' operational model, noting that the separation of powers did not mean that the "departments ought to have no *partial agency* in, or no *controul* over the acts of each other. [Montesquieu's] meaning, . . . can amount to no more than this, that where the *whole* power of one department is exercised by the same hands which possess the *whole* power of another department, the fundamental principles of a free constitution, are subverted."[10]

Historically speaking, the doctrine of the separation of powers entered American constitutionalism as a fairly simple and matter-of-fact division of the agencies of the national government rather than as a subtle effort to differentiate powers in terms of their innate characteristics. The President exercised judicial power (pardons) and legislative power (the veto); the legislature undertook executive functions (approval of appointments, treaties) and judicial functions (amnesties), and the courts to a lesser degree dabbled in executive and legislative activities. Moreover, there is no empirical evidence to suggest that the maxim about delegated power not being subject to further delegation had any standing; the statutes of the first twenty years of the Republic are full of laws delegating national authority to state institutions; state courts, for instance, were given the power to naturalize aliens and to handle a number of offenses against the laws of the United States.

There were a number of disputes in the early nineteenth century that touched marginally on the doctrine of the separation of powers. President Jackson, for example, justified his employment of the veto on policy grounds (his predecessors had felt that the veto should be reserved for legislation the chief executive believed to be unconstitutional) by asserting the full autonomy of the presidency. And, of course, a similar concept of institutional independence underlay Chief Justice Marshall's exercise of judi-

9 Alexander Hamilton, James Madison and John Jay, *The Federalist* (1788), ed. with intro. and notes by Jacob E. Cook (Middletown, Conn., 1961), p. 324.
10 *Ibid.*, pp. 325–326.

cial review over acts of Congress. But a careful search of the precedents suggests that the separation of powers, although it occupied an honored position in the polemical literature, was not articulated as a serious principle of constitutional interpretation until the 1850s, when Justice Benjamin Curtis invoked it in two leading decisions.

Denying the practice of sixty years, Curtis asserted in *Cooley v. Board of Wardens of Port of Philadelphia*[11] that "if the States were divested of the power to legislate on [interstate and foreign commerce] by the grant of the commercial power to Congress . . . Congress cannot regrant, or in any manner reconvey to the States that power." Suddenly *delegata potestas non potest delegari* attained constitutional status—and by *ipse dixit:* Curtis did not linger to justify his pronouncement. Nor did the justice stipulate the precise constitutional foundation for his views. Further reflection presumably indicated to him that a violation of the separation of powers fell afoul of the due-process clause of the Fifth Amendment; at least this was the thrust of his presentation in *Murray's Lessee et al. v. Hoboken Land and Improvement Co.*[12] Ignoring Adams' model, Curtis attempted to define the separation of powers in terms of substance; embarking on an elaborate gloss on the *nature* of judicial authority, he rejected the time-honored operational definition of judicial power as that power exercised by judges.

It would be pointless to catalogue the subsequent instances where the separation of powers turned up as a *ratio decidendi* in Supreme Court litigation. What is important is to note that this doctrine became a major theoretical roadblock to the development of administrative law, regulatory commissions and delegations of emergency authority to the President. The nub of the argument was that Congress could not delegate "legislative" or "judicial" power to administrative officers (whether located in the executive branch or in the so-called independent regulatory commissions)—a contention which, if accepted by the Court, would have destroyed the whole regulatory apparatus that developed in the wake of the industrial revolution and the growth

[11] 53 U.S. 299 (1851).
[12] 59 U.S. 272 (1855).

of a national economy. An agency such as the Interstate Commerce Commission, for example, clearly fuses executive, legislative and judicial power. It administers, it makes rules and it engages in enforcement.

The Supreme Court, however, was seldom prepared to fortify this high ground. Instead, the justices devised various escape mechanisms from the logical chains of separation doctrine. On one hand, they found that the powers exercised by administrative bodies were not legislative and judicial, but "quasi-legislative" and "quasi-judicial"[13] on the other, they held that when Congress delegated authority to various administrative instruments, this did not constitute delegation of "legislative power" if meticulous standards of administration were specified[14]—it was merely an implementation of legislative power.[15] Indeed, in 1934 the leading authority on the question, Edward S. Corwin, declared the doctrine of the separation of powers moribund.[16]

Ironically, in 1935 the corpse arose from its bed and provided the Supreme Court with the basis for striking down the Oil Code promulgated under the National Industrial Recovery Act[17] and for several other subsequent judicial forays against the evils of the New Deal. But later decisions by the "Roosevelt Court," notably that reached in *U.S.* v. *Rock Royal Co-operative, Inc.,*[18] seem to have put this tumultuous spirit finally to rest. The closest the Supreme Court came to a separation-of-powers ruling in the years since 1941 was in *Sweezy* v. *New Hampshire,*[19] when Chief Justice Warren, while denying the applicability of the separation of powers, seemed to suggest that New Hampshire had violated due process of law by delegating to its Attorney General plenary authority to act as a subcommittee of the state legislature.

To conclude, the separation of powers is thus back where it began in 1789 as an abstract affirmation of the independent con-

---

[13] See Rathbun v. U.S., 295 U.S. 602 (1935).

[14] See J. W. Hampton Co. v. U.S., 276 U.S. 394 (1928).

[15] Robert E. Cushman, *The Independent Regulatory Commissions* (New York, 1941).

[16] Corwin, *The Twilight of the Supreme Court* (New Haven, 1934), p. 145.

[17] Panama Refining Co. v. Ryan, 293 U.S. 539 (1934).

[18] 307 U.S. 533 (1939).

[19] 354 U.S. 234 (1957).

stitutional existence of the President, the Congress and the Supreme Court. And the notion that delegated power can not be further delegated has been demolished by constitutional logic drawn from John Marshall; that congressional power where it exists is plenary, and that plenary jurisdiction includes the power to give power away. Limits on delegation do exist, but they are political, not constitutional, in character.[20]

[20] Roche, *op. cit.*, pp. 127–161.

The Expatriation Decisions: A Study in Constitutional Improvisation and the Uses of History

ON FEBRUARY 18, 1963, in the cases of *Francisco Mendoza-Martinez* and *Joseph Henry Cort*,[1] the Supreme Court struck down as unconstitutional a provision of the nationality code which said that "departing from or remaining outside of the jurisdiction of the United States" during wartime or a period of national emergency "for the purpose of evading or avoiding training and service in the land or naval forces of the United States"[2] created in effect an irrebuttable presumption of a voluntary decision to expatriate, i.e., to extinguish one's American nationality. The reader who winces at this convoluted formulation should brace himself. Worse is yet to come. Indeed, it would be hard to discover an area of American public law in which the premises and logic of action have been so absurdly attenuated, or in which

Reprinted, with permission, from *The American Political Science Review*, Volume LVIII, No. 1, March 1964, pages 72–80.

[1] 83 S. Ct. 554 (1963).
[2] 58 Stat. 746 (1944) as amended by 66 Stat. 163 (1952).

the historical record has been so flagrantly distorted. (Unless it is in the similar area of denaturalization, which is excluded from discussion here.)[3]

The crucial difficulty has arisen from the fact that a set of improvisations, formulated on an *ad hoc* basis over a century and a half, was in 1940 promoted into an ideology. Since all good ideologies must have historical foundations, there was a hasty movement to the archives and, with appropriate selectivity, a History was concocted. Opponents of the expatriation formula, of course, needed a history of their own, or, let us call it, an Anti-History. These two versions of the development of expatriation in the United States have appeared like siamese twins in all subsequent litigation: the United States maintaining that deprivation of citizenship is not a "penalty" but merely a formalization of voluntary individual action; opponents claiming that deprivation of nationality except on a clearly voluntary basis is an unconstitutional innovation, a break with all the traditions of the past.

We are suffering, in short, from an acute case of hardening of the categories; perhaps the time has come to explore the history and logic of expatriation from a wholly dispassionate standpoint. This does not imply that I have no opinions on the validity or wisdom of the expatriation statutes, but rather that they will be, to the best of my ability, stated as such rather than guised as "historic truths." The historian, unlike the brief-writer, can never proceed on the assumption that history unfolds backwards in neat legal categories; his task, whatever his opinions on the merits of contemporary policies, is to analyze the past on its own terms. I have elsewhere chronicled the problems of loss of citizenship,[4] and will confine myself here to a summary of historical developments which provide the background for current chaos.

---

[3] For the similar development of legal improvisation in this field see Roche, "Pre-Statutory Denaturalization," *Cornell L.Q.*, vol. xxv (1949), p. 120 and "Statutory Denaturalization," *Pittsburgh L.R.*, vol. xiii (1952), p. 276.

[4] Roche, "Loss of American Nationality: The Years of Confusion," *Western Pol. Q.*, vol. iv (1951), p. 268; "Loss of American Nationality: The Development of Statutory Expatriation," *U. of Pa. L.R.*, vol. ic (1950), p. 25; and the studies of denaturalization cited *supra* fn 3.

I

There is an ancient Talmudic caveat that the existence of a question does not necessarily require the existence of an answer. Yet when the Supreme Court comes to grips with the constitutionality of a statute written in 1940 or 1952, it commonly assumes that there is an answer concealed in the corpus of American constitutional history, that there is a "logic of constitutionality" which makes it possible for events in 1963 to be squared with the intentions of 1787. There is, in short, an assumption of equivalence which serves as the rationale of judicial review, and this juridical fiction in turn activates the brief-writers in their desperate quest for History, or Anti-History. It would hardly do for the Supreme Court, asked how the Framers would feel about expatriation, property rights in space, or the obligation of commitments to the United Nations, to pass—though it might be the course recommended by sophisticated intelligence. Instead, an elaborate *gestalt* is promulgated with the key question: how would the Framers have reacted to the issues of 1963 if they had been given the opportunity? In practice, the views of the Framers thus construed often bear a striking resemblance to those of the justices writing the opinions.

The apparent outcome of this role-playing is, I suspect, that Justice Black knows a good deal more about what James Madison had in mind when he introduced the First Amendment into the House of Representatives than James Madison did at the time. And all legal practitioners are surely aware of the esoteric divination that frequently goes into the construction of statutes—a technique which, by the way, achieved something of a high point in the recent *Cort* case when the Supreme Court gave the McCarran-Walter Immigration and Nationality Act of 1952 a *liberal* construction.[5] What must be emphasized is that the history of expatriation in the United States does not fall into anybody's *post hoc* categories. On this subject our ancestors were neither "liberal" nor "conservative" by contemporary standards; confronted by issues of citizenship, they dealt with them ex-

[5] Rusk v. Cort, 369 U.S. 367 (1962).

temporaneously in terms of their value systems. In fact, before the Civil War there was a conspiracy among the political leadership to *avoid* a clear definition of United States citizenship. This was not perversity, but was founded on a recognition that the status of the Negro, notably of the free Negro, was a great source of conflict between North and South and, in the interests of political harmony, had best be left "unclarified."[6]

If citizenship itself was juridically obscure, what can one expect with respect to loss of citizenship? The United States was a nation of immigrants and it is in this context that one must understand the significance of the "natural right of expatriation": It was American policy to deny the doctrine of indefeasible allegiance *in the international forum*. When our spokesmen talked of the right of expatriation, they were not concerned with loss of *American* citizenship; they were combating in specific situations—e.g., the British impressment of British-born, naturalized Americans from our ships[7]—the traditional doctrine that a citizen could not shift his allegiance without the consent of his sovereign. Yet ironically *in the municipal forum* the United States, like the British, endorsed the doctrine of indefeasible allegiance. In other words, we claimed the right to naturalize immigrants but denied Americans the right to give up their American nationality—a classic nationalist posture.[8]

In *Shanks* v. *Dupont* (1830), the Supreme Court gave its conclusions on the subject; said Justice Story, "The general doctrine [governing American law] is that no persons can by any act of their own, without the consent of the government, put off their allegiance and become aliens."[9] And Chancellor James Kent in

---

[6] See Roche, *The Early Development of United States Citizenship* (1949).

[7] See Anthony Steel, "Impressment in the Monroe-Pinckney Negotiation, 1806–1807," *Amer. Hist. Rev.*, vol. LVII (1952), p. 352 and "Anthony Merry and the Anglo-American Dispute about Impressment," *Cambridge Hist. J.*, vol. IX (1948), p. 331.

[8] Steel, *Amer. His. Rev.*, vol. LVII at p. 357 fn. 20; Tsiang, *The Question of Expatriation in America Prior to 1907* (1942); Morrow, "Early American Attitudes towards the Doctrine of Expatriation," *Amer. Jour. Int. Law*, vol. XXVI (1932), p. 552.

[9] 3 Peters 242, 246 (1830). As his correspondence reveals, John Marshall was a supporter of indefeasible allegiance: "it is a question upon which I

his *Commentaries* concluded a discussion of expatriation by stating:[10]

> From this historical review . . . the better opinion would seem to be that a citizen cannot renounce his allegiance to the United States without permission of the government, to be declared by law; and that, as there is no existing legislative regulation on the case, the [perpetual allegiance] rule of the English common law remains unaltered.

Only Congress (or the state legislatures?) could validate expatriation for Americans, but after several abortive efforts, the last of which was in 1818, the legislature dropped the topic.[11] Living as we do in the shadow of the Fourteenth Amendment, it is difficult for us to appreciate the disruptive force of states' rights in the *antebellum* period. A legislative examination of the problem of citizenship, and its loss, automatically opened up into a bitter debate on the nature of sovereignty. Thus those who argued that citizenship in the nation was derived from state citizenship would insist that provision for expatriation also lay within state jurisdiction; the abolitionists, who were urging the primacy of national citizenship,[12] assigned the expatriation authority to Congress; and those interested in peace and quiet simply kept the dilemma off the floor. This may seem quaintly abstract, but it should be recalled that the heart of the *Dred Scott* decision,[13] which touched off a furor North and South, was the theoretical question of Scott's citizenship in Missouri, i.e., his standing to bring action for trespass in the federal forum under the diversity clause of Article III of the Constitution.

---

never entertained a scintilla of doubt; and have never yet heard an argument which ought to excite a doubt in any sound and reflecting mind." Marshall to Pickering, April 11, 1814, cited by Albert J. Beveridge, *Life of Marshall* (1916–19), vol. IV, p. 54.

[10] Kent, *Commentaries* (1827), vol. II, pp. 49–50.

[11] See Roche, "Loss of American Nationality: The Years of Confusion," *op. cit.*, pp. 274–277.

[12] See tenBroek, *Anti-Slavery Origins of the Fourteenth Amendment* (1951).

[13] Scott v. San[d]ford, 19 Howard 393 (1857).

According to the standard mythology,[14] the right of expatriation *for Americans* was finally established in 1868 when Congress passed an "expatriation act." True, this statute began strongly enough by asserting that:[15]

> Whereas the right of expatriation is a natural and inherent right of all people, indispensable to the enjoyment of the rights of life, liberty, and the pursuit of happiness. . . .

But a persistent reader, who continued beyond this rhetorical flourish, could get a different sense of legislative intent (one consonant with the title of the bill, an "Act concerning the Rights of American Citizens in Foreign States"); it stated:[16]

> and whereas in the recognition of this principle this Government has freely received emigrants from all nations, and invested them with the rights of citizenship; and whereas it is claimed that such American citizens, with their descendants, are subjects of foreign states, owing allegiance to the governments thereof; and whereas it is necessary to the maintenance of public peace that this claim of foreign allegiance should be promptly and finally disavowed: Therefore any declaration, instruction, opinion, order or decision, of any officers of this Government which denies, restricts, impairs, or questions the right of expatriation is hereby declared inconsistent with the fundamental principles of this Government, and therefore null and void.

In other words, the "expatriation act" of 1868 was merely another affirmation of the rights of foreign nationals to expatriate, i.e., to become naturalized *American* citizens, and an announcement to the world at large that the United States considered these adopted citizens fully within its protection.

Naturally there was a certain amount of feedback from this luminous pronouncement; for the rest of the nineteenth century,

---

[14] As incorporated, for example, in Justice McKenna's opinion of the Court in MacKenzie v. Hare, 239 U.S. 299 (1915), or Justice Jackson's in Mandoli v. Acheson, 344 U.S. 135 (1952).

[15] Stat. 223 (1868). It is perhaps worth recalling that preambles have no legal force, Jacobson v. Mass., 197 U.S. 11 (1905).

[16] *Ibid.;* see Roche, *op. cit., supra* fn. 11, pp. 282–285 for a discussion of the legislative history of this enactment.

the President, the Secretary of State and the courts engaged in desultory excursions on whether Congress had intended the right of expatriation to extend to Americans.[17] The preponderant opinion was that Congress had so intended, but nobody got particularly wrought up on the subject because of its marginal character.[18] Many problems arose in connection with the marriage of American women to aliens, and here an ingenious improvisation, too illogically delightful to pass over, was employed to dispose of the question: the citizenship of an American woman married to an alien went into a specially designed limbo. Thus while living abroad her American citizenship was "in abeyance" or "inactive" for the duration of her foreign residence and coverture, but she could regain it by "returning to and dwelling in the country of her maiden allegiance."[19] This was a neat halfway station between two contending and inconvenient legal traditions: the first asserting the rule of perpetual allegiance, and the second maintaining the primacy of the husband's status.

In 1906 and 1907, Congress finally took official notice of the legal problems created by nonstatutory denaturalization and expatriation and passed two statutes which for the first time systematized immigration and nationality procedures. The Expatriation Act of 1907, which alone concerns us here, essentially gave statutory validity to the administrative law of expatriation which had been developed in the years preceding.[20] An American who became a naturalized citizen of a foreign state, or who took an oath of allegiance to another sovereign; a naturalized American who returned to his native land or took up permanent residence in another foreign state; an American woman who married an alien; were all held to have voluntarily given up their American citizenship. This is an oversimplification[21]—naturalization abroad, for example, established an irrebuttable presump-

---

[17] See *ibid.*, pp. 286–294 for an analysis of the interpretations of the 1868 statute.

[18] *Ibid.* There was no authoritative judicial determination.

[19] *Ibid.*, p. 289.

[20] 34 Stat. 1228 (1907). The companion legislation dealt with naturalization, 34 Stat. 596 (1906).

[21] For detail see Roche, "The Loss of American Nationality" *op. cit., supra* fn. 4.

tion of expatriation, whereas foreign residence by a naturalized citizen created a rebuttable presumption (and the citizenship of women was put into the limbo described earlier). But the important point for our purposes is that Congress adopted the basic syllogism that has underpinned expatriation legislation ever since: 1) expatriation must be "voluntary"; and 2) the United States can establish the outward and visible standards of such volition and force an individual to accept the consequences of the freely willed decision thereby imputed to him.

At the same time, it should be carefully noted that the expatriation categories of the 1907 statute were all related to a putative *transfer* of allegiance. They established criteria, that is, for determining when an American had taken up a new nationality (or reverted to his original status); the proviso on women had, indeed, a quaintly arrogant ring: "Any American woman who marries a foreigner shall take the nationality of her husband." In other words, the 1907 enactment was not designed to penalize Americans for their sins; it may have had that impact in marginal cases, but its main purpose was to regularize the arrangements by which the United States took notice that an American national had *sua sponte* abandoned his citizenship for another. The Supreme Court viewed the matter in this light: after stipulating that "it may be conceded that a change of citizenship cannot be arbitrarily imposed, that is, imposed without the concurrence of the citizen," the Court held the statute to be part of the "inherent power of sovereignty":

> As a government, the United States is invested with all the attributes of sovereignty. As it has the character of nationality it has the powers of nationality, especially those which concern its relations and intercourse with other countries.[22]

We can stop our summary of this aspect of expatriation here. We have a firm category: those who have by their actions indicated that they have voluntarily abandoned American nationality in favor of citizenship in, or at least allegiance to, a foreign sovereign. In 1940 this category was expanded to include one who took service in a foreign army if "he has or acquires the nationality of such foreign state," one who accepted or performed "the

[22] MacKenzie v. Hare, 239 U.S. 299, 311 (1915).

duties of, any office, post or employment under the government of a foreign state or political subdivision thereof for which only nationals of such state are eligible," and one who voted in a political election in a foreign state.[23] The 1952 statute retained these provisions with slight modifications.[24]

II

With this background, we can now turn to another set of criteria for expatriation, those involved in *Trop* v. *Dulles*[25] and in the 1963 cases. Beginning in 1940 the Congress added several new provisions to the section setting forth the standards of voluntary expatriation, and they were qualitatively distinct from those described above. They were not recognitions of a transfer of allegiance except in the most abstract ideological sense; they were punishments for sins against the sovereign. An American was held to have expatriated himself by committing treason,[26] by deserting from the armed forces in wartime,[27] by leaving the country or remaining outside of the country to avoid military service (1944 amendment)[28]; and by attempting, conspiring, etc. to teach and advocate the overthrow of the United States government by force or violence (1954 amendment).[29] Conviction for treason, desertion or sedition thus carried with it automatic denationalization; the proviso on draft-dodging, involved in the *Cort* and *Mendoza-Martinez* cases, was not triggered in this fashion: It was not feasible to convict absentees in criminal actions.

[23] 54 Stat. 1169 (1940). There was also a special provision for renunciation of American nationality, designed for use by dual nationals living abroad.

[24] 66 Stat. 163 (1952). There were some additions and changes. Service in the armed forces of a foreign state was held to expatriate without regard to the stipulation of the 1940 act quoted in the text. Accepting service for a foreign government cost one his nationality if a) he had or acquired the nationality of such state, or b) if he were required to declare allegiance to such foreign power as a prerequisite for employment. Sec. 349, Immigration and Nationality Act of 1952, 8 U.S.C. 1481.

[25] 356 U.S. 86 (1958).

[26] 54 Stat. 1169 (1940).

[27] *Ibid.*

[28] 58 Stat. 746 (1944).

[29] 68 Stat. 1146 (1954).

Indeed, only when an individual, like Mendoza-Martinez, returned to the United States and was apprehended for draft
evasion could a trial take place. In Cort's instance, for example,
an indictment had been turned in against him in federal court
and a warrant was out for his arrest for draft dodging, but until
he returned to the jurisdiction no further action was possible.
The decision that an individual had departed from, or remained
outside of the United States to avoid military service was thus
left in the hands of the administrative authorities: the Immigration and Naturalization Service, which could exclude an individual from the United States on the ground that he had
expatriated himself by evading military service, and the Department of State, which could withdraw an individual's passport
and inform him of his loss of nationality under this clause. It was
not an easy provision to administer, but Congress in 1952
stepped in with a helpful presumption: "failure to comply with
any provision of any compulsory service laws . . . shall [in the
instance of an American abroad] raise the presumption that the
departure from or absence from the United States was for the
purpose of evading or avoiding training. . . ."[30]

I have so far taken for granted the very issue which was *sub
judice* in *Trop* v. *Dulles*,[31] *Rusk* v. *Cort*,[32] and *Kennedy* v.
Mendoza-Martinez (and was evaded on technical grounds in
Perez v. *Brownell*),[33] namely, that deprivation of nationality
under these rubrics was in fact a punishment, a criminal sanction,
rather than a mere recognition of transfer of allegiance, an official
imprimatur on a private, voluntary act of expatriation. The
Solicitor General labored mightily[34] in *Cort* and *Mendoza-
Martinez* to demonstrate that "punishment" was not involved,
but this was obviously an effort to distinguish the current cases
from *Trop*, where the Court had invalidated the desertion provision, and to fit them into the mold of *Perez*, where the Court

[30] Sec. 349 (a) (10), Act of 1952.
[31] 356 U.S. 86 (1958).
[32] 83 S. Ct. 554 (1963).
[33] 356 U.S. 44 (1958).
[34] Kennedy v. Mendoza-Martinez, 83 S. Ct. 554 (1963), Brief for Appel-
lant, pp. 53–64. The Solicitor General did not reargue this issue in his brief
in the Cort case.

sustained the voting-in-a-foreign-election category. The historian, fortunately, is not bound by the deductive requirements of pleading, and can confidently call a spade a spade.

Had it not been for the eccentricities of precedent, one and all would surely have admitted what is patent on the face of the legislation: that it is essentially penal in character. Indeed, both historically and contemporaneously denationalization has been widely employed as a punishment for "bad" behavior.[35] At this moment one may be deprived of his Nicaraguan citizenship for "expounding political doctrine running counter to the ideal of the Fatherland, affecting its national sovereignty or tending to destroy the republican system of government."[36] In Albania and Yugoslavia it is sufficient to refuse "to do one's duty"[37]; in Brazil, to engage in activities "against the public interest"[38]; and in a number of states one is thus penalized for indications of disloyalty, disaffection or a mentality contrary to the national spirit.

The United States, happily isolated and isolationist, had no statutes of this kind on its books in the nineteenth century. Having no external politics of any consequence, no peacetime conscription, and little competitive nationalism, we had no need for such sanctions. But one early effort in this direction suggests that it was the lack of motivation rather than virtuous principles which prevented denationalization from being used punitively: the proposed and never-ratified Thirteenth Amendment. Introduced in 1810, this measure provided that:[39]

If any citizen of the United States shall accept claim, receive or retain any title of nobility, or honor, or shall, without the consent of Congress, accept or retain any present, pension, office or emolument, of any kind whatsoever, from any Emperor, King, Prince, or foreign power, such person shall cease to be a citizen

[35] See summary of various provisions for denationalization in U.N. General Assembly Doc. No. A/CN.4/66, 6 April 1953, Section 9.

[36] *Ibid.*

[37] *Ibid.*

[38] *Ibid.* See also *Laws Concerning Nationality*, U.N. Doc. No. ST/LEG/SER. B/4 (1954).

[39] Ames, "Proposed Amendments to the Constitution," *Annual Report of the American Historical Assoc. 1896*, vol. II (1896), pp. 186–187.

of the United States, and shall be incapable of holding any office of trust or profit under them or either of them.

As originally introduced, the amendment also penalized inter-marriage with a person of royal blood![40] (It may seem strange that this was cast in the form of a constitutional amendment, but the dominant Jeffersonian view held that citizenship was within the jurisdiction of the states—a statute would thus have been a federal usurpation of states' rights.) The proposal received the necessary two-thirds vote in the House of Representatives without debate, and with only slight changes in the Senate, and fell but one state short of the three-quarters necessary for adoption.[41]

In 1864 Congress did pass a measure—the Wade-Davis bill—which *inter alia* provided (§14) that "every person who shall hereafter hold or exercise any office, civil or military, except offices merely ministerial, and military offices below the rank of colonel, in the rebel service, . . . is hereby declared not to be a citizen of the United States."[42] Lincoln pocket-vetoed the enactment, but it still seems to spoil Justice Black's case that the Fourteenth Amendment made citizenship an "absolute," i.e., that the authors of the Amendment would never have dreamed of employing denationalization as a penalty. It also supplies evidence that Civil War legislators were aware of the distinction between "citizenship" and "rights of citizenship"—the issue to which we now turn our attention.

The statutory ancestor of the punitive provisions of the Nationality Act of 1940 was not this obscure enterprise, but a Civil War measure aimed at draft-dodgers and deserters. In 1865, an amendment was added to the Enrollment Act which stipulated that draft-dodgers and deserters who did not return to military service within sixty days of the passage of the act were "deemed and taken to have voluntarily relinquished and forfeited their rights of citizenship."[43] There has been a great deal of argument in recent years over whether this statute deprived deserters of

[40] 11 *Annals of Congress* 549 (1810).

[41] Ames, *op. cit.*, p. 187.

[42] See Richardson, *Messages and Papers of the Presidents* (1899), vol. VI, p. 223.

[43] 13 Stat. 490 (1865).

their citizenship or merely of their civil rights (right to vote, hold office, etc.).[44] No one can read the minds of the dead with certainty, but in the context of the measure it seems that when Congress said "rights of citizenship," it meant precisely that; the Chairman of the House Military Affairs Committee, who guided the bill through that chamber, presented this section as a disfranchisement.[45] But even if, improbably, Congress meant to deprive deserters of their nationality, there is no escaping the conclusion that this was a punitive sanction. It was so treated after the close of World War I when President Calvin Coolidge, on March 5, 1924, issued a "Proclamation of Amnesty" in which he granted "amnesty and pardon to all persons who have heretofore [been convicted of desertion in wartime] to the extent that there shall be . . . fully remitted as to such persons any relinquishment or forefeiture of their rights of citizenship."[46]

In 1940 the desertion proviso served as a model for the section of the Nationality Act which "expatriated" (to convert an intransitive verb into the active mood) traitors, and later those who left or stayed out of the United States to evade military service, and later still those convicted under the Smith Act. The "rights of citizenship" employed in the old law were quietly converted to "citizenship"; when queried on this change during the Hearings on the 1940 Act, State Department Counselor Richard Flournoy stated that the Department had always construed the Act of 1865 as depriving Americans of their nationality, and that seemed to settle the question.[47]

[44] As already noted, the distinction between citizenship and rights of citizenship was not lost on Civil War legislators. In 1865 Congressman Ashley of Ohio introduced a measure to deprive high Confederate officials of their *citizenship*, *Cong. Globe*, 38th Cong., 2d sess., p. 280. This was immediately forestalled when Congressman Eliot of Massachusetts noted that "A person cannot commit treason if he is not a citizen." *Ibid.*, p. 299.

[45] *Cong. Globe*, 38 Cong., 2d sess., p. 643 (Schenck of Ohio).

[46] 43 Stat. 1940 (1924). For whatever it may be worth, Coolidge referred to those in this category as "fellow citizens." See generally Gathings, "Loss of Citizenship and Civil Rights for Conviction of Crime," *Am. Pol. Sci. Review*, vol. XLIII (1949), p. 1228.

[47] 2 *Hearings before Committee on Immigration and Naturalization on H.R. 6127*, 76 Cong., 1st sess., vol. II, p. 38 (1940). But see *In the Matter of P————*, 1 I. & N. Dec. 127, 132 (Board of Immigration Appeals, 1941).

Thus in the present nationality code we find, in addition to the category examined earlier which provided for the loss of American citizenship for those who concretely evidenced a shift of allegiance to a foreign sovereign, a second category based on the proposition that "Bad Americans" should be deprived of their nationality. The first category had a rational foundation in international law; the second operates purely in the municipal forum to create stateless persons—it provides a mode of punishment superadded onto those provided by the criminal law for certain heinous offenses against sovereignty. Admittedly one can conjure up abstract arguments that a traitor has opted for another allegiance, but in the context of *nationality law* this is essentially absurd: he is merely a technically stateless inmate of a federal penitentiary. Again one can claim that Communists convicted under the Smith Act have indicated by their own free will their superior loyalty to the Soviet Union, but then what does one do with convicted Trotskyites who can at best be described as would-be nationals of a nonexistent foreign power? And most deserters from the armed forces, far from demonstrating a superior loyalty to the enemy, are simply interested in a quiet life away from gunfire and the rigors of military existence. Perhaps, as in the case of Mendoza-Martinez,[48] special provisions could be formulated to deal with the problems created by dual nationals who evade military service by moving to the state of their alternative citizenship, but generally speaking—as in Cort's instance—draft-evaders have violated the national service laws, without any concomitant indication of allegiance to another sovereign. Let us now examine the constitutional problems that these two major categories have created over the last decade.

When the Supreme Court was confronted with the constitutionality of these two expatriation categories, it had singularly few guidelines to follow. History provided no answer—or, perhaps, too many, conflicting answers. The founders of the nation were no help because they were preoccupied with a different question: Was admission to the community a state or a national prerogative? The burden of evidence indicates to me that na-

[48] Who was by birth a dual national of the United States (*jure soli*) and Mexico (*jure sanguinis*).

tional citizenship was originally viewed as derivative from state citizenship, and all early discussions of loss of nationality came to grief on the reef of states' rights.[49] The Fourteenth Amendment settled this issue, and presumably thereby vested any jurisdiction over expatriation in the national government, but still there was no authoritative doctrine on the reach of the expatriation power. The states in the revolutionary period had deprived Tories of their state citizenship (and everything else in their possession)[50] —and the working definition of "Tory" was often pretty loose— but aside from the abortive "Thirteenth Amendment" of 1810 and the Wade-Davis bill there were no later examples of efforts to employ expatriation in a punitive fashion. The 1865 desertion statute left a shambles of conflicting interpretations in its wake. In short, to reiterate, there was no "theory" of expatriation because the problem simply was not important enough to warrant serious jurisprudential effort.

In the twentieth century, after the passage of the 1907 statute, the federal courts had been confronted with a number of problems, but all of these arose from litigation in the first category, i.e., they were concerned with issues of transfer of allegiance. The provisions of the 1907 law on loss by marriage to an alien husband, for example, were, as already noted, sustained as a legitimate exercise of congressional authority over international relations.[51] In *Perkins* v. *Elg*,[52] the leading modern case, the Supreme Court overruled the administrative authorities by holding that the American-born child, of naturalized American parents who subsequently reverted to their former nationality and took her with them to Sweden, had not lost her citizenship. In the course of the opinion, Chief Justice Hughes provided the widely cited rationale.[53]

> Expatriation is the voluntary renunciation or abandonment of nationality and allegiance. It has no application to the removal

[49] Roche, *op. cit., supra* fn. 6.
[50] See Van Tyne, *The Loyalists in the American Revolution* (1929); Hurst, "Treason in the United States," *Harvard Law Review,* vol. LVIII (1945), pp. 226, 268–272.
[51] MacKenzie v. Hare, 239 U.S. 299 (1915).
[52] 307 U.S. 325 (1939).
[53] *Ibid.* at 334.

from this country of a native citizen during minority. In such a case the voluntary action which is the essence of the right is lacking.

Hughes, however, did not invoke constitutional grounds; indeed, he was careful to state the basis of the decision narrowly:[54]

> As at birth she became a citizen of the United States, that citizenship must be deemed to continue unless she has been deprived of it through the operation of a treaty or congressional enactment or by her voluntary action in conformity with applicable legal principles.

This still left the judiciary with no constitutional bearings on loss of nationality imposed by law or by treaty—and it might be added that a number of treaties dating from the Bancroft Treaty of 1868 with the North German Confederation[55] did, in effect, impose loss of American citizenship upon naturalized citizens who returned to North Germany or other former sovereignties for two years or more.

Thus the Supreme Court, when it turned to the problem of loss of nationality by desertion, voting in foreign political elections, or leaving the nation to evade military service, was really writing on a blank constitutional slate. All previous decisions tended to support the proposition that the United States could "expatriate" its nationals as an inherent coefficient of sovereignty, but in no previous holding had a punitive proviso (in the sense described above) been under litigation. History was useless, and the existing body of patchwork administrative and judicial improvisations provided no baseline, no logical line of development. (Indeed, it was not unknown for the Department of State to take one position, and the Department of Labor—which then had jurisdiction over the Immigration and Naturalization Service—to take the opposite.[56]) There was a loose tradition that expatriation had to be "voluntary," but this word had been given a peculiar, disembodied gloss: An individual did not have the option of deciding whether he wanted to lose his citizenship; one merely had the

[54] *Ibid.* at 329.

[55] 15 Stat. 615 (1868). See Roche, *op. cit., supra* fn. 11, pp. 285–286.

[56] Such dissension was part of the background of the Elg case, see Roche, *op. cit., supra* fn. 21, pp. 30–31.

freedom to decide whether or not to undertake a commitment which carried with it denationalization, e.g., marriage to an alien husband. Consequently voluntary marriage could, and did, lead to involuntary expatriation, i.e., to a loss of citizenship which was in subjective terms unwanted. Curiously this technique had been anticipated by Representative Lowndes of South Carolina in 1818; opposing a bill to enounce the "right of expatriation," Lowndes told the House, "If you pass this bill, you have only one step further to go, and say that such acts shall be considered as presumption of intention of the citizen to expatriate, and thus take from him the privileges of a citizen."[57]

Elsewhere I have examined in greater detail the chaos which has emerged from recent Court encounters with problems of expatriation.[58] Suffice it here to say that it is perhaps too easy to be critical of the Supreme Court's handling of expatriation issues; as Justice Jackson, with his usual insight, remarked, "it would be unrewarding to point out conflict in precept and confusion in practice on this side of the Atlantic, where ideas of nationality and expatriation were in ferment during the whole nineteenth century."[59] Practice simply outran theory and because the whole problem of loss of nationality was so trivial, so marginal to the main concerns of public policy, a legal tradition developed on the basis of pragmatic accretion. A special problem was met by an *ad hoc* remedy, and the *ad hoc* remedies, in aggregate, constituted the law on the subject. Nobody worried about the constitutionality of the Bancroft Treaties, any more than the congressmen who passed the Wade-Davis Bill tossed in their beds wondering what constitutional power to hang Section 14 on. If there had to be a constitutional justification, the Attorney General could doubtless conjure one up, or find a professor of constitutional law to do the job for him.

However, in the past half-century nationality matters have moved from the littoral to the center of public policy. There has been continuing dispute over immigration issues, a tightening up

[57] 15 *Annals of Congress* (1818), p. 1050.

[58] See Roche, "The Expatriation Cases: Breathes There the Man with Soul So Dead . . . ?," in Kurland, ed., *1963 Supreme Court Review* (1963).

[59] Mandoli v. Acheson, 344 U.S. 133, 135 (1952).

of standards for naturalization, and finally in the last twenty-five years two major campaigns for codification and rationalization of nationality practices—the first resulting in the Nationality Act of 1940 and the second in the Immigration and Nationality Act of 1952. In the specific context of this paper, a mass of earlier statutes and administrative regulations were codified into the section regulating loss of nationality, Section 401, of the Nationality Act of 1940. And a few new provisions were added, with no furor, that were allegedly patterned on existing provisos. Let us take, for example, the desertion case: Here the old Civil War statute was assimilated, but where the 1865 enactment deprived deserters (and draft-evaders: in the Civil War, an individual was automatically in the service as of the date he was ordered to enroll) of their "rights of citizenship," the 1940 revision forfeited "citizenship." Then, on the model of the desertion provision, a similar provision denationalized traitors, and was extended in 1954 to include those convicted under the Smith Act. Had someone proposed that Americans convicted of gambling or traffic violations be denationalized, there would undoubtedly have been a heated controversy, but no congressman could get very interested in the problems of traitors, deserters, draft-dodgers or sedition-mongers. These provisions had to be constitutional; the precedent, after all, was an act of 1865. Moreover, it was not *really* a punishment; like denaturalization,[60] deportation[61] or (later) depriving those deported on security grounds of their social security benefits,[62] it was merely a civil action which small-minded litigants persisted in branding as punitive.

The federal courts had the perplexing burden of making constitutional sense out of this corpus of improvisation. And it was not a simple task. To borrow a classic instance from the area of naturalization law, when the Supreme Court was confronted with the problem of *res judicata* involved in a denaturalization suit under the 1906 statute, it sustained the reopening of an earlier naturalization judgment on the ground that before 1906 naturali-

[60] Luria v. U.S., 231 U.S. 9 (1913).
[61] Mahler v. Eby, 264 U.S. 32 (1924); Fong Yue Ting v. U.S., 149 U.S. 698 (1893).
[62] Flemming v. Nestor, 363 U.S. 603 (1960).

zation had been an *ex parte* matter which though "conducted in a court of record . . . [was] not in any sense an adversary proceeding . . . [but] was closely analogous to a public grant of land. . . ."[63] Or, to put the matter differently, Justice Pitney declared that a naturalization judgment had, for a century or more, not been a "case or controversy"! This remarkable announcement raised a few judicial eyebrows,[64] but Justice Brandeis explained in a later case that the commotion on the subject was unfounded: "If the proceedings were not a case or controversy within the meaning of Article III, Section 2," he said, "this delegation of power upon the courts would have been invalid."[65] This masterly injection of circular logic put an end to the argument.

When the courts came to grips with expatriation legislation, they found themselves dealing with a mixed bag. As already elaborated above, they discovered two fundamentally different types of expatriation provisions, the first relating to transfers of loyalty, the second concerned with betrayals of allegiance. Yet the two were interwoven in one statute and alleged to be rested on the same constitutional foundation: the right of an American citizen voluntarily to abandon his nationality. Moreover, the Constitution and early precedents are totally useless on the subject. What then is perhaps surprising is that the Court has, in its own fashion, so closely approximated the objectives of what I would take to be a rational expatriation policy, one which treats denationalization as a dimension of foreign relations rather than of the penal code, one which minimizes the creation of stateless persons, one which recognizes that depriving an American of his citizenship is not a casual legal undertaking which can be left, without review, in the hands of virtually invisible administrative bodies or justified by the illogical whimsy of over-zealous congressional committees.

And finally, to revert to the question raised at the outset, the political scientist must inquire as we move into 1964 how much longer American public law will labor under the burden of his-

---

63 Johannessen v. U.S., 225 U.S. 227, 236–38 (1912).

64 See e.g., Judge Geiger's comment in U.S. v. Kamm 247 Fed. 968, 974 (E.D. Wis. 1918).

65 Tatun v. U.S., 270 U.S. 568, 577 (1926).